DECIDING *WHAT'S* TRUE

DECIDING
WHAT'S
TRUE

THE RISE OF POLITICAL FACT-CHECKING
IN AMERICAN JOURNALISM

LUCAS GRAVES

COLUMBIA UNIVERSITY PRESS   New York

COLUMBIA UNIVERSITY PRESS

PUBLISHERS SINCE 1893

NEW YORK   CHICHESTER, WEST SUSSEX

CUP.COLUMBIA.EDU

Library of Congress Cataloging-in-Publication Data

Names: Graves, Lucas, 1970– author.

Title: Deciding what's true : the rise of political fact-checking in American
journalism / Lucas Graves.

Description: New York : Columbia University Press, [2016] | Includes
bibliographical references and index.

Identifiers: LCCN 2016005306 (print) | LCCN 2016009516 (ebook) |
ISBN 9780231175067 (cloth : alk. paper) | ISBN 9780231175074
(pbk. : alk. paper) | ISBN 9780231542227 (e-book) | ISBN 9780231542227 ()

Subjects: LCSH: Journalism—Objectivity. | Journalistic ethics.

Classification: LCC PN4784.O24 G73 2016 (print) | LCC PN4784.O24
(ebook) | DDC 302.23—dc23

LC record available at http://lccn.loc.gov/2016005306

COVER DESIGN: CHANG JAE LEE

COVER IMAGE: JON GREENBERG

References to websites (URLs) were accurate at the time of writing. Neither the author
nor Columbia University Press is responsible for URLs that may have expired or
changed since the manuscript was prepared.

CONTENTS

ACKNOWLEDGMENTS

THIS BOOK WOULDN'T EXIST WITHOUT THE INDULGENCE OF MANY people, beginning with its protagonists. The exceptional candor and generosity of the fact-checkers and other journalists featured in these pages opened a window onto a new professional world. I owe special thanks to Bill Adair and Angie Drobnic Holan of PolitiFact, Brooks Jackson and Eugene Kiely of FactCheck.org, and Glenn Kessler of the *Washington Post*.

The research for this book began at Columbia University, where two mentors provided invaluable guidance and support. Michael Schudson was the ideal advisor, patient and wise, always knowing more than he said and saying exactly what was needed. I hope these chapters reflect the influence of his unusually graceful way of thinking. David Stark never failed to ask the question that cast everything in a new light; his interest, advice, and sharp eye were an enormous asset. I also benefited from the incisive comments and questions of Todd Gitlin, Victor Pickard, and Stephen Reese, and of Herb Gans, who volunteered to read the final product. All of these thoughtful critiques helped greatly to carry the project forward.

At Columbia I received valuable support in David Stark's CODES seminar and from many friends in the Sociology Department, which became a second home; thanks especially to Monique Girard and Josh Whitford. On the remarkable faculty in our small, boundary-crossing Communications Program, I owe special thanks to Andie Tucher and Frank Moretti, whose confidence made all the difference early on. Frank had a wide embrace and he is missed by all of us. Chris Anderson, Jonah Bossewitch, Laura Forlano, Tom Glaisyer, Phil Kay, John Kelly, Rasmus Kleis Nielsen, Ruth Palmer, Ben Peters, Soomin Seo, Julia Sonnevend, Olivier Sylvain, Madiha Tahir, and Joost van Dreunen were valued comrades in and out of the J-school basement.

A number of organizations have supported this project directly or indirectly. Funds for research, travel, and writing came from the Poynter Institute, the Open Society Foundations, the Democracy Fund, the Omidyar Network, the Wisconsin Alumni Research Foundation, and the Mellon Graduate Fellows program at the Institute for Social and Economic Research and Policy. A fellowship with the New America Foundation in Washington, DC, provided crucial support at an early stage; I'm indebted to Steve Coll and Tom Glaisyer for their interest. Special thanks also go to Tom Rosenstiel, Jane Elizabeth, and Jeff Sonderman at the American Press Institute in Reston, Virginia, whose engagement has been vital for researchers who study fact-checking. In that community I've benefited from conversations and collaboration with Brendan Nyhan, Jason Reifler, Michelle Amazeen, Emily Thorson, Ashley Muddiman, and Talia Stroud.

An army of friends in New York and Madison read parts of this book at various stages. Peter Asaro, Chris Anderson, Katherine Brown, Emily Callaci, Kathryn Ciancia, Biella Coleman, Judd Kinzley, Nicole Nelson, Ruth Palmer, Laura Portwood-Stacer, Sue Robinson, Annie Rudd, Julia Sonnevend, Molly Wright Steenson, and Stephen Young all gave valuable feedback on chapter drafts. Christina Dunbar-Hester influenced this undertaking from start to finish and was always ready with a raised eyebrow when I needed it most. My editor at Columbia University Press, Philip Leventhal, has been a calm and sure guide; thanks also to Miriam Grossman. Patti Bower and Michael Haskell performed remarkable feats of copyediting. I owe a tremendous debt to two anonymous reviewers and to my friend Rasmus Kleis Nielsen for their incisive and thoughtful comments on the final draft. This book is far better as a result.

Many others aided and abetted this work at various points. My colleagues in the School of Journalism and Mass Communication at UW–Madison helped in ways great and small; thanks especially to Sue Robinson, Lew Friedland, Shawnika Hull, Al Gunther, and the late, extraordinary James L. Baughman. Jessica Faule, Rich Garella, Omar Serageldin, Ranjit Singh, and Alix Burns put me up (and put up with me) during numerous research trips. Ingrid Erickson lent me her apartment in Harlem. Meghan Chua and Caitlin Cieslik-Miskimen assisted ably with editing, research, and transcription. Kate Fink and Patrice Kohl handled successive versions of the content analysis in chapter 6. Patricia Connelly offered to copyedit the whole thing one Christmas, and then did it. My mother, Janice Olson, lent her editing and design talents, her reassuringly strong views, and her unflagging support. Anjali Bhasin was patient, cheerful, and wise. Molly Steenson and Emily Callaci commiserated often and well.

I've been lucky throughout to be surrounded by an extended family that's close by even when I'm not—Patricia, Jessie, Alan, Greta, Mardi, the Olsons, and most of all my parents, Dave and Jan. This is for them.

In memory of Michael Graves.

DECIDING *WHAT'S* TRUE

PART I
THE LANDSCAPE OF
FACT-CHECKING

INTRODUCTION

A Brazen Lie?

THE 2012 U.S. PRESIDENTIAL RACE ENDED ACCORDING TO THE forecast, with a decisive victory for Barack Obama. But the closing days did bring one unusual development: the most emphatic collective debunking of a major campaign claim in the modern history of American journalism. The episode presaged what would be ubiquitous political fact-checking in the primaries four years later, when reporters' instincts were sharpened by unusually wild rhetoric from several political outsiders—in particular a famous real estate mogul and reality TV star. In hindsight, it was all the more remarkable for centering on a comparatively mild campaign claim from the consummate establishment candidate.

At the tail end of October, with Election Day less than two weeks away, the campaign of Republican contender Mitt Romney began airing a tough new ad in the crucial swing state of Ohio. Polls showed President Obama performing unusually well among white working-class voters there, bolstered by the evident success of the government's 2009 bailout of U.S. automakers. In his own commercials, Obama mercilessly exploited his opponent's very public opposition to the bailout, which had included a *New York Times* op-ed with the unfortunate title "Let Detroit Go Bankrupt."[1] Romney's new attack ad, called "Who Will Do More?," seized on a news bulletin out of Detroit to cast the government's role in a different light. Over images of old sedans being flattened by an industrial press, a male voice offered a harsh appraisal of the White House's record: "Obama took GM and Chrysler into bankruptcy and sold Chrysler to the Italians, who are going to build Jeeps in China." As evidence for the last point, the ad flashed an out-of-context excerpt from a recent financial news item reporting that Chrysler "plans to return Jeep output to China."

The attack finessed a charge Romney had made more bluntly two days earlier at a campaign rally in Defiance, Ohio, just an hour's drive from a major Jeep plant. "I saw a story today that one of the great manufacturers in this state, Jeep, now owned by the Italians, is thinking of moving *all* production to China. I will fight for every good job in America," Romney declared to enthusiastic applause. The candidate didn't name his source, but earlier that day a blog at the *Washington Examiner* had reported, and the *Drudge Report* had repeated, that Jeep "is considering giving up on the United States and shifting production to China."[2] Those reports pointed back to the same *Bloomberg Business* article which, despite some awkward wording, stated clearly that Chrysler's reentry into Chinese manufacturing would *not* mean "shifting output" from the United States.[3] Even before Romney took the stage in Defiance, a Chrysler vice president had posted an online response to what he called "biased" reports: "Let's set the record straight: Jeep has no intention of shifting production of its Jeep models out of North America to China." The Obama campaign quoted Chrysler prominently in its own response to Romney's charge, e-mailed to reporters after the rally in Defiance. Armed with that direct refutation, papers in Ohio and Michigan characterized Romney's error in stark language. An article in the *Detroit Free Press* opened this way after referring to Romney's "false claim" in the headline: "Republican presidential candidate Mitt Romney repeated a false claim Thursday night that Chrysler Group may move all Jeep vehicle production to China, drawing criticism from the Obama campaign, which said the Michigan native had blatantly skewed a news wire story."[4]

With this narrative already in place and media attention trained on Ohio, the reaction to Romney's new commercial was swift and decisive. "Who Will Do More?" began airing in Toledo on a Saturday. The debunking started the next day at the *Free Press* and the *National Journal*, whose headline announced matter-of-factly, "Romney Ad Wrongly Implies Chrysler Is Sending

Jobs to China."⁵ By Tuesday a handful of national outlets as well as the *Toledo Blade*, the *Des Moines Register*, the *Cleveland Plain Dealer*, and the *Columbus Dispatch* had issued fact checks; a blogger at the *Washington Post* marveled at the "brutal headlines" brought on by "Romney's Jeep-to-China lie."⁶ By the end of the week, the controversy had been covered across national newspapers and TV networks. "How out there is Mitt Romney?" Jon Stewart asked *Daily Show* viewers. "A car company—the people who convince you you need 'undercoating'—are coming after him for his dishonestly." Meanwhile President Obama turned the controversy into a laugh line in a stump speech:

> You've got folks who work at the Jeep plant who have been calling their employers worried, asking is it true, are our jobs being shipped to China? And the reason they're making these calls is because Governor Romney has been running an ad that says so—except it's not true. Everybody knows it's not true. The car companies themselves have told Governor Romney to knock it off.⁷

Journalists emphasized that Romney had aired the attack despite the controversy over his earlier remark. The *New York Times* addressed the deception in an editorial, a column, and at least five separate news reports as the attack drew new condemnations from Washington and Detroit.⁸ A front-page campaign analysis in the *Times* called the TV ad "misleading" in the first sentence, in the reporter's voice.⁹ A segment on National Public Radio (NPR) played competing clips from the Romney ad and from Obama's counterattack claiming Jeep was adding jobs in Ohio. The host, Robert Siegel, put the question to an NPR correspondent on the campaign trail: "Well, which is it, Don: they're adding jobs in Ohio or sending them to China?" The reporter left no doubt that the facts were on the president's side. Romney's attack, he explained, reflected the need to "shake things up and really hurt President Obama" in a state that might well decide the election.¹⁰

The most thorough debunking came from three elite national outlets that specialize in fact-checking political statements: FactCheck.org, PolitiFact, and the *Washington Post*'s Fact Checker. Journalists at these sites had investigated thousands of statements like this one and, as is almost always the case, they reached similar conclusions. All three reconstructed in detail the circumstances of Romney's claim and the wider history of Chrysler's bankruptcy and bailout.[11] All three found the ad deeply misleading although it avoided the outright falsehood of Romney's original speech. And all three fact-checkers went on to include the episode in their end-of-year reviews of the worst "whoppers" of 2012. PolitiFact named the claim its "Lie of the Year," stressing that even though Jeep issued "a quick and clear denial," Romney made it into a TV commercial that was "brazenly false." The analysis continued:

> And they stood by the claim, even as the media and the public expressed collective outrage against something so obviously false.
>
> People often say that politicians don't pay a price for deception, but this time was different: A flood of negative press coverage rained down on the Romney campaign, and he failed to turn the tide in Ohio, the most important state in the presidential election.[12]

Of course, it is impossible to say precisely what effect the controversy had on the Ohio results. Media and campaign professionals called Romney's attack a strategic blunder for inviting a torrent of negative coverage. "It was a very high-risk strategy, and it backfired," the Obama strategist David Axelrod declared.[13] More interesting than the immediate political impact, though, is what the episode said about prevailing attitudes in political journalism. The immediate and nearly unanimous reaction in the press showed clearly how much has changed in the profession over the last quarter-century, and especially the last decade. It showed how comfortable reporters have become challenging routine political claims—even in straight news reports and often in their own voice. In this way it reflected the growing influence of professional fact-checkers and of the wider fact-checking movement in American news.

This book is about that movement. It tells the story of a group of journalists inventing a new style of political news, one that seeks to revitalize the "truth-seeking" tradition in journalism by holding public figures to account for the things they say. Whether the fact-checkers make any real difference in public discourse is often debated. But their success in building a new journalistic institution can't be denied. Practically every national news organization in the United States offers some kind of political fact-checking today. Dozens of outlets across the country specialize in the new genre either as independent websites or as permanent features of a newspaper or news broadcast. All but a handful were established since 2010; scores more have taken root overseas.[14]

Newsrooms have long employed fact-checkers, of course, who verify the information in an article before it goes to print. References to proofreaders first appeared in U.S. periodicals early in the nineteenth century, with copy editors following a century later.[15] Full-fledged fact-checking departments emerged at national magazines in the 1920s and 1930s.[16] The women's section of the classifieds in midcentury newspapers advertised for fact-checkers alongside typists, secretaries, file clerks, and "his girl Fridays." One can find examples from as early as the 1940s of a curious kind of inside-journalism story: rueful letters of praise from journalists to the obsessive, nitpicking fact-checkers who disturb their evenings and weekends and keep them honest.[17] Today these paeans usually come tinged with concern that too many newsrooms no longer practice robust fact-checking.[18] "Being fact-checked is not very fun," the *Atlantic*'s Ta-Nehisi Coates chided in 2012 after an embarrassing episode prompted *Newsweek*—which had shuttered its fact-checking department in the 1990s—to explain that its writers checked their own work. "Good fact-checkers have a preternatural inclination toward pedantry, and sometimes will address you in a prosecutorial tone. That is their job and the adversarial tone is even more important than the actual facts they correct."[19]

This highlights a key aspect of traditional, internal fact-checking: it takes aim at the reporter, not the people being reported on. When a news outlet insists on verifying a source's claims instead of simply reporting them *as* claims, the choice upon discovering a mistake has usually been to fix it or to cut it.[20] In his own ode to fact-checkers, the *New Yorker* writer John McPhee tells the story of the heroic efforts by one of the magazine's researchers to verify a single paragraph in a sixty-thousand-word article—a nuclear physicist's startling anecdote about a Japanese incendiary balloon blown halfway across the world to land on the very reactor making the plutonium that would soon destroy Nagasaki.[21] McPhee had resigned himself to "kill" the passage when, just hours before press time, the fact-checker tracked down another source. Reached at a shopping mall—with the help of the police—the new source confirmed the story and the paragraph lived. The routines of internal fact-checking respond to the imperative to eliminate untruth, not call attention to it.

The new fact-checkers do just the opposite. They investigate claims that are *already* in the news and publish the results as a new story. The fact-checking movement asks political reporters to do something that can be quite uncomfortable for them: to challenge public figures by publicizing their mistakes, exaggerations, and deceptions. It asks them to intervene in heated political debates and decide who has the facts on their side. "After being trained for years not to take sides, you will now have to choose which side is right," instructs a training manual for journalists new to the genre.[22] This kind of fact-checking has precursors in American news, most directly in the "adwatch" reports on campaign commercials that proliferated in the 1990s. Over the last decade, however, political fact-checking has become a staple of professional news reporting in the United States. Fact-checkers now operate year in and year out, not only during elections. They investigate questionable claims wherever they surface, from political memoirs and Facebook posts to speeches on the floor of Congress. And they see themselves as a distinct professional cohort—a self-described fact-checking *movement* within journalism. Increasingly, fact-checkers have their own rules, routines, and "best practices," hammered out in their own conferences and mailing lists. They promote their style of journalism tirelessly and celebrate its achievements vocally. "Fact-checking is not a fad. Fact-checking is not a novelty. It is absolutely here to stay," PolitiFact's publisher declared triumphantly at the first "global summit" of fact-checkers, in 2014. "At PolitiFact, we are reminded of our reach and importance every day as we spread this mantra: Words matter. What a politician says matters. What the government says matters. And when they make a promise or a claim, fact-checking journalists will check it out."[23]

This book investigates fact-checking through the three U.S.-based organizations that have done the most to establish it as a practice and as a movement: FactCheck.org, launched in 2003, and PolitiFact and the *Washington Post*'s Fact Checker, both founded in 2007. These outlets are now well-established voices in national political discourse, cited constantly in venues from NPR to the *Daily Show*. They have won numerous awards for their work; in 2009 PolitiFact received a Pulitzer Prize, U.S. journalism's top honor, for its coverage of the 2008 presidential campaign.[24] (FactCheck.org was also a nominee.) Since then newsrooms around the country, large and small, have embraced the genre. The major broadcast networks—ABC, CBS, NBC, CNN, Fox, and MSNBC—all regularly offer on-air fact checks, sometimes in partnership with the full-time outlets. NPR coproduced a fact-checking series with PolitiFact and delivers its own fact checks of campaign claims as well as major political events like the State of the Union address. The Associated Press and the *New York Times*, standard-bearers of print journalism, have invested heavily in the new genre and now offer fact checks well beyond campaign season.[25] *USA Today* covers the movement avidly, cites fact-checkers often, and in 2012 began posting videos and reprinting articles directly from FactCheck.org, whose reporters appear in the paper under their own bylines. Only one major national paper, the *Wall Street Journal*, has not embraced the trend.[26]

The fact-checking movement also includes journalists working in local and regional news outlets around the country. These efforts come and go, and no reliable count exists. But serious fact-checking initiatives can be found in traditional newspapers, like the "Truth Needle" at the *Seattle Times* and the *Reno Gazette-Journal*'s "Fact Checker," as well as in online-only outlets like the Voice of San Diego and the Michigan Truth Squad. In 2012 and 2014, local TV newsrooms in markets from Elmira, New York, and Madison, Wisconsin, to Phoenix, Denver, and San Francisco ran segments under names like "Fact Check," "Truth Test," and the popular "Reality Check." Several ventures are the product of unusual local partnerships, like AZ Fact Check, run jointly by the *Arizona Republic*, an NBC affiliate, and the journalism school at Arizona State University. More than a dozen news outlets have signed up to run state-level PolitiFact franchises since the site began to license them in 2010.

Several vital threads come together in the fact-checking movement and the organizations that lead it. Theirs is a story of shifting institutional norms and practices: Fact-checkers enact a deliberate critique of conventional reporting and its practice of objectivity. It is also a story of technological change. Fact-checking as a genre and fact-checkers as news organizations are finely adapted to today's networked news ecosystem. Finally, this is a story about contemporary ways of knowing—about the limits of rational debate in the postbroadcast public sphere. Fact-checkers are a product of the same fractured and fragmented media world they seek to repair. Their work shows every day how the facts in political life depend on institutional knowledge-building regimes and how difficult public reasoning becomes when those regimes lose authority.

Deciding What's True charts the emergence of a new style of newswork, updating a long tradition of newsroom studies whose landmark is Herbert Gans's *Deciding What's News*. Fact-checkers say political reporting must be more assertive in a world where journalists no longer control access to the public sphere—where they have lost the ability to decide what's news. At the center of the book is a detailed picture of the day-to-day work of fact-checking: how these reporters mine the daily news for claims to investigate, how they find original data and trustworthy experts, how they reach decisive verdicts, and how they respond to their many critics. Fact-checkers think about their audience and their mission in more than one way. They try to balance the daily realities of highly partisan, often vicious political discourse online with their formal commitment to inform a reasoning democratic public. They promise to resolve factual debates in an objective way but also say that, in politics, the truth is not black and white.[27]

This new style of journalism offers a window onto changes in the newsroom and in the wider news ecosystem. Fact-checking combines traditional reporting tools and a commitment to objectivity with the annotative, critical style first associated with bloggers. Fact-checkers practice journalism in the network mode. They link promiscuously to outside news sources, encourage other reporters to cite their work, and strike distribution deals with major media organizations. Fact-checkers have achieved a high profile in elite media-political networks. This affirms their status as objective truth seekers but also places surprising limits on their political critique. Fact-checkers vocally reject "false equivalence" in the news. At the same time, they insist that neither major party has a greater claim to truth in U.S. politics—though their own rulings point to more egregious falsehoods from the right.

Themes and Arguments

Journalism does not simply hold a mirror up to the world: This is the common point of departure for almost all academic research about news production.[28] Journalists deem some events and people newsworthy while ignoring others. They privilege particular sources and viewpoints, fashioning this material into narratives that fit basic formulas and often reproduce establishment perspectives.[29] They do all of this in ways that vary markedly across different genres or national traditions of journalism. That is, reporters and editors *make* the news—though as Michael Schudson has emphasized, they do not make it up.[30] Fact-checking brings the problem of the institutional basis for public truth claims into sharp relief. The journalists studied in this book make a sincere and remarkably successful effort to get at the facts behind political claims. But facts depend on particular interpretive schemes. They can be unmade in the face of new evidence or a different way of looking at the world. Fact-checking thus highlights the deeper problem with the journalism-as-mirror metaphor: Not just the news but the human institutional reality it reports on is socially constructed.

Three overarching themes run through *Deciding What's True*. The first major focus is on the history and practice of objective journalism in the United States. Organized political fact-checking by professional journalists is barely a dozen years old. The organizations studied here were born into an industry already in crisis, roiled by economic, technological, and professional challenges. They are witnesses to and products of what has been called the "slow-motion collapse of the industrial work model" in journalism.[31] In the last decade a new wave of newsroom studies has examined changes in the production of news in the digital age, in the United States and overseas.[32] The rise of fact-checking as a style of news and a movement in the news adds an important chapter to this story. Fact-checkers practice a kind of journalism that is undeniably of this moment but also claims to revitalize the truth-seeking ideals so vital to the field's self-understanding. Their novel mission returns our attention to the question that animated canonical studies of American journalism by Gaye Tuchman, Michael Schudson, Herb Gans, Daniel Hallin, and others: the understanding and practice of objectivity among professional reporters.

Understanding is just as important as practice in this account. The events and texts brought together here are meant to show how fact-checkers do their work but also how they *talk* about it—to one another and also to fellow journalists, academic researchers, media and political reformers, and the public. A norm like objectivity is more than just a pattern of behavior: "Explaining the *articulation* of a norm is part of explaining the norm."[33] More than that, formally articulated norms and day-to-day practices exist in a sort of dialectic.

Norms inform practices but don't entirely explain or lie "behind" them. Like the rest of us, journalists reinterpret their ideals and sometimes invent new ones as circumstances change. They understand their own work differently depending on the situation and the audience. Thus, an important current in these pages is "metajournalistic" discourse, today and in the past—the conversation journalism has with itself about its successes and failures and about how to adapt to the demands of a changing political world.[34] Reporters began to push at the bounds of objective practice even before the norm became fully entrenched.[35] Fact-checking continues a decades-long turn toward more assertive, analytical reporting that claims the authority to interpret politics for readers.[36] Like earlier journalistic reformers, fact-checkers say their approach corrects for the failures of conventional reporting— although they almost never criticize fellow journalists in published articles. Their understanding of objectivity and their vital ties to other news organizations—two factors more closely related than we might suppose— keep the focus on politicians.

Those links between news organizations point to a second major theme: the shifting media-political environment for news production. Fact-checkers offer an exceptionally clear view of systemic changes in the media in recent decades: the fragmenting of news audiences and the proliferation of journalistic genres and roles that accompanied the rise of first cable and then the Internet as news platforms. The world of more or less "mass" audiences in which journalism became a profession no longer exists. The notion of a single consensus "story" around major events, never completely accurate, is all but defunct. Much of the news ecosystem today is occupied by outlets and formats that exist in relation to other outlets and formats—news offered as an alternative or a corrective to "mainstream" accounts, whether on Fox News or *Democracy Now!*[37] Fact-checkers appreciate these realities as well as anyone working in the media today. They study the media in every story, tracing the origins of political rumors and mapping their spread through the news ecosystem. Their own work sparks frequent controversies that ripple out across media networks.

In this way fact-checking makes explicit the "intermedia" links that traditional reporting practice tends to obscure and that journalism research has dealt with only episodically.[38] Formally, fact-checkers adhere to traditional ideas about journalism's public, writing for an idealized audience of democratic citizens. They say their mission is simply to provide information, not to change public discourse. At the same time, these journalists pay close attention to their own media footprint. Their work is designed to be incorporated into future news stories. Their authority as objective fact-checkers depends in part on the network of elite media outlets that cite and quote and interview them—relationships that demand effort and attention. Because fact-checking tries to institutionalize a new practice of objectivity, it makes visible the web of material, organizational, and institutional ties in which a norm like objectivity has meaning.

Finally, this book raises the question of how we negotiate public facts in a divided political moment. What counts as a hard fact of political reality for journalists or for the rest of us? What are the limits of public reasoning in a fractured media environment where consensus is rare? Fact-checkers believe in facts. They trust their own methods for seeking them out. But they necessarily operate in a difficult zone between accuracy and truth and admit that the facts in politics can be a matter of interpretation. The debate over Romney's controversial campaign ad captured the paradox well. By one standard, at least, "Who Will Do More?" was accurate—Chrysler *was* going to build Jeeps in China, Romney's defenders pointed out, dismissing the mainstream consensus as evidence of liberal media bias.[39] A fact check by Fox News argued that the real issue was that "after getting bailed out by American tax dollars, a company was deciding to create jobs somewhere *other* than in the US."[40] But professional fact-checkers read the ad differently. They carefully reviewed the economic, policy, and political circumstances around Romney's claim. In that context, the clear intent was to create the impression that the bailout was costing American jobs, when the best evidence indicated the opposite was true. Romney's *message* was a lie even if his words were not.

The question of how to separate fact from opinion—of what kind of truth is even possible in politics—stokes the frequent public controversies over fact-checking. It runs under most of the episodes reviewed in these chapters. It may not have any simple, definitive answer, but studying professional fact-checkers does shed light on the practical realities of building durable facts in today's public sphere. These organizations afford an unusually clear view of the ways that factual reasoning is "embedded"—in material practices, social relations, and systems of value. The world of journalistic work that emerges here offers little evidence for the existence of incontestable facts or absolute truth. This does not mean, however, that objective journalism's injunction to separate facts from values is pointless. On the contrary, the work of nonpartisan fact-checkers attests every day to the value of a practical commitment to objectivity. On almost every page of this book we find evidence that one argument is not as good as another, that experience and understanding do count for something, and that fair and honest inquiry brings us closer to the truth.

Organization of the Book

The seven chapters that make up *Deciding What's True* are organized into three parts. The first part introduces the fact-checkers and considers fact-checking broadly as a form of journalism, political discourse, and factual inquiry. The key question here is where this new kind of news reporting fits both in today's media world and in the history of professional journalism in the United States. Chapter 1 profiles the three news organizations at the heart of the book: FactCheck.org, PolitiFact, and the *Washington Post*'s Fact Checker. These "ink-stained fact-checkers" form the core of a professional reform movement that sees the new genre as a response to the fragmentation of American public life over the last three decades. However, fact-checking is contested terrain—bloggers, media critics, and politicians all lay claim to it. I survey the fact-checking landscape and introduce the partisan media "watchdogs" who act as a kind of permanent counterpart to journalistic fact-checkers. This wider institutional milieu is vital to understanding how professional journalists define and patrol the boundaries of legitimate fact-checking.

How should we understand fact-checking as a form of factual inquiry? Chapter 2 begins by reviewing the institutional history that has taken shape among practitioners, vital to their sense of fact-checking as a reform movement, and then considers the genre as part of the longer "interpretive turn" in American news. This leads to the question of what separates fact-checkers from other journalists: What are the particular epistemological challenges of investigating claims from public political discourse? Drawing on science and technology studies, I offer a framework based on the surprising instability of "institutional facts." Fact-checkers operate in an institutional world that is messier than we might think and reach their verdicts by making reasoned judgments about the right standard to apply in a given context. But they work in the open, without the mechanisms that regulate and protect factual inquiry in more specialized areas like science or law. Comparisons to both scientific work and investigative journalism illuminate the ways that judgments of fact and value are woven together while highlighting the special challenge of building durable facts in the political world.

The second part of the book offers a close study of the day-to-day work of the elite fact-checking organizations—how these journalists go about, and think and talk about, the contentious business of deciding what's true. It opens with the story of one of the political lies that first put fact-checkers on the map of mainstream news, the surprisingly persistent rumor that President Obama is not a natural-born U.S. citizen. Chapters 3 and 4 explore the newswork routines that make up this investigative work, from choosing claims to check to "triangulating the truth" when experts disagree. Although the elite fact-checkers differ in some respects, a body of common rules and procedures has taken shape around their fraught enterprise, visible in office work, training sessions, editorial meetings, and public and private documents. The analysis in these chapters highlights how fact-checkers navigate a deeply politicized field of experts and data, how they rely on one another's work, and how they come together in moments of controversy. It also introduces what fact-checkers call the problem of "context"—the difference between literal and implied meaning that always troubles their work.

Chapter 5 turns from institutional routines and norms to the murkier epistemological terrain at the heart of fact-checking. It explores this with a close study of the operation and occasional breakdowns of PolitiFact's "Truth-O-Meter," the fictional instrument that helps to organize and routinize the group's investigations while also giving fact-checkers a way to critique their own methods. I develop these themes and apply the framework introduced in chapter 2 with an extended case study: a fact check of Glenn Beck that I wrote as a participant-observer at PolitiFact and that provoked a public confrontation with the conservative media icon. The case highlights once again what objective factual inquiry means in practice for these journalists: not testing political claims against undisputed facts but rather drawing on judgment and reason—and, inevitably, *values*—to interpret a contested institutional reality and make a coherent argument about where the truth lies.

What kind of difference can fact-checking make in the world? The third part of *Deciding What's True* looks outward to the fact-checkers' relationships with readers, with other reporters, and in the political realm. It begins with a scene from the 2014 midterm elections: one more case in the vivid catalogue fact-checkers cite to show that what they do will never stop politicians from telling lies. While in practice fact-checkers pay close attention to their effect on political discourse, they insist that the only legitimate mission for journalists is to provide information to citizens. Chapter 6 details the fact-checkers' ties to their audience: how they cultivate traffic, how they communicate with readers, and how they reconcile an idealized vision of the public with the charged partisan dynamics that drive attention week by week. But fact-checkers also have a second vital audience. They strive for relevance and achieve their widest impact by managing formal and informal relationships across the media world, especially with high-status news outlets. These relationships magnify the impact of fact-checking while affirming its authority and legitimacy as objective journalism.

The final chapter of *Deciding What's True* takes up the objective status of the fact-checkers as a function of their position in the media-political networks they navigate every day. Their status as objective journalists depends on the way that others use and talk about their work; it is reproduced in formal and informal relationships and in the pattern of outlets that cite and quote and link to them. This helps explain the limits of their truth-telling mission: fact-checkers focus deliberately on discrete claims and individual political actors, carefully avoiding any conclusion that would assign blame for political controversies or for the state of public discourse as a whole. They refuse to talk about the largest conclusion to be drawn from a decade of fact-checking in the United States: Republicans distort the truth more often and more severely than Democrats. I conclude with an epilogue examining recent changes in the world of fact-checking and what they mean for the future of this new genre.

A Note About the Research

My first contact with professional fact-checkers came in 2010 as a graduate student at Columbia University. I was working on a dissertation about the emerging news ecosystem, using a handful of case studies to examine how major stories unfold today in the critical interplay among different kinds of news venues: elite newspapers, alternative media, talk shows, political bloggers, and so on. Various fact-checking sites—I did not yet understand the vital differences among them—kept turning up in my cases. These organizations seemed to have an especially clear view of online discussion and debate. So late that year I made two trips to Washington, DC, to visit Media Matters for America, PolitiFact, and FactCheck.org (which until 2011 also had its headquarters there). Almost overnight, my project changed shape. More than offering a view of the changing news ecosystem, these fact-checking groups embodied it in their unusual mission, their work practices, and their organizational structures. Fact-checkers produced the kind of link-driven analysis usually associated with political blogging. But more interesting was what seemed to set them apart from bloggers: deep ties to the world of elite journalism and a vocal commitment to its reigning ideal. Even before I'd seen the behind-the-scenes work of investigating political claims, listening to fact-checkers hinted at an occupational world that bridged old and new media in surprising ways.

Deciding What's True is the first in-depth study of the fact-checking movement in professional journalism. It draws on a mix of textual and ethnographic methods: participant observation, formal and informal interviews, content analysis, and some historical research. It is based on more than two hundred hours of fieldwork and interviews conducted over the course of five years in the newsroom and in various public and private forums. I also rely on close textual analysis of published fact checks and other news reports, reading these in light of the historical events they relate to. In practice these methodological lines became quite blurred. The media actors studied here produce a stream of documents—newspaper articles, editor's notes, blog posts, media transcripts, conference transcripts—that defy easy categorization as news texts or ethnographic "texts." Debates about fact-checking often include journalists, media critics, and press scholars engaging with one another directly and publicly. I suggest in the introduction to part 2 that professional fact-checkers perform an unusual variant of the reporter's role as witness: they witness *mediated* events. Similarly, this book reports on an intensely mediated discourse of and about fact-checking.

The initial phase of the research, between 2010 and 2012, spanned fieldwork in Washington, DC, Philadelphia, and another East Coast city that was the site of professional training for a new PolitiFact partner. I interviewed editors, reporters, and interns at the fact-checking organizations as well as traditional journalists, media critics, partisan fact-checkers, and political strategists. As a researcher embedded with PolitiFact and FactCheck.org, I observed training sessions for reporters and interns, took part in editorial meetings, accompanied fact-checkers on media visits, performed a range of staff and intern duties, and wrote two bylined articles for publication. I sat in with fact-checkers as they met to rule on dozens of political claims from the 2012 presidential cycle and then tracked these rulings as they spread across the media landscape. This mix of news analysis and ethnographic research forms the core of chapters 3, 4, and 5. It allowed me to follow controversies as they unfolded both inside and outside of the newsroom, and to read published articles in light of the actual newswork and internal deliberations that produced them.

At the end of 2011, with funding from the New America Foundation, I co-organized a fifty-person, daylong conference that featured professional fact-checkers as well as journalists, researchers, activists, educators, and foundation officials.[41] This was a rare opportunity for a qualitative researcher—a chance to have my "informants" respond to vital questions about the history, norms, practice, and political effects of fact-checking, in a real-world setting involving important constituencies for their movement. This marked the start of a longer engagement in the fact-checking milieu that informs this book. I've participated in more than a dozen conferences, panel discussions, and other public events with fact-checkers. I helped to plan the first international fact-checking summit, which took place in London in 2014, and presented research there and at the next international conference a year later.[42] I've been involved in several research initiatives that brought together scholars and journalists interested in the growth of fact-checking and the effects it can have in the world. I have also taken part in private forums organized by fact-checkers to solicit feedback about new initiatives. This view of how fact-checkers talk about their work in different contexts and to different constituencies is especially important in framing the analysis in chapters 6 and 7.

Deciding What's True offers a glimpse of a new kind of news at a moment of rapid change. Fact-checking is a moving target—an evolving field that connects the worlds of journalism, academia, and politics. This protean quality makes it a fascinating subject and has made it possible for me to both observe and participate in different registers as the field has taken shape. (One anthropologist has coined an evocative term for this sort of engagement in an emerging area: "participant figuring out."[43]) At the same time, being involved in the fact-checking milieu in multiple contexts can produce conflicts of interest. For instance, programming the 2011 summit meant trying to meet the priorities of funders—liberal foundations interested in media reform, including George Soros's Open Society Institute—while also pursuing my own research agenda and protecting my relationships with fact-checkers. One major point of tension was the guest list: Some funders felt strongly that the progressive fact-checking outlet Media Matters for America should be present, and professional fact-checkers worried about the political slant of the event (especially given Soros's involvement) and insisted that conservative outlets also be invited if Media Matters was. As the journalists hoped, the solution was not to invite any partisan outlets.[44]

This sort of political tension runs through the fact-checking world and surfaced in many different ways during the research for this book. Another example: although I make a point of it here, during fieldwork I did not challenge these journalists on the question of why Republicans fare worse in their ratings. (At the same time, I made no secret of my own views and invited several key informants to critique an earlier draft.) More generally, it is fair to note that I have had some small role in the discourse this book examines. A major theme of what follows is how fact-checking has been influenced by contact with adjacent professional fields, in particular the academic and nonprofit worlds. However, I hope it will be clear that close engagement in this emerging journalistic world has been a crucial source of insight and perspective, one I try to be reflective about here.

A Note on Consistency

Finally, a note about consistency—my own and that of the journalists this book reports on. Fact-checking remains a contested practice, unclaimed and unstable. What it means is still to some extent up in the air. Various participants and observers, often a difficult line to draw, see it in different ways. This book focuses on the work of professional, journalistic fact-checkers. A major goal—less straightforward than it sounds—is to understand this emerging phenomenon as they do and to communicate that sense to the reader. But I also try to trace the contours of a wider discourse that sprawls across the media and political worlds.

As noted earlier, fact-checkers talk about their work in different ways depending on the situation and the audience. Their vision of what fact-checking can accomplish is sometimes narrow and sometimes broad. These journalists claim not to want to change people's minds but seize eagerly on any sign that fact-checking makes a difference in the world. They purport to offer decisive factual judgments but also say reasonable people can disagree with their conclusions. They avoid some topics altogether. Throughout this book I draw attention to the limits and internal contradictions of the fact-checking movement. This is where one begins to see the tensions that always inform such a professional project—the difficult questions it raises and the provisional answers fielded by different actors in an emergent area of practice. But I don't mean to present these inconsistencies as a fault or even out of the ordinary. On the contrary, this sort of inconsistency seems basic to human affairs. None of us could get by without it in our professional lives (certainly not in academia). The contradictions we rely on tend to become visible whenever something interesting happens in the life of an organization or a wider professional field—when previously stable and unquestioned arrangements become unsettled.[45]

Fact-checking continues to generate remarkable enthusiasm in the worlds of journalism and politics. It also invites regular critiques, some quite thoughtful, from observers who think fact-checkers confuse public discourse more than they clarify it or that they fall prey to the same sort of false balance they so often condemn.[46] Advocates of meaningful structural change in the conduct or content of American politics may be forgiven for concluding that fact-checking, on the whole, reinforces the centripetal tendencies of U.S. media and political elites—a bipartisan consensus that delegitimizes strong political views as against a more reasonable, "moderate" center. Meanwhile, the earnest people involved in the hard work of political campaigns often don't recognize themselves in the picture that fact-checkers offer of a world ruled by dishonesty and lacking in conviction.[47]

I am sure this book will not completely satisfy such critics, but I hope it sheds light on these complicated questions. It may be worth saying outright that I am sympathetic to the broad fact-checking project, if not always to the conclusions these journalists reach. I treat the fact-checkers as sincere in their commitments. I see the contradictions they present as something to understand rather than condemn. Fact-checking is a reform movement, but one distinctly tethered to the ideology of professional journalism. These are not outsiders—perhaps the key fact in explaining both their success and the limits of their media and political critique. Like earlier generations of journalistic reformers, fact-checkers aim to revise their profession's reigning ideal in order to defend it.

1

INK-STAINED
FACT-CHECKERS

Early in the summer of 2014 an unusual gathering took place at the London School of Economics, near the city center: the first-ever international conference of political fact-checkers.[1] Attendees came from more than twenty countries on six continents. They represented twenty-six different fact-checking operations. Several of these ran out of major national newspapers, such as *Le Monde* in Paris, *El Mercurio* in Chile, and London's *Guardian*. Others had ties to broadcast operations, like the Fact Check desk of the Australian Broadcast Corporation, or like Pagella Politica—literally, "Political Report Card"—an independent site whose research drives a live, weekly fact-checking program on Italy's public broadcaster, RAI. Most, however, were independent websites with no formal ties to news organizations. All but three of the outfits represented had been launched in the last five years.[2]

On the first morning of the summit, the fact-checkers met in a cramped classroom to introduce themselves. Roughly half had backgrounds in journalism, but others came from the worlds of politics, academia, and technology; two were college students in the Czech Republic. Many saw themselves as political reformers. The founder of India's FactChecker.in, which relies on academic researchers to investigate claims and journalists to edit their work, explained that the initiative grew out of a nationwide anticorruption movement. Egypt's MorsiMeter emerged from a wave of volunteerism that accompanied the Arab Spring, "when people became insanely optimistic and . . . we decided to build a line of tools that helps to empower the average citizen," said its co-creator, an "information activist." Some fact-checkers targeted statements by political figures while others focused on correcting errors in the press or offering a counterpoint to state-run media. Ukraine's StopFake, a site launched just months before the summit that specialized in exposing doctored photographs and bogus news accounts, had the narrowest mission: to counter "Russian propaganda."

Fact-checkers with reporting backgrounds described themselves as seeking to improve the profession. "I believed that journalism in Italy was ill, and fact-checking is good medicine to try to save our journalism," declared the founder of Il Politicometro, another Italian site. The *Guardian*'s Reality Check columnist echoed that view with a comment on her own career: "It rather surprised me that after twenty years of being a reporter I then go off into a little corner of the web site to do what I kind of got *into* journalism to do."3

The veterans in the room, comparatively speaking, were the three U.S. fact-checking outlets this book focuses on: FactCheck.org, founded in 2003, and PolitiFact and the *Washington Post*'s Fact Checker, both launched in 2007. Each was represented at the summit by its second generation of leadership (although the founders remained active in the movement and had advised many of the overseas ventures that attended the summit).4 The modern fact-checking movement arguably began at a much smaller meeting seven years earlier, when the founder of FactCheck.org, Brooks Jackson, invited his two new rivals to a conference on "the rise of media fact-checkers." He welcomed them warmly to the fold; both in turn credited FactCheck.org for inspiring their new ventures. "Well, thanks very much, Brooks, and you're certainly the father of this movement," said Michael Dobbs, the *Washington Post*'s original Fact Checker columnist. "It's great that we're now a fraternity. We're not just ink-stained wretches, we're ink-stained fact-checkers, and we're proud of our calling."5

This book tells the story of these ink-stained fact-checkers. As noted in the introduction, over the last decade a surge in fact-checking has swept over American newsrooms, from the major broadcast networks and prestige venues like the *New York Times* and National Public Radio (NPR) to scores of smaller newspapers, television stations, and online news outlets across the country. While controversial fact checks still draw criticism in some quarters, the profession's standard-bearers have almost universally embraced the new genre. Debates about whether fact-checking is appropriate in objective news reports seem to be settled. In 2012 the incoming public editor of the *Times*, Margaret Sullivan, dedicated her very first post to a full-throated call for more fact-checking, distancing herself from concerns raised by her predecessor just nine months earlier: "Whatever the conclusions, whatever the effectiveness, of challenging facts, the idea that we have to debate the necessity of doing so strikes me as absurd. What is the role of the media if not to press for some semblance of reality amid the smoke and mirrors?"[6]

But the landscape of fact-checking is contested terrain. Its shifting borders include not just professional journalists but also bloggers, media critics, comedians, elected officials, government agencies, corporations, and other public voices. This chapter offers an overview of that landscape, profiling the three elite fact-checking organizations and the professional milieu that has formed around them. This is a milieu grounded in news reporting but with important ties to the academic and nonprofit worlds—links that have helped to shape fact-checking as a subfield of professional journalism. The second half of the chapter profiles a handful of partisan organizations that fact-check from a political point of view, and that frequently criticize the work of sites like PolitiFact and FactCheck.org. These partisan outlets aren't seen as peers by professional fact-checkers. But they figure prominently in the controversies that envelop this new form of journalism. They are essential to understanding the practices and discourse of the fact-checking movement.

Fact-Checking as Political Discourse

For professional journalists, fact-checking refers to a certain set of reporting practices and to the stories these yield. It increasingly denotes a genre, like "news analysis" or "Q&A," involving a more-or-less standard set of conventions for research and presentation. News outlets signal the shift in convention by giving fact checks a special label or assigning them to a designated page—or simply, as the Associated Press (AP) does, by inserting the phrase "FACT CHECK" into the headline.

But in everyday usage, especially online, fact-checking denotes a mode of address. A "fact check" in this wider sense refers to any analysis that publicly challenges a competing account. This mode of public critique helped to define what has been called the Internet's first native genre, the blog. On December 9, 2001, two months after the 9/11 attacks, a conservative blogger incensed at coverage of the U.S. war effort in Afghanistan issued a call to arms against mainstream journalism: "It's 2001, and we can Fact-Check your ass."[7] That phrase left a wide footprint in online discourse among bloggers of all political stripes. It became shorthand for bloggers' practice of line-by-line analysis of questionable claims, especially claims from journalists. It emphatically captured the shared belief that the Internet had changed the balance of power between reporter and reader. "The Internet is also a venue for press criticism," Nicholas Lemann, dean of Columbia's Journalism School, observed in a 2006 *New Yorker* piece. " 'We can fact-check your ass!' is one of the familiar rallying cries of the blogosphere."[8] While fact-checking has a distinct history within journalism, it is fair to say that the political fact check represents blogging's legacy to the contemporary public sphere, a discursive move available to anyone participating in online discussion and debate.

Examples abound in contemporary public discourse. For instance, in mid-2014 a Walmart executive issued a public fact check of a column in the previous day's *New York Times*, which had argued that the business model of the world's largest public corporation depends upon various forms of public assistance to supplement its "humiliating wages." Walmart's response treated the *Times* column like a first draft submitted to an editor, marking up the text in red ink and challenging its claims with hand-scrawled margin notes; an introduction explained, "We saw this article in the New York Times and couldn't overlook how wildly inaccurate it is, so we had some fun with it. We hope you will too." The debunking won immediate attention from conservative outlets like the *Daily Caller* and the *Wall Street Journal*. And predictably, within days it drew detailed, point-by-point rebuttals from writers at *Salon* and the *Huffington Post*, the latter titled simply "Fact-Checking Walmart's Fact Check of the New York Times." As is often the case, the dispute turned on earlier fact-checking: how to interpret a PolitiFact piece that questioned similar claims about Walmart.[9]

The language of fact-checking has been taken up with particular enthusiasm in the political world. Fact checks now appear routinely not only from campaigns but on the websites of Democratic and Republican party organizations and in press releases from congressional committees and individual lawmakers. (A search on congressional web domains turns up more than seven thousand results, with the earliest appearing to date from 2007 and 2008.) These texts often copy the structure of journalistic fact checks, presenting suspect claims in quotes and linking back to multiple sources. "Fact Check: Why What Speaker Boehner Just Said Is Completely Wrong," announced a late 2013 dispatch from Nancy Pelosi, then the House Democratic leader, whose site dedicated a page to fact-checking. To debunk the claim that members of Congress enjoyed a special exemption from new health care rules, the piece cited two conservative sources and a liberal think tank as well as a respected health news site, PolitiFact, and FactCheck.org.[10] Fact-checking by parties and politicians peaks around the same political events that draw journalists, like debates and major speeches. (Since 2012, House Republicans have offered "real-time" fact checks of the president's State of the Union address on a dedicated site.[11]) But it also clearly reflects partisan electoral imperatives. The day Hillary Clinton released *Hard Choices*, a memoir of her tenure as secretary of state that laid the ground for her 2016 presidential run, Republicans (clearly working from an advance copy) responded online with six "volumes" of fact-checking organized around the major foreign policy challenges the book addressed.[12]

Barack Obama's political staff have been avid fact-checkers. During the 2008 presidential race, the Obama campaign unveiled a website called "Fight the Smears" to combat various rumors about the candidate: that he was a Muslim, that he refused to say the pledge of allegiance, that Michelle Obama used the word "whitey" in church, and so on. In 2009, as the debate over health care reform took shape, the White House established a "Reality Check" page to debunk "myths" about the Affordable Care Act.[13] During its first term, the Obama administration published fact checks on areas as diverse as energy policy, the automobile bailout, and the fate of a bust of Winston Churchill, which the president had supposedly sent back to the British—and which Republican presidential contender Mitt Romney promised to return to its rightful place in the White House.[14] For the 2012 race the Obama campaign unveiled a new site, AttackWatch.com, which invited supporters to become part of the president's "Truth Team": "When you're faced with someone who misrepresents the truth, you can find all the facts you need right here—along with ways to share the message with whoever needs to hear it."[15]

In this wider sense as a mode of public discourse, fact-checking reflects a several-decade shift: the diminished differentiation or more complex inter-penetration of the institutional fields of journalism and politics in the face of technological and economic change.[16] It is well established that rising media abundance has made untenable the gatekeeper role journalists enjoyed in the midcentury heyday of "high-modern" journalism, dominated by three national broadcast networks and powerful metropolitan newspapers.[17] Scholars attribute any number of changes in journalistic practice to this shift; for example, some argue that news organizations abandoned "sac-erdotal" approaches to politics in a more competitive and fragmented me-dia environment.[18] But media abundance also invited a proliferation of news roles and formats that intermingled journalism and politics in new ways. This includes blogs, of course, but before that expanded op-ed pages in the 1970s, political talk radio in the 1980s, and a host of debate, analysis, and com-mentary formats on cable news networks through the 1990s. A thoughtful recent analysis finds that "the space of opinion" in American journalism—meaning venues for elite opinion, analysis, and argument, from policy jour-nals to the *Daily Show*—has expanded dramatically since the introduction of the modern op-ed page at the *New York Times* in 1970. This space of "media intellectuals" bridges the fields of journalism, politics, and academia, the authors argue, and today "is characterized by an incredible diversity of for-mats linked together in a nested a series of multimedia conversations and citational references."[19]

Professional fact-checkers reject the argument that what they do amounts to commentary or opinion journalism, a criticism they hear often. Their identification as reporters who adhere to the objectivity norm is central to the enterprise. However, fact-checking as a whole belongs to the "space of opin-ion" in this broader sense of a sphere of elite contestation over politics and policy. In that space, one class of organization deserves special attention as a kind of permanent institutional counterpart to the professional fact-checkers: partisan media "watchdog" groups who publicize, criticize, and sometimes copy journalistic fact-checkers. Four of these watchdog outlets will be intro-duced after profiles of the elite professional fact-checking organizations.

The Elite Online Fact-Checkers

The first site dedicated to online fact-checking appeared quite early in the history of the web. Snopes.com was founded in 1995 by a pair of self-described "amateur folklorists" with no background in journalism. Today it is the most popular online fact-checker by far, with more than 6 million visitors per month. The site relies on ad support and reportedly yields a comfortable living for Barbara and David Mikkelson, the husband-and-wife team who still run it aided only by a pair of editorial assistants.[20] Snopes.com is not news-driven and addresses itself broadly to online rumors and "urban legends"; major site categories include, for instance, 9/11, Hurricane Katrina, and "Cokelore." However, Snopes.com also debunks rumors and myths from the world of politics, sometimes by citing specialists like FactCheck.org and PolitiFact.[21] Although the founders don't identify as journalists, they have responded to accusations of bias—an elemental feature of the fact-checking world—by pointing to the site's financial independence and political neutrality. The "About" page of Snopes.com declares that David Mikkelson is "wholly apolitical, vastly preferring his quiet scholarly life in the company of his cats and chickens to any political considerations."[22]

The first nonpartisan fact-checker focused strictly on U.S. politics appears to have been Spinsanity, launched in 2001 by three recent college graduates. The site was billed as a "nonpartisan watchdog dedicated to unspinning misleading claims from politicians, pundits and the press."[23] The founders saw themselves as press critics as much as journalists. As one would explain to *Daily Show* host Jon Stewart, "Me and my co-editors were sitting around after the 2000 election, and we were just disgusted with the way it all went, and really disgusted with the media coverage, and disgusted with what happened in Florida."[24] Spinsanity ran through the 2004 presidential campaign, ultimately producing more than four hundred fact checks. Its work was syndicated in media outlets including *Salon* and the *Philadelphia Inquirer* and yielded a best-selling 2004 book about the news media and the Bush White House, *All the President's Spin*. (As told to Stewart, the book described how the administration took advantage of one of the "weaknesses" of the news media: "the objectivity that journalism aspires to, where they won't call a lie a lie.") In a sign of the disciplinary lines that overlap in fact-checking, after Spinsanity closed, one of the founders became a reporter, another joined the staff of a journalism review, and the third, Brendan Nyhan, became a political scientist who studies political misinformation and fact-checking.[25]

Although not run by professional reporters, both of these early fact-checking sites practiced journalism in the broadest sense: they tried to offer authoritative, factual accounts of issues of public concern and interest.[26] This is particularly true of Spinsanity, which, despite its overt media critique, embraced journalism's core mission of helping people to understand public debates and make informed political choices. This is the mission entailed in what Herb Gans has called "journalism's theory of democracy," the self-understanding of American reporters that places the information they provide at the center of democratic citizenship.[27] The fact-checking operations that followed brought new resources to bear on that mission—larger staffs, professional training and experience, and access to elite media and political networks. But they also shared Spinsanity's critique of conventional journalism, a critique with deep roots within the profession.

FactCheck.org: A "Consumer Advocate" for Citizens

The first dedicated U.S. fact-checking site staffed by professional journalists was FactCheck.org, a nonprofit founded by veteran political reporter Brooks Jackson and communications scholar Kathleen Hall Jamieson. Jackson had begun producing fact-checking segments as a political correspondent a decade earlier at CNN, where he consulted Jamieson's work to refine the format. (This history is reviewed in more detail in the next chapter.) Housed at the Annenberg Public Policy Center at the University of Pennsylvania—its original name was the "Annenberg Political Fact Check"—FactCheck.org announced itself in 2003 as a "nonpartisan, nonprofit, 'consumer advocate' for voters that aims to reduce the level of deception and confusion in U.S. politics."[28] The site was conceived as a project for the 2004 election but proved unexpectedly popular and became a year-round venture. (Its fame grew after being cited by Vice President Dick Cheney—as "factcheck.com"—in a debate with his Democratic challenger John Edwards.)[29]

Today an editorial staff of six, assisted by undergraduate interns, produces roughly five fact checks per week. These often investigate multiple claims related to a current political controversy and may run to several thousand words. Unlike many newer peers, FactCheck.org does not use a rating system or meter to grade the truth of political claims, but its fact checks describe political deception in blunt language and often deliver sharply worded verdicts. ("Kentucky Sen. Rand Paul claimed that 20 million jobs were created after President Ronald Reagan's dramatic tax cuts in the 1980s, and that this was the 'last time' such job growth took place. Paul is wrong on both counts," began a typical item from mid-2014 titled "Rand Paul's Supply-Side Distortion.") The group focuses its analysis on "major U.S. political players," meaning in practice government officials, electoral candidates, and various party organizations, including outside groups such as political action committees. However, it also investigates online rumors and chain e-mails related to political themes.

The FactCheck.org site carries no advertising and relies on foundation support. Funding from the Annenberg Foundation averaged almost $750,000 since 2010 but began to fall off in 2014, as a ten-year grant establishing the site came to an end.[30] In 2010 the organization also began accepting private donations, which totaled $139,000 in 2014, an election year, and $58,000 the following year. FactCheck.org does not take money from corporations, labor unions, or advocacy groups. In 2011 the Annenberg Public Policy Center launched FlackCheck.org, a companion site focused on "political literacy." The venture is separately staffed and operated but relies on FactCheck.org's research to produce videos and analysis highlighting "patterns of deception" in political speech.

Its nonprofit status and ties to a research university set FactCheck.org apart to a degree from peers based in traditional newsrooms. A mission statement explains that the site aims to apply "the best practices of both journalism and scholarship"; staff sometimes invoke an academic mindset, for instance, to explain their refusal to use "unscientific" rating systems.[31] More strikingly, the site's copyright policy invites anyone to reproduce or distribute its fact checks free of charge, so long as appropriate credit is given and "editorial integrity" is preserved. In this way, foundation support helps to resolve the usual tension between journalism's democratic and commercial goals, ensuring the widest possible audience for the group's fact-checking. "Being stolen or plagiarized is fine with us," founder Brooks Jackson told me. Eugene Kiely, who succeeded Jackson as director in 2013, echoed this view: "Our copyright essentially says 'steal our stuff.'" FactCheck.org has established informal dis-

FactCheck.org Fellowship Program

FactCheck.org, the award-winning political website at the Annenberg Public Policy Center of the University of Pennsylvania, is now accepting applications for its 2011–2012 fellowship program. The next class of fellows will be trained during an eight-week, paid summer program at FactCheck's offices at APPC from June 5–July 30. Those who are trained this summer must agree to work 10 to 15 hours per week at FactCheck.org during the fall and spring semesters, if their work merits continued employment.

We are a nonpartisan, nonprofit "consumer advocate" for voters. The fellows at FactCheck.org help our staff monitor the factual accuracy of claims made by political figures in TV ads, debates, speeches, interviews and news releases. They help conduct research on such claims and write articles for publication on our website under the guidance and supervision of FactCheck.org staff. The fellows must have an ability to write clearly and concisely, an understanding of journalistic practices and ethics, and an interest in politics and public policy. The fellows also must be able to think independently and set aside any partisan biases.

The deadline for applications is Feb. 28. For more information, contact FactCheck.org Philadelphia Director Eugene Kiely at Eugene.kiely@factcheck.org.

THE ANNENBERG
PUBLIC POLICY CENTER
OF THE UNIVERSITY OF PENNSYLVANIA

FIGURE 1.1 A call for interns for FactCheck.org's fellowship program describes the group's mission and indicates the qualities it looks for in student interns, including "the ability to set aside any partisan biases." *Source: Courtesy of FactCheck.org.*

tribution partnerships to increase its reach, for instance, with *USA Today, Yahoo News,* and the *Huffington Post,* which frequently reproduce its articles.[32]

Despite these ties to the academic and philanthropic worlds, though, FactCheck.org identifies unmistakably as a journalistic enterprise. The site has won numerous journalism awards and was a nominee for a Pulitzer Prize. Its editorial staff come almost exclusively from backgrounds in political reporting. (Both Jackson and Kiely are veteran political reporters. The former worked for CNN, the *Wall Street Journal*, and the AP, and the latter for the *Philadelphia Inquirer* and *USA Today*.) This core identification is reaffirmed constantly in both public and private settings. Thus, for instance, a call for student interns stressed that they must be able to "think independently and set aside any partisan biases" (see figure 1.1). To the dismay of some, interns are discouraged from participating in political causes or events or from adorning their workspace with political materials.[33]

PolitiFact: Fact-Checking as a Database

PolitiFact appeared in May 2007 as a joint project of the *St. Petersburg Times* and its then-sister publication, the *Congressional Quarterly*. The nonprofit Poynter Institute owns the newspaper, now called the *Tampa Bay Times*. But both the *Times* and PolitiFact operate as commercial, ad-supported media ventures, and select fact checks run in the print edition of the paper. (*CQ*'s role in the site diminished quickly, and in 2009 it was sold to the Economist Group.) The idea for PolitiFact came from Bill Adair, then the newspaper's Washington bureau chief. He proposed it to his editors—with the tentative name "Campaign Referee"—as a version of FactCheck.org built around a database, rather than a blog. "My idea was, take what FactCheck was doing and package it in a way that was less of a blog, and takes advantage of the web," Adair explained. "By building it from scratch we were able to create what I think is truly a new form of journalism."[34]

PolitiFact's database hinges on its trademarked "Truth-O-Meter," which scores every political claim along a six-point scale running from "True" to "Pants on Fire." The site's original mission statement played up this difference from its predecessor: "PolitiFact . . . is bolder than previous journalistic fact-checking efforts because we'll make a call." PolitiFact also differs from FactCheck.org in the targets of its fact-checking, who from the outset have included not just political but media figures: pundits, analysts, columnists, editorial writers, and so on. In 2013 the organization spun off Pundit-Fact, a sister site dedicated to claims by media personalities. Truth-O-Meter verdicts become part of a database that can be accessed according to the topic, the rating, and, crucially, the speaker, making it possible to look up the lifetime record of public figures tracked by the site. "This is a working database and over time it will grow more valuable," the site promised at launch.[35]

By 2015 that database had grown to more than five thousand fact checks. Today seven editors and reporters produce roughly twenty items per week for PolitiFact's national site and for PunditFact. Since 2010 PolitiFact has also licensed its brand and its methodology to state media partners—typically flagship newspapers—who pay roughly $30,000 the first year and annual renewals of about $10,000. State franchises operate independently after being trained in the Truth-O-Meter method. They commit to producing several items per week, which run on a dedicated state page at the PolitiFact site and become part of the master Truth-O-Meter database. In return, state media partners sell advertising against their stories at the site and have the right to carry PolitiFact stories in their print editions or to syndicate them to other news outlets in their state.[36] The franchise network grew quickly in its first two years but saw defections after the 2012 presidential race. As the next election approached, it began to recover, however, and by the end of 2015 included fourteen states: Texas, Florida, Georgia, Rhode Island, Wisconsin, Virginia, New Hampshire, Missouri, California, Iowa, Arizona, Nevada, Colorado, and Ohio.[37]

Despite its origins in a commercial newspaper, it would be a mistake to understand PolitiFact mainly as a for-profit venture. Ad revenue at the site has never yielded more than a fraction of the costs of what is a staff-intensive form of journalism. Likewise, from the start of its state licensing program, PolitiFact acknowledged that the "modest amount of revenue" from the media partnerships would not yield a profit and was, instead, a way to defray costs while increasing the audience for PolitiFact's fact-checking. Asked about revenues after the first partners joined in 2010, Adair stressed the site's journalistic mission: "Ultimately, this is a public service play."[38] That sense of mission runs through training sessions for new state partners, who are invited to practice a more demanding and more honest form of journalism. In editor's notes the group often celebrates the depth of the Truth-O-Meter database and the growth of the PolitiFact network around the country. Reporters and editors from across the network gather each year for a celebration they call "PolitiFact Palooza."

Beginning in 2010 PolitiFact sought to build ties to the nonprofit sector, where a number of foundations have supported fact-checking and research about fact-checking as a means of improving the quality of public discourse. These efforts bore fruit in 2013 with a $625,000 grant from the

Ford Foundation and the Democracy Fund that financed the launch of PunditFact.[39] The money allowed PolitiFact to add three full-time fact-checkers to its national staff. It also came with a requirement to "analyze the reach and impact" of the new venture, a common practice in the philanthropic world.[40] This evaluation requirement would be fulfilled by the Poynter Institute rather than by PolitiFact directly. Still, it illustrates a recurring theme: how the disciplinary lines that cross in fact-checking—journalistic, philanthropic, academic—push professional reporters to think and talk about their work in new ways.[41]

The Fact Checker: Translating Political "Code Words"

In September 2007, four months after PolitiFact appeared, the *Washington Post* unveiled its own dedicated fact-checking venture. Political reporter Michael Dobbs, who had retired from the *Post* but was invited back to cover the presidential race, proposed the Fact Checker as a way to correct "some of the flaws in political reporting, the focus on the horse race and the 'he said, she said.'" He envisioned the column awarding some sort of "Pinocchio" prize to dishonest politicians, perhaps with a nose that grew to match the scale of the deception.[42] As Dobbs would later write, he prepared for a heated discussion with his editors: "Was it the place of a *Post* reporter to referee campaign debates, and rap erring politicians over the knuckles? Would we be sacrificing our cherished 'non-partisan' status and 'balance' if we came down on one side or the other in factual arguments?"[43]

Instead the idea met with swift approval. The Fact Checker ran on the *Post*'s website through the presidential election, with an "unofficial quota" of one item per day. A dozen or so columns also ran in the print edition of the newspaper, usually a few pages into the "A" section. The ratings system awarded political claims from one to four "Pinocchios" depending on the degree of distortion; true claims earned a "Gepetto" checkmark. Three months into his tenure Dobbs invented a new category, "True but False," for claims that are "technically accurate" but nevertheless "create a misleading impression that can be as powerful as an outright lie."[44] Looking back on the experience, Dobbs has said that he felt overwhelmed by the "deluge of misinformation," which required him to become an "instant expert" in areas he had never covered before, and that he was able to do more probing reporting during the 2004 race by focusing on a handful of issues.[45]

In 2011 the *Post* revived the Fact Checker as a permanent feature under Glenn Kessler, a longtime politics and policy reporter with the newspaper. Kessler has called this an ideal assignment for a journalist with his background in covering most major policy areas, and especially with experience on the diplomatic and foreign affairs beat, long friendly to analytical reporting.[46] The column's mission statement describes fact-checking as a form of explanatory journalism: "We will seek to explain difficult issues, provide missing context and provide analysis and explanation of various 'code words' used by politicians, diplomats and others to obscure or shade the truth." The rebooted Fact Checker left the Pinocchio scale intact and, at the end of 2011, began compiling average Pinocchio scores for major presidential candidates, a small step toward the "database" approach used by PolitiFact. At the same time, whereas his predecessor occasionally investigated claims from the opinion pages, Kessler hews more narrowly to statements "by political figures and government officials."[47]

Kessler and one other fact-checker produce roughly one item per day for the *Post*'s website, with a column also running in the news section of the print newspaper each Sunday. In 2013 the newspaper unveiled an experimental "instant fact-checking" platform called Truth Teller, funded with a $50,000 grant from the Knight Foundation. The application used an algorithm to identify political claims in recorded speech from video clips and matched these in real time to fact checks from the *Post* as well as PolitiFact and FactCheck.org, displaying the verdict as the video ran.[48] As part of the project, Kessler gained an additional assistant to help produce prerecorded versions of Fact Checker columns for the newspaper's video outlet, PostTV. The rationale mirrored that for FlackCheck, FactCheck.org's companion site: to animate fact-checking in a compelling format that will reach a wider audience than lengthy written analyses.[49]

The Fact Checker differs from its two national peers in its day-to-day ties to a traditional newsroom. The contrast with PolitiFact is notable: While both ventures are attached to print newspapers, PolitiFact runs its own website and is headquartered in a Washington bureau dominated by fact-checkers. Meanwhile Kessler works out of the *Post*'s newsroom, publishes on its website, and does not operate the Fact Checker as a business unit with its own revenue. In this way the venture more closely resembles fact-checking initiatives by other national news outlets like the *New York Times*, the AP, and NPR. However, the Fact Checker is a year-round operation not focused on campaign season. Kessler and his staff work on fact-checking full time, unlike political reporters assigned to check an occasional speech or debate. And, just as important, both Kessler and his predecessor have participated avidly in the professional discourse that argues for the importance of this uncomfortable and often controversial style of journalism. For these reasons, it makes sense to consider the Fact Checker in the same terms as dedicated outlets like PolitiFact and FactCheck.org.

Reformers in the Journalistic Field

These three dedicated fact-checking outlets, with one or two counterparts at traditional news organizations, have become a recognized professional cohort in elite journalism. They meet several times a year at conferences or private gatherings that bring together journalists, researchers, and funders interested in the fact-checking phenomenon. They appear together on panels and are quoted in the same articles. "Call it the Fact-Checking Summit," announced a journalism review's report on a mid-2012 meeting at the National Press Club, continuing:

> The key players in journalism's burgeoning fact-checking movement were on the scene: pioneer Brooks Jackson, who launched and runs FactCheck.org; Bill Adair, editor of the Pulitzer-winning PolitiFact, the Tampa Bay Times initiative that also has regional branches around the country; Glenn Kessler, who writes the The Fact Checker for the Washington Post; and longtime D.C. correspondent Jim Drinkard, who oversees accountability reporting for the Associated Press.[50]

The three elite fact-checkers see themselves as a kind of fraternity. "We're friendly," a group of state PolitiFact reporters were told during a training session—an unusual lesson for journalists to hear about their main rivals.[51] The three sites cover much of the same material, cite one another in their work, and band together against their critics. As noted earlier, when his new counterparts emerged in 2007, FactCheck.org founder Brooks Jackson held a meeting to celebrate the surge in fact-checking. "I am so glad . . . that we have company in this area now," he declared, calling PolitiFact "a breath of fresh air" and praising the skills and experience the *Washington Post* brought to its venture.[52] When Kessler took over the *Post*'s fact-checking column in 2011, Jackson and Adair took him to lunch in Washington, welcoming the new fact-checker to their very small club.[53] "I wouldn't say we're competitors, I think we view each other as part of the same peer group," Kessler would later explain in a PBS interview.[54]

These three organizations are rivals joined in a very self-conscious project of pioneering a new kind of journalism. They offer a reformer's critique of conventional political news, rejecting what is often called "false balance" or "he said, she said" reporting.[55] "I am a journalist of many years—a recovering 'he said, she said' reporter, I suppose," Jackson joked at the opening of a fact-checking summit in late 2011.[56] That reformist identity has taken shape in critical venues like conferences and journalism reviews which, as Barbie Zelizer noted two decades ago, help to "build authority for practices not emphasized by traditional views of journalism."[57] This book draws heavily on such metajournalistic discourse and especially on a series of public and private meetings of fact-checkers over the last decade (listed in table 1.1). These gatherings have been vital to the fact-checking movement in three ways: first, as opportunities for the journalists involved to recognize their shared mission as a movement; second, as sites to negotiate the tensions and contradictions implicit in that movement; and third, as sources of cross-pollination between journalism and adjacent fields, like academia and the nonprofit world, which have been important sources of financial and intellectual support.[58]

On first analysis, fact-checking appears to be simply another specialized journalistic subfield, like sports reporting, with its own subset of norms and practices within the wider professional field. Many practitioners would describe it this way. What sets it apart is a self-conscious orientation to the rest of the field: fact-checkers seek fairly openly to *fix* political journalism by introducing new practices, revising prevailing norms, and building institutional resources for what they see as an essential and undervalued form of public-affairs reporting. Like earlier instances of journalistic "field repair," such as the public journalism movement of the 1990s, fact-checking justifies

TABLE 1.1 Building a Movement: Fact-Checking Events Since 2007

Event	Sponsor	Place	Date
Pants on Fire: Political Mendacity and the Rise of Media Fact-Checkers	Annenberg Public Policy Center	Washington, DC	November 9, 2007
The Future of Fact Checking	City University of New York	New York	November 15, 2011
Fact-Checking in the News	New America Foundation	Washington, DC	December 14, 2011*
"The Facts of Political Life"	New America Foundation	Washington, DC	February 28, 2012*
Truthiness in Digital Media	Harvard Berkman Center	Cambridge, MA	March 6–7, 2012*
"Fact Checking the 2012 Election: Views from the Trenches"	Annenberg Public Policy Center	Washington, DC	May 22, 2012
Countering Misinformation and Strengthening Online Discourse	New America Foundation	Washington, DC	February 8, 2013*
"Challenges for the Fact-Checking Movement: 2013–2016"	New America Foundation	Washington, DC	March 5, 2013
"Fast Food & Fact-Checking: Lessons from PolitiFact"	South by Southwest	Austin, TX	March 11, 2013
"Fact-Checking Goes Global"	South by Southwest	Austin, TX	March 10, 2014
"Fact-Checking Goes Global"	International Journalism Festival	Perugia, Italy	May 3, 2014
"API Fact-Checking Scholars' Meeting"	American Press Institute	Washington, DC	May 30, 2014*
Global Fact-Checking Summit	Poynter Institute	London	June 9–10, 2014*
Latam Chequea	Chequeado	Buenos Aires	November 6–8, 2014
Truth in Politics 2014: A Status Report on Fact-Checking Journalism	American Press Institute	Washington, DC	December 10, 2014*
"Examining PunditFact and Its Role in Journalism"	Poynter Institute	Washington, DC	February 10, 2015*
Global Fact-Checking Summit	Poynter Institute	London	July 25–25, 2015*

Note: There may be other fact-checking events since 2007 not included in this list.

* Events attended by the author.

its unconventional approach in terms of a fundamental failure of the profession.[59] A recurring theme in the chapters that follow is how their common mission both binds rival fact-checkers together and makes their emerging subfield open to influences and discourses from outside of journalism.[60]

Contrasts and Convergence

The three elite U.S. fact-checkers are not identical. Comparing their organizational backgrounds and structure helps to account for some of the differences in their approaches. Consider the contrast between FactCheck.org and PolitiFact. Foundation support and university ties at the older outlet anchor what its own journalists describe as a straightforward, no-frills approach to fact-checking. For instance, FactCheck.org vocally rejects the ratings systems developed by its newer rivals. Brooks Jackson has said there's no "academically respectable way" to rate the truth of political claims— "We're part of an Ivy League university here"—and that he sees meters mainly as marketing tools: "It's flashy, it's eye-catching, it gets people involved, and it helps sell it to an audience that might find our stuff more pedantic."[61] In contrast, PolitiFact's status as an independent, revenue-seeking business unit has encouraged a more entrepreneurial mindset. From the outset the site eagerly courted publicity (by one account, Bill Adair gave more than two hundred on-air interviews during the group's first year) and developed partnerships with broadcasters to promote its work.[62] This media-hungry approach dovetailed with its easily citable Truth-O-Meter, a device that reflects both journalistic and business goals. The humorous rating system makes PolitiFact's analysis easier for readers to digest—it adds flavor to what Adair calls "eat your vegetables" journalism—and also helped to build a national brand.[63] The site's media profile eased the launch of the PolitiFact franchise network, built around licensing the trademarked Truth-O-Meter. Running that network, in turn, has shaped journalistic practice, for instance, by requiring PolitiFact to codify its methodology in order to train new fact-checkers and to promote consistency across franchises.

At the same time, the field of professional journalism is ample and diverse enough to account for the differences between these groups. It would be a mistake to see a strong causal link between funding arrangements (or other organizational features) and newsroom practice among the fact-checkers.

While editors at FactCheck.org attribute their approach to a scholarly mind-set, truth meters are used by other university-linked fact-checkers, such as AZ Fact Check. Conversely, many traditional news organizations such as the AP and the *New York Times* have been reluctant to use rating systems, not-withstanding the example set by the *Washington Post* and the *Tampa Bay Times*. In a 2012 panel discussion with his fact-checking peers, Jim Drinkard, accountability editor at the AP, pointed to the inherent "squishiness" of me-tered ratings.[64] It is equally hard to trace a clear link between organizational roots and the use of a meter among overseas fact-checkers.[65]

In this respect, organizational circumstances influence journalistic work mainly by shaping the context within which editorial choices should make sense. Being based at an Ivy League university adds to the institutional-cultural repertoire the journalists at FactCheck.org can draw on to understand and justify their approach to fact-checking and in this way has shaped their identity and their practice. But the group can also fairly be described, de-spite its nonprofit status and academic home, as journalistic traditionalists—an identity both Jackson and his successor, Eugene Kiely, embrace. "I'm old school," Jackson told me, a phrase he has used in other interviews.[66] Differ-ent rationales would have been available to stay away from rating political claims had FactCheck.org taken root not at a university but in one of the media outlets Jackson worked for previously.

Indeed, while important differences persist, the three elite fact-checkers have shown clear signs of convergence in both business and editorial prac-tice. Editors at FactCheck.org have remarked several times on the sharper deadline pressure the group faced once its national rivals appeared; in 2009 a major site redesign introduced the "FactCheck Wire" for shorter, more timely articles. Both FactCheck.org and the *Post*'s Fact Checker have taken pages from the highly visible PolitiFact. Since 2012, for instance, FactCheck .org has sought to boost its public profile with an aggressive campaign to partner with print and broadcast news outlets.[67] And, as noted earlier, soon after relaunching Fact Checker, Glenn Kessler took a step toward PolitiFact's database model with a "Pinocchio Tracker," which compared the fact-checking records of major presidential candidates.[68] Meanwhile, and perhaps most important in terms of fact-checking's development as a journalistic institution, PolitiFact and Fact Checker have begun to benefit from philan-thropic interest in fact-checking, following the path laid down by FactCheck.

org. This sort of convergence may or may not be the result of deliberate imitation in particular cases, but it unfolds against the backdrop of a set of common constraints—economic, editorial, political—shaping the decisions these organizations take.[69]

This is arguably what it means for a distinct field or subfield of practice to take shape: practitioners begin to identify with one another, even as rivals, and to identify common techniques, concerns, values, and so on. Even where contrasts persist, fact-checkers increasingly have a common language for talking about those differences and what they mean, developed over years of contact in both public and private settings. Take again the question of rating claims, the most visible and contentious dividing line in the fact-checking world. In a 2012 farewell post looking back on nearly a decade at the helm of FactCheck.org, Brooks Jackson mixed praise for his fellow fact-checkers with sharp words about the pitfalls of "inflexible rating systems."[70] The post identified a trade-off that fact-checkers who use ratings systems have conceded openly: meters draw increased attention and simplify analysis that can be forbiddingly dense but also seem to hold out the promise of a mechanical objectivity that defies the messy reality of journalistic fact-checking. (Even the editor of the *Tampa Bay Times*, PolitiFact's parent newspaper, has called the Truth-O-Meter a journalistic "gimmick," albeit a valuable one.)[71] Rating systems bring the tensions in fact-checking into sharp relief and have made PolitiFact and the Fact Checker the focus of intense criticism from both political figures and fellow journalists.

The tradeoffs of rating systems became a central theme of the 2014 Global Summit of fact-checkers. Reprising a debate from an earlier journalism conference, Bill Adair staged a "steel-cage death match" with the director of Full Fact, a London-based fact-checking outlet that abandoned its own five-point rating scheme (indicated by a magnifying lens) as lacking precision and rigor. Will Moy explained that Full Fact decided to forgo "higher attention" in favor of "long-term reputation," adding that "a dodgy rating system—and I'm afraid they are inherently dodgy—doesn't help us with that." PolitiFact's two top U.S. rivals also took part in the debate, which Adair opened with a light-hearted vow to convert the new director of FactCheck. org to his way of thinking.[72] After someone wondered why the scales tend to be comical, Glenn Kessler defended the *Washington Post*'s rating system: "Those Pinocchios, at least in Washington, have tremendous power. I mean

I have members of Congress that call me up, directly, and say, 'What do I need to do to stop getting Pinocchios?'" Of roughly two dozen fact-checking groups in the room, just over half used some sort of meter to assess claims or political promises, and forceful arguments were offered both for and against. But the most striking feature of the discussion was the easy agreement about the virtues and limits of rating claims and the repeated affirmation that the fact-checking world needs multiple approaches.[73]

A major goal of the meeting was to establish an association of fact-checkers from around the world. This promised to be a delicate task. Many different kinds of organizations were present, including a dozen without strong ties to journalism. Surprising methodological differences emerged over the course of the two-day meeting. Some overseas fact-checkers were astonished to learn that their U.S. counterparts always call the subjects of their investigations before publishing; they wondered whether this invites reprisals, or gives public figures the chance to change their story. Meanwhile, veteran journalists in the room couldn't believe that some academically minded peers checked every single factual claim in a debate or speech rather than just the interesting ones. With so many different understandings of what counts as a fact check or a fact-checker, the organizers would have to decide who qualified for membership in the new association. Only one clear principle emerged: Partisan fact-checkers with direct ties to political parties or other interest groups could not take part.[74]

Fact-Checking from a Political Point of View

As noted earlier, fact-checking offers a clear illustration of the institutional blurring or mixing of the media and political fields in recent decades. This is true in at least two important ways. First, journalism that challenges public statements makes it harder in practice for reporters to claim a clear separation from political actors. To contest a claim in public is a political act. It invites political criticism and risks drawing reporters into partisan fights— precisely the kinds of fights that the defensive tactics of objective journalism, such as "he said, she said" framing, are designed to avoid.[75] (It is worth noting that the day-to-day work of fact-checking bears at least a superficial resemblance to the opposition research that has long been a feature of U.S.

political campaigns.) Of course one can argue, as fact-checkers do, that true objectivity means taking the side of truth even when that favors one point of view. But this produces a more "political" journalism in the sense of reporting that advances an argument and predictably sparks counterarguments.

Second, fact-checking as a genre has invited particularly exuberant forms of media activity from political actors and from organizations that bridge the media and political spheres. It is an active site of what some political communications scholars call the "mediatization" of politics, meaning the tendency for political activities or processes—campaigning, activism, and etc.—to "assume media form."[76] This is sometimes described as the penetration of "media logic" into other spheres of activity: to pursue political goals in an organized and strategic fashion means, increasingly, to think and behave like a media producer.[77] This sort of logic can be read, for instance, in strategies used by political actors to go "around" traditional news media. (Journalists and media critics have objected loudly to the use of such strategies by the Obama administration: "They become publishers, they become journalists, they become their own advertising agency," an ABC White House reporter complained in an NPR segment on this question.)[78] The mediatization of politics is arguably neither as new nor as complete as the most overheated rhetoric suggests.[79] Nevertheless, it offers a useful frame for thinking about fact-checking by political actors who very visibly imitate journalistic techniques and presentation even as they challenge professional journalism.

Beyond journalism, one area where fact-checking finds institutional purchase—where it is practiced in a sustained and organized way—is among press critics. Media criticism, like fact-checking, links journalism to adjacent professional fields. In the United States, it has two main centers of gravity. What might be called establishment press criticism straddles the border between professional journalism and media scholarship. It is embodied by publications like the *Columbia Journalism Review* and the *American Journalism Review*, both based in schools of journalism. Various publications and centers occupy different points along the spectrum between reporting and academia; Harvard's Nieman Journalism Lab, to take another example, takes a more scholarly approach than the established professional reviews. However, all of these venues offer a space for professional self-examination and critique—for instance, of "he said, she said" reporting—and have helped to incubate the fact-checking movement. (Two articles in the *American Journalism Review*, the first from 2004, appear to have been the first to use the phrase "fact-checking movement."[80]) In addition to covering and generally celebrating the new genre, establishment press critics sometimes offer their own fact checks. For instance, the *Columbia Journalism Review*'s "Campaign Desk" site, which first appeared in 2004 and has called itself "the conscience of the political press," often evaluates political claims in the course of scrutinizing campaign coverage.[81]

A separate and quite vibrant tradition of media criticism in the United States emerges from the political world and has yielded organized fact-checking efforts on both the left and the right. Partisan media watchdog groups—early examples are the conservative Accuracy in Media, established in 1969, and its liberal counterpart Fairness & Accuracy in Reporting, operating since 1986—engage in a shifting mix of media and political activities. They conduct research and issue reports documenting media bias. They produce various forms of in-house media that report on the news industry, such as newsletters, blogs, and sometimes video segments. And they publicize all of this work through interviews and articles in conventional news outlets. In this respect, they might be considered a subset in the wider category of American "think tanks" that, as Thomas Medvetz argues, bridge the political, academic, economic, and media fields, drawing resources selectively from each of these worlds in order to negotiate institutional challenges.[82] Like other kinds of think tanks, media watchdog groups have adapted to the digital media environment by emphasizing media production and newslike story forms. This includes regular efforts at fact-checking.

Media Watchdogs as Fact-Checkers

Any number of partisan media critics engage regularly with the professional fact-checkers, from lone bloggers to writers with well-known partisan journals like the *Weekly Standard*, *Washington Monthly*, and the *American Prospect*. One site, PolitiFact Bias, exists solely "to expose the defective fact-checking apparatus at PolitiFact, with special focus on the problems that help show PolitiFact's marked ideological bias."[83] But four established media watchdog groups deserve special attention as critics of professional fact-checkers and sources of partisan fact-checking.

Accuracy in Media

Founded in 1969 by Reed Irvine, then an economist with the Federal Reserve, Accuracy in Media (AIM) established a prototype for media watchdog organizations that would follow on the left as well as the right. The group can be seen as part of the wider network of "movement conservatism" that emerged to challenge the orthodoxies of the liberal welfare state in the wake of Barry Goldwater's disastrous 1964 presidential campaign. AIM was an early beneficiary of conservative philanthropic networks and helped to develop the critique of the "liberal media" that has been an anchor of modern conservatism. In 2009, the last year for which figures were available, the nonprofit took in $500,000 in contributions.

AIM focuses squarely on identifying bias in the news, describing its mission as "to promote accuracy, fairness and balance in news reporting."[84] Its signal campaigns over more than four decades include forcing PBS to air a rebuttal to the network's thirteen-part 1983 documentary on the Vietnam War; a long effort to "Impeach Dan Rather" (or "Can Dan") by exposing the CBS anchor's alleged leftward slant; and a critique of the *New York Times*'s reporting on the "El Mozote" massacre perpetrated by the U.S.-backed military regime in El Salvador, which prompted the paper to reassign its correspondent there.[85] While distinct from contemporary fact-checking, these efforts point up the sometimes hazy line between checking facts and finding bias. The campaign against the *Times*'s reporter, for instance, turned in part on challenging the facts of his account of the massacre (details that would be vindicated a decade later). Similarly, AIM's day-to-day output often questions claims in news reports and uses the language of fact-checking—but with journalists rather than the sources they quote as the target of the investigation. As a 2014 *AIM Report* piece on the *Times*'s Benghazi coverage summarized, "Accuracy in Media has, time and again, disproven these points. But, given the misinformation put forward by the Grey Lady, the facts bear repeating."[86]

Media Research Center

Founded in 1987 by the conservative activist L. Brent Bozell, the Media Research Center (MRC) has succeeded AIM as the most active nexus of conservative media criticism. A mission statement explains that "MRC's sole mission is to expose and neutralize the propaganda arm of the Left: the national news media." In 2013 the group took in more than $13 million in contributions and dedicated $4 million to its "news analysis" division, claiming a staff of sixty-three dedicated to "monitoring, analyzing, and reporting the most egregious examples of media bias." As with AIM, the MRC's media analysis has often involved a kind of fact-checking through the lens of conservative politics. Thus, in a report from the mid-1990s, MRC researchers reviewed a year of Medicare coverage in national newspapers and magazines and turned up 1,060 "errors"—meaning references to program "cuts" that were in fact only reductions in growth. The MRC's monthly newsletter *Media-Watch*, published until 1999, featured a "Janet Cooke Award" (named after the *Washington Post* Pulitzer Prize recipient who was later exposed as a fabricator) to "distinguish the most outrageously distorted news story of the month."

In 2005 the MRC launched a separate site, NewsBusters, to provide a rapid-fire outlet for its analysts, who use banks of digital video recorders to monitor the daily news diet on broadcast and cable networks. The site has roughly a dozen people on staff, assisted by numerous outside contributors, posting twenty to thirty brief items each day in response to mainstream news accounts. NewsBusters scored a major fact-checking coup in 2008 when, after Hillary Clinton referred on the campaign trail to landing "under sniper fire" on a trip to Bosnia a decade earlier, the MRC found taped news video in its archive that showed the First Lady being greeted in a happy ceremony on an airport tarmac.[87] (As reviewed in chapter 4, mainstream fact-checkers picked up the story several days later—without crediting the conservative outlet that broke it.) The MRC enjoys a prominent profile across conservative media networks, with Bozell and other key figures frequently appearing on Fox News programs and similar outlets.

Fairness & Accuracy in Reporting

The group Fairness & Accuracy in Reporting (FAIR) appeared in 1986 as a "progressive" counterpart to Irvine's AIM. In an essay on FAIR's first birthday, founder Jeff Cohen, a former ACLU attorney, pointed to a rising rightward tilt in the "major media" due to corporate consolidation and to conservative media critics "harassing journalists who uncovered unpleasant truths about poverty, inequality, government corruption or U.S. military and nuclear policy."[88] FAIR's mission emphasizes three related strands: documenting conservative or corporate bias in the news media, increasing the presence of progressive or "dissenting" voices, and advocating structural media reforms that favor this sort of diversity. FAIR criticizes the establishment press—and especially the *New York Times*—as relentlessly as conservative critics. One academic profile argues that FAIR has earned "a reputation as an authoritative press critic and media analyst among the MSM"; its studies of sources and guests on news programs have been credited with prompting editorial shifts at outlets like ABC's *Nightline* and PBS's *NewsHour*.[89] (After a 1990 study, for example, the PBS program began to feature prominent left figures such as Noam Chomsky and Edward Said.) The nonprofit has a staff of seven today and a relatively meager budget, just under $600,000 in 2013. It does not accept advertising or corporate funding and claims that 60 percent of revenue comes from contributions and subscriptions, with foundations providing the rest.

FAIR's activities mix research with activism and media production. The group puts out a monthly magazine, *Extra!*, and a weekly radio show, *CounterSpin*; it also prompts public phone and e-mail campaigns with "action alerts" to a mailing list of more than fifty-five thousand. FAIR's media critique often rests on close factual analysis to contest the phrasing or framing of news reports, sometimes citing nonpartisan fact-checkers. Its blog and radio program occasionally feature pieces billed directly as fact checks that take aim at journalists as sources of misinformation or misrepresentation. ("Well, let's factcheck Factcheck," FAIR announced in a reply to FactCheck .org's finding that Social Security was not created by Democrats.)[90] The group also frequently criticizes fact checks from established news outlets for false balance: "One of the problems with media 'factchecking' is the notion that all things must be 'checked' equally."[91]

Media Matters for America

The media watchdog whose work most closely resembles mainstream fact-checking is Media Matters for America. The group describes itself as "a progressive research and information center dedicated to comprehensively monitoring, analyzing, and correcting conservative misinformation."[92] It was founded in 2004 by David Brock, a journalist best known for sensational exposés of the Clintons before publicly renouncing his conservative views in the late nineties. After his conversion, Brock became active on the left, and Media Matters enjoys close ties to Democratic funding networks. In 2010 the group had seventy employees and a budget of $10 million.[93] The organization regularly publishes research documenting conservative or corporate bias in the news, or analyzing coverage of issues such as climate change. It has also run high-profile campaigns against conservative media figures (most famously, a successful push for CBS to fire Don Imus after the radio host referred to a women's basketball team as "nappy-headed hoes").

Week to week, Media Matters operates as a kind of permanent political campaign, with staffers scanning broadcast, print, and online news outlets in three shifts spanning an eighteen-hour day.[94] This results in hundreds of articles each week calling attention to errors and distortions, especially on Fox News, which Media Matters clips avidly. The group focuses more directly on issues of fact than other media watchdogs and produces lengthy, meticulously documented analyses that often rely on the same sources employed by mainstream fact-checkers, whom it also regularly cites. (In a 2010 interview, Tate Williams, then chief of staff, described the organization's mission to me as "to stop a smear in its tracks," arguing that this involves doing the investigative work that reporters too often neglect.[95]) At the same time, though, reports on Media Matters slip into the sort of ideologically freighted language that nonpartisan journalists avoid. The site's debunking takes aim exclusively at conservative media figures and politicians, a point professional fact-checkers invariably make to show that Media Matters is not a trustworthy source.[96]

Drawing Boundaries in the Fact-Checking Universe

Journalists who produce fact checks in traditional newsrooms or at dedicated sites like PolitiFact and FactCheck.org do not view partisan media critics as legitimate peers. On the contrary, professional fact-checkers take pains to distinguish their own objective newswork from what they see as political argument making. They do not cite partisan outlets like Media Matters or the MRC in published articles, nor do they link to these sites in their snapshots of fact-checking around the web. (PolitiFact, FactCheck.org, and the Fact Checker all publicize the work of rival fact-checkers via their websites or Twitter feeds. This sometimes includes nonjournalistic outlets, such as Snopes.com, but never partisan sites.) Professional fact-checkers go to great lengths to avoid being associated with counterparts in the political world, for instance, by avoiding joint appearances in panel discussions or news interviews. Fact-checkers can be quite frank about this aversion. At a 2011 meeting the *Washington Post*'s Glenn Kessler told other journalists, "I actually have a really sinking feeling if I start to fact-check something and I see, oh, God, Media Matters has already looked into this, and sometimes I'll just not even touch it 'cause it feels like it's already been tainted."[97]

Still, partisan media critics participate vocally in daily political discourse in the United States, and understanding their role helps to shed light on the work of professional fact-checkers. This is true, first of all, precisely because the latter disassociate themselves from their partisan counterparts so strenuously. The understanding and practice of fact-checking by professional journalists have been shaped, in part, by this kind of "boundary work."[98] The contrast with partisan sites gives mainstream outlets both another reason and another way to articulate their own vision of what legitimate fact-checking looks like. This professional line drawing takes place in public and in private—for example, in training sessions, new staff or interns are told very clearly who counts as a fact-checkers and who does not. As in classic examples of boundary work, professional rewards and resources are at stake here: status, autonomy, career advancement, and so on. However, in contrast to some other cases of boundary drawing noted by journalism scholars— between "serious" and tabloid reporters, for instance, or between traditional and "participatory" news—fact-checkers are not warding off a direct professional challenge from media watchdogs.[99] The outsiders in this case are truly that; partisan media critics have little prospect of and less desire for recognition in the journalistic establishment. Rather, in constantly affirming the divide between fact-checking and partisan critique, fact-checkers shore up the professional claims of their *own* new and sometimes controversial genre. The intended audience is other elite journalists.

For their part, media watchdog groups are among the most eager consumers and sharpest critics of journalistic fact-checking. They publicize rulings that support their own arguments and vehemently dispute those that don't. Media Matters has referred to the three national fact-checkers in thousands of posts, usually in order to cite their work as evidence of conservative misinformation. But Media Matters also regularly accuses fact-checkers of "false balance" (and even ran an editorial cartoon directly mocking Politi-Fact founder Bill Adair, pictured blithely defending a controversial Truth-O-Meter ruling about Medicare as Republicans dismantle the program).[100] The less prolific NewsBusters has made hundreds of references to the fact-checkers and includes PolitiFact on its list of "people and organizations" tracked. After PolitiFact greeted the news of U.S. House member Michele Bachmann's 2013 retirement with a review of her terrible Truth-O-Meter record, NewsBusters attacked the fact-checker's "extremely skewed methodology."[101] At the same time, the conservative site has reported with delight on the "years-long pissing contest" between PolitiFact and the liberal MSNBC host Rachel Maddow. When that dispute flared again in June 2014 (after PolitiFact challenged Maddow's recollection of the controversy over rescued prisoner of war Jessica Lynch a decade earlier), NewsBusters came to Politi-Fact's defense with its own fact check of the liberal pundit.[102]

A Division of Critical Labor

Professional fact-checkers prefer to ignore the attention they receive, favorable or otherwise, from partisan media watchdogs. They almost never engage directly with these critics. In contrast, fact-checkers carefully tend their relationships with mainstream media outlets and often respond publicly to praise or censure from that quarter. After the 2012 presidential race, for example, both PolitiFact and FactCheck.org ran letters from their founders answering the charge, leveled by figures like the late *New York Times* media reporter David Carr, that fact-checking hadn't made a difference.[103] But sites like Media Matters and NewsBusters can't be ignored completely. They are busy nodes in online media-political networks, covering the same ground as the fact-checkers day after day. They turn up in broadcast transcripts and op-ed pages and search results, influencing the fact-checkers if only by the "taint" they attach to certain issues or arguments. Like other journalists today, fact-checkers read their professional status in the media footprint of their own work. Their standing as legitimate, objective voices is reflected in and reproduced by the shifting pattern of media-political actors who cite and quote and link to them. Partisan media critics are an unavoidable feature of that network landscape.

Looking broadly at a fact-checking universe that includes journalists as well as media watchdogs and other political voices highlights the way the new genre bridges adjacent professional domains. Almost any deceptive claim that gains traction in public discourse can be debunked in two distinct modes: as uttered by a misleading politician or as reproduced by irresponsible journalists. Perhaps the best-known episode in the history and lore of fact-checking is the controversy over "death panels" sparked by a 2009 Facebook post from vice presidential candidate Sarah Palin. Claims that President Obama's health care reform plan envisioned some kind of euthanasia for unproductive members of society met a wide array of fact-checking responses. FactCheck.org and PolitiFact challenged Palin's claim directly; Media Matters fact-checked the "Fox News personalities" who promoted it; and FAIR faulted *USA Today* and other mainstream news outlets for failing to debunk the claim and thus helping to legitimize outlandish rhetoric.[104] The fact checks by professional journalists noted in passing how rhetoric about death panels had caught fire in the news media, but they did not fault their peers for fanning the flames.

This consistent pattern underscores a fairly simple division of critical labor between the fields that overlap in fact-checking: media actors focus their critique on politics while political actors direct theirs at the media. Journalists by instinct and by charter tend to attribute faults in the public sphere to the behavior of politicians or to the nature of politics, episodes of professional self-flagellation notwithstanding. Fact-checkers share the occupational cynicism of political reporters generally; they are quick to argue that lying is a basic feature of politics and that no amount of fact-checking will change that. Meanwhile, political actors—including campaigns, party organizations, issue groups, and activists—see the news media as a primary arena of political contestation. Political campaigns measure their own progress, justifiably or not, through day-to-day media coverage.[105] Perhaps as a result, the institutional logic of politics tends to blame adverse outcomes on inadequate or unfair coverage and, often, to see reforming the media as the most hopeful route to political change.

The fact-checking organizations this book focuses on are led and staffed by reporters with long backgrounds in print and broadcast news. They place themselves squarely in the tradition of objective journalism and subscribe to norms that wall reporting off from the political realm. They see themselves as journalists and not media critics. Still, I will argue throughout that fact-checking represents a serious and sustained critique of conventional political reporting. Fact-checkers organize and understand their work around this shared critique, one with a long history in and out of journalism that they have carried into practice in a new way online. This is why it makes sense to understand fact-checking as a kind of professional reform movement—as an argument about how objectivity *should* be practiced, a point developed in the next chapter. Michael Schudson's description of an earlier generation of upstart reporters (who led the resurgence of investigative journalism in the sixties and seventies) applies equally well to the new fact-checkers: "They make a case for a journalism true to an ideal of objectivity and false to the counterfeit conventions justified in its name."[106]

This chapter has surveyed the landscape of fact-checking in order to understand how this professional movement fits into the journalistic field and into the wider sphere of elite political communication. Fact-checkers represent a distinct cohort at the center of political journalism—one with recognized leaders, with its own emergent subset of journalistic norms and practices, and with an increasingly stable vocabulary to address recurring internal debates and points of tension. I've argued that fact-checking appeals to the profession's core democratic values while also reflecting particular sources of outside influence. First, as a subfield of U.S. journalism, fact-checking has unusually close ties to the nonprofit and academic worlds. Fact-checkers have grown increasingly comfortable speaking the language of these neighboring fields and seeking funding and legitimacy through them—although, as we shall see, these links are also sources of tension in defining the mission and practice of fact-checking. And second, the practices and discourse of professional fact-checking reflect these journalists' constant efforts to distinguish themselves from partisan counterparts. As both competitors to and critics of professional fact-checkers, partisan media critics are an unavoidable feature of online political discourse. Boundary drawing helps fact-checkers to articulate and define correct practice and to reinforce their own claim to journalistic legitimacy. All of these influential outsiders—political actors, media critics, and academics—figure prominently in the cases and episodes developed in the following chapters.

2

OBJECTIVITY, TRUTH SEEKING, AND INSTITUTIONAL FACTS

"TRUTHFULNESS HAS NEVER BEEN COUNTED AMONG THE POLITICAL virtues," Hannah Arendt observed drily in her disquisition on "lying in politics," penned after the release of the Pentagon Papers.[1] Professional fact-checkers bear witness to this day after day, cataloging the great and small distortions, misrepresentations, and lies that are part of the regular business of politics. Like other journalists in the decades since Vietnam and Watergate, they begin with the assumption that all politicians lie and will lie brazenly when the stakes are high enough. Fact-checking is the product of a half-century shift that has seen political reporters as a class grow less trusting of officials and more willing to subject their claims to skeptical analysis. As routine as lying in politics may appear, however, exposing it is rarely straightforward. Fact-checking constantly draws journalists off the ground of hard fact into muddier territory of evaluation, interpretation, and opinion. What look like obvious deceptions usually turn out to be defensible by some standard—enough at least to make the fact-checkers concede, as they always do, that readers may see the matter differently.

Consider the controversy over Mitt Romney's attack on the White House's auto industry bailout in the final days of the 2012 campaign, reviewed at the opening of this book. "Obama took GM and Chrysler into bankruptcy and sold Chrysler to the Italians who are going to build Jeeps in China," Romney's ad claimed. The three elite U.S. fact-checkers called that one of the most dishonest political attacks of the year, a desperate bid to make Ohio autoworkers fear for their jobs. An unusually large number of journalists across the country also saw it that way. But that meant looking past the literal meaning of Romney's ad to its implied message, that Chrysler's expansion in China would cost American jobs. It meant staking out a position on what exactly *counted* as costing American jobs—which in turn involved subtle judgments about the health of the auto industry and the viability of exporting U.S.-made cars to Chinese consumers.[2]

The same question comes up over and over in verdicts from PolitiFact, FactCheck.org, and the Fact Checker. What counts as "ending Medicare"? (Fact-checkers said turning the program into a block grant would not end it; liberal critics called that a matter of opinion.) What counts as a "government takeover" of health care? (Fact-checkers argued that President Obama's plan hardly qualified; conservatives said that depends on one's viewpoint.)[3] What, for that matter, counts as a "death panel"? Even Sarah Palin's outrageous charge about the White House's health care reform plan has been defended on the grounds that it accurately described a move toward "rationed" health care.[4]

Critics have called this constant slide into interpretation a problem of the sorts of claims fact-checkers choose to investigate, arguing that they stray too easily into the realm of opinion. But it is really a problem of language and truth—more precisely, of our casual notion of a body of universal truth that rests on indisputable facts that can be defended without recourse to argument and interpretation.[5] Before South Carolina finally heeded calls to lower the Confederate battle flag at its state capital in the wake of the 2015 shootings in the Emanuel African Methodist Episcopal Church, fact-checkers and other critics soundly debunked the argument, made by some of the flag's defenders, "that the Civil War was not fought over slavery."[6] That defending slavery was the South's principal war aim is today widely accepted by historians of the period (though it was not a half-century ago). By any reasonable standard it counts as a firm historical fact—but one unavoidably tied into a particular set of arguments about how to read the economic and political circumstances of the conflict. In practice, even what look like straightforward questions of scientific fact can turn on subtle judgments of context. At the height of the 2014 Ebola epidemic, PunditFact ruled "False" a frightening claim by the well-known political analyst George Will: that new science pointed to possible airborne transmission of the lethal virus. The conservative pundit was correct that a recent lab experiment suggested Ebola could be transmitted through the air—but not under circumstances that *count* as airborne to epidemiologists. "This is still a form of direct contact," one of the scientists explained.[7]

This chapter takes up the problem of objective truth as confronted by fact-checkers. The first section places fact-checking within the longer history of the objectivity norm in journalism. I begin by reviewing the fact-checkers' sense of where their style of reporting comes from and then consider the genre as one strand of the well-established turn toward interpretive, critical reporting since the 1960s. The second section of the chapter considers the problem of truth more generally, comparing fact-checkers to other kinds of fact-seekers, especially in science. Drawing on perspectives from the sociology of science, I argue that the key problem here is the instability of "institutional facts." This discussion lays the ground for a closer look at the day-to-day routines of fact-checking in the chapters that follow.

An Interior History of Fact-Checking

The elite national fact-checkers sit at the center of a wider circle of journalists and news organizations who take part in the fact-checking movement to varying degrees. In this milieu a kind of institutional history has begun to cohere in which fact-checkers trace the roots of their practice through common people and events in their own careers, reaching back to the 1980s. This shared history chronicles the failures of conventional objective reporting but also shows the profession responding with new ideas and techniques. It establishes a library of common references that undergirds fact-checkers' sense of themselves as journalistic reformers. This history also offers another instance of the sort of metajournalistic discourse by which journalism as a community reproduces itself, establishes boundaries, and asserts or contests professional values—in particular, the objectivity norm.[8]

Reporting that debunks claims by political figures has a long history on op-ed pages, in investigative journalism, and in the alternative press. Beginning in the late 1950s, for instance, the leftist journalist I. F. Stone carried boxed items that look like stripped-down fact checks in his muckraking newsletter, *I. F. Stone's Weekly*.[9] However, to directly challenge exaggerations and deceptions by public figures was rare in straight news reports through most of the twentieth century. At least as early as the 1950s reporters talked about this as a kind of Achilles' heel of objective journalism. "For decades the American press has worshipped the God of objectivity," one newspaper editor wrote in 1951, at the height of the Red Scare. "This seemed to keep the voters informed on all sides of a question until the invention of the technique of the big lie."[10] That is, the commitment to objectivity meant unscrupulous politicians such as Wisconsin senator Joseph McCarthy could count on reporters to faithfully transmit even their wildest claims—or especially those, given journalism's affinity for conflict and controversy. As another contemporary observed, "under pressure of McCarthy's methods, objective reporting serves simply as a transmission belt for outrageous falsehood."[11]

During the 1980s American journalists became more comfortable attaching doubt to political claims in the news, partly in response to a mounting critique of the failures of stenographic reporting in previous decades.[12] A precursor of modern fact-checking emerged with the election of Ronald Reagan in 1980. His later reputation as the "Great Communicator" makes it easy to forget that Reagan came to the White House with a well-established reputation for error and exaggeration.[13] On the campaign trail, he had famously claimed that trees caused more pollution than automobiles and that there was more oil in Alaska than Saudi Arabia. He consistently mangled the details of government programs he pledged to eliminate. Reagan responded to this attention by accusing reporters of "journalistic incest," but the theme carried over into coverage of his presidency.[14] "The White House Press conference has been converted by Ronald Reagan into a forum for inaccuracy, distortion, and falsehood," the *Columbia Journalism Review* declared in 1986.[15] One media critic noted after Reagan's death, "Major newspapers would run stories on all the facts he had mangled, a practice that faded as it became clear that most Americans weren't terribly concerned."[16]

The *Washington Post* was one of the newspapers challenging the president's facts. When Reagan took office the *Post* began to experiment with brief analytical pieces, sometimes offered as sidebars to straight news, highlighting his misstatements.[17] The paper pointed to the president's record to justify the scrutiny: "Press Conference by Reagan Follows a Familiar Pattern," announced the headline over a September 1982 story detailing his "numerous factual mistakes" in a discussion of the economy.[18] A striking example came after a 1985 radio interview in which Reagan defended the progress made by South Africa's white regime in dismantling apartheid. The *Post* reported Reagan's remarks in a highly skeptical front-page story; a sidebar by the paper's Johannesburg correspondent highlighted four key claims in bold type and fact-checked each in turn.[19] The former *Post* editor Len Downie has explained that Reagan's reputation pushed the paper to embrace the new approach: "I thought it was important for readers to know when he was inaccurate," he told Michael Dobbs, the paper's first Fact Checker columnist. According to Dobbs, however, fact-checking fell off sharply in the later years of Reagan's presidency.[20] Another *Post* reporter has said the paper abandoned the format after readers objected. "We stopped truth-squadding every press conference," Walter Pincus recalled in a 2007 interview. "And we left it then to the Democrats. In other words, it's up to the Democrats to catch people, not us. We would quote both sides."[21]

The Rise of "Adwatch" Coverage, 1988

A crucial turn toward fact-checking, today's practitioners argue, came with the 1988 presidential contest between Vice President George H. W. Bush and Massachusetts governor Michael Dukakis.[22] Even before the race had finished, it was seen as a nadir in American political campaigns. "The level of fact and accuracy is far below the norm for a presidential campaign," communications scholar Kathleen Hall Jamieson declared late in the contest. "This is the first presidential election I can remember in which there are major errors of fact being asserted as if they were true."[23] After the election, journalists and media critics argued that coverage had become irrelevant by continuing to focus on speeches and policy papers while mostly ignoring the vicious, truth-distorting "air war" that absorbed the candidates' money and perhaps decided the outcome.[24] *Washington Post* columnist David Broder, the so-called dean of the Washington press corps, wrote a series of columns about the debacle that today's fact-checkers claim as founding documents.[25] Broder called for reporters to start "truth-squadding" campaign ads. He took aim at the political consultants whose ties to reporters softened campaign coverage. And he gave a platform to other voices in journalism and academia arguing for more aggressive campaign coverage (notably, Jamieson and Larry J. Sabato, who became regular sources on these questions).[26] "We should treat every ad as if it were a speech by the candidate himself," Broder wrote as the 1990 campaigns took shape. "In fact, it will be seen and heard by far more people than any speech he gives to a live audience." He offered a recipe for reporters to avoid past mistakes:

> Demand the supporting evidence from the candidate airing the ad, get rebuttal information from his opponent and then investigate the situation enough ourselves that we can tell the reader what is factual and what is destructive fiction.
>
> And we ought not to be squeamish about saying in plain language when we catch a candidate lying, exaggerating or distorting the facts. The consultants have become increasingly sophisticated about insinuating— visually or verbally—charges that they avoid making in literal terms.[27]

The 1988 race had offered prototypes. Late in the contest, Dukakis made an issue of false charges leveled by his opponent in a pair of harsh television spots.[28] One was the Bush campaign's now-legendary "Tank" ad, which accused Dukakis of opposing "virtually every defense system we developed"; a litany of major defense programs scrolled onscreen over an unflattering video of the candidate riding in a tank. The charges were almost entirely baseless, and an ABC News segment two weeks before Election Day took the commercial apart. The segment began by highlighting Dukakis's complaints but segued into an authoritative debunking of each of the commercial's claims. Inspired by that piece, a *Washington Post* article two days later dissected the Tank ad and Bush's racially charged spot blaming Dukakis for crimes committed by prisoners on weekend furlough (such as convicted murderer Willie Horton, made famous by the campaign).[29] The news outlets framed their fact checks as analyses of distortions from both sides, although Bush's tactics were manifestly worse. "The problem [is] you always want to find two sides of a story," the producer of the ABC segment would complain in a panel discussion with Jamieson four years later. "In this case there was only one side of the story."[30]

During the 1990 midterm campaigns, adwatch pieces multiplied on television and in newspapers, where they were informally known as "truth boxes."[31] Journalists described the format as a kind of professional innovation made necessary by ever-baser campaign tactics. "This is the year a genuine rebellion against the cheapening of our politics may take place," Broder wrote after surveying instances of truth-squadding from around the country.[32] Another hopeful review of the trend, by media reporter Tom Rosenstiel, invoked the ur-text of campaign reporting to explain the innovative genre: "This year, the American news media have embarked on what many campaign professionals and journalists consider *the first real advance in press coverage of politics* since Theodore White began looking behind the scenes at the mechanics of campaigning in his landmark book, 'The Making of the President 1960.'"[33]

In the 1992 election, more than half of the largest U.S. newspapers ran at least one adwatch report. (The figure would reach 80 percent in 2006.[34]) TV newsrooms eagerly embraced the format, led by the 24-hour CNN, which put its special assignment desk on the fact-checking beat. "We're attempting to police the process," a CNN news director told NPR that year as the campaigns began in earnest. The broadcast networks followed suit in the final months of the race; CBS took the label "Campaign '92 Reality Check" and used a dramatic stamp logo to introduce its segments.[35] "Thank goodness, the networks have a fact check so I don't have to just go blue in the face any more," Bill Clinton declared during a 1992 presidential debate. The trend spread to local newsrooms as well: A 2007 survey of local TV news directors found that the number airing adwatch segments rose from below 10 percent in the mid-1990s to nearly 40 percent a decade later.[36]

Year of the Fact Check, 2004

FactCheck.org was a kind of stepchild of the surge in adwatching. Brooks Jackson, then a political correspondent at CNN, was drafted by the network in 1991 to work on adwatch segments. He had misgivings about the assignment: "I was reluctant to do it because it didn't fit what I had by training and long experience at the AP and the *Wall Street Journal* come to think of as objective journalism, because it called for a little bit of editorializing—calling things false or misleading and stating a conclusion."[37] He embraced the new format, though, and it became popular at the network; soon the segments began to challenge claims beyond political advertising, taking the name

"Fact Check." To refine the format, Jackson worked closely with Kathleen Hall Jamieson, whose research suggested that poorly designed fact checks might reinforce the messages they intend to debunk.[38] By 2003, however, CNN's interest in the format had waned. Jackson and Jamieson launched FactCheck.org that year with funding from the Annenberg Foundation. In an *On the Media* interview before the Iowa caucuses, Jackson presented the site as a course correction for political journalism:

> Well, you know, ever since Teddy White wrote that wonderful book, *The Making of the President, 1960*, reporters have been, I think, tilting too far in the direction of reporting campaigns as horse races, reporting the inside skinny on what the campaigns are up to, how they're using polling, how they're raising money, who's in, who's out.
>
> I think the pendulum swung a generation or even two ago a little too far in the direction of reporting process. If FactCheck.org makes a small effort toward nudging that pendulum back in the direction of covering substance, then I think we will have accomplished something worth accomplishing.[39]

The launch of FactCheck.org was accompanied by a wider surge in fact-checking by newspapers and TV stations. One journalism review dubbed 2004 the "Year of the Fact Check," pointing to efforts at the *Washington Post*, the *New York Times*, the *Los Angeles Times*, ABC News, and many smaller outlets. Journalists described the new efforts as a reaction to unusually harsh campaigning that year, epitomized by the "Swift Boat" ads questioning the Vietnam War record of Democratic presidential nominee John Kerry. "I think the Swift Boat Veterans for Truth is really what caused the rebirth or certainly the explosion of fact-checks that's now taking place," a CNN news director commented after the race. "It sort of gave a second life to some of the tools that maybe hadn't been used as much in recent campaigns."[40] In a 2007 meeting with other fact-checkers, then–ABC News correspondent Jake Tapper recalled his own embrace of the format: what began with the investigation into the Swift Boat campaign became a regular feature after a "histrionic" speech by Sen. Zell Miller of Georgia at the 2004 Republican National Convention, another episode that comes up often in this milieu. For the final months of the race, Tapper ran a dedicated "Fact Check desk" on the network's flagship program, *World News Tonight*.[41]

PolitiFact and the *Washington Post*'s Fact Checker also took shape partly in response to the 2004 campaign, although they wouldn't emerge until the next presidential cycle. PolitiFact founder Bill Adair recalls the 1990s surge in fact-checking as intense but short-lived, stifled by a backlash from politicians and the public. (Studies suggest that use of the format fell off in 1996 but began to recover in 2000.[42]) "I think that journalists got scared in the 1990s that to say something's false was to be biased, was to take a side," he told me in an interview.[43] A personal turning point came while covering Zell Miller's 2004 convention speech. Miller ran through a litany of military programs John Kerry had voted against as senator, to suggest he was weak on defense—though, as reporters well understood, many were procedural votes against versions of bills Kerry ultimately supported.[44] "The speech by Zell Miller . . . was kind of an epiphany for me, where I did nothing but write a horse-race story and really felt guilty about it," Adair told fellow fact-checkers at a 2011 meeting.[45] He explained PolitiFact's origins this way on another occasion: "This grew out of my own guilt. I had covered political campaigns and felt that I had been a passive co-conspirator in sort of passing along inaccurate information and hadn't fact-checked it the way I should and so I went to my editors with a proposal that we create a web site where we would do fact-checking full time."[46]

The Fact Checker column at the *Washington Post* has a similar prehistory. On the 2004 campaign beat for the newspaper, Michael Dobbs investigated the Swift Boat allegations as well as the controversy over *60 Minutes*' botched report on President George W. Bush's National Guard service. Dobbs has said those stories convinced him of the need to "institutionalize" fact-checking at the paper for the next presidential race.[47] Glenn Kessler, who succeeded Dobbs as the paper's resident fact-checker in 2011, has likewise pointed to his experience investigating campaign claims in 2004 and previously—including a front-page debunking of Zell Miller's "slashing convention speech."[48] "The level of the attacks at the Republican convention focused everyone's attention on the need to provide context to our readers," Kessler told the *Columbia Journalism Review* late in the 2004 campaign.[49] Both Kessler and Dobbs also note their backgrounds covering diplomacy and international affairs, beats that demand interpretation by the reporter.[50] "I covered this extraordinary story, the collapse of communism," Dobbs told fellow fact-checkers in 2007:

> Now, when we were covering that story, we did not try to be fair and balanced; we tried to be fair, but we didn't try to be balanced. . . . We tried to tell the truth as we saw it, and if we had abided by the strict conventions of American journalism, you know, we wouldn't have been able to describe this incredible story that was unfolding in front of us very truthfully.[51]

In this way practitioners make sense of fact-checking as part of the see-sawing balance of power between journalists and politicians. A common narrative about the successes and failures of political reporting anchors their sense of fact-checking as an evolving professional response to new tactics and technologies in the political world. This sort of history-making project is nothing new, of course. Barbie Zelizer, Michael Schudson, and others have pointed to the cultural work accomplished when reporters talk to one another about heroic and less-than-heroic episodes in the history of journalism: the Kennedy assassination, the Vietnam War, Watergate, and so on.[52] Journalists "come together by creating stories about their past that they routinely and informally circulate to each other," Zelizer has argued. This "recycling of stories" serves to reaffirm common values and practices but also to legitimate new ones—to "build authority for practices not emphasized by traditional views of journalism."[53] Thus, later reporters looking back on the mostly uncritical reporting at the peak of McCarthyism wove that embarrassing history into a morality tale justifying a turn toward more assertive, interpretive journalism.

It is not surprising, then, that one other story comes up often when fact-checkers talk about their movement: the Iraq War.[54] Journalists have drawn this connection over and over, pointing to fact checks as an antidote to the stenographic reporting that helped the Bush administration build its case for war in 2002 and 2003. "Just as the Vietnam War destroyed the cozy relationship between presidents and the White House press corps, the [weapons of mass destruction] fiasco caused many mainstream journalists to become much more cautious about accepting uncorroborated claims by politicians of all stripes," Michael Dobbs wrote in a report on the rise of fact-checking.[55] The connection makes little sense in practical terms; political fact-checkers would have had few concrete resources to debunk White House allegations about Iraq's weapon's programs.[56] But it makes a great deal of sense when we understand fact-checking as a reaction against the credulous insider culture responsible for the media's performance—as a self-conscious effort to restore the balance of power between reporters and officials.

The Analytical Turn in U.S. News

What accounts for the rise of political fact-checking? The genre very clearly extends what Kevin Barnhurst has evocatively called "the new long journalism."[57] This is the well-documented turn over the last half-century toward more interpretive, analytical, and assertive reporting, especially about politics. Scholars have mostly read this analytical turn as a shift in the culture of journalism, one that reflects changed social attitudes but also embodies reporters' quest for professional status and authority. This account is nicely fleshed out by the story journalists tell about fact-checking—by their self-conscious sense that it represents an innovation or evolution of political reporting. The fact-checking movement reflects and reproduces the professional culture tied to more analytical journalism.

Numerous studies confirm the point, basic to histories of American journalism, that news reporting since the nineteenth century has become less stenographic and more interpretive.[58] "Since emerging as a distinct occupation, journalism has had an explanatory urge," Barnhurst offered in a recent overview of the "interpretive turn."[59] Especially after the 1950s, newspaper reports grew longer and more analytical; they focused increasingly on issues and trends rather than isolated events; and they became more skeptical of official claims, highlighting the political motives and interests of public figures.[60] One recent analysis, by Kate Fink and Michael Schudson, finds that "conventional" news—classic, inverted-pyramid reports on a discrete event—claimed 85 percent of front-page news in 1955 but had fallen to less than half by 2003, replaced mostly by "contextual" reports that "focus on the big picture, providing context for other news."[61] This trend has reached new heights in the recent wave of "explanatory journalism" ventures such as Vox and "The Upshot" from the *New York Times*.[62] In a 2014 column, the *Times*'s public editor noted the near absence of hard news on the paper's front page and aired complaints from unhappy readers. As one objected, "It's all news analysis and interpretive journalism—very good, indeed, but still not news as such."[63]

Broadcast news echoes this pattern. The launch of CBS's 60 *Minutes* in 1968 heralded waves of documentary-style "news magazine" programs dedicated to investigative or analytical news (and of tabloid imitators). Meanwhile, after the 1960s daily news on television and radio grew more interpretive; public figures were relegated to ever-shorter "sound bites" or "image bites" while journalists claimed a rising share of the limited airtime for political coverage.[64] Barnhurst's study of the flagship news programs on NPR between 1980 and 2000 captures the shift very well. The earliest reports on *Morning Edition* and *All Things Considered* tended to use short narrated clips to transition between roomier statements from public figures; later magazine-style segments reversed that formula, with brief quotes from newsmakers dropped in to illustrate the reporter's narration. Barnhurst found NPR's political correspondents asking fewer and fewer questions over the two decades while offering many more statements of opinion: "Journalists interpreted politics by looking for the hidden agenda at work behind overt acts and by engaging in a critique of policies."[65]

The analytical turn in journalism can be understood in a number of ways. One underlying factor is the profession's embrace of increasingly sophisticated perspectives and methods from the social sciences, propagated in journalism schools and buttressed by the general rise in college education among reporters and readers alike. This shift dovetailed with a wider scientific turn in public and private administration; over the course of the twentieth century, journalism has had recourse to more and better information from public institutions in government, academia, and beyond.[66] In this sense, the profession has responded to the critique issued by Walter Lippmann in 1922 and echoed by the Hutchins Commission twenty-five years later: reporting became more scientific, more comprehensive, and more critical in order to cover a complex and interconnected world.[67] The wave of reform legislation beginning with the 1966 Freedom of Information Act improved the flow of public information to newsrooms and enshrined a greatly expanded norm of public access to official records.[68]

A second vital factor is the political disenchantment of Americans generally and reporters especially beginning in the 1960s—what Schudson has called the rise of a "critical culture." Watergate remains the iconic case of journalism's loss of innocence. But that scandal followed a decade that provided ever more striking instances of official willingness to deceive—most notably the routine, organized mendacity of the war effort in Vietnam, which "drained the reservoir of trust between the government and the press."[69] One vivid comparison of metro newspapers in the early 1960s and late 1990s declares that to read the earlier coverage "is to roll back a gigantic cultural loss of idealism"; to modern eyes the stories seem "naively trusting of government" and to advance "an unquestioned, quasi-official sense of things."[70] Daniel Hallin argues that this "high-modernism" of American journalism, a midcentury interlude of mostly untroubled alignment between the views of professional reporters and government officials, was grounded in the Cold War political consensus and in widespread economic prosperity. Both of these anchoring conditions began to erode in the 1960s and 1970s, the first quite dramatically. As American political life became more fractured and less coherent, Hallin explains, the "interpretive role of the journalist" grew to fill the vacuum.[71]

Finally, the analytical turn must also be read through the lens of journalism's professional project. It continues the quest for public authority and social respectability that first took shape at the turn of the century, anchored in Progressive Era faith in science and public reason.[72] Making sense of the world is a higher calling than simply recording events and transmitting claims. Whether exposing public misdeeds, spotting social trends, or reading political tea leaves, journalism that makes visible the unseen forces in our lives confers greater status on the profession. Analytical reporting allows more play for reporters' political, intellectual, and literary ambitions. It gives rise to areas of specialized expertise and training that help to legitimate reporters' claims to be news "professionals"—areas such as "precision journalism" in the 1970s or "data journalism" today.[73] And it simultaneously fulfills and celebrates journalism's mission as a democratic watchdog, elevating the reporter vis-a-vis the public figures she reports on. The post-1960s turn toward analytical and investigative reporting helped to underwrite new career horizons that opened up for reporters as news programming multiplied and diversified, especially on cable television.[74] A late-1990s journalism review would argue that Watergate launched "the era of the journalist as celebrity."[75] That simplifies a complex history but points to the rising fortunes of a widening class of media professionals—journalists, pundits, experts— who would claim national fame and prestige after the 1970s.

Rejecting the "Strategy Frame"

The analytical turn clearly finds new expression in the surge in fact-checking over the last decade, and especially in the emergence of full-time, professional fact-checkers. The commitment to assess rather than simply report what politicians say positions journalists as the arbiters of political truth. It violates the norm against making arguments or "drawing conclusions" (which is why some journalists say fact-checking belongs on the opinion pages).[76] Even simple fact checks may require thousands of words of explanation and analysis; practitioners often describe the genre as part of a wider trend toward both "accountability journalism" and "explanatory journalism."

At the same time, fact-checkers reject particular kinds of analysis. They describe the genre as an antidote not only to "he said, she said" reporting but also to another oft-criticized feature of American news: its focus on the political "horse race." (Hence their conflicting references to the original behind-the-scenes campaign narrative, *The Making of the President, 1960.* Fact-checking builds on that journalistic "advance" but also corrects for the preoccupation with "process" it ushered in.) At a conference in 2011, one media scholar asked fact-checkers whether the "culture of fact-checking"— meaning the constant tit-for-tat of claims and counterclaims—amplified the "horse-race politics" that causes citizens to tune out. The journalists objected strenuously. "I mean, I think we're the antithesis of horse-race journalism, which is covering who's ahead, who's behind, what does the last poll show," FactCheck.org founder Brooks Jackson countered. Glenn Kessler, the *Washington Post*'s Fact Checker, agreed: "I think that the horse-race coverage of politics, when I covered politics, it's the part that I hated most about it, and in fact, it's why I didn't want to cover politics anymore."[77]

The crucial paradox here is that both fact-checking and the horse-race coverage it rejects can be understood as strains of interpretive journalism. Both qualify as what Hallin calls more "mediated" genres that foreground the journalist at the expense of his or her subjects.[78] What scholars call the "game frame" or "strategy frame" (usually in contrast to a focus on substantive political issues) emerged as a companion to increasingly skeptical, analytical journalism.[79] Its appeal is precisely that it allows reporters to be critical of political actors—to draw on their own acumen and take readers behind the veil of public life—while avoiding charges of bias.[80] The indictment against horse-race coverage can leave the impression it merely performs journalistic "savviness," encouraging public cynicism while skirting any substantive questions voters might care about.[81] But the reality is more complex than that. News reports blend questions of politics and of policy in ways that are hard to reduce to a simple litmus test. It is better to say that strategic framing offers one device for managing the political risks of adversarial reporting but in ways that also may blunt the impact of that reporting.

These dynamics emerged with unusual clarity in a case that American journalists today point to as a grave professional failure: coverage of the run-up to the 2003 U.S. invasion of Iraq. The various forms of political pressure experienced by reporters in the aftermath of 9/11 have been well documented.[82] In that environment, newsrooms applied exacting rules of evidence to any reporting that cast doubt on official claims. In January 2003, to take one example, the Associated Press reported that two months of inspections by UN weapons experts readmitted to Iraq had found no evidence of forbidden arms, even at sites singled out by officials in Washington and London. The reporter on the story complained later that he could not go further and assert what he by then considered established fact: that the White House lacked firm evidence of Iraq's weapons programs. He explained in a 2007 interview, "That would be stricken from my copy because it would strike some editors as tendentious. As sort of an attack or some sort of allegation rather than a fact."[83] This underscores the way rules of evidence in journalism are embedded in real-world social and political relations. Gaye Tuchman has made this point starkly: "Facts about the powerful are treated with more care than those about the powerless."[84]

Meanwhile, strategic framing offered a way to modulate the tone of potentially incendiary reporting on the march to war. In late 2002, 60 *Minutes* aired a review of the White House case for invading Iraq. The report highlighted experts' doubts about Iraq's nuclear weapons program and about alleged links between Saddam Hussein and al-Qaeda. However, 60 *Minutes* framed the segment as an analysis of the marketing effort for the invasion. "It's not the first time a president has mounted a sales campaign to sell a war," correspondent Bob Simon announced to open the piece, reviewing slogans for U.S. war efforts through history.[85] Simon would later explain the approach in a PBS interview that is worth quoting at length:

> BOB SIMON: And, I think we all felt from the beginning that to deal with a subject as explosive as this, we should keep it in a way almost light. If that doesn't seem ridiculous.
>
> BILL MOYERS: Going to war, almost light.
>
> BOB SIMON: Not to present it as a frontal attack on the Administration's claims. Which would have been not only premature, but we didn't have the ammunition to do it at the time. We did not know then that there were no weapons of mass destruction in Iraq.
>
> We only knew that the connection the Administration was making between Saddam and Al Qaeda was very tenuous at best and that the argument it was making over the aluminum tubes seemed highly dubious. We knew these things. And therefore we could present the Madison Avenue campaign on these things, which was a sort of softer, less confrontational way of doing it.[86]

That response helps to illustrate the subtle interweaving of concerns about evidence and about political risk. The CBS investigation lacked the definitive proof to mount a "frontal attack." Focusing on White House strategy was a way to raise questions about the case for war without taking a decisive factual position as to its soundness—and without raising the ire of the White House and its defenders. As a consequence, though, the import of the story changed. An investigative report driven by doubts about evidence in the Bush administration's case for war became a strategic analysis whose central claim was already self-evident: that the White House was making a case for war.

Fact-checkers lack the flexibility to modulate their truth-telling in this way. This is perhaps the most important thing to understand about their work and the reactions it provokes: Fact-checking as a genre forecloses the ability of journalists to shift into a strategic register in order to finesse evidence and manage risk. This is not to say fact-checkers don't care about questions of political strategy. Published fact checks often discuss what politicians want to achieve with particular claims and, as we shall see in chapter 4, this guides the factual analysis in subtle ways. But the dominant frame of a fact check *is* always one of factual analysis, constrained by the formal commitment to reach a verdict expressed in the language of truth and falsehood. Fact-checkers can't have it both ways, gesturing at a conclusion without standing behind it.

Fact-Checking as a Form of Knowledge Production

Fact-checkers confront thorny epistemological questions more often and more directly than many other journalists for the simple reason that they set out to resolve factual disputes rather than to relay a set of facts about the world. This demands an added measure of coherence. A fact check should make sense not just as one reasonable account of the world but as the correct account. Fact-checking often invites comparisons to other kinds of factual inquiry, especially in the sciences.[87] At the same time, the institutional world these reporters move in sets their work apart from scientific inquiry—itself not as straightforward as we often assume. Considering fact-checking broadly as a form of knowledge production helps to illuminate the peculiar epistemological challenges these journalists face.

A basic feature of the informational universe fact-checkers operate in is that simple and settled questions seem to become more complicated and less settled on close inspection. This sounds like a commonplace, along the lines of "every answer only brings more questions." Nevertheless, it cuts against our intuitive picture of how fact-checking might work to ground public discourse on a bed of hard facts. We think of facts as the Cartesian building blocks of logical reasoning, the basis for true statements and sound arguments about the world. This commonsense view matches "correspondence" theories of truth.[88] It fits what phenomenology calls our "natural attitude" to the world around us, the taken-for-granted sense of an external reality that others perceive the way we do.[89] "Every fact is a brick in the wall of an argument," one fact-checker told me to explain why even trivial matters deserve scrutiny. "If it can't bear the weight of the wall, it doesn't deserve to be there."[90] How can we meaningfully debate the merits of any position if we can't even agree on the basic facts?

In practice, though, fact-checking rarely proceeds in neat Cartesian steps to a set of hard, elemental facts that either support a statement or don't. The facts available to test a public claim are typically incomplete, conditional, disputed, or otherwise uncertain. This is a more normal state of affairs than we tend to think; humans navigate the world quite effectively with imperfect facts, and by treating as settled matters that—at the margins, at least—may not be. In most situations we don't need precise definitions in order to communicate and do very well with only roughly overlapping senses of what a word or concept stands for in a given context.[91] Think of the simplest sort of factual assertion: "This is an apple." We can make it in most cases with utter confidence despite having no idea of how to define an apple. Moreover, we can make it even if no settled definition exists across various disciplines— for instance, if botanists and plant geneticists and orchard growers draw the boundary around "apple" in different ways. Whose definition is the right one? It simply does not matter unless we find ourselves in the unusual position of having to justify our assertion.

Meanwhile, turning to a specialist to resolve a factual dispute often reveals that the question itself is oblique to the specialist's way of understanding the subject. Expert knowledge tends to break up the objects and categories we take for granted in stating everyday facts about the world (a reliable source of tension between reporters seeking a usable quote and specialists who supply only qualifications and reservations). Consider pundit George Will's frightening claim about Ebola transmission, mentioned at the start of this chapter. To laypeople, the question of whether the disease was "airborne" sounds straightforward: can it be transmitted by a sneeze or cough? But scientists interviewed by PolitiFact asked other questions: Does the virus itself promote sneezing and coughing? (Ebola doesn't.) How sick does someone have to be for transmission to occur this way? (Sick enough to be bedridden rather than walking the streets.) Do disease-causing particles remain suspended in the air for long? (Not in Ebola's case.) For epidemiologists, the category "airborne" entails judgments about a cluster of disease characteristics that, in an assumed context of human behavior and social relations, speak to the ease of transmission.[92]

The Instability of Institutional Facts

The informational universe that fact-checkers inhabit consists of what philosopher John Searle has called "institutional facts."[93] Unlike the "brute facts" of the material world, these concern things—like money, or borders, or last month's joblessness rate—which exist and have meaning only by virtue of some institutional rule-making apparatus. Searle stresses that institutional facts are for reasoning purposes no less certain than facts of nature.[94] The fact that parts of the Rio Grande mark the border between the United States and Mexico is *ontologically* subjective: the boundary, unlike the river itself, does not exist independent of our collective understanding. But the existence of the border is nevertheless *epistemically* objective by this approach. It can be factually verified; it is a matter not of opinion or loose convention but of "systems of constitutive rules."[95] At the same time, Searle argues that complex structures of institutional reality, like legal currencies or political boundaries, can evolve more or less by accident. Facts about these institutions obtain even in the face of false beliefs about *why* they do.[96]

Political fact-checking depends on probing the institutional structures that underlie public claims. To test the truth of a campaign claim about tax rates or immigration policy or any other area of public life, these journalists ask exactly the questions Searle's theory would suggest: Who is the relevant authority here? What are the constitutive rules? But the answers often turn out to be surprisingly unclear. The picture of social reality that emerges is less well ordered—which is not necessarily to say less well functioning—than the one Searle paints and than most of us might naïvely suppose. Institutional facts obtain in some contexts but not others. Very often more than one relevant standard or definition exists, and a fact-checker must decide which to use. The constitutive rules may not be articulated precisely until *after* a disagreement arises. The institutional world harbors a great deal of latent uncertainty: what looks from afar like a settled policy may turn out to be based in ignorance or inattention, quickly unraveling in the face of new circumstances.

A good way to capture this is by saying that well-established institutional facts—"waterboarding is a form of torture," to take a controversial example—prove to be only frozen arguments when circumstances change and constituencies shift. American journalists could refer unthinkingly to waterboarding as torture through the twentieth century.[97] They didn't need to consult legal experts or to choose one decisive rationale for drawing the link. It had support in both American and international law; it reflected journalistic precedent, mainly in writing about far-off authoritarian regimes; and perhaps most important, who was going to object? But that firm institutional fact came undone once it emerged that the United States had waterboarded its prisoners. Now, important people *would* object to the designation; now reporters *would* have to justify their choice of words. Secret legal memos released to the public clarified (but did not fundamentally change, officials insisted) the legal boundary around torture: what counted was not just the act of waterboarding but the circumstances in which it was done, the degree of pain inflicted, and so on. While organizations such as the Red Cross and the United Nations continued to describe waterboarding and related methods as torture, U.S. officials placed them in the new category of "enhanced interrogation techniques."

For journalists, this presented a dilemma not unlike that scientists face when experiments don't produce the results predicted by theory.[98] Should reporters assess the evidence about U.S. actions by what had been a well-established standard? Or, on the contrary, did the surprising new data argue for refining the rules they had previously applied? Most responded by dropping the word "torture" or qualifying it in ways they hadn't before—"according to opponents" or "under international law." Editorial pages continued to assert the link as fact but news reports could only detail the more particular facts it was based on: the terms of international antitorture agreements, historical prosecutions for the crime in U.S. courts, and so on.[99] The editor of the *New York Times* explained the shift this way: "When using a word amounts to taking sides in a political dispute, our general practice is to supply the readers with the information to decide for themselves."[100] The connection had been demoted from fact to argument. Now, with the controversy past, the fact appears to be stabilizing once again. In a mid-2014 policy shift, the *Times* declared that since prosecutions don't seem to be in the offing, the everyday understanding of torture is once again more relevant than the "disputed legal meaning." Therefore, "from now on, The Times will use the word 'torture' to describe incidents in which we know for sure that interrogators inflicted pain on a prisoner in an effort to get information."[101]

Of course, *every* fact is also always an argument, open at least in principle to qualification or refutation. This applies no less in hard science than in political life. A project of the sociology of science has been to understand the work that goes into "hardening" scientific facts, work that is not only technical or scientific (in the everyday sense of those terms) but also institutional, discursive, *social*. Our fundamental mistake, argues the sociologist Bruno

Latour, has been to conceive of facts as "elementary building blocks" made of "primitive, solid, incontrovertible, indisputable material," when in reality they are just the opposite: complex, carefully elaborated, and deeply collective.[102] By this light, in effect, all facts are institutional facts. This approach to scientific knowledge sometimes has been controversial.[103] But by stressing the collective nature of fact-making, it offers a valuable perspective for thinking about the world and the work of professional fact-checkers.

In practice, we tolerate a great deal of uncertainty, or assume certainty where none exists, until something gives us a reason not to. One might say that a degree of uncertainty or imprecision is part of the normal functioning of institutional reality. Consider a political border, one of Searle's favorite examples of institutional fact: Our ability to invoke a single notional border differently in various local contexts arguably helps to structure coherent activity at different registers or scales. (For instance, tolerating a certain amount of disagreement allows us to point at a clean line on a map to plan a route but also place a road sign where it will be most visible to drivers and organize utility districts in line with geography or infrastructure.) The idea that elision of difference helps to coordinate action or meaning is at the center of the metaphors—like "translation," "black boxes," and "boundary objects"—which sociologists use to describe how different actors, even with incompatible views of the world, work together in coherent scientific or technical initiatives.[104] "Consensus is not necessary for cooperation nor for the successful conduct of work," Susan Leigh Star and James Griesemer have famously written. "This fundamental sociological finding holds in science no less than in any other kind of work."[105] Journalists involved in fact-checking routinely uncover the hidden inconsistencies and disagreements lurking in institutional arrangements. But their own project is less forgiving of difference. Fact-checkers highlight the different definitions available to test a claim about the world—and then they have to endorse one standard.

Uncivil Discourse and Uncertain Meaning

Another defining feature of the world fact-checkers move in is its inhospitability to anything that looks like reasoned, factual inquiry. Their experience reminds us that careful deliberation in public contexts does not happen often or easily. Consider one of the historical examples that best expresses our ideal for public talk about politics today. The public sphere of coffees houses and print journals in eighteenth-century Europe seizes the democratic imagination precisely for locating reasoned political discourse in social spaces that were at least partly open, often mediated, and cultural or civic rather than political. But it is vital to recall that this celebrated early modern public sphere took root under strong, elite-derived norms of civility, and that debate centered on the narrow concerns of an emerging commercial class.[106] Shared norms and interests underwrote the bracketing of social status in the coffeehouse—the idea that the best argument would carry the day, no matter who made it—and the presumed bracketing of class interest across a wider, imagined public sphere.[107] We might assume this tension between inclusivity and reason disappears upon moving from the political realm to the scientific, but this is not the case. Historian Steven Shapin has shown how norms of civility and gentility offered a scaffold for the scientific revolution.[108] A civility norm grounded in shared class and culture defined the boundaries scientific discourse in the Enlightenment—both *who* could speak scientifically and *how* to speak scientifically. It cemented a wider "trusting system" without which individual acts of scientific distrust, such as replicating experiments and verifying results, would be impossible.[109]

These histories underscore the link between civility and reason, where civility is understood as a highly constrained mode of public discourse predicated on trust and the mutual assumption of good faith. As Shapin writes, "The ultimate incivility is the public withdrawal of trust in another's access to the world and in another's moral commitment to speaking the truth about it."[110] Explicit mechanisms enforce civility and regulate factual discourse in the modern institutional settings we associate with rigorous fact-finding work, like a laboratory or a courtroom or a congressional committee. Fact-finders in these environments can compel testimony from their subjects, human or otherwise. They observe strict protocols for gathering and presenting evidence. And they communicate according to formal rules whose violation may carry harsh professional or legal penalties.[111]

The hope that fact-checking can help to fix a broken public sphere, often disavowed by the fact-checkers themselves, imagines something like the Habermasian ideal of rational-critical discourse. But building hard facts is a collective effort. It becomes more difficult in the absence of social or institutional mechanisms to regulate public talk. Journalistic fact-checkers have no authority to make others cooperate, and they operate in a political world where good faith cannot be assumed. As media critics often complain, being factually incorrect or openly hypocritical seems to carry little cost for politicians, pundits, and other "professional communicators" who populate the media-political landscape.[112] Instead, experts who may reason carefully in their own academic domains learn to argue more colorfully and glibly to succeed as public intellectuals.[113]

The lack of civility in public discourse points to another basic feature of the fact-checkers' world: uncertain meaning. Their work is complicated by an immediate problem of interpretation that doesn't exist in the same way for fact-makers in more specialized areas with narrower constituencies. The public always becomes a third term in the fact-checking equation because these journalists evaluate statements made to or in front of a wider polity. As we shall see in case after case, this opens a potential distance between the literal truth of a statement and what it might mean or be designed to convey to its audience. Fact-checkers police false claims as well as misleading ones, terms they use almost interchangeably. "A politician can create a false, misleading impression by playing with words," notes the guide to the Fact Checker's "Pinocchio" scale. That rating system, like PolitiFact's Truth-O-Meter, assigns intermediate scores to statements that are simultaneously accurate and misleading. This approach treats such claims in effect as *somewhat* false; it fuses accuracy and dishonesty into a single ordinal scale.[114]

Other fact-finders also wrestle with problems of meaning and interpretation, of course. But they conduct their investigations within narrower interpretive or epistemic communities: of law, of a scientific discipline, of a particular area of policy, and so on.[115] Again, the hard sciences offer a useful counterpoint. The central insight of Thomas Kuhn's notion of scientific paradigms is that social-linguistic context structures scientific discovery: facts hold together, or fail to, against the backdrop of shared systems of interpretation.[116] Studies of laboratory work emphasize that different scientific fields or even subfields (for instance, experimental and theoretical physics) have very different ways of thinking about evidence and argument.[117] What Karin Knorr-Cetina calls "epistemic cultures" in the sciences define and reproduce themselves partly by shared vocabularies and common practices that regulate exchange within the group while also walling it off from the lay public and from powerful outsiders.[118]

Reporters, in contrast, have little of the equipment—rigorous education, specialized techniques, formal licensing—that we associate with objective inquiry in domains like law, medicine, and science. Journalism is an "uninsulated profession," easily buffeted by market and political forces.[119] This vulnerability guides the essentially defensive routines of objective practice in conventional journalism. It underlies the norm against taking sides in political disputes and becomes visible when reporters apply more demanding standards to stories about powerful subjects. The most famous instance of this, and one that does a lot of work in journalistic culture, is the apocryphal story that during the *Washington Post*'s Watergate investigation, editors required two corroborating sources for every anonymous claim.[120]

It is important to recognize how closely related the mechanisms of factual stabilization and professional protection are here. To say a field like journalism lacks scientific precision or rigor is, at least in part, to say that nonjournalists exert influence on it. Outsiders who want to address some area of scientific knowledge or practice typically need to engage the science on its own terms by mastering the terminology or speaking through credentialed experts. Laypeople can be remarkably successful in shaping expert discourse. Steven Epstein shows how AIDS activists in the 1980s and 1990s gained the authority to make moral claims on the direction of biomedical research after establishing themselves as "credible participants in the process of knowledge production."[121] One of the activists he interviews remarks, "Oh, this is like a sub-culture thing, you know, it's either surfing or its medicine, and you just have to understand the lingo, but it's not that complicated once you sit through it."[122]

That claim would hardly sound so surprising applied to a defenseless field like journalism. Members of the public face relatively few hurdles in challenging reporters' interpretations of the world. Fact-checkers are in the difficult position of offering decisive conclusions about controversial matters that anyone may feel qualified to weigh in on. This raises the tricky question of where fact-checkers' own expertise lies; I will suggest in chapter 4 that they consider themselves specialists in navigating diverse sources of expertise and teasing out useful facts from ideological arguments.

Fact, Value, and the Problem of Fairness

Another way to understand the problem of interpretation is that the fact-checkers studied in this book assess not only accuracy but also fairness. They are often criticized for confusing the two. As a critic at the *Columbia Journalism Review* complained after what progressives saw as an epic fact-checking blunder, "the fact-checkers have set their sights on identifying not only which statements are true, but which are *legitimate*."[123] In everyday thinking, we invoke the modern divide between two senses of "right," separating factual or scientific judgments from moral ones.[124] *How* to build an atomic weapon is a fundamentally different sort of problem than *whether* to build one. We can disagree about values but not about facts: this assumption is at the core of how we usually think about facts, and of professional journalism's practice of objectivity. (Whether we can truly separate fact from value is a more controversial question in philosophy than in everyday thinking.[125]) Disciplinary lines and technical vocabularies help to sustain the divide between fact and value in many kinds of specialized fact-finding work, purging morality (or at least lay morality) from the pursuit of knowledge in the lab, for instance.[126] In one sense, what makes language technical or scientific is precisely the bracketing out of particular concerns or kinds of discourse. A certain scheme of value is normalized and made invisible.

Fact-checkers adhere to this principle of separation in some respects: they distinguish factual claims from expressions of opinion and often say that to find a particular statement true or false is not to take a position on the rightness of the policies it is meant to promote. However, fact-checkers cannot bracket out the fairness of a statement itself from their factual analysis. In effect, they are concerned with not just right information but right communication.[127] In real-world political debates the two become very difficult to disentangle.

Fact-checkers defend professional journalism's commitment to objectivity. But by threading together arguments about truth and about fairness, they defy the injunction to separate facts and values. This suggests a surprising affinity with investigative journalism, which relies on very different tools and procedures. In their remarkable portrait (discussed in chapter 5) James Ettema and Ted Glasser show how investigative reporters defer to the ideal of objectivity even as their truth-seeking mission "leads them to challenge the limits of journalistic practice."[128] Like fact-checkers, investigative reporters can't take official claims at face value. As a result, Ettema and Glasser argue, their work reveals how values are woven into verification procedures and editorial judgment—it reveals the "inherent interdependence of human interest and human knowledge."[129] It thus points up the inadequacy of the "naïve realism" most of us casually subscribe to when it comes to understanding the real work of investigating facts. Ettema and Glasser outline a position "between realism and relativism" that is useful here as well:

> We do not deny that there is truth to seek. We contend, however, that those who seek a truth defined in terms of a naive metaphysical realism attempt the impossible, and therefore they attempt far too little. This paradox is easily resolved: because naive realism demands an exact correspondence between value-independent statements and a mind-independent reality, it subverts thoughtful consideration of what practical truth seekers must actually try to do.[130]

This chapter has placed fact-checking in the evolving tradition of objective practice in journalism while also considering the peculiar epistemological challenges confronting this kind of news reporting. Fact-checking as a movement has coalesced around a particular reading of journalism's failures over the last several decades, continuing a long history of revisions to the objectivity norm. I've argued it should be seen as part of the broader "interpretive turn" in news, even as fact-checkers explicitly reject particular styles of political analysis. And I've suggested that the fact-checkers' mission makes them unusually sensitive to the tensions and contradictions implicit in objective journalism. To understand the challenge of fact-checking means recognizing the features of the institutional world these reporters operate in, one characterized by unstable facts, uncivil discourse, and uncertain meaning. Fact-checkers investigate statements relating to an institutional reality that is far messier than we might suppose, one where even simple facts may rest on unclear or contested standards. They investigate claims that are often designed to deceive, made by political actors committed to instrumental advantage rather than coherent reasoning discourse.

This discursive environment sets fact-checkers apart from fact-finders in other fields—especially in science, which these journalists hold up as an ideal—and, I will argue, helps to explain the difficulty of settling factual disputes in public affairs. The next section of this book turns to the practical realities of checking facts as a form of newswork. As we shall see, the day-to-day routines of fact-checking—the procedures used, sources consulted, rules observed—are compellingly transparent and straightforward. They reflect the experience and consideration of professional journalists who are committed to their mission. At the same time, even simple fact checks leave room for disagreement, and this style of journalism invites an extraordinary degree of conflict and controversy.

PART II

THE WORK OF
FACT-CHECKING

"Born in the U. S. A."

THE PERSISTENT RUMOR THAT BARACK OBAMA WAS NOT BORN IN the United States may have begun with a fact-checking error. In 1991, according to one news report, a brochure put out by a literary agency included this mistake in the future president's biography: "Barack Obama, the first African-American president of the Harvard Law Review, was born in Kenya and raised in Indonesia and Hawaii."[1] Others have traced the rumor to a chain e-mail circulated by supporters of Hillary Clinton during the Democratic primary race in the spring of 2008.[2] What is undisputed is that doubts only gained force after the Obama campaign tried to quell them by releasing a digital copy of the candidate's Hawaiian birth certificate, in June of 2008. As PolitiFact would write soon after, "then the firestorm started."[3] The document provoked a string of new questions: Why wasn't it signed? Where was the embossed seal? Why was the certificate number blacked out? Shouldn't there be creases, from folding?

By their own accounts, fact-checkers at FactCheck.org and PolitiFact went to unusual lengths to address rumors about the president's real name, birthplace, and background. PolitiFact sought copies of every public record it could find on Barack Obama: his marriage certificate, driver's license file, property records, and official attorney's registration with the Supreme Court of

Illinois. A reporter e-mailed the birth certificate released by the Obama campaign to Hawaii's Department of Health; "it's a valid Hawaii state birth certificate," a spokesman confirmed. A Hawaiian colleague produced her own birth certificate so the two could be compared. Nevertheless, the fact-checkers conceded that conspiracy theorists could always raise some new doubt. The resulting article, one of the most-viewed in PolitiFact's history, concluded this way: "It is possible that Obama conspired his way to the precipice of the world's biggest job, involving a vast network of people and government agencies over decades of lies. Anything's possible. . . . But step back and look at the overwhelming evidence to the contrary and your sense of what's reasonable has to take over."[4]

FactCheck.org went one step further, contriving to have two reporters visit the Chicago headquarters of the Obama campaign in August of 2008 to look at the candidate's physical birth certificate.[5] This was largely a matter of good fortune. A press contact for the campaign, who had resisted calls to release a new version of the certificate, finally relented and invited FactCheck.org to see the document; as it happened, two staffers were going to Chicago for a conference. The journalists held the document in their hands and felt the raised seal. They took pictures of the seal, of the signature from Hawaii's registrar of vital statistics, and of the official certificate number, and posted these online in high resolution for readers to examine. Titled "Born in the U.S.A.," the article testified that

> FactCheck.org staffers have now seen, touched, examined and photographed the original birth certificate. We conclude that it meets all of the requirements from the State Department for proving U.S. citizenship. Claims that the document lacks a raised seal or a signature are false. We have posted high-resolution photographs of the document as "supporting documents" to this article. Our conclusion: Obama was born in the U.S.A. just as he has always said.[6]

Fact-checkers were forced to revisit the question many times as it surfaced over the next several years and could now point to the conclusive testimony from that visit to Obama's headquarters. "Our friends from FactCheck.org went to Chicago, held the document in their questioning hands and examined it closely. Their conclusion: It's legit," asserted a PolitiFact item in 2009,

written after a correspondent for the conservative news site WorldNetDaily
.com raised the issue again in the White House press room.[7] Two years later,
Donald Trump and Sarah Palin once again hinted at doubts about the president's natural-born status during the tentative early days of the Republican
presidential primary. The *Washington Post*'s Fact Checker columnist noted the
"fine work" of his two fact-checking rivals in debunking such "'birther' nonsense," and linked to FactCheck.org's piece as decisive proof that the birth
document featured a raised seal and a signature.[8]

Conventional news outlets could, in turn, cite the work of the fact-checkers
to challenge the rumors. After then–CNN host Lou Dobbs questioned
Obama's birthplace on his program in 2009, NPR's *Morning Edition*
featured FactCheck.org founder Brooks Jackson to offer an authoritative
rebuttal. "This is nonsense," Jackson declared on the air. The NPR narra-
tor continued:

> That's Brooks Jackson, a former senior investigative reporter for the *Wall
> Street Journal* and for CNN itself. He now runs FactCheck.org, a non-
> partisan outfit associated with the University of Pennsylvania's Annenberg
> Center. His researchers examined and held candidate Obama's Hawai-
> ian certificate of birth during last year's presidential campaign. Jackson
> says President Obama was born where he says he was.[9]

The professional fact-checkers have been cited and interviewed hundreds
of times in connection with the "birther" controversy, across the United
States and overseas, in outlets from the *New Yorker* to the *New Zealand Herald*.
During the 2012 campaign, U.S. journalists would grow more comfortable
challenging the rumors in their own voice. A CNN segment from May 2012
featured a testy live exchange between anchor Wolf Blitzer and Donald
Trump. "Donald, you and I have known each other for a long time, and I
don't understand why you're doubling down on this birther issue after the
state of Hawaii formally says this is the legitimate birth certificate," Blitzer
said. He did not cite the fact-checkers but ran through the evidence they and
other journalists had compiled over five years of research, including 1961
birth announcements in the *Honolulu Advertiser* and the *Honolulu Star-Bulletin*.
Trump countered that parents may run false birth announcements in hopes
of securing citizenship for their children. "Donald, you're beginning to

sound a little ridiculous, I have to tell you," Blitzer chided at one point. "Let me tell you something, I think you sound ridiculous," Trump shot back.[10]

The "birther" controversy captures with unusual clarity the fact-checker's role as testifier: "Jackson says President Obama was born where he says he was." This is the most basic rationale the new professional fact-checkers offer for their own existence—to be a trusted authority weighing in on factual questions readers don't have the time or ability to resolve for themselves. But the actual reporting work involved in certifying Barack Obama's background was quite atypical. Fact-checkers rarely have call to travel or even to leave their desks. Their articles don't feature datelines or on-the-scene descriptions from inside the courtroom or the campaign headquarters. Fact-checkers *testify* but rarely *witness*. "It's desk work," Angie Drobnic Holan, since named PolitiFact's top editor, said in an interview:

> When I do my fact-checking, I don't go out to meetings. I sit at my desk, I read reports, I read transcripts, I use the phone all the time. . . . A lot of reporters like the idea of going out and eye-witnessing things. I like that too, but I don't think that's what's needed for political fact-checking. I don't think you get closer to the truth with politics actually being at the press conference.[11]

Consider a much more typical example of what fact-checkers do every day. During my research at FactCheck.org in Philadelphia, a delegation of Russian journalists on a tour of the United States visited the group. An editor explained fact-checking to them this way: "It's standard journalism practices that should be used more by more journalists, but sometimes they don't have the time or they're on deadline, and . . . so it becomes 'he said, she said,' and the reader is left confused and not really knowing what's the truth. And that's where we try to come in."[12]

To illustrate, the editor mentioned an article encountered while reading the *New York Times* on the way to work just a few weeks earlier. It was a report on a speech by the then-governor of Mississippi Haley Barbour, a rumored presidential contender. Three paragraphs in the reporter quoted an attack line directed at President Obama: "In the last two years, the federal government spent $7 trillion and our economy lost seven million jobs. I guess we ought to be glad they didn't spend $12 trillion. We might have lost 12 million jobs."[13] A quick trip to the Bureau of Labor Statistics website would have revealed that actual job losses under the current White House were less than half of what Barbour claimed. "It doesn't take a lot to get that information," the FactCheck.org editor stressed—and yet, "it was a fact that went completely unchallenged by the *New York Times* reporter, and the *New York Times* is the best paper that we have in the country."[14]

The case offered to the visiting journalists in Philadelphia was typical in a number of ways that will be developed in the next three chapters. First, it centered on a well-known politician who was a possible candidate for high office. Professional fact-checkers hew closely to what sociologist Herb Gans has called "journalism's theory of democracy" and see their core mission as helping citizens to make well-informed choices at the ballot box.[15] They call what they do a form of "accountability reporting"—as an editor's note put it, "one of the few places in American journalism where elected officials . . . are held accountable for what they say."[16] That mission does *not* extend, however, to holding fellow reporters accountable for their work. The piece FactCheck .org published the day after Barbour's speech stated flatly that he had "grossly exaggerated" the real job-loss numbers. It linked to the *New York Times* report as evidence of what the governor had said. But it did not fault the paper of record for failing to challenge the easily checkable claim.[17] The elite fact-checkers see themselves as journalists, not media critics. They want to cure the profession of its bad habits but almost never directly fact-check their fellow reporters.[18]

Second, the Barbour episode illustrates very well the "desk work" fact-checkers routinely engage in even as it advertises an idealized version of that work. The analysis in this case could not have been simpler: The governor cited two statistics, and the fact-checkers compared these to authoritative data. To confirm the $7 trillion in spending, FactCheck.org linked to the Budget of the United States Government, as issued by the Office of Management and Budget. To show that the job-loss figure was "not even close," the article linked to a data sheet at the Bureau of Labor Statistics website: "Table B-1. Employees on nonfarm payrolls by industry sector and selected industry detail." Fact-checkers always seek official data and often point to examples like this to explain what they do. In practice, though, finding claims to check and establishing their truthfulness is not always so straightforward.

Fact-checkers traffic in institutional facts, like birth certificates and jobless-ness rates, which rest on a tangle of definitions, conventions, and bureau-cratic practices. These facts are more fragile than they seem.

Finally, the "birther" and Barbour fact checks both show how deeply me-diated is the journalism of fact-checking at every stage. Fact-checkers scan the news and pore over transcripts looking for suspicious claims to investi-gate. They use search engines and news archives to trace the origins of po-litical rumors and bogus statistics. And they promote their conclusions ea-gerly to other journalists, encouraging news outlets to cite their findings and to invite them on the air. Fact-checkers do, in one sense, assume the journal-ist's traditional role as witness: they witness and report on *mediated* events. Fact-checkers are both students of and active participants in the emerging media ecosystem.

This section of *Deciding What's True* examines the day-to-day work of fact-checking—its rules and routines, both formal and informal, as practiced by the three elite national U.S. outlets. Where do fact-checkers find claims to investigate? Who in public life do they focus on? What sources of infor-mation do they use? How do they deal with politically aligned experts and think tanks? Chapters 3 and 4 focus on the daily routines of finding and checking political claims while chapter 5 considers the epistemological questions this investigative work raises through an extended ethnographic case study.

3

CHOOSING FACTS
TO CHECK

THE FACT-CHECKER'S JOB BEGINS WITH CHOOSING CLAIMS TO CHECK
from countless public utterances made every day on matters large and small.
Editors at PolitiFact sometimes call this "the art of finding a checkable
fact." Like assembling a newspaper or a newscast out of the day's events, it is
a trickier and more fraught process than the routine cases can make it seem.
Public figures seem to stretch the truth more or less as a matter of course,
and fact-checkers complain all of the time that they can't keep up. At a panel
discussion after the 2014 elections, FactCheck.org's managing editor, Lori
Robertson, called this the organization's biggest challenge. "We'll never feel
like we have enough staff and enough resources to do all of the fact-checking
that we'd want," she said, pointing to an "avalanche" of questionable
claims in 2014. "We always wish we could do more." Her fellow panelists
all agreed. A fact-checker from Alaska noted that his state had just finished
the most expensive election in its history: "We were dealing with just a
huge amount of speech or discourse or whatever you want to call it, and we
didn't really come close to checking everything, or even a significant pro-
portion of what was out there."[1]

How, then, to choose the relative handful of statements to investigate each
week with sharply limited resources? Public discourse today involves a wide

range of professional communicators whose words shape politics and policy.[2] Should fact-checking focus on candidates for public office? Should it be balanced along party lines? Should fact-checkers take a scientific approach—choosing statements by some fixed rule or even at random? Finding facts to check involves judgments of newsworthiness, fairness, and practicality. For fact-checking groups, it means formulating policies about what kinds of claims can be checked and who merits this sort of scrutiny. It also constantly invites charges of bias from critics who ask whether we can draw any meaningful conclusions from fact-checkers who choose claims subjectively.[3] Meanwhile these reporters trust their own news sense in making judgments about what is interesting or important enough to check. "We are journalists, not social scientists. We select statements to fact-check based on our news judgment," PolitiFact's Bill Adair wrote in response to one outside tally that accused the site of systematic bias against Republicans.[4]

This chapter reviews the routines used in choosing facts to check at FactCheck.org, PolitiFact, and the *Washington Post*'s Fact Checker. Their formal policies vary somewhat but converge in prioritizing "checkable" statements by officeholders and political candidates. I consider their policies and practices through the lens of professional news values, the sometimes unspoken criteria journalists use to prioritize news coverage. Fact-checkers apply this familiar language in choosing claims to check but deemphasize breaking news and scoops in favor of a methodical, comprehensive approach. Finally, I try to convey a sense of the search for checkable facts as form of digital newswork, one that involves submitting to a torrent of online political communication. This perspective underscores how fact-checking depends on the routine transcription of political speech, a basic but unremarked feature of the modern media world.

The Art of Finding a Checkable Fact

For a news organization, finding a steady diet of factual claims to investigate begins by answering a basic question: Who in public life qualifies for fact-checking? The elite U.S. fact-checkers all focus their attention on political figures, especially officeholders and candidates. "It is my commitment that every politician in America should face the Truth-O-Meter," PolitiFact founder Bill Adair declared, quite earnestly, during a visit to a classroom of journalism students.[5] This focus is in keeping with the fact-checkers' core mission of providing a tool that citizens can use to make informed political choices. Brooks Jackson, the founder of FactCheck.org, explained that mission to me this way: "Our job, it seems to me, and the only job that any journalist can really properly aspire to, is to be a resource for those citizens who honestly are bewildered and confused and looking for help in sorting out fact from fiction."[6]

This democratic mission echoes clearly in the official literature of the fact-checking sites and comes up constantly in formal and informal settings. It is embodied in the permanent report cards maintained by PolitiFact and, during some races, by the *Washington Post*'s Fact Checker. Like a baseball card, these pages offer key statistics summarizing the performance of an individual political figure, making it easy to compare different candidates in an election.[7] The fact-checkers operate year-round but find their highest purpose during presidential races. Only a few months into 2015, all three sites were running special sections pegged to the election more than a year and a half away. PolitiFact greeted each campaign launch with a review of the candidate's Truth-O-Meter record—in a March report, Rand Paul had the best record—while the Fact Checker unveiled a graphical gallery for reviewing presidential hopefuls. Although in practice the fact-checkers also write with politicians and journalists in mind (as I argue in chapter 6), formally speaking, they work on behalf of an idealized public of information-hungry voters.

The *Washington Post*'s Fact Checker has the narrowest focus of the three sites, targeting "statements by political figures and government officials."[8] FactCheck.org's site explains that the group focuses on "major U.S. political players," including officeholders and candidates but also political action committees, labor unions, trade associations, and other political entities. The organization also puts real energy into debunking chain e-mails and responding directly to readers who ask about the political rumors they encounter online. "I had no idea when we started out the extent to which people were being bamboozled by this stuff," Brooks Jackson explained in an interview. "It's just under the surface, and the mainstream news organizations don't pay much attention to it. But an awful lot of people are getting what they think is information this way."[9] On the first day of a training session I observed, interns were armed with a detailed protocol for responding to these reader queries, including an eleven-page list of the most common Internet rumors and how they had been debunked.[10]

PolitiFact casts the widest net, challenging anyone "who speaks up in American politics."[11] The group interprets this mandate playfully at times. In addition to political groups and chain e-mails, PolitiFact has taken to task, for instance, Kareem Abdul-Jabbar, "a yard sign," and "18% of the American public" (who, as measured by one poll, continued to believe President Obama was a Muslim).[12] During one of my visits, PolitiFact's national staff had fun rating a claim about gun deaths made in the funny pages by "Doonesbury" character Mark Slackmeyer.[13] The fact check featured a colorful panel from the comic strip, and the analysis turned mainly on an e-mail interview with strip creator Garry Trudeau. (Trudeau clarified that in citing the number of deaths by gunfire "at home," his fictional radio host meant Americans killed in the United States, not necessarily in their dwellings.) Now "Doonesbury" appears—between David Dooley, president of the University of Rhode Island, and Chris Dorworth, a Florida state legislator—in PolitiFact's database of nearly three thousand public figures who have faced the Truth-O-Meter. The accompanying headshot is of Slackmeyer, not Trudeau.

Professional fact-checkers differ most sharply in their stance on scrutinizing fellow media figures. None of the three elite sites will directly challenge a reporter or a news outlet as the source of a claim, in the manner of partisan media watchdogs like Media Matters or the Media Research Center. However, PolitiFact does examine statements by pundits, columnists, and editorial writers, and in late 2013 launched a new site, PunditFact, to focus on such media personalities. This means challenging fellow journalists, which can complicate the group's vital relationships with other news outlets. For instance, ABC's *This Week*, which had a fact-checking partnership with PolitiFact in 2010, initially balked at including fact checks of its own pundits in the Truth-O-Meter feed on the show's website. Similarly, PolitiFact's rulings against progressive pundit Rachel Maddow have drawn vehement attacks from her and other hosts on MSNBC, a source of friction with a network that had frequently featured PolitiFact on its news programs. During a review of PunditFact's first year of operations, one editor noted the challenge of partnering with media outlets whose stars may also be put under the microscope: "It's a delicate thing because they say to your face, 'Yeah, sure, we're open to it, but are you going to fact-check our people too?'"[14]

Meanwhile, neither FactCheck.org nor the *Post*'s Fact Checker normally take on claims made by pundits or opinion journalists. At FactCheck.org this was explained to me as a matter of resources—it would require additional staff to check "the talking heads" when it is hard enough keeping up with falsehoods peddled by politicians.[15] Excluding pundits also seems to be conflated with a general ban on challenging opinion. During a training session, an editor at FactCheck.org walked interns through the transcript of a recent episode of ABC's *This Week*, looking for claims to check. When economist and *New York Times* columnist Paul Krugman appeared on the page, the editor skipped past his remarks: "We don't care what Paul Krugman says. He's a liberal economist, and he's got an opinion, and he's not running for office."[16] In contrast, Krugman's claims have been assessed more than a dozen times by PolitiFact, where he has earned unusually high marks.

Defining Checkable Facts

If they differ slightly on the question of who deserves their scrutiny, the elite fact-checkers agree emphatically on a basic rule about *what* can be checked: facts, not opinions. This is a constant refrain. In the training session just noted, the FactCheck.org editor turned from Krugman's comments to an extended *This Week* interview with Republican presidential hopeful Mitt Romney, an obvious candidate for fact-checking. Asked about his stance on the federal government's 2009 "bailout" of American automakers, Romney declared that billions of dollars would have been saved had the automakers moved more quickly into bankruptcy. "That's an opinion, there's no way to fact-check that," the staffer told the interns, explaining that Romney hewed to a "different philosophy" economically from the Obama administration. In contrast Romney's next claim, that the president had promised unemployment would stay below 8 percent, was easy to check and provably false. A segment featuring a former White House economic adviser yielded a quick flurry of checkable facts, such as the assertion that the economy had added a million private-sector jobs in the last six months. The editor seized on the remark: "*That's* something we can fact-check. It's a fact, it's a number."[17]

The same point was driven home during a three-day training session for state political reporters being inducted into the PolitiFact network.[18] Every Truth-O-Meter item begins with the "ruling statement," the precise claim being checked. This is usually a brief, verbatim quote, although it may also paraphrase a claim for clarity; what it can't ever be is a statement of opinion, trainees were told. The Truth-O-Meter "owner's manual" prepared for PolitiFact franchises repeats the lesson: "So what's a good fact to check? First, needless to say, it can't be an opinion."[19] The manual goes on to explain that there's no way to check the assertion that, for instance, taxes should be lower; reporters should focus instead on statements used to buttress those opinions, like the oft-repeated line that the United States has the highest corporate tax rate in the world. ("Mostly True," according to PolitiFact.) In practice, the line between factual claims and statements of opinion can be difficult to draw—a key issue in the fact-checking controversies discussed in chapters 4 and 5.

Claims about facts may also prove impossible to verify, making what these journalists call "checkability" a basic criterion. Fact-checkers rely whenever possible on public data sources and independent experts, and have little to work with when authoritative sources aren't available. Many important but unverifiable claims emerge in the area of national security; two examples I heard were the claim that more al-Qaeda members operate in Pakistan than Afghanistan and President Obama's assertion that the United States no longer tortures prisoners.[20] (There is an irony in this, as fact-checkers have called their movement a response to the failures of the American press before the Iraq War. As noted in the last chapter, they would have been hard pressed to challenge official claims about Iraq's "weapons of mass destruction.")

The high "spike rate" for pieces that can't be verified is treated as a point of pride at PolitiFact. At one training session I observed, an editor described to a group of new fact-checkers the work that went into investigating whether Barack Obama's first presidential campaign had lied about the candidate's real stance on the North American Free Trade Agreement. This became an issue after reports surfaced that an Obama adviser had reassured Canadian officials that the candidate's rhetoric about renegotiating NAFTA wasn't sincere. "I don't think it's appropriate to go to Ohio and tell people one thing while your aide is calling the Canadian ambassador and telling him something else," Republican candidate John McCain declared after the story broke.[21] However, a Truth-O-Meter item about the episode was spiked by a higher-up who said simply, "You don't have it. You don't have the proof." "And I was proud," the PolitiFact editor continued, "because I think it showed our high standards."[22] The Truth-O-Meter training manual echoes the point: "There's no shame for the reporter who wrote an item that got spiked. There simply weren't enough facts for the Meter."[23]

The three elite fact-checkers all focus on statements that *may* be false. There is little point in confirming, say, that there are fifty states in the union. They differ in their approach to suspect statements, however. FactCheck.org only publishes analyses of claims that turn out to be false. If a reporter knows or if research shows that a budget statistic is accurate, for instance, the work stops there. (Exceptions may be made when something widely thought to be false turns out to be true, according to Jackson.) More than once I heard this explained as matter of resources—to write up an analysis of truthful claims would leave less time to debunk false ones. "We're not going to write when they're right because we don't have enough time," an editor instructed during a training session. "We're only looking for stuff that's wrong."[24] The focus on falsehood colors the selection process from the beginning. "We look for things that don't sound right," Brooks Jackson has explained.[25]

Fact-checkers who issue formal ratings, like the Truth-O-Meter and the *Washington Post*'s Pinocchio scale, take a different approach—one that models, in principle at least, an experimental protocol. At PolitiFact, choosing a claim to check initiates a somewhat formalized set of procedures that always results in a ruling, unless insufficient evidence is found. This is deliberate. As a statement of principles I was shown argues, "Fact-checking journalism has often focused on falsehoods, which paints a distorted picture of the political discourse. . . . Our goal is to rate the claims that people are curious about. If a claim ends up being True, we still publish an item." (Just over one-third of published Truth-O-Meter items receive a rating of "True" or "Mostly True."[26]) Rating true statements as well as false ones lends some validity to the statistical "report cards" on individual politicians and to other, sometimes playful measures PolitiFact has developed.[27] However, PolitiFact stops short of claiming scientific rigor in its selection process. Asked by a student journalist how the group chooses facts to check, Bill Adair offered a formulation I heard several times: "We're guided by news judgment. And we are all journalists, we're not social scientists."[28]

In my own experience at PolitiFact finding claims to check, it was very tempting to focus on items that I thought were probably false—to behave more like a policeman than a scientist. Veteran fact-checkers have reported

something similar. Glenn Kessler, the *Washington Post*'s Fact Checker columnist, has said the main piece of advice his predecessor offered was to run more
"Geppettos," the label given to truthful claims on the site's four-Pinocchio
scale. Nevertheless, Kessler lamented, he managed to give only four or five
such ratings in the course of a year—"the problem is there's so many untrue
statements out there that I haven't really found the opportunity to do it."[29]
Like other journalists, fact-checkers think about their own work by overlapping but not always compatible standards. They seek to shed light on
complex policy questions and to inform electoral choices but also to expose
public deception and hypocrisy.

News Values and Fact-Checking

Even discarding statements of opinion and those that are obviously true or
seem impossible to verify, fact-checkers have many more claims to choose
from than they can possibly examine. To sort through them, they apply a
version of journalism's familiar "news sense"—the principles of story selection, difficult to articulate, which reporters and editors pride themselves on
acquiring on the job.[30] Fact-checkers focus first on claims about important
policy matters, claims that highlight the choice between political candidates
(usually accusations leveled by one candidate against another), and claims
that have caused controversy or received media attention. Although their rulings frequently turn on narrow questions of phrasing, fact-checkers also
purport not to challenge verbal slips or mistakes made "under the klieg
lights."[31] "I make a distinction between statements that are made in prepared
speeches versus things that might be said off-the-cuff," the *Washington Post*'s
Glenn Kessler has explained.[32] The same point was emphasized in training
sessions at PolitiFact as well as FactCheck.org, whose interns were told,
"We're not here to poke anybody in the eye."[33]

Fact-checkers temper this news sense with a deliberate effort to take into
account what average citizens understand or care about. All of the sites solicit statements to check from their readers and point out when an item ran
by popular demand. At PolitiFact, roughly one-third of Truth-O-Meter items
originate in reader queries, I heard. Internally, staffers sometimes refer to
"the Mabel test," invoking a hypothetical middle-income American far from

Washington, DC. The statement of principles explained, "Our most important principle in choosing a fact to check is whether a typical person who heard the statement would wonder, *Is that true?*" Similarly, when visiting journalists asked how FactCheck.org selects facts to check, an editor explained the group's news judgment this way: "Is this of some national significance? Is it something that most people would be interested in knowing? . . . Or is it just so outrageous and crazy that it'd be something that we should do?"[34]

Fact-checking thus embodies distinct elements of "accountability" journalism as well as "explanatory" or "service" journalism, all terms I heard fact-checkers use to describe what they do. Fact-checkers also cultivate their own occupational sense of items that will be fun or challenging to investigate. Like other journalists, they seize the opportunity to interview interesting people or to write about unusual subjects. The "Doonesbury" fact check mentioned earlier is a good example. Although the analysis was straightforward, the piece offered a chance to talk to a famous cartoonist and to describe the strip panel by panel, including the visit from a space alien that sets up a final wisecrack. Humor and even local boosterism find a place in fact-checking. PolitiFact Georgia has investigated the "claim" by Atlanta's celebrity groundhog, General Beauregard Lee, to be more accurate than Pennsylvania's better-known Punxsutawney Phil. (The boast was judged "Mostly True" based on weather service data and an interview with a human meteorologist.[35])

In other cases the analysis itself holds appeal. While I visited PolitiFact, the site issued a "Barely True" rating (since relabeled "Mostly False" in a sitewide revision) to Vice President Joe Biden's claim that shutting down Amtrak's Northeast Corridor would require seven new lanes on highway I-95.[36] Nobody had proposed to shut down the rail line. Biden's comment was meant to illustrate the importance of the nation's rail infrastructure, a point PolitiFact's analysis (concluding the real figure would be as little as one lane in each direction) hardly disputed. But the piece, which took a day and a half to report, raised all kinds of challenging questions: Would all of the displaced Amtrak riders take to their cars? What about bus and plane travel? How should you account for peaks and valleys in ridership? How does population growth figure into the math? The panel of editors who reviewed the item remarked on its complexity and joked about trying to get their heads around all of the variables.[37]

The news sense developed by traditional newspaper editors or broadcast news producers embraces these elements as well. Some stories seem self-evidently important; others are justified in terms of audience appeal or utility; and still others aim for peer recognition or tickle a shared journalistic sensibility. But the fact-checker's news sense also differs from the deadline reporter's, most markedly in a diminished emphasis on timeliness, originality, and exclusivity. The elite fact-checking outlets routinely issue verdicts days or even weeks after the statement being checked was made. And fact checks run regardless of whether another news outlet or fact-checker has already covered the same ground.

Timeliness

Fact-checkers take pride in the work that goes into each piece and the time it takes to produce. They often say that what distinguishes their brand of journalism from deadline reporting is having the time and the space to investigate an issue thoroughly. "This is not one-call journalism," one editor told a group of state reporters, including seasoned veterans, being trained in the PolitiFact method. Trainees learned that Truth-O-Meter items can take days to report thoroughly.[38] The group celebrates a willingness to tackle complex questions that might put off other fact-checkers. One example mentioned several times was the claim by Republican presidential hopeful Herman Cain, a business-man, to have saved Godfather's Pizza when he was CEO of the restaurant chain. This could have been dismissed as impossible to verify or a matter of opinion—what counts as rescuing a struggling business? Nevertheless, Politi-Fact largely confirmed Cain's boast in a 1,600-word fact check that cited more than thirty distinct sources and took two weeks to research.[39]

FactCheck.org founder Brooks Jackson has made the same point many times. "If you're going to do it right, it takes time," he told me in an interview, mentioning a just-posted piece on federal salaries that had gone through two weeks of reporting and revisions.[40] The group, based at the University of Pennsylvania, prides itself on methodical research and careful, nuanced articles that go through a rigorous vetting process—a word-by-word internal fact-checking in the style of the *New Yorker*—before being published. Interns heard the message on the first day of their training: "Take your time. We have the luxury of time. We're not trying to beat the clock. . . . One of our luxuries is that we can be thorough."[41]

The standard explanation for the failure of traditional reporters to challenge false claims is that deadline pressures simply don't permit it. I heard this many times, from nearly every fact-checker I spoke to. As noted earlier, group of overseas journalists visiting FactCheck.org was told that fact-checking is "standard journalism practices that should be used more by more journalists, but sometimes they don't have the time . . . so it becomes 'he said, she said.'"[42] In reality, this is only one factor—and maybe not the most important one. Reporters working a beat or a campaign often don't bother to check an official claim even when the evidence is only a click away. When asked, many fact-checkers will speak eloquently about the perils of "access journalism," anonymous sources, and an insider culture that promotes "false balance" in the news. But the idea of writing quickly under deadline is basic to journalism's identity and becomes an easy and natural way for fact-checkers to emphasize what they do differently.

Originality

In the same way, fact-checkers worry less than their traditional peers about getting "scooped" or about finding a new angle for an item that has been challenged before. False claims resurface all of the time. Campaign-trail rumors that have been thoroughly debunked may return four years later with even more force, as with the doubts about President Obama's birth certificate. All three of the major fact-checking sites regularly run new items rehashing their own research from weeks or months earlier. At a training session for state political reporters writing their first Truth-O-Meter items, a Politi-Fact editor explained that the rhythms of fact-checking require a different mindset:

> The old way of thinking in the newsprint era was, if it was in the paper we just assumed everybody had read it. How many times have you heard that from an editor—"We had that, let's move on." You don't want to repeat the news, it doesn't seem as fresh. But in the case of fact-checking, it's really not a good answer to say, "Well, we ran that."[43]

The same applies to items that have been already refuted by another site. A tremendous amount of overlap exists in the claims checked by FactCheck .org, PolitiFact, and the *Washington Post*'s Fact Checker, who often cite one another in their published articles.[44] "That's the nature [of fact-checking]," Glenn Kessler has explained. "It doesn't really matter that they've done it before and I haven't."[45] The fact that the three sites return over and over to the same questions becomes a running theme in their published articles. "What night of presidential foreign policy debate would be complete without the rehashed claim from Romney that Obama embarked on an 'apology tour' of the world soon after being elected president," joked a FactCheck.org report on the final Obama-Romney debate in October 2012. The piece linked to FactCheck.org's earlier story and to "our fact-checking colleagues" at Politi-Fact and the *Washington Post*.[46]

PolitiFact's top editor, Angie Drobnic Holan, emphasized this point to overseas fact-checkers in a 2014 discussion of "best practices": "Glenn and Eugene and I, we all watch each others' sites, and we will repeat each others' fact checks with our own process," she explained. New reporters sometimes complain about this, Holan noted, but "we don't all have the same readers, so not all of our readers have seen that fact check." When overseas fact-checkers expressed surprise that U.S. sites rehash the same material, their American counterparts argued that the impact of a fact check is greatest when they reach the same conclusion independently. "If we all say this person's full of beans, it can have a dramatic impact," Kessler argued.[47] The advice was later distilled into an article on PolitiFact:

> We all like to be original, but it's rare to be the absolute first fact-checker looking at a claim. More often than not, someone else has researched and written what you're investigating, or at least something similar.
>
> At PolitiFact, we check our archive of more than 8,000 fact-checks to see what we've written on a given topic. We also look at the work of our friends at Factcheck.org, the *Washington Post*'s Fact Checker, Snopes and other fact-checking sites—and we credit appropriately. We will look at what they found and then verify the evidence for ourselves.[48]

Fact-checkers generally reach the same conclusions and admit that disagreement in their rulings can cause real discomfort.[49] "We sometimes get a little ruffled when we come to different conclusions," Kessler noted in a C-SPAN interview after his first year on the job. "But generally we tend to see eye-to-eye on things."[50] In rare cases, a fact check may be revised to reflect the wider consensus. In late 2011, for instance, PolitiFact reconsidered a ruling on White House rhetoric linking budget cuts to rising crime after both readers and the other major fact-checkers saw it very differently. "It was a disconcerting schism for us. It's much more satisfying when the major fact-checking organizations agree, because we know we've reached the same conclusions independently," an editor's letter remarked.[51] This kind of journalism draws frequent criticism from well-known media and political figures, and fact-checkers take refuge in one another's work when controversy arises. A dramatic instance, reviewed in the next chapter, came when the sites faced heavy fire for challenging Democratic claims that a Republican budget plan would "end Medicare." To defend themselves, the fact-checkers all pointed to their unanimous verdicts condemning "Mediscare" tactics.[52]

This is not to say that fact-checkers don't see one another as competitors. Staffers have a sense of which outlet checked a claim first, or best. Jackson, who launched FactCheck.org in 2003, has commented ruefully on the increased pressure to turn items around quickly since his rivals appeared on the scene: "When we're fact-checking a debate, for example . . . we used to wait and go through the transcript, but now there's so much competition from these other guys, people expect us to get our stuff up in less than 24 hours."[53] PolitiFact takes pride in being a little quicker than its peers, managing to weigh in on public controversies while they are still unfolding in the news.[54] But, as noted earlier, this is the friendly competition of rivals collectively pioneering a new enterprise.

Relevance

Even as they downplay competitive pressure and tell staffers to slow down, not speed up, fact-checkers clearly do strive to be timely and relevant. They package fact-checking stories around current events—campaign debates and political conventions but also major holidays, sporting events, and so on. They pay close attention to trending topics in the news. Thus, in the spring of 2012, as U.S. gas prices spiked, all three sites ran features checking the "gassy rhetoric" (Fact Checker) of the "gasoline price blame game" (PolitiFact).[55] This topicality jibes with the mission of explanatory journalism that helps readers to make sense of public affairs. "For me a fact is worth checking if it's in the news and it can tell a broader story about policy," the *Washington Post*'s Glenn Kessler explained at a conference after the 2014 U.S. midterm elections. "If the national conversation is about immigration, let's do some immigration fact-checks. . . . If Ferguson is happening, let's fact-check things going on in Ferguson. So I think it has to be rooted in the news and hopefully it's part of a broader conversation you have with your readers about difficult complex policy issues."[56]

Like most journalists, fact-checkers take for granted that their readers value such timeliness. They pay close attention to daily and hourly traffic statistics and to the challenges of SEO, or search engine optimization. Posting a fact check while an issue is still in the news can bring in new readers who find an item via Google or another search engine. To make sure its coverage of a major debate or speech ranks highly on Google, PolitiFact may post a story "shell" with a descriptive headline—such as "Fact-Checking the Presidential Debate"—before the event has even begun.[57]

A rapid response also boosts a fact-checker's chance of being cited by political figures or by fellow journalists and thus—although they sometimes disavow this goal—of influencing public debate. While I visited PolitiFact, a veteran reporter known for his ability to quickly fact-check complex issues took just a few hours to produce a 1,200-word rebuttal of a claim by President Obama about the debt relief promised in his new budget. The piece was quickly vetted and went live just after 4:30 P.M. on the same day as the president's speech.[58] The next morning, during his inaugural press briefing, the incoming White House press secretary Jay Carney repeated the president's claim. ABC correspondent Jake Tapper bluntly challenged his math, citing PolitiFact. In the official transcript, the president's spokesman seems to have been caught off balance:

> JAKE TAPPER: Right, but when PolitiFact says it's false for the President to say that he's not adding to the debt, it doesn't matter? This White House is still going to continue to make the claim that you're not adding to the debt, even when nonpartisan people have looked at it and said you actually are?

JAY CARNEY: Well, look, I would just refer you to the statements of Jack Lew explaining this. I'm not an economist. I know you've heard phrases like that before. (Laughter.) But I'm not. And we absolutely stand by the budget.[59]

In choosing claims to check, fact-checkers are always a step behind the news cycle. These organizations serve competing aims. One is to draw readers—and perhaps to make a difference in public discourse—by weighing in when it counts. Speed is a factor here. But another goal is to build a permanent database of carefully checked facts and political records that citizens can consult whenever they need to. "We are not just about producing a daily product with the political news of the day," founder Bill Adair explained shortly after PolitiFact launched. "We are serving voters by creating a database that they can go to before the election to say, 'Huh, I'm kind of interested in Obama or Biden, or whoever. Let me see how they stack up.'"[60]

A database has a longer shelf life than a news story. At both FactCheck .org and PolitiFact I heard reporters remark on sudden spikes in traffic to old items that have become relevant again. In addition to running lengthy thematic features and a "wire" for shorter, breaking items, FactCheck.org curates the research in its own archive through an "Ask FactCheck" form and a "Viral Spiral" page that focuses on popular online rumors. One of the primary tasks for interns is to respond to the hundreds of e-mail queries the group receives every day, pointing readers to the relevant fact checks or summarizing their findings. The group takes this work very seriously. On the first day of training, interns received a lengthy tutorial on "inbox procedures," along with a list of dozens of the most common questions and links to the responses. Accuracy is paramount even in these one-on-one exchanges with readers, an editor stressed.[61]

Meanwhile, PolitiFact addresses the tension between old and new with the "layered" structure of its website, organized around the Truth-O-Meter. As noted, the site was conceived as a more database-like version of FactCheck .org. Each Truth-O-Meter ruling is a news story but also a data point, factored automatically into various statistical measures and available for editors to pull into topical feature stories. A Truth-O-Meter item I wrote as a participant-observer in 2011, about Indiana governor and Republican

Tampa Bay Times

PolitiFact.com

Winner of the Pulitzer Prize

SATURDAY, SEPTEMBER 12TH, 2015

NATIONAL   TRUTH-O-METER™ ˅   STATES ˅   ARTICLES   PROMISES ˅   PEOPLE ˅   PUNDITF/

Hillary Clinton's file

Democrat from New York

Hillary Clinton is a candidate running for president of the United States in 2016. She served as U.S. Secretary of State during the first four years of the Obama administration. She is formerly a U.S. senator from New York, first elected in 2000. She was a candidate for president in 2008. She previously served as first lady when her husband, Bill Clinton, served two terms as president. She was born in Chicago in 1947, graduated from Wellesley College and earned a law degree at Yale Law School. She and her husband have one daughter.

Clinton's statements by ruling

Click on the ruling to see all of Clinton's statements for that ruling.

True		38 (31%)
Mostly True		24 (20%)
Half True		25 (20%)
Mostly False		21 (17%)
False		13 (11%)
Pants on Fire		2 (2%)

FIGURE 3.1 The PolitiFact file for Hillary Clinton as of September 12, 2015. The site's database compiles a running report card for every person or group whose claims have been checked. *Source: Courtesy of the* Tampa Bay Times.

presidential contender Mitch Daniels, offers a good illustration.[62] This was the first time PolitiFact rated a claim by Daniels; posting the piece required a new entry for him in the master database, including a headshot and a brief biographical note. The site's content management system automatically generated a page called "Mitch Daniels's file," where his career statistics are automatically tabulated (as of mid-2015, these include three "False" rulings and one "Pants on Fire") and any stories involving him are listed.[63] (Figure 3.1 shows the file for a more frequent fact-checking target, Hillary Clinton.)

My Truth-O-Meter piece was posted at 5:00 P.M. on February 17, nearly a week after Daniels made his claim (about interest on the national debt) at the annual Conservative Political Action Conference. It immediately appeared on the news feed at the front of PolitiFact's site as a rectangular data box including Daniels's picture, the statement being checked, and the Truth-O-Meter ruling. Clicking on that data box brought up the full 670-word article. The ruling also was quickly folded into two topical stories: one about the conservative event and another about a flurry of budget-related claims.[64] Truth-O-Meter items may be pulled into new topical round-ups months or even years later. In my case, both of the topical stories actually ran before the Daniels item was ready. An editor simply tacked a new paragraph onto the articles, and added the data box to the other Truth-O-Meter rulings listed on the side of the page.[65]

Balance

A final question fact-checkers wrestle with in choosing statements to examine is balance. Professional fact-checking groups vocally reject what journalism critics call "he said, she said" reporting. At the same time, they make a point of their commitment to check "both sides" of the American political arena, unlike partisan media critics who fact-check from the left or from the right. In a report on the fact-checking movement, Michael Dobbs, the *Washington Post*'s original Fact Checker columnist, wrote that "if you criticize only one side (in the manner of the left-leaning Media Matters, for example), you are no longer a fact checker. You are a tool in a political campaign."[66] The elite fact-checkers reinforce this distinction constantly. "They are rebutting people they don't agree with," Brooks Jackson said of partisan sites. "When I say fact-checking, I am talking about neutral, nonpartisan critiques of false statements, whoever makes them. They don't fit my definition of fact-checking."[67] PolitiFact's "Beyond the Truth-O-Meter" feature, a round-up of fact-checking from around the web, never links to Media Matters, the conservative NewsBusters, or similar sites.[68]

In practice, the commitment to monitor "both sides" requires a different sort of balancing act, one designed to achieve rough parity in checking liberal and conservative claims but without enforcing strict counts. Running more items about one party may accurately reflect political reality—during a primary race, for instance—but also risks the appearance of bias. Kessler has said that he strives for balance but does not keep a running tally by party until an end-of-year review.[69] He described the dilemma at a 2011 conference on fact-checking:

> If I end up writing a number of columns that are just on Republicans, and it's kind of the season because of the primaries, I start getting lots of emails from readers saying, "When are you going to write about, you know, 'Obummer?'" . . . I try to kind of balance it as much as I can [though] it depends what's in the news. . . . Because, you begin to lose credibility with your readers if they feel like you're only writing about one side.[70]

The same problem came up in training sessions for new PolitiFact journalists in an important primary state. The state had begun to be deluged by speeches and advertisements from various Republican contenders. But with no real competition in the other party, the danger existed that there simply would not be enough Democratic claims to check. Reporters were encouraged to unearth statements by Democrats wherever they could—from labor unions, party leaders, local officeholders, columnists, and so on. At the same time, they were instructed never to count, which leads to second-guessing and artificial balance.[71] The same policy applied at PolitiFact's national newsroom. Although staff aim for rough balance, no formal procedure exists to make sure equal numbers of claims are being checked from the left and the right. While I visited PolitiFact, a political scientist at the University of Minnesota published a detailed statistical analysis of the site's rulings over the previous year.[72] Staffers were relieved to find the analysis showed they checked Democrats and Republicans at roughly the same rate.[73] "We try to check roughly the same number of claims by Democrats as we do for Republicans, but we have to go where the claims are and lately there have been more made by Republicans," Bill Adair told an interviewer during the 2012 election.[74]

Finding Facts as Newswork

The problem of finding facts to check raises questions that go to the heart of the genre's bid for acceptance as a legitimate form of objective reporting. However, it is also important to consider the constant search for checkable political claims as *work*. Paying attention to the routines and resources involved in this digital labor highlights how fact-checking fits into the contemporary media-political environment. Some of the work of finding facts to check takes place in the background, performed as a matter of course by journalists who follow politics closely and consume the news avidly. Professional fact-checkers develop an eye (or ear) for good claims to check and may show up at the office with a story idea plucked from the morning's newspaper. Other items "come in over the transom," in the words of one PolitiFact editor. Readers frequently suggest claims to check, as do reporters in traditional newsrooms and political operatives eager to see their opponents challenged.[75] But finding facts to check can also be tedious and tiresome. It involves not just reading the newspaper but poring over it, and over press releases, speeches, congressional testimony, and TV and radio transcripts. It means watching and sometimes transcribing political ads and other campaign videos as well as debates, press conferences, interviews, speeches, and similar events.

Both FactCheck.org and PolitiFact have routinized the process, though in different ways, in order to cover campaigns thoroughly and to maintain a steady flow of checkable items. Both organizations rely on student interns to do much of this work. During campaigns, FactCheck.org uses a monitoring system that embodies the two-party logic of American politics. During the 2010 midterm elections, for instance, staff and interns were each given a list of ten candidates to track culled from a list of competitive races in *Cook's Political Report*.[76] The training sessions I observed in the summer of 2011 took place as Republicans were beginning to campaign in earnest for the party's presidential nomination. On the first day interns received a handout, neatly divided into "Democrats" and "Republicans," that listed their tracking assignments for the summer. In addition to seven declared and suspected Republican contenders, the list included the congressional leadership of both parties as well as the organizations that would be "spending the money": the three national campaign committees for each party and also well-monied outside groups allied with them, such as the AFL-CIO, the U.S. Chamber of Commerce, Moveon.org, Crossroads GPS, and so on.[77]

Assignments in hand, and before learning what makes a good claim to check, the interns received a detailed lesson in "setting up your system" for monitoring candidates. This consisted, first, of signing up for the myriad electronic channels employed by modern political campaigns: Twitter feeds, Facebook pages, YouTube channels, e-mail lists, and news feeds on campaign websites. (One of the interns became alarmed at this—would she have to "friend" or "like" the candidates to track them on Facebook? Would *real* friends see? No, fortunately.) Interns also learned how to set up alerts on YouTube and Google Video to automatically find new videos by or about their campaigns. And they were guided through the various news and politics sites they should visit at least once a day, sites that cover the minutiae of political campaigns and aggregate video clips, transcripts, and so on—"the source material you need to do your job." These included news outlets (Politico, the Daily Note, Real Clear Politics) but also some party-oriented sites, such as GOP.gov and GOP12. As a FactCheck.org editor explained, "a fact is a fact, a video is a video, this is what he said." Sites run by political groups can't be trusted for analysis but are perfect for harvesting claims.[78]

Discovering a new speech, campaign ad, or other political text via one of these channels only begins the process of identifying suspicious claims. During my visit, two interns were led by a blog at the political newspaper the *Hill* to investigate Democratic "robocalls" being conducted in a number of contested congressional districts. The website of the Democratic National Campaign Committee had a sample of the robocall script; an editor helped them to identify several dubious statements in the text, bolding the suspicious language—like the claim that a Republican budget plan would "end Medicare."[79] The binary logic of American politics pervades this selection work completely. Walking interns through the transcript of a Mitt Romney interview, a FactCheck.org editor drew their attention to a comment the candidate made about the need for government to invest in basic research. The editor said the remark should be saved, predicting that at some point Romney would contradict himself by criticizing President Obama for such public investments. "There's no wasted reporting," interns learned.[80]

Most striking, though, was the way in which monitoring a campaign meant submitting to a torrent of political communication. Every public statement by a candidate today leaves traces across multiple channels: an e-mailed press release, key quotes tweeted by the campaign staff, a bulletin on Politico, perhaps a video clip on YouTube or a news site. "You know what they're doing, you know where they're going, you know what they're saying pretty quickly," interns were told. Twitter was described as by far the most useful monitoring tool, one that had transformed fact-checking. Fact-checkers "follow" (subscribe to tweets by) not just their candidates but also the other reporters and political sites covering those candidates—"that's how news is broken now, sometimes even before the AP starts writing a story about it." One editor told me that the expensive ad-tracking service FactCheck.org subscribed to had become almost redundant: As soon as a new campaign ad "drops," somebody—usually the campaign itself—will tweet about it.[81]

"Stocking the Buffet" at PolitiFact

PolitiFact uses a different method to organize the process of finding facts to check. Suspect statements reside in a monthly spreadsheet called "the buffet," maintained on Google Docs. All week long, staff and especially interns add entries to this spreadsheet, consisting of a verbatim quote to be checked along with the speaker, the date, and the name of the media outlet, with a link if possible. At PolitiFact's national office, this was called "stocking the buffet" or "trawling for shrimp"; the point of the metaphor, trainees learned, is being able to pick and choose from an assortment of delectable items. A four-page list of useful "buffet sources" I was given included many of the same party leaders and political groups that FactCheck.org's interns covered as well as pundits, editorial pages, and television programs. However, the first sources on the list were two transcription services and the *Congressional Record*. Every entry included a link to the pages that fact-checkers care about: press releases (for politicians) and transcripts (for broadcast programs). Asterisks marked programs that don't provide a full transcript online, meaning LexisNexis would have to be used. In other words, this was not mainly a list of political actors but a library of textual resources, of places to find statements.[82]

PolitiFact's buffet grows quickly, sometimes with dozens of items added in a single day. The sources mined depend on the day's news. During my fieldwork, for instance, the president gave an interview to Fox News when the network hosted the Super Bowl. This yielded eight statements for the buffet, five of which became Truth-O-Meter items, published individually and aggregated into a topical story about the interview.[83] But staff also rely on routine weekly political programming. Mondays and Tuesdays see many items culled from the "Sunday shows," like NBC's *Meet the Press*, while later in the week the buffet fills with statements made on prime-time political programs on CNN, Fox, and MSNBC. PolitiFact editors periodically scroll through the buffet to highlight (literally) promising items and assign them to fact-checkers. Reporters may also circumvent the buffet by proposing a fact check directly to an editor.[84]

Stocking the PolitiFact buffet proved more difficult than one might think. It is possible to read through dozens of pages of transcripts from a speech or a television program and turn up only a handful of checkable claims—and fewer interesting or important ones. White House press briefings, fact-checkers joked, are especially fruitless. The question to be researched must be reducible to a distinct and verifiable claim. PolitiFact calls this the "ruling statement": the precise point being checked, which appears at the top of every Truth-O-Meter item. However, politicians and pundits are practiced at building arguments that resist such analysis—as one staffer put it, at "lying with facts."[85]

My first day "trawling for shrimp" reinforced this lesson. My visit coincided with the uprisings in Egypt's Tahrir Square, and I began by looking for claims relating to those events. The buffet was already filled with material from the Sunday political shows, so I turned to Fox and MSNBC transcripts from the previous week. I was especially interested in Glenn Beck's show on Fox News: the pundit was being ridiculed by liberals and some fellow conservatives for a series of broadcasts making the case that leftists in the United States and popular uprisings in the Middle East were linked in a global project of Islamic socialism.[86] As neoconservative commentator Bill Kristol wrote in his magazine,

> When Glenn Beck rants about the caliphate taking over the Middle East from Morocco to the Philippines, and lists (invents?) the connections between caliphate-promoters and the American left, he brings to mind no one so much as Robert Welch and the John Birch Society. He's marginalizing himself, just as his predecessors did back in the early 1960s.[87]

Although Beck plied this fascinating theme for many days, I could not find a distinct claim to address via the Truth-O-Meter. Beck's broadcasts joined the Muslim Brotherhood (and their so-called offspring, al-Qaeda) together with elements as diverse as American labor unions, the Weather Underground, the sociologist Frances Fox Piven, and the radical protest group Code Pink. But Beck hedged his rhetoric—"I'm not saying they are plotting together"—even as he painted a picture of a "strange alliance between the left and the Islamists."[88] Beck's larger message amounted to an opinion: that these elements *should* be discussed together because of their shared critique of the West. Was that objectively absurd? It seemed so to me, but not in a way that could be straightforwardly fact-checked.[89]

Meanwhile, I also read through transcripts of MSNBC's political programming for claims about the uprisings. What immediately stood out was how the network's liberal hosts had taken on the same "Beck" episodes, using clips from his own show to mock him and to challenge his entire premise rather than specific factual claims. All week long MSNBC pundits (and guests from Media Matters and the *Nation*, among other outlets) constructed a counternarrative in which Beck's distortions were held to illustrate the danger Fox News posed to meaningful political discourse: "Can you imagine how stupid our debates are going to be about foreign policy in this country for the next few months after Fox spent the entire week of the Egypt revolution broadcasting these conspiracy theories day after day after day?"[90] Pundits and opinion journalists enjoy more latitude than professional fact-checkers in the claims they can challenge and the arguments they can make.[91]

The Routine Transcription of Political Speech

The experience of "stocking the buffet" illustrated the point that fact-checkers don't operate in a political vacuum. Statements emerge in political contexts—often in rancorous public arguments—which color their perceived importance or interest. But it also illuminated an important shift in the material environment in which news is produced, one that makes FactCheck.org and PolitiFact possible and pervades contemporary journalistic work more generally. This could be called the *routine transcription* of political speech. To a remarkable degree today, words uttered in public or on the air by political figures quickly become searchable text on the Internet, ready to be copied and quoted and linked to.

At the time of my research, PolitiFact subscribed to two commercial databases of news and political events. LexisNexis offers transcripts of most

U.S. news programming within a few days of the broadcast. The *Congressional Quarterly*'s CQ.com provides nearly instantaneous transcripts of remarks made by political figures in a range of forums, from speeches and conferences to interviews on cable news networks. CQ.com's feed updates with surprising speed; a new transcript appears every few minutes. But most items in PolitiFact's "buffet" don't come from these services, as government agencies, campaign offices, and news outlets increasingly publish their own transcripts online. NPR and CNN, for instance, post the transcribed text of almost all of their news programming. MSNBC and Fox News publish transcripts most of their political programs and of special event coverage, though not of daytime news broadcasts.

It would be hard to overstate how much fact-checking relies on—is a creature of—this routine transcription. It pervades the day-to-day work at FactCheck.org and PolitiFact. Fact-checkers constantly hunt for transcripts, read through them, and send one another links to them. Much of the training for new fact-checkers deals with where to find and how properly to handle transcripts. Trainees at both organizations were told to never assume that a newspaper article reported a quote accurately but always to go back to the transcript if possible. At PolitiFact this was illustrated with a cautionary tale: a false accusation leveled against Florida's attorney general that turned out to be the result of misattributed quotes in a newspaper article.[92] The accuracy of the transcript itself is a trickier issue. "If we have access . . . listen to the video itself, because the transcripts can be wrong," FactCheck.org interns were told. (One intern found a transcript of *Fox News Sunday* that quoted Sarah Palin as referring to $46 billion when she had said $4 to $6 billion.)[93]

Where transcripts don't exist, finding a steady supply of facts to check becomes difficult. This challenge came up in training sessions for state PolitiFact reporters covering early primaries: Many local campaign events would be only lightly covered and take place in informal or semiprivate settings, like fundraisers and house parties. No records would be available from the usual sources—the national news media, the campaigns, and the transcription services. A PolitiFact editor encouraged the reporters to record these events themselves and transcribe them as necessary in order to find new claims to check.[94]

Transcripts of political speech are not new to journalism. Reporters have long relied on the text of prepared remarks distributed on paper at events such as a campaign speech or congressional hearings. For decades, major newspapers like the *New York Times* employed transcription services to cover, for instance, the Sunday political shows, which usually generated an article or two in the newspaper on Monday. But the volume of routine transcription today marks a sea change. Now publicists for the Sunday shows not only post same-day transcripts online but also mail out choice quotes each week to any reporter or blogger who subscribes to their mailing list. (An interview with a former publicist for ABC's *This Week* confirmed the obvious: the goal of this aggressive transcribing is precisely to be reported on, blogged about, tweeted, forwarded, and etc.[95]) Fact-checking as a genre of news is profoundly dependent on this constant, electronic flow of political texts. And of course fact-checkers contribute to the same flow, offering raw material—data, text, quotes—for politicians, bloggers, and other journalists to build into new texts.

Choosing claims to check is just the first step in the fact-checking process. But it is a vital step, raising basic questions about the proper conduct and mission of this emerging style of newswork that will surface again and again. Examining how fact-checkers harvest interesting or important political claims from each day's news clarifies their position both in professional journalism and in a wider ecology of political communication. Fact-checkers see themselves as fulfilling journalism's Fourth Estate role and prioritize coverage that helps citizens to choose between political candidates or understand important policy issues. Like other reporters, they balance this with some regard for what might amuse and engage readers, and themselves. At the same time, the fact-checkers' news sense sets them apart from other journalists: They emphasize methodical coverage over speed and novelty and downplay the competitive aspects of journalism. These modified news values befit a genre that must always slightly lag the news cycle. As noted earlier, fact-checkers report on mediated events. Although they differ in outlook and method from political bloggers, both genres share this quality of annotating events reported elsewhere.[96]

Finally, it is worth noting that finding facts to check doesn't have to be an "art." One site in Eastern Europe, Demagog, has experimented with an overtly scientific approach, checking every single factual claim in the weekly political debates it monitors.[97] More systematic selection methods could be applied in the United States as well. "I think it's possible the fact-checkers leave themselves open to being criticized by political people because there isn't always a transparent methodology for which claims are selected," press critic Tom Rosenstiel observed at a 2014 meeting of fact-checkers in Washington, DC. "You sort of watch for claims you think might be fishy and then you fact check them. . . . What's the argument against a more social-science approach?"[98] While fact-checkers admit the potential for selection bias, however, they reject out of hand the idea that they should discard news judgment in favor of a standardized selection process. This is a recurring theme in the next two chapters: Fact-checkers freely acknowledge that theirs is a fallible human endeavor, but they also believe it offers a meaningful picture of political reality.

4

DECIDING
WHAT'S TRUE

IN THE SUMMER OF 2009, TO CAPITALIZE ON ITS ROLE IN DOCUMENTING events like student protests in Iran, the video-sharing site YouTube launched a "Reporter's Center" designed to support citizen journalism with instructional videos submitted by professionals from various corners of the news industry. Videos on the channel ran from heady explorations of the craft—"Ira Glass on Storytelling"—to mundane tips for shooting "stand-ups" and using Google Maps in stories. To support the launch, YouTube recruited contributions from CBS's Katie Couric, the *Washington Post*'s Bob Woodward, and other high-profile journalists and news organizations—including PolitiFact. Then just two years old, the site had won national attention and Pulitzer Prize for its reporting on the 2008 presidential contest. "PolitiFact's Guide to Fact-checking" walked viewers through the mostly commonsense steps the organization uses to assess political claims: contacting the author of the claim, using original data from nonpartisan sources, and so on. But the four-minute video betrayed a certain reluctance as a how-to guide, showcasing PolitiFact's methodology without really inviting viewers to try it for themselves.

Professional fact-checkers rely on public information sources available to anyone. They have no credentials beyond their bylines as working reporters.

Their most important research tools are Google, e-mail, and the telephone. On the face of it, any reasonably news-literate person with access to the Internet has what she needs to start fact-checking. But none of the journalists I spoke to at FactCheck.org, PolitiFact, and similar outlets expressed very much faith in the average citizen's ability to put aside political preferences and research claims methodically and fairly. "There are a lot of nuances in this stuff," PolitiFact's Bill Adair told me the first time I interviewed him. "I just think professional journalists do the best fact-checking." These doubts are only amplified by the suspicion and hostility so often directed at the fact-checkers by members of the public. As one of the very first responses to PolitiFact's online tutorial asked, "who is this person to debunk jack shit?"

What gives a group of journalists the authority to not only report facts but publicly decide them? What special knowledge or skills do fact-checkers possess? This chapter explores the protocols of fact-checking—the fairly consistent body of routines and procedures the elite professional fact-checkers have developed to render verdicts about public political claims. Fact-checkers pride themselves on a "show your work" approach to reporting. In broad strokes, their methodology adheres to a few simple rules and straightforward steps. But this simple sequence masks more subtle judgments involved in finding reliable experts and data, in assessing the intent or subtext behind a piece of partisan rhetoric, and thus in weighing claims not only for technical accuracy but also for their *meaning* in the context of a particular political debate.

An "Uninsulated" Profession

One easy answer to the question of what qualifies fact-checkers for their work lies in the nature of the material they have to work with. Even on the national stage, political figures distort the truth in obvious ways. Many will continue to repeat an absurd claim as long as it yields some political advantage. It hardly takes an expert in health policy to discover that the Affordable Care Act does not provide for "death panels" with the authority to terminate care for people deemed unworthy based on their "level of productivity in society," as Sarah Palin famously claimed in a 2009 Facebook post—a charge that echoed widely through the 2010 and 2012 elections. Still, even that outrageous and widely debunked claim hints at the care required in fact-checking. The florid charges about President Obama's health care reform plan did not emerge in a vacuum. The law contemplated difficult choices about the wisest use of limited health care resources, including in the costly area of end-of-life care. To sort out the facts from the demagoguery required nuance, judgment, and a good working knowledge of the research and policymaking landscape of Washington, DC.[1]

The question of how fact-checkers go about their work brings up journalism's conflicted status as both a profession and a craft. The markers of the field's professionalization over the last century are well established: among others, the adoption of institutional codes and standards, the spread of journalism education, and, especially since the 1950s and 1960s, the rise of an Ivy League–dominated top tier earning high salaries and firmly entrenched in elite society.[2] At the same time an element of craft or trade identity remains stubbornly at the center of journalism's self-conception, closely tied to an ideal of the reporter as outsider. The tension between these two poles can be read in the recurring debate over who counts as a journalist or, for instance, in the disdain for journalism degrees that remains a part of newsroom culture. A decade before the rise of blogs and "citizen journalism," a nasty exposé of Columbia's elite journalism school in the *New Republic* railed against the "the desperate futility of journalism instruction," revealed in pseudoscientific jargon and reporting formulas. The author compared J-school to McDonald's Hamburger University in the effort "to dignify a trade by tacking onto it the idea of professionalism"—something antithetical to the doubting, disrespectful, muckraking instinct of good reporters.[3]

But to call journalism a trade is not to say anyone can do it, much less do it well. On the contrary, to journalists of various stripes it places the emphasis on instincts and techniques that can't be taught in school and that may be dulled when reporters become too established and comfortable. This comes through clearly in the episodes at the center of American journalism's professional mythology, most famously the Watergate investigation at the *Washington Post*—pursued doggedly by two hungry Metro reporters, the object lesson holds, while more established colleagues at the National Desk scoffed.[4] Historian Robert Darnton's remarkable essay on his own "occupational socialization" at the *New York Times* in the 1960s draws a detailed sketch of the reporting tricks and unwritten rules young reporters learn on the way to developing "a sense of mastery over their craft."[5] Darnton peered into newsroom culture to reveal the sometimes unflattering habits and self-justifying rhetoric of reporters and editors producing copy that at its worst was formulaic and pandering. But he also took seriously reporters' competitiveness, on-the-job experience, and tacit behavioral codes as a source of what is best in journalism.

Journalism is an "uninsulated profession," in Michael Schudson's phrase.[6] It lacks the esoteric knowledge, technical language, and formal accreditation that protect doctors and lawyers from the lay public. This is nowhere more evident than among political fact-checkers, whose conclusions and methods come under relentless scrutiny. Anyone can disagree with their work, and everyone does: politicians, pundits, media critics, and, in a ceaseless torrent of comments and tweets and posts, members of the general public who fact-checkers say it is their mission to inform. Fact-checking brings the paradox of journalistic authority into sharp relief. It rests on a contradictory claim that reporters can render judgments involving complex technical questions well beyond their formal expertise—and that they can do this more expertly and reliably than the average person.

Fact-checkers lack the expertise to approach complex areas of social or economic policy on their own. However, they do claim a particular, second-order expertise in sorting through arguments offered by knowledgeable sources and in distilling decisive facts from political rhetoric and "spin." "I bring a unique perspective of having listened to bullshit in Washington for thirty years," the *Washington Post*'s Fact Checker told me.[7] The fact-checkers' sense of their own ability to filter the politics out of a factual argument is of a piece with the formal commitment to remain neutral and objective. To reporters, this hard-to-define skill is what makes the commitment to objectivity meaningful for journalists and hard for outsiders to understand. This kind of expertise falls squarely in the domain of tacit knowledge.[8] It's the sort of thing that's difficult to lay out in a textbook but that, fact-checkers say, distinguishes their work from that of partisan critics unable to see that their own convictions are ideological, not factual. Invoking this sort of knowledge or skill is a way to erect professional boundaries, to disarm critics, and sometimes to paper over contradictions in the fact-checking project. At the same time, the day-do-day experience of fact-checking and the working knowledge it produces deserve to be taken seriously.

Going to the Source

Fact-checking starts with mining the news for important or interesting statements to investigate. As noted in last chapter, this can be time-consuming work: the claim should provoke readers' curiosity but must also be "checkable" and come from someone deemed fair game for fact-checking, most often an officeholder or political candidate. Having found an intriguing statement, the fact-checker looks for a way to demonstrate, as authoritatively as possible, whether it is true. Usually this process begins with a phone call or an e-mail to the author of the claim.

This is partly a matter of journalistic fairness—the subject of a piece must be given the chance to respond. Even a claim that directly contradicts official data merits a call to the author. Consider the attack by Mississippi governor Haley Barbour on the Obama administration's economic record, reviewed in the introduction to part 2: Barbour claimed 7 million jobs had been lost since President Obama took office at the peak of the "Great Recession," but Labor Department data showed the real number was just half that. Still, the analysis by FactCheck.org stressed that the governor's staff had the chance to tell his side of the story. "We are waiting for a response and will pass it along if we get one," the piece concluded, though it was hard to imagine what sort of reasonable explanation Barbour could provide.[9]

As that case illustrates, the burden of proof rests with the author of a claim. Both FactCheck.org and PolitiFact will publish a piece even if the person being checked never responds. "People who make factual claims are accountable for their words and should be able to provide evidence to back them up," PolitiFact's statement of principles explains. "We will try to verify their statements, but we believe the burden of proof is on the person making the statement."[10] And, having contacted a statement's author, fact-checkers are under no obligation to air his or her views with a standard "response quote." "We include a response from the person making the claim only if it's relevant, only if it speaks to the facts you're checking," trainees were told. "We don't allow them to use PolitiFact stories to score their talking points. We are about the facts."[11]

More than journalistic fairness, though, contacting the author of a claim is a matter of reporting method. It offers the chance not only to clarify what the speaker meant but to begin to trace the origins of a questionable fact or figure—as we shall see, the decisive analytical step in many fact checks. Contacting the claim's author may also point the fact-checker to relevant documents, experts, or other sources of authoritative research. Especially in thorny cases, it helps to frame the research and analysis. An editor at FactCheck.org stressed this when a visiting journalist asked about the group's methodology: "In terms of process . . . one of the things we do here is go to the people who make these kinds of claims and say, 'Well, back it up. What evidence do you have?' . . . [Then] at least we've got a basis to start from. . . . We've got some parameters and we can check the information and prove them right or wrong."[12]

PolitiFact requires its fact-checkers to contact the author of a claim and asks them to make that the very first step in checking it. The Truth-O-Meter training manual explains that this makes the research easier by providing a "road map to the facts." It also reinforces the distinction between fact-checking and standard political reporting. As an editor told me and explained to trainees, calling the statement's author first encourages fact-checkers to keep an open mind. It inhibits the reporter's reflex of amassing evidence for a final "gotcha" interview—which, from a fact-checker's point of view, is not only unfair but unscientific.[13] Fact-checking in this way inverts the logic of other forms of "accountability reporting." Investigative reporters have good reason to save difficult interviews for the end of the research and difficult questions for the end of the interview, standard tactics taught in journalism school. There may be only one chance to ask the key question that yields a quotable response or a vital piece of information. For fact-checkers, on the other hand, the most important quote is already on the record: the statement being checked.

The effort to verify a claim sometimes provokes a confrontation with its author. This may take place behind the scenes. After President Obama quoted Ronald Reagan to defend a new minimum tax rate for the wealthy—the so-called "Buffett Rule"—the *Washington Post*'s Fact Checker wrote that the Republican hero had been taken out of context.[14] As Glenn Kessler explained in an interview, before the column went live, a White House official called his editor at the *Post* to try to kill it.[15] (The piece ran anyway.) In rare cases, the subject may publish a preemptive attack on the fact-checker. In 2011, the conservative pundit Michelle Malkin charged a Democratic congresswoman with arguing that abortion "is better for unplanned babies than having to eat Ramen noodles." Contacted by PolitiFact to back up the claim, Malkin responded on her blog. She posted the entire e-mail from the PolitiFact reporter as well as her own response, which accused him of having made up his mind already; of not understanding blogger "snark"; and of failing to recognize the difference between opinion and fact, a critique fact-checkers hear often. "I am an opinion journalist who has always been transparent about my ideology," Malkin wrote. "You are opinion journalists who masquerade as neutral arbiters of fact. Nice work if you can get it."[16] PolitiFact trainees were told to assume any e-mail they send in the course of research might become a public document.[17]

Tracing False Claims

The crucial step in investigating almost any political claim is to trace it back to its origin. This helps in two ways. First, finding the original news report or policy paper from which a statistic was plucked often shows that it has been used deceptively. Fact-checkers care not only about whether a statement is accurate but whether it is misleading. And second, sources come with varying degrees of authority: blog posts, newspapers, think tanks, government agencies, academic experts, and so on. The rules of formal logic may forbid "arguments from authority," but in public political discourse these judgments are impossible to avoid. Showing where a claim originated and who helped to spread it can offer a powerful case for skepticism.

Public figures and especially political campaigns now expect to be contacted by fact-checkers and usually have lists of sources at the ready to support the points they make in advertisements, debates, and major speeches, like the State of the Union address. "You'll find that the presidential campaigns are accustomed to [us], they know us, they have respect for what we do even if they don't agree with every ruling we make," I heard during one training session. Fact-checkers accord a working respect to campaigns that deal with them in this "professional" manner and joke or complain about politicians whose staff don't return calls.[18]

Documentation provided to support a political claim is called the "backup sheet" or sometimes just the "backup."[19] The backup documents for campaign advertising often follow a standard format: a full-page grid with verbatim quotes and, sometimes, visual descriptions from the advertisement arrayed against explanation and sources relevant to each claim. Presidential campaigns have prepared backup sheets to document claims in television ads since at least the 1992 election, in response to the rise of adwatch stories.[20] (In addition, television stations have some discretion to reject ads that make unsupported claims.) As a well-known Republican political consultant explained at a 2007 forum on fact-checking,

> When we're putting together a campaign . . . we are the original fact-checkers. Real professional campaign operatives do not put out an ad that they haven't fact-checked. For twenty years, I have not delivered an ad to a television or radio or newspaper without the documentation package with it because we know we will be tasked to be truthful."[21]

However, very often the official backup directly undermines the claim being made. Nearly every fact-checker I spoke to remarked on this. One example that became part of office lore at PolitiFact came from the 2008 presidential race, when the site was less than a year old. On the campaign trail and again during a primary debate, Mitt Romney blamed President Bill Clinton—and, thus, Democrats—for weakening the U.S. military in pursuit of a "peace dividend." To back up the claim, a Romney staffer e-mailed a page from the federal budget that showed reductions in defense spending under the Clinton White House. But the very same budget page showed clearly that those declines had actually started earlier, under the first President Bush. The fact that the campaign had willfully misrepresented the evidence only strengthened the indictment; the Truth-O-Meter verdict noted that "Romney is selectively choosing numbers that make it appear the military cuts were Clinton's alone."[22] Romney's remark was rated "Half True," reserved for claims that are "partially accurate" but leave out crucial details or take something out of context.

A fact check I wrote as a participant-observer, checking Indiana governor Mitch Daniels, followed the same pattern.[23] Daniels had claimed in a speech at the Conservative Political Action Conference that interest payments on the U.S. debt would soon outpace national security spending. Obeying PolitiFact protocol, I began by calling the governor's press secretary. She didn't answer, so I left a message and immediately sent a follow-up e-mail. I then wrote to several economists to ask for help dissecting the claim. Four hours later the press secretary wrote back, explaining that the current defense budget was close to $700 billion, and that by the end of the decade, according to White House estimates, interest on the debt would top that; she documented the second point with a link to a two-year-old article in the *Washington Examiner.* But Daniels had said "in a few years," not by the end of the decade. And he referred broadly to "national security" spending, not to the defense budget. Even before verifying the data or talking to any economists, I knew the governor had taken some rhetorical license.[24]

The backup sheets provided with campaign ads, I was told, are particularly egregious in taking sources out of context. During a visit to FactCheck.org, one of the group's most experienced interns pointed me to a piece she had written the year before dissecting an attack ad against Arkansas senator Blanche Lincoln.[25] The ad, by a rival in the Democratic primary, claimed Lincoln had cut Social Security and spliced together her statements from a recent debate to suggest she planned to do so again. But the backup documents could only point to Lincoln's "yes" vote sixteen years earlier on an amendment, never passed, that would have reduced spending across all entitlement programs, not just Social Security, and only under very specific conditions. This was clear evidence of an intent to mislead by creating the "illusion" that Lincoln favored cuts to Social Security, FactCheck.org found. Soon after, the challenger was questioned about that fact check and denied taking his rival out of context; the fact-checkers responded with another piece debunking the new interview.[26]

Fact-checkers often see their own rulings distorted by political campaigns. Trainees at both FactCheck.org and PolitiFact heard colorful examples meant to reinforce the lesson that politicians will say anything to get elected. One notable instance came after PolitiFact Ohio awarded House Republicans a "Barely True," just a notch above "False," for a press release blaming Democrats for the "spending spree" that made it necessary to boost the federal debt limit.[27] One day after the piece was published, Republicans issued a new press release trumpeting that ruling: "POLITIFACT OHIO SAYS TRUE: 'Betty Sutton and Her Fellow Democrats Went on a Spending Spree and Now Their Credit Card Is Maxed Out.'" PolitiFact responded just four hours later with another fact check, which began, "Is up down? Is red blue?" The new press release received a "Pants On Fire," the lowest possible rating.[28] (Partly in response to episodes like this one, the "Barely True" rating on PolitiFact's Truth-O-Meter was later changed to "Mostly False.")

Political operatives have a strong incentive to "weaponize" fact checks, a 2015 report argued, because "all those eye-catching Pinocchios and Truth-O-Meter ratings are perfect material for a 30-second political response or attack."[29] In an earlier survey of local TV news directors, 29 percent of those who ran adwatch stories (and nearly half in large TV markets) reported that those stories were used in future campaign advertisements. In one-third of those cases, news directors said, the new ads distorted the adwatch segments they cited.[30] Several political operatives I interviewed stressed that tactical considerations govern what kind of claims go into a campaign ad. The question is always whether the possible cost of being challenged outweighs the perceived political benefit of making the claim. The standard in opposition research, one told me, is not whether a claim is true but whether it is "defensible."[31]

If no backup is available from the author of a claim, fact-checkers turn to the Internet and to proprietary news databases such as LexisNexis. False claims and dubious statistics usually emerge from news articles that a politician has cited glibly or taken out of context. "Often they'll rely on some news report that itself is flimsy, or they'll take a report from a blog that supports their point of view," new fact-checkers were told in a Politi-Fact training session.[32] One trainee then chose an odd figure from Minnesota representative Michele Bachmann for his first fact check: because of the president's economic policies, she had claimed in a radio interview, families were paying 29 percent more for their Memorial Day barbecues. Bachmann's staff did not return his calls, but searching online he came up with a *New York Post* article titled "That Cookout Will Cost You 29 Percent More This Year." A call to the reporter revealed that the figure was based on the newspaper's own calculations, using food prices in New York City. So PolitiFact reconstructed the analysis ingredient by ingredient—hamburger, hot dogs, buns, potato salad, etc.—with national figures from the Consumer Price Index, resulting in a price jump of just 10 percent for the typical American barbecue. Economists interviewed further suggested that White House policy had little to do with rising food prices; Bachmann earned a "False."[33]

As this suggests, finding the origin of a suspicious claim or statistic usually begins by typing it into Google. "When I encounter a weird [or] strange fact, one of the first things I do is Google the figures, which is an amazingly efficient way to figure out where it comes from," Glenn Kessler said in an interview.[34] He offered the example of a statistic that then–House Speaker John Boehner wielded in a speech to business leaders and in a public letter to the White House: that the Obama administration had 219 new regulations in the works that would cost the economy more than $100 million apiece. How had he arrived at 219 federal rules? Kessler searched the Internet for the curiously precise figure. It appeared to originate in an opinion piece by an expert in "regulatory studies" who had served in the Bush administration. In an interview, she walked Kessler through her analysis of "major" rules from the federal government's Regulatory Information Service Center. Kessler found that many of the regulations would not be implemented for years, if ever; some had been on the list since before Obama took office. And many were considered major because they would generate $100 million or more in economic activity or consumer benefits rather than imposing new costs. A spokesman for Boehner conceded the language was misleading; the Speaker earned three Pinocchios.[35]

In this way much of the work of assessing a claim lies in discovering where it originated and how it spread. Even the most outrageous claims have some sort of provenance, a media-political career that fact-checkers try to reconstruct. A now-classic example among fact-checkers was the explosive statistic that President Obama's late-2010 trip to India would cost U.S. taxpayers $200 million per day. FactCheck.org and PolitiFact (along with other news outlets and blogs) traced that figure to a single article in the *Press Trust of India,* quoting an unnamed official in Maharashtra. The analysis by FactCheck.org helpfully reproduced the statistic's media trajectory, from the conservative news aggregator Drudge Report to Rush Limbaugh's radio show and the *Washington Times.*[36] PolitiFact rated the claim "False" after Michele Bachmann repeated it on CNN and likewise traced its path "in the blogosphere and over conservative airwaves."[37] Both sites made a tentative effort to estimate the actual costs of such trips, which it is government policy not to disclose. But the force of their refutation lay in revealing the claim's unlikely source and the way it had spread, unsubstantiated, across partisan regions of the modern media landscape.

Evidence and Experts

As the cases reviewed so far suggest, checking facts often turns on a contest of sources. The examples I heard cited time and again to explain what fact-checkers do underscored the simplicity and reliability of the enterprise. They seem to require no interpretation and leave little room for disagreement. A public figure deploys a statistic about jobs, or the budget, or taxes; a fact-checker consults the authoritative data; the politician either has or hasn't distorted the "real" numbers. Well-established conventions usually guide fact-checkers in choosing these sources and using their data. Why only count "nonfarm" jobs in assessing a claim about unemployment, a FactCheck.org intern wanted to know? Because that's the standard everyone uses, she was told.[38] But not every case is so clear-cut. Inevitably, seams appear in the consensus about what data are appropriate and which experts can be trusted.

Relying on official, public data is basic to the fact-checkers' claim to objectivity. "We are neutral and scrupulously fair," PolitiFact trainees were told. "We examine all sides of an issue, we use the most unbiased sources we can find, and then we reach a decision."[39] In practice, this means using government data whenever possible. A statement of principles emphasized that "the best sources are independent and nonpartisan. At the national level we often rely on federal agencies such as the Bureau of Labor Statistics, the Census Bureau, the Government Accountability Office and the Congressional Budget Office. At the state level, we seek similar independent government agencies."[40]

Likewise, new interns at FactCheck.org received a four-page list of trusted "web resources" that consisted largely of such government agencies. Training at both organizations stressed the need to consult these original data sources rather than relying on a news report or policy paper about, for instance, joblessness or the federal budget. In part this is because reporters make mistakes. But it also reflects a general sense that the further a statistic travels from its original source, the greater the risk that it will be distorted or taken out of context. "We want to make sure we're working with primary sources of information like the Bureau of Labor Statistics, and not secondary information, or worse," a staffer at FactCheck.org emphasized to interns.[41]

The claim to objectivity also rests on what fact-checkers call a "transparent" approach to journalism. Every Truth-O-Meter item features a sidebar listing the sources consulted and every person interviewed during the research, even those not mentioned directly in the body of the article. Like an academic bibliography, this source list includes publication and interview dates, with web links provided whenever possible. The typical ruling relies on five to ten sources, but some cite many more. The source list for a piece I wrote checking a claim by conservative pundit Glenn Beck (reviewed in the next chapter) ran to eighteen different items, including news outlets, policy reports, four expert interviews, and the website of the Muslim Brotherhood.[42] FactCheck.org offers a similar bibliography at the end of its feature articles; shorter "wire" pieces only include links in the body of the text. The *Washington Post*'s Fact Checker also links to documents cited but does not publish a separate list of sources.

The need to be transparent was stressed constantly during training sessions at PolitiFact and in internal documents like the Truth-O-Meter training manual, with a section on "sources and our commitment to transparency." The source list attached to each article serves as a constant reminder that this is a "new kind of journalism," a phrase I heard many times. Revealing sources very self-consciously performs the idea of scientific reproducibility. The practice of "showing your work" acts simultaneously as a way to argue and persuade and as a defense against critics who remain unconvinced. One editor explained to me, "when you publish links to the original report, when someone else can follow your reporting and really take it apart, it's more scientific. It's not perfectly scientific, but anyone can verify it." (At one point the group considered publishing research and interview notes along with each piece, but reporters objected that sources would stop taking their calls.)[43]

In keeping with this "transparent" approach, both FactCheck.org and PolitiFact use only on-the-record sources. (In contrast, the Fact Checker sometimes quotes government officials anonymously in providing context for a claim.) FactCheck.org has no stated policy but, as Brooks Jackson explained, "we don't cite anonymous sources as proof of anything factual. Why would anyone believe it if we did? . . . We think of our pieces as meeting the high standards of academic scholarship." He went on to volunteer his own view that conventional journalism too easily indulges requests for anonymity, which should be granted only in the most extreme circumstances.[44] Meanwhile, PolitiFact policy emphatically bans off-the-record or on-background sources. "The phrase 'sources said' should not appear in a PolitiFact item," the Truth-O-Meter manual instructs, adding that officials who refuse to be quoted by name have been "tolerated for too long" by Washington journalists. Trainees were told that anonymity violates the basic logic of fact-checking—"you can't have an anonymous source debunking a fact"—and that nothing would upset editors more than violating this rule.[45]

Although fact-checkers favor original data from public agencies, in practice these statistics are rarely enough to render a verdict. Even straightforward numerical comparisons raise questions that a reporter may not feel qualified to answer. My fact check of Governor Daniels offered a case in point.[46] Daniels claimed that interest on the debt was about to exceed national security spending. Official data were easy to find but hard to decipher: Should I use interest payments as projected in the latest White House budget, as Daniels had? Doesn't Congress hold the "power of the purse"? And what counts as "national security" spending? The official Defense budget excluded the cost of ongoing wars. And what about the Central Intelligence Agency, the National Security Agency, and the Department of Homeland Security? Was there some sort of convention? I interviewed two experts who walked me through various permutations: one from OMB Watch, a budget watchdog, and another from the Concord Coalition, which advocates deficit reduction. Happily, both budget experts agreed that the governor's math did not add up. The fact that one hailed from a group associated with deficit reduction only seemed to make the case stronger.[47]

"Triangulating the Truth"

The need to consult experts presents a real problem for fact-checkers, pulling them inevitably into the busy national market of data and analysis retailed in service of ideological agendas. "You're going to seek independent, nonbiased sources—of which in today's world there are none," a PolitiFact editor joked during training. Similarly, interns at FactCheck.org were warned to watch out for "think tanks in Washington" that pursue political agendas—although "there are some good ones that at least provide information in addition to their spin." Navigating this landscape is a matter of getting at the facts while ignoring the spin, trainees at both groups were told. It is also a matter of tacit journalistic knowledge. As I heard repeatedly, certain groups and specific experts are "academically solid" and can be trusted to provide honest data or thoughtful analysis despite their ideology.[48]

Like other news organizations, fact-checkers attach political labels—"left-leaning," "pro-Republican," and so on—to various think tanks to guide their readers. "In a political atmosphere that is sharply polarized along party lines, it can be difficult to find an expert who is truly independent," Politi-Fact's statement of principles explained. "Many groups that are technically nonpartisan, such as think tanks, are actually aligned with a political party. We disclose their leanings if we quote them." Assigning these labels is a matter of loose convention, however, and the think tanks sometimes object.[49] Fact-checkers also come under attack for choosing particular experts or for failing to disclose possible sources of bias. An especially vivid example came in the spring of 2012, after PolitiFact challenged a job-loss statistic Mitt Romney was wielding to bash the White House.[50] The policy director for Romney's campaign responded with a stern, one-thousand-word e-mail attacking PolitiFact's sources: one had donated to the Obama campaign while another, identified only as a Princeton professor, was previously the chief economist in Obama's Labor Department. Accusing the fact-checkers of "embarrassing bias and lack of journalistic standards," the Romney official admonished them to reconsider:

> I have no way of knowing whether PolitiFact was aware of this and failed to disclose it, or whether she failed to identify her role in the Administration—frankly, I am not sure which would be worse. . . . I hope you will agree that this rating was inappropriate and that the piece does not reflect the journalistic standards to which your organization intends to hold itself. Please retract the piece and issue a correction as soon as possible.

PolitiFact responded by publishing the e-mail, interviewing four additional economists, and adding a seven-hundred-word reporting "addendum" to the original Truth-O-Meter article, which now concluded this way: "We considered the Romney campaign's complaints but do not see any evidence that warrants changing our ruling."[51]

The elite fact-checkers negotiate this terrain of politicized expertise in different ways. PolitiFact reporters are encouraged to interview multiple sources when researching a claim. Nearly every Truth-O-Meter item cites at least two or three experts, and some use a dozen or more. One article consulted fourteen different historians and military experts in awarding a "Pants on Fire" to Mitt Romney, who had said the U.S. Navy and Air Force under President Obama were the smallest they had been since 1917 and 1947, respectively.[52] A small controversy erupted when one of those experts disagreed with the verdict. He published a lengthy critique that included his own e-mail exchange with the PolitiFact reporter, complaining that he'd been asked "leading" questions; a media critic at Politico covered the disagreement in a snarky post.[53] In response, an editor's letter from PolitiFact trumpeted the research that had gone into the piece and the number of experts interviewed:

> After interviewing those 14 people and reading reports from the Naval History and Heritage Command, the Heritage Foundation, the Mitchell Institute and the Government Accountability Office, we concluded that while the numbers were largely correct, they do not back up Romney's point. We rated the claim Pants on Fire because, as one expert told us, It "doesn't pass 'the giggle test.'"[54]

PolitiFact items often feature analysis from experts or groups with opposing ideologies, a strategy described internally as "triangulating the truth." "Seek multiple sources," an editor told new fact-checkers during a training session. "If you can't get an independent source on something, go to a conservative and go to a liberal and see where they overlap." Such "triangulation" is not a matter of artificial balance, the editor argued: the point is to make a decisive ruling by forcing these experts to "focus on the facts."[55] As noted earlier, fact-checkers cannot claim expertise in the complex areas of public policy their work touches on. But they are confident in their ability to choose the right experts and to distill useful information from political arguments.

The emphasis on outside experts is less pronounced at FactCheck.org, although most features do include one or two such interviews. As at PolitiFact, the group's fact-checkers generally note the political leanings of the think tanks they consult and factor this into their analysis. This can mean citing groups with different orientations or simply emphasizing where an expert has diverged from the party line. For instance, FactCheck.org has twice firmly refuted the "supply-side" notion that tax cuts can stimulate enough additional economic activity to offset the loss in government revenue, grounded in the Laffer Curve.[56] In each case, the analysis highlighted testimony from economists with conservative think tanks and who had worked in the Bush administration. Among economists, "there's no dispute" that tax cuts lead to lower revenues, one expert at the American Enterprise Institute was quoted as saying. The subtext was clear: even conservative economists won't stand behind supply-side claims.

Glenn Kessler, the *Washington Post*'s Fact Checker columnist, cites outside experts far less frequently than his peers. Kessler explained that, while he may interview an economist or a policy analyst to make sure he understands an issue completely, he tries not to quote such sources for validation in the published column. "I'm the kind of reporter who is reasonably confident in his judgments," he said in an interview, pointing to his long experience covering the White House, Congress, the State Department, the economy, and national politics: "I like to speak with my voice, because I have actually covered just about everything in Washington. . . . You can see my bio, you can see what I've covered."[57] Experience as a foreign correspondent is particularly good training for a fact-checker, Kessler averred, because reporters covering diplomacy and international affairs are expected to be more interpretive. Keeping expert testimony to a minimum is meant to give the column a distinct, matter-of-fact voice that sets it apart from its rivals. But it also helps to shield the site from the inevitable critics who read bias into the sources fact-checkers use. "You can get so easily burned," Kessler explained, pointing to the controversy after PolitiFact relied on economists tied to the Obama administration. His own analysis of the same claim from Mitt Romney roughly echoed PolitiFact's. But the presentation was different: Kessler's piece included a response quote from a Republican official and did not cite any economists to support its argument.[58]

"You Can't Really Trust What They Say"

Finally, the selection of evidence and experts becomes a way for professional fact-checkers to draw boundaries that separate their own work from that of politically motivated rivals. The three national fact-checking sites check many of the same statements. They frequently cite one another as sources, along with established outlets like Snopes.com, and highlight how often they reach the same conclusions. However, the elite fact-checking organizations almost never point to the work of politically aligned sites like Media Matters and the Media Research Center (MRC).[59]

This holds even when a partisan group leads the way on a high-profile story. In 2008, for instance, after the comedian Sinbad cast doubt on Hillary Clinton's recollections of "landing under sniper fire" during a 1996 trip to Bosnia, MRC research director Rich Noyes used the organization's own news archive to offer the first thorough debunking of Clinton's claim. Noyes published his research on the *NewsBusters* blog, with a damning video clip from an original CBS report that showed the First Lady and her daughter being greeted by a large, friendly crowd at the NATO-controlled Tuzla Air Base.[60] Four days later the *Washington Post*'s Fact Checker column looked into the claim, awarding the First Lady four Pinocchios; PolitiFact followed with its own Truth-O-Meter item building on the *Post*'s report.[61] Both fact checks essentially reproduced the MRC analysis, combining news searches with the video evidence from CBS. (The network had by then released the 1996 report from its own archive—apparently prompted by an e-mailed link to the MRC version.)[62] Neither the *Washington Post* nor PolitiFact cited MRC's work, but the conservative group was quick to both take and give credit as the story spread into the mainstream media:

> The Washington Post is aligning its Fact Checker with Rich Noyes of NewsBusters. . . . We at MRC are often skeptical of major-media fact checkers as we are of the politicians they're checking. But this Hillary story is easily dismissed, and it's a credit to the Post when they apply the Pinocchios on both sides of the political fence.[63]

Meanwhile, as noted earlier, the professional fact-checkers take any opportunity to draw a bright line between their own nonpartisan research and that of politically motivated research operations. Several fact-checkers remarked to me that sites like Media Matters can be a useful source of raw material, such as transcripts or video clips, but cannot be counted upon to investigate issues fairly and without bias. The question came up unexpectedly during intern training at FactCheck.org. An editor was using Google to search for a recent fact check and instead came across a parallel analysis by Media Matters. This prompted a quick lesson for the new interns:

> There's a lot of groups out there that claim to be fact-checking when they're not. They're just fact-checking the opposition, like Media Matters. . . . They're coming from a bias, either right or left. They're out to expose the other side. They conveniently leave out the truth or distort the truth for their own purposes. . . . They're coming from a certain point of view, and it's going to be distorted. You can't really trust what they say.[64]

The leading fact-checkers all echoed this argument at a 2011 fact-checking forum I helped to organize in Washington, DC. As noted in the introduction, the one-day conference had support from the Open Society Foundations, which also funded Media Matters, and some participants thought the group should be present—until professional journalists objected that the meeting was taking on a partisan cast. Still, Media Matters came up repeatedly during the discussion. The group often debunks the same claims as the nonpartisan fact-checkers and regularly cites their articles as evidence. (The site also vocally criticizes rulings it objects to.) In some cases the analysis across these outlets is indistinguishable; why not cite Media Matters when their work is sound?[65] "It's just so one-sided, and that I think is why they are not a credible source," PolitiFact's Bill Adair explained. "If I were a liberal I would, I'm sure, look at Media Matters all the time and treasure it, but I really think our role as journalists is to dig to the original stuff and do our own analysis."[66] The *Washington Post*'s Glenn Kessler agreed:

> The one thing I will say about Media Matters is that it is impressive the amount of data that they collect in terms of really watching these networks and radio stations in ways that I cannot possibly keep up with them. But the fact that they only look at one side is a real problem for them. . . . I don't think that anyone can really take them that seriously. . . . So it's not at all reliable, they go through their particular partisan frame.[67]

The reluctance to cite partisan media critics is of a piece with a wider aversion to using blogs as authoritative sources. This is not a firm policy, but elite fact-checkers generally will not credit a lesser-known blog in the way they would a fellow fact-checker. In one instance I observed, a PolitiFact trainee investigated the claim, made by the White House press secretary, that Republican presidential hopefuls had not once used the terms "middle class" or "education" during a recent debate.[68] Verifying this meant scanning the entire 22,000-word transcript for those terms or their analogues. (Although technically accurate, the claim earned a "Barely True" because the candidates were never asked about education, and they used other words to talk about the middle class.) In the course of doing the research, the reporter found a blog that had conducted a parallel analysis and included it in the source list with her first draft. An editor took it out, explaining, "You did the work, they also did it."[69]

This raises an important point: in general, the elite fact-checkers see the blogging world—and the Internet as a whole—as a carrier of political misinformation rather than a corrective to it. This default view is reinforced by their day-to-day experience tracing false claims and by the steady torrent of criticism and invective directed at them online. Cases in which the fact-checkers do cite a blog only confirm the preference for establishment sources. Both FactCheck.org and PolitiFact have several times drawn on legal analyses by SCOTUSblog and the Volokh Conspiracy, for instance. But these are respected outlets run by well-known legal scholars who teach at top-ranked law schools and have argued cases before the Supreme Court. Like prominent think tanks, they may have points of view. (The Volokh Conspiracy, for instance, is considered to have a libertarian outlook.) But their academic credentials and establishment status—and the perceived quality of their work—distinguish them from what fact-checkers otherwise see as a stew of online vitriol and partisanship.

Context and Consistency

The most difficult question professional fact-checkers face, and the most controversial, is how to address the divide between what words say and what they seem to mean. Fact-checking almost always involves plucking a statement from the context of a wider public debate. For this reason, fact checks often include a disclaimer explaining that to find a claim true or false is not to take a policy position. But not every phrase can be cleanly severed from the language around it and the circumstances that produced it. For fact-checkers, the problem of "context" becomes an all-purpose way to talk about what a statement was designed to convey or how reasonable people are likely to interpret it. It raises the question of intent and makes it difficult to separate evaluating a statement from evaluating the person who made it.

Training sessions at FactCheck.org and PolitiFact constantly emphasized the need to look beyond the literal truth of a statement. One of the two core principles that guide the operation of PolitiFact's Truth-O-Meter is "context matters." A FactCheck.org editor made the same point to new interns: "Context is everything. They're very cute with how they word things." To illustrate, he pointed to a boast President Obama had just made at an auto plant in Toledo, Ohio: "I'm proud to announce the government has been completely repaid for the investments we made under my watch by Chrysler because of the outstanding work that you guys did." In fact, the government would never see $1.3 billion of the $12.5 billion funneled to the automaker under the Bush and Obama administrations; the new president simply wrote off the losses and then put them in his predecessor's column. "The 'under my watch' is the fudge word here," the editor explained. Assessing the claim meant in part understanding how it had been constructed to advance a political goal. To the White House, though, the analysis seemed to unfairly pick apart a claim that had been worded very carefully in order to satisfy fact-checkers. The editor told me that an Obama press officer called to complain that, in effect, "we're damned if we do and we're damned if we don't."[70]

This is a common complaint about the interpretive latitude fact-checkers assert in finding defensible statements misleading. A striking example came up in an interview with Glenn Kessler, the *Washington Post*'s Fact Checker columnist, who had just challenged a statistic from Senate Majority Leader Harry Reid.[71] To defend a proposed minimum tax rate for the wealthy, Reid declared on the floor of the Senate that in 2011 "there were 7,000 millionaires who didn't pay a single penny in federal income taxes. Instead, ordinary Americans footed the bill—and that's not fair."[72] Kessler could only find much lower figures by consulting IRS data and the nonpartisan Tax Policy Center, so he asked a spokesman for Reid to explain. The spokesman pointed to a different study by the Tax Policy Center—one counting millionaires by the less restrictive standard of "cash income" rather than adjusted gross income. Kessler gave the Senate leader two Pinocchios, explaining the ruling this way: "Faced with a choice between using an actual IRS figure cited by the White House or using an inflated statistic with little relevance to the definitions in the bill, Reid chose the latter." But Reid's spokesman objected strenuously. He wrote by e-mail, as quoted in the *Post* column, "The fact Senator Reid cited is correct. You checked it, I provided you with a citation proving that it is correct. End of story. . . . If you consider a true statement for which I can provide a clear citation to merit even a single 'Pinocchio' then the raison d'être of your blog is beyond me."[73]

What is the right way to count millionaires? When more than one standard exists, as is usually the case in policy debates, questions of accuracy become colored by judgments about how appropriate a particular measure is in context. To a veteran economic reporter well versed in tax policy, adjusted gross income was clearly the relevant standard, tied to the "definitions in the bill." A simpler, everyday measure more familiar to the average reader looked like an "inflated statistic" meant to mislead the public—enough at least to earn two Pinocchios. Dealing with context presents a special problem for fact-checkers who rate statements numerically. As noted in chapter 1, FactCheck.org avoids using a meter for exactly this reason. "There are many cases where statements will be literally true yet give a misleading picture," Brooks Jackson told me. The need for nuance militates against trying to rate statements in any scientific fashion, he argued, pointing to FactCheck.org's home at a research university: "Somebody would say, 'Well exactly what scale did you use to determine that?' So we have always stayed away from trying to assign some sort of 'mendacity index' to things."[74]

A dramatic example of this conundrum emerged when the campaign of Mitt Romney, by April 2012 the presumptive Republican presidential candidate, devised a counterattack to Democratic rhetoric about a Republican "war on women." In campaign speeches and interviews, Romney began to repeat a disturbing statistic: more than 92 percent of U.S. jobs lost since President Obama took office were lost by women. "His policies have been, really, a war on women," the candidate asserted in an interview on Fox News. The job-loss figure, derived from Bureau of Labor Statistics data, was perfectly accurate. But it was also deeply misleading, fact-checkers and other observers argued: Men accounted for 60 percent of total jobs lost in the recession that began in 2007. The first two years saw heavy declines in male-dominated economic sectors, such as construction and manufacturing, while the damage took longer to spread to government, education, and health care. This is a typical cycle seen in earlier recessions, economists noted.

The three fact-checkers all provided that context but approached the central paradox in different ways. Unburdened by the need to assign a rating, FactCheck.org noted simply that "Romney's statistic is accurate, as far as it goes. But it's not the whole story."[75] The piece quoted a conservative economist arguing that Obama's "antigrowth" policies were, if anything, hurting male-dominated sectors such as coal mining and oil drilling, while his health care law would boost women's employment. In an unusual move, meanwhile, the *Post*'s Fact Checker declined to rate Romney's claim, calling the statistic "true but false." Predictably, conservative bloggers and the media watchdog *NewsBusters* read this attempt at nuance as clear evidence of liberal media bias.[76] And PolitiFact explained that "the numbers are accurate but quite misleading," rating the claim "Mostly False" for ignoring "critical facts that would give a different impression."[77] The Romney campaign objected in a widely publicized letter, and conservative news outlets and bloggers lampooned PolitiFact's analysis. "I don't get it," wrote one blogger, continuing: "It's true, but nevertheless 'Mostly False,' because . . . because what? Because Obama isn't responsible for the numbers?! How does that make the assertion 'Mostly False'? The assertion is simply a number, and you've said the number is correct. The conclusion should be 'Completely True.'"[78]

The ratings used by PolitiFact and the *Post*'s Fact Checker are designed to address literal and contextual meaning by providing multiple grades of truth. As I heard from all of the fact-checkers, the truth is not always black and white. But scoring context-sensitive claims in a consistent way has proven difficult. Kessler explained that the crucial divide on his four-Pinocchio scale, and the trickiest to judge, lies between two Pinocchios (defined as "significant omissions and/or exaggerations") and three ("significant factual error and/or obvious contradictions"). This marks the line between claims that are contextually misleading and those that shade into outright factual deception, a distinction that can be hard to make. "I freely admit, the difference between two and three Pinocchios is hard to say," Kessler told me.[79]

Editors at PolitiFact have tried to devise clear internal policies for dealing with claims that are misleading in context. The most difficult cases, which I heard discussed many times, concern implied responsibility: politicians often take credit or assign blame for some shift by stating that it happened since they took office, or since the person they hope to unseat did. Mitt Romney's claim about women's job losses was an example—an accurate statistic was deployed to create the false impression that White House policies were hurting women. During its first few years, PolitiFact had no consistent approach to these statements, which might earn a "True" or "Mostly True" so long as the figures were accurate. In 2010, for instance, the mayor of Providence, Rhode Island, made that city's falling crime rate—the lowest in thirty years—the centerpiece of his successful bid for Congress. Crime rates fell sharply in cities across the United States over the same period, a trend some experts attribute to an aging population. But the mayor received a green light from PolitiFact Rhode Island: "Even though . . . it's not clear how much he or his administration is directly responsible for a rate that began dropping during the [previous] administration, we rate his statement as True."[80]

This approach is easy for politicians to "game," however, and leads to fact-checkers certifying as true messages that may mislead the public. In May of 2011 an e-mail from the editor-in-chief to all PolitiFact reporters and franchises drew attention to this problem: "We've had lots of ratings in the past few months on claims about job losses and job gains, the price of gasoline and countless other statistics that are intended to make a simple point"— that the "president/governor/senator/mayor is to blame." A new approach was instituted to take into account how "reasonable people" interpret such statements.[81] As Bill Adair would explain in an editor's note, called "Tuning the Truth-O-Meter,"

> About a year ago, we realized we were ducking the underlying point of blame or credit, which was the crucial message. So we began rating those types of claims as compound statements. We not only checked whether the numbers were accurate, we checked whether economists believed an office holder's policies were much of a factor in the increase or decrease.[82]

In practice, as the editor's letter also acknowledged, this results in many rulings of "Half True."[83] But the bigger risk of such a policy is that it will be applied too formulaically. Even subtle shifts in language or setting may undercut what seemed a clear standard. In his 2012 State of the Union address, for instance, President Obama offered the following hopeful employment statistics: "in the last 22 months, businesses have created more than 3 million jobs. Last year, they created the most jobs since 2005."[84] The day of the speech, following its established rationale, PolitiFact rated that claim "Half True." As the ruling explained, "Obama is correct on both counts when using private-sector job numbers. But he went too far when he implicitly credited his administration policies."[85] Both readers and pundits objected strenuously, however, and some editors felt the verdict was too harsh. In a rare revision, the next morning PolitiFact changed the ruling to "Mostly True" after deciding the president wasn't "implicitly crediting his own policies" as strongly as they had initially believed.[86]

The president's choice of words played a role here: he hadn't used one of the trigger phrases, such as "on my watch," which PolitiFact has interpreted as implied credit-taking. But the ritual logic of the State of the Union address also cut against PolitiFact's analysis. Political custom requires the president to give the address. He is expected to offer an honest assessment but also a hopeful one. The president hadn't inserted the phrase into a campaign ad. To an extent the institutional political context blurred the distinction between stating a trend and taking credit for it. The new ruling hardly satisfied PolitiFact's critics, however. In a scathing five-minute segment, MSNBC's Rachel Maddow, a frequent detractor, played the relevant clips from the State of the Union address and then walked viewers carefully through PolitiFact's original and revised analysis. She concluded:

> What is their chastened, revised, new rating for their fact-check of the president saying two things that they admit are true? What's their new rating? Mostly true? Mostly true. PolitiFact, you are fired. You are a mess. You are fired. You are undermining the definition of the word 'fact' in the English language by pretending to it in your name. The English language wants its word back. You are an embarrassment. You sully the reputation of anyone who cites you.[87]

In these cases, observers faulted the fact-checkers for willfully ignoring the literal truth of a statement. How can a claim that's perfectly accurate not be rated completely true? But the roles of literalist and contextualist are often reversed, with the journalists accused—by the very same critics on the left and the right—of letting attention to technical details or semantics blind them to the larger truth of a question. The most powerful example of this, and one that has had lasting consequences for the way fact-checkers fit into U.S. politics, was the controversy over what Republicans planned to do to the fifty-year-old Medicare program that insures elderly Americans.

Did Republicans Plan to Kill Medicare?

Beginning in the spring of 2011, the three elite national fact-checkers issued a string of articles contesting a widely repeated Democratic attack line: that health care changes envisioned in the budget proposed by Wisconsin representative Paul Ryan would "end" or "abolish" or "kill" Medicare.[88] Their analysis was remarkably consistent. The fact-checkers explained that Ryan's proposal left the current system intact for today's Medicare recipients and for those qualifying over the next decade; under a new "premium support" system, later retirees would have to cover more but by no means all of their medical expenses. They noted that a *Wall Street Journal* article frequently quoted as proof that the plan would "essentially end Medicare" was being taken out of context. (The words "as a program that directly pays bills" were left out.) PolitiFact and FactCheck.org took issue with the apparent age of seniors in TV ads that showed them stripping to pay for medical expenses, or being wheeled over a cliff by a Ryan lookalike. (The seniors depicted were too old to be affected by the proposal.) The fact-checkers all argued that adding a simple qualifier, like "as we know it," would make the claim more defensible.[89]

The rulings touched on a crucial issue in the 2012 election, and the reaction from critics of the Ryan proposal was ferocious.[90] The furor peaked after PolitiFact made the claim its "Lie of the Year" for 2011.[91] (FactCheck.org and the Fact Checker included it on similar end-of-year lists.[92]) The day of the announcement, in a post titled "PolitiFact, R.I.P.," *New York Times* columnist Paul Krugman wrote, "This is really awful. Politifact, which is supposed to police false claims in politics, has announced its Lie of the Year— and it's a statement that happens to be true, the claim that Republicans have voted to end Medicare."[93] A critic writing at Harvard's Nieman Watchdog site drafted a one-thousand-word letter of apology for PolitiFact founder Bill Adair to issue; in it Adair would admit that the fact-checkers had been so eager to "cast a pox on both houses" that they treated a claim that was "essentially true" as an egregious falsehood.[94] Media Matters accused the fact-checkers of promoting falsehoods that "act as a cancer on American democracy."[95] "Fact checkers are under assault!" Glenn Kessler wrote in the introduction to his own piece on the worst lies of the year, adding for emphasis this nasty quote from the media-insider website Gawker: "Politifact is dangerous. Stop reading it. Stop reading the 'four Pinocchios' guy too. Stop using some huckster company's stupid little phrases or codes or number systems when it's convenient, and read the actual arguments instead. You're building a monster."[96]

The liberal analysis was also remarkably consistent. Critics accused the fact-checking sites, and especially PolitiFact, of allowing a slavish literalism to obscure the truth of what the proposed Medicare changes would mean. The *essential* nature of the health entitlement for seniors would be lost in converting it to some kind of subsidy for private insurance plans. "Capping costs to beneficiaries, closing the traditional fee-for-service program, and forcing seniors to enroll in new private coverage, ends Medicare by eliminating everything that has defined the program for the last 46 years," wrote an observer at the Center for American Progress.[97] A *Washington Monthly* article likened the change to taking the metallic badge from a Ferrari and attaching it to a golf cart:

"Where's my Ferrari?" the owner would ask.

"It's right here," I'd respond. "This has four wheels, a steering wheel, and pedals, and it says 'Ferrari' right there on the back."

By PolitiFact's reasoning, I haven't actually replaced the car—and if you disagree, you're a pants-on-fire liar.[98]

Episodes like this can seem to defy decisive factual analysis. Many observers suggested the question was a matter of opinion and thus unsuitable for fact-checking.[99] "Does the Republican plan indeed end Medicare? I would argue yes. But it's obviously a question of interpretation, not fact," said a critic at *New York* magazine.[100] This echoed the argument made one year earlier in a *Wall Street Journal* editorial responding to PolitiFact's previous "Lie of the Year," the Republican claim that President Obama's health care reform plan amounted to a "government takeover of health care." "PolitiFact's decree is part of a larger journalistic trend that seeks to recast all political debates as matters of lies, misinformation and 'facts,' rather than differences of world view or principles," the paper declared.[101]

But how should we distinguish claims that can be fact-checked from those that are matters of worldview? The rhetoric about a "government takeover" of health care, repeated widely by Republicans in the 2010 and 2012 races, offers a telling case. Fact-checkers pointed out that the Affordable Care Act would actually expand the private insurance market and would not feature public doctors or public insurance. As FactCheck.org explained, "it doesn't come close to establishing a government-run system like those of Britain or Canada."[102] The analysis implied a "reasonable person" standard: What counts as a "government takeover" is not a matter of opinion but of reasoned argument that takes into account the actual shape of the world. Such interpretive judgments pervade fact-checking. As noted, even deciding how many millionaires pay no taxes turns out to be controversial. More precisely, it requires statements of qualification and definition—by this standard, not that one—that demand interpretation. Checking only statements that nobody could *object to* as matters of political opinion would leave a very narrow field.

The furious response to the "end Medicare" rulings brought these questions into sharp relief. From the fact-checkers' point of view, the analysis was straightforward and supported by dozens of experts of various backgrounds and affiliations. Consider this formulation: if reducing Medicare coverage by a certain amount at a certain date in the future "ends" the program, what would one say of a plan that *actually* ended it?[103] Crucially, the attack line earned harsh ratings from the fact-checkers at least partly for contextual reasons having to do with the way they encountered it in the wild. The charge echoed for months no matter how often it was debunked. It ran in harsh ads that nakedly took sources out of context and showed a wizened grandmother being thrown from a cliff. And it clearly was part of a deliberate, coordinated national strategy.

Professional fact-checkers do not assess claims in the abstract. They evaluate statements made by actual people in particular ways under specific circumstances, contingencies that necessarily inform their factual analysis. To many critics, they overreach in interpreting claims contextually.[104] But in the day-to-day work of fact-checking, the content of a message, the form it takes, and the political context that produced it are all bound up in its truth value. Fact-checkers agree that matters of opinion can't be checked, but they object to partisans who use that label as a license for deceptive claims. "Don't be tempted to dismiss this sort of thing as a mere difference of interpretation," Brooks Jackson wrote in a book about political "disinformation." "There is more to it than that. Both sides are actively working to deceive the public."[105]

To fact-checkers, the "end Medicare" rhetoric was just one more instance of what journalists and political operatives call "Mediscare"—the time-honored two-party tradition of frightening senior citizens, who are among the most politically engaged and reliable voters in the country. "Readers should simply just turn off the TV or mute the TV whenever there's any ad involving Medicare, because both sides are going to demagogue that as much as they can," Kessler argued in a TV interview.[106] All three fact-checking groups made knowing references to this long political tradition in their analyses. FactCheck.org reviewed the controversy this way after the claim resurfaced in March of 2012, rallying to the defense of its fellow fact-checkers:

> Scaring seniors with bogus claims about their retirement benefits is an old tactic, used again and again and again, by both parties. . . .
>
> We later called the claim one of the "Whoppers of 2011," and our friends at Politifact.com and the Washington Post agreed. Politifact called it the "Lie of the Year," and the Post's "Fact Checker" columnist Glenn Kessler called it an untruth worthy of four Pinocchios—his worst possible rating—and later one of the "The biggest Pinocchios of 2011."
>
> Politifact's "Lie of the Year" rating drew howls from liberal commentators and left-leaning news outlets, including MSNBC's Rachel Maddow, not to mention Democratic operatives, as though they collectively held a trademark on the name "Medicare."
>
> So, here we go again. But facts are still facts, and we still find these claims to be deceptive, even if Democrats find them to be politically useful.[107]

Like many other journalists, fact-checkers see political claim making through the left–right prism of U.S. two-party politics. Constant references to "two sides" or "both sides" are a way to assert their objectivity and to organize the daily routines of researching political speech. The scorn dispensed by supporters of whichever party has been fact-checked only reinforces these reflexes. At a panel discussion I participated in, Bill Adair was asked directly about the controversy over the "Lie of the Year" selection. He acknowledged the furious response from critics and readers—more than 90 percent of e-mails disagreed with the ruling. He walked through PolitiFact's reasoning, emphasizing what a common strategy "scaring seniors" has been for both parties. He pointed out that FactCheck.org and the Fact Checker reached the same verdict. And then he explained, as fact-checkers almost always do in these situations, that when they don't get it from one side, they get it from the other: "This is a gutsy form of journalism, and making these calls . . . you're going to face a lot of criticism. That's why not many people get into this business. Because, we're in a business where in a single day, with two ratings, we can alienate both halves of our audience. You know, what kind of a business model is that"?[108]

Controversy like this is a basic and recurring feature of the fact-checking world. Fact-checkers attempt to settle public questions by establishing a set of basic facts that reasonable people can agree should serve as firm pegs for future debates. To do this, they rely on a consistent and quite reasonable set of rules and procedures: interviewing the author of a claim, using data from official sources, consulting independent experts, and so on. As noted in chapter 2, their project embodies our taken-for-granted sense of "facts" as something like the epistemological equivalent of atoms: elementary particles that can be assembled into true arguments about the world, with little room for interpretation or doubt. Fact-checkers sometimes advertise a streamlined version of their job, underscoring how often they come to the same conclusions.

But checking facts is more slippery work than that idealized picture suggests. Fact-checkers must be relentless skeptics, questioning every reference that politicians cite to back up their claims. And they have few perfectly reliable sources of information to turn to in their own research. Fact-checkers rely on tacit journalistic knowledge to identify trustworthy sources, to "triangulate the truth" from competing experts, and to distill solid information from tendentious ideological arguments. These journalists operate in a world where statements often mean more than they say, and where facts only cohere in the context of particular institutional arrangements. Their analysis is always open to challenge in ways that cast the fact-checkers as political actors and question their claim to objectivity. The next chapter turns directly to these epistemological questions with a close study of PolitiFact's Truth-O-Meter.

5

OPERATING
THE TRUTH-O-METER

FACT-CHECKING IS A CONTROVERSIAL ENTERPRISE. AS WE'VE SEEN, fact-checkers weather constant criticism from politicians, pundits, and everyday readers who disagree with the conclusions they reach. The practice of "showing their work" does not insulate these journalists from accusations of bias; on the contrary, it offers reliable fodder for critics who take issue with their sources or their methods. Fact-checkers often hear the charge that they favor one party or the other, or that they strive for "false balance" between the two. Other critics accept that this is a difficult job carried out by well-meaning journalists but point to basic flaws in the enterprise.

One frequent observation is that fact-checkers don't choose statements to investigate randomly or in any scientific fashion.[1] As noted in chapter 3, this is a point they make themselves: "We are journalists, not social scientists."[2] But fact-checkers also believe their reporting captures real patterns in political discourse. "We've fact-checked Clinton more than 100 times since we began operations in 2007," announced a mid-2015 review of Hillary Clinton's PolitiFact record, the day before a campaign launch event.[3] Readers comparing the 2016 candidates could see that Clinton and rival Jeb Bush had earned "Half True" or better on more than two-thirds of their Truth-O-Meter verdicts, compared to less than one-third for Ted Cruz, and just 5 percent for

Donald Trump. Fact-checking appears to do a good job of catching out those politicians who exhibit a flagrant disregard for the truth.[4]

A second and more fundamental critique is that fact-checkers treat as questions of fact what are really matters of opinion or ideology. This argument has been made often by both liberal and conservative critics, along with the related point that fact-checkers confuse accuracy and fairness in analyzing political claims.[5] Political scientist Brendan Nyhan, a former fact-checker, cautions that journalists should "only invoke the authority of facts when assessing claims that can be resolved on evidentiary grounds, rather than straying into subjective judgments about the political process or semantic debates over terminology."[6] Other political scientists have called the entire project flawed, arguing that fact-checkers betray a "naïve political epistemology" based on the "tacit presupposition that there cannot be genuine political debate about facts, because facts are unambiguous and not subject to interpretation."[7]

Fact-checkers do speak the language of truth and falsehood. But they also insist, paradoxically, that people may legitimately disagree with their rulings and that, in politics, the truth is never black and white. "Facts can be subjective," one fact-checker explained to me.[8] In effect, the fact-checkers attach an asterisk to each of their rulings, conceding that this is an imperfect human undertaking carried out in a political realm where facts can be elusive. The same can be said about professional journalism as a whole. The objectivity norm that came to define the field after World War I was a response to the failure of what Michael Schudson calls "naïve empiricism"—an effort to reclaim a modest, working truth grounded in rules and procedures rather than in the notion that reporters can hold a mirror up to the world.[9] At the same time, fact-checkers believe in what they do. Like other journalists, they reconcile doubt about the ability to achieve perfectly objective truth with a faith in the value of trying.

These paradoxes emerge clearly in the operation of PolitiFact's Truth-O-Meter. The fictional truth-telling instrument has been called a gimmick, even by other fact-checkers.[10] But the Truth-O-Meter plays a complex role: it organizes and routinizes the work of checking facts while also giving fact-checkers a way to talk about the limits of their project. This chapter begins with a review of the rules for "operating" the Truth-O-Meter and then turns to an extended case study: a fact check I researched and wrote as a participant-observer at the group's headquarters, investigating a claim by the conservative pundit Glenn Beck. The case draws our attention to the instability of institutional facts, discussed in chapter 2. It shows how judgments of fact and value necessarily come together in fact-checking—and how that is consistent with a practical approach to finding the truth.

"Congratulations on Your Purchase of a Truth-O-Meter!"

Of the professional fact-checking groups, PolitiFact has the most carefully articulated process for researching political claims and rendering a verdict. In part, this stems from the group's franchise model. In order to license the PolitiFact method to state partners, the group had to codify that method; it had to develop policies and procedures that could be imparted in training sessions and incorporated into official literature. This effort yielded PolitiFact's most important repository of organizational knowledge, the Truth-O-Meter "owner's manual." The roughly twenty-page training manual was originally developed for PolitiFact Texas, launched in 2010 by the *Austin American-Statesman*. The overarching goal of the manual is to ensure that rulings remain roughly consistent across a growing number of semi-independent PolitiFact newsrooms. However, in my observation, the evolving document is also a key institutional resource when PolitiFact faces controversy or criticism. It offers a kind of master text for resolving internal debates and for crafting the public statements the group sometimes issues to explain its methods.[11]

The focus on process also jibes with PolitiFact's notion of pioneering a new kind of database journalism, compiling records and statistics that will be relevant far beyond the current news cycle. In a training session I observed, new fact-checkers were told not to forget to include the full date—day, month, and year—in all of their work for this reason. "We're going to be around in one hundred years," an editor proclaimed. This database model is central to PolitiFact's mission. As I heard repeatedly, the archive of Truth-O-Meter rulings gives voters a new way to assess candidates for public office, a resource that grows deeper and richer with each election cycle. An added benefit of licensing franchises to state newspapers is the ability to track promising local politicians early in their careers; by the time they reach the national stage, PolitiFact will already have a detailed record of their statements in the database. For this aggregate data to be meaningful, the methods used to generate each ruling have to be as consistent and well-reasoned as possible.[12] This sets up a parallel editorial hierarchy for newsrooms in the PolitiFact network. Although the goal is for partners to operate independently, the lines of authority always point to PolitiFact's top editors as the keepers of the Truth-O-Meter methodology.[13]

The trademarked Truth-O-Meter anchors PolitiFact's fact-checking routine. Every ruling the group publishes rates the veracity of a claim along the six-point scale. "The goal of the Truth-O-Meter is to reflect the relative accuracy of a statement," PolitiFact's website explains to readers, describing the individual ratings this way:

> The meter has six ratings, in decreasing level of truthfulness:
>
> TRUE—The statement is accurate and there's nothing significant missing.
>
> MOSTLY TRUE—The statement is accurate but needs clarification or additional information.
>
> HALF TRUE—The statement is partially accurate but leaves out important details or takes things out of context.
>
> MOSTLY FALSE—The statement contains an element of truth but ignores critical facts that would give a different impression.
>
> FALSE—The statement is not accurate.
>
> PANTS ON FIRE—The statement is not accurate and makes a ridiculous claim.[14]

Although PolitiFact's methodology has evolved significantly since the site launched in 2007, the language of the Truth-O-Meter remains almost unchanged. One substantial revision took place in mid-2011, when the original rating of "Barely True" was changed to "Mostly False" in response to frequent complaints that the original label gave too much credit to misleading statements.[15] Such tweaks always threaten the integrity of the database, however, and for that reason are not undertaken lightly. The switch to "Mostly False" applied retroactively to all statements in the Truth-O-Meter database (an editor's note was appended to affected rulings). Although the original definition of the rating remained intact, reading through the relabeled rulings it seems likely some would have been rated more generously—perhaps earning a "Half True"—if the tougher rubric already had been in place.[16]

As the name suggests, journalists at PolitiFact regard the Truth-O-Meter with some playfulness. The capital "O," with its hint of kitschy midcentury futurism, reminds us that a machine for reliably and scientifically determining what is true doesn't exist. (Calling it simply the "Truth Meter" would have conveyed something more earnest.) In interviews and in office banter, PolitiFact staff often made joking references to the fictional device. After a political scientist accused the site of selection bias, one staffer suggested an editor's note reminding the world that the Truth-O-Meter "is not a scientific instrument." The "owner's manual" also plays with this ambiguous status. Like a real product manual, the front page of the version I saw congratulated the user for the purchase of this instrument: "If operated and maintained properly, your Truth-O-Meter will give you years of enjoyment! But be careful because incorrect operation can cause an unsafe situation." A list of safety instructions followed, with a reminder not to take politics too seriously—and to disconnect the Truth-O-Meter during electrical storms.[17] This playfulness is in keeping with one of the fact-checking principles stressed in the manual and in PolitiFact's other literature: that "reasonable people can reach different conclusions about a claim."[18] As trainees learned, "this is a human enterprise, and the truth is not black and white. The very philosophy behind the Truth-O-Meter is shades of gray."[19] Similarly, one of PolitiFact's first editor's notes told readers that "our goal with the Truth-O-Meter is to give the truth of a claim, but we recognize that truth is not always black and white."[20]

In this way, the Truth-O-Meter captures a reflexivity that fact-checkers bring to their novel enterprise. At the same time, the fictional device plays a vital organizational role at PolitiFact. The Truth-O-Meter lies at the center of PolitiFact's appeal to potential media partners to invest in a new and more rigorous form of journalism. It is literally what a state franchise licenses and the basis for the training sessions its reporters receive. Broadcast partners who air PolitiFact verdicts are encouraged to display the symbol (some use animated versions with sound effects). The Truth-O-Meter is also the basis for the modularity of PolitiFact's website, the hinge that lets it function as both a news feed and a database. This modularity helps to resolve a recurring tension between making news and keeping records, as past rulings can be pulled from the database to create topical news stories. Modularity also helps to resolve a potential tension between the state sites and PolitiFact National. The main news feed can list interesting items from state newsrooms while ensuring that credit and advertising revenue accrue to the outlet that did the work.[21]

Principles of the Truth-O-Meter

PolitiFact's reporters take the "proper operation" of the Truth-O-Meter very seriously in their day-to-day journalism. The fictional instrument is the principal means of organizing the work of checking facts and the basis for their claim to consistency and objectivity. As the training manual stated,

> We often say we've created a new form of journalism. That's especially true when we have to make a Truth-O-Meter ruling. The procedure for making a ruling is not something you'll find in a journalism textbook. We've essentially had to create a new type of journalistic jurisprudence, a set of principles that guide our Truth-O-Meter rulings and make them solid and consistent.[22]

The proper operation of the Truth-O-Meter can be divided into two phases. First, a fact check must be reported and written consistent with the PolitiFact procedures described in chapters 3 and 4: identifying a clear "ruling statement," giving its author the chance to supply evidence, consulting original data sources over secondary reports, and so on. Although the research that goes into a Truth-O-Meter item can be tricky and time-consuming, writing these pieces was, in my experience, straightforward and quite fun. Most PolitiFact stories follow a fairly simple, expository recipe. Several times I heard this described as the "inverted pyramid upside-down": items open with the context for a statement, proceed through the detailed analysis, and conclude with the most important information, the ruling. (This expository formula works because the ruling is also visible at a glance in the Truth-O-Meter graphic.) The training manual distilled this writing process into a paragraph-by-paragraph template for new fact-checkers to apply while learning how to write for the Truth-O-Meter.[23]

The key to this formula is that Truth-O-Meter items enact for the reader the process of researching a claim. The reporting itself supplies the narrative arc, including key paragraph transitions: we wondered whether that was true, we found this data, we called these experts, and so on. (PolitiFact relies heavily on the first-person plural.[24]) Like a legal argument—a comparison that comes up constantly at PolitiFact—a fact check repeatedly justifies itself to the reader, explaining why a claim was chosen and how the final ruling was reached. As we've seen, fact-checking articles are often stories about the news, examining the spread of misinformation across media networks. But every Truth-O-Meter item is also a story about reporting work—about the conduct of journalism.

In the course of researching and writing a Truth-O-Meter item, the reporter assigns a tentative rating to the claim being checked. Once an item has cleared the first round of edits, the second phase in the operation of the Truth-O-Meter begins. PolitiFact reporters and editors jokingly call this the "star chamber": an ad hoc panel of three PolitiFact editors (not including the original author) who decide the final ruling by applying the published definitions of the Truth-O-Meter ratings and a set of guiding principles for interpreting those definitions. These guiding principles were developed in 2010, drawing on the "case law" of existing rulings and on the experience of the three PolitiFact editors who had made all of the rulings up to that point. "It's not like there are principles that you learned in J-school about how to do Truth-O-Meter rulings," trainees were told. "We invented the Truth-O-Meter and therefore we had to invent the principles on how to use it."[25] An editor's letter in 2011 introduced the principles to the public and in a 2013 follow-up PolitiFact described them this way:

Words matter—We pay close attention to the specific wording of a claim. Is it a precise statement? Does it contain mitigating words or phrases?

Context matters—We examine the claim in the full context, the comments made before and after it, the question that prompted it, and the point the person was trying to make.

Burden of proof—People who make factual claims are accountable for their words and should be able to provide evidence to back them up. We will try to verify their statements, but we believe the burden of proof is on the person making the statement.

Statements can be right and wrong—We sometimes rate compound statements that contain two or more factual assertions. In these cases, we rate the overall accuracy after looking at the individual pieces.

Timing—Our rulings are based on when a statement was made and on the information available at that time.[26]

In my observation, the guiding principles came up frequently in star chamber sessions, invoked by name or implicitly. Many rulings turn on the tension between the two core principles, "words matter" and "context matters." (As trainees learned, the principles are listed in order of importance.) Previous rulings may also be invoked to clarify how a principle applies, again on the analogy of common law. Most star chamber sessions last just ten or fifteen minutes and involve little controversy; of the more than twenty-five I observed, only a handful proved at all contentious. Two of three panelists must agree on the final ruling, although unanimity is strongly preferred and usually achieved. But some sessions become quite heated. In one case I witnessed, the disagreement lasted most of an afternoon and the panel was forced to reconvene twice.[27]

In the Star Chamber

Even agreeable star chamber sessions proved revealing. Consensus toward a final ruling builds in path-dependent and not perfectly consistent ways; as fact-checkers freely admit, the process is as much art as science. The line between adjacent Truth-O-Meter ratings can be hard to draw. This can make numerical claims surprisingly tricky to rule on: How accurate does a quoted statistic have to be to qualify as "True"? Or as "Half True"?[28] In a very early Truth-O-Meter item, from 2007, Texas's Ron Paul earned a "Mostly True" for claiming that five thousand Americans had died in Iraq and Afghanistan.[29] As the "owner's manual" explained, though Paul had exaggerated the figure by 13 percent, his larger point was that a lot of Americans had died in the wars—a fact the correction did not undercut. Conversely, my fact check of Indiana's Mitch Daniels, reviewed in the last chapter, awarded him a "False" for anticipating a budget event by perhaps six or seven years.[30] Arguably, the fact that U.S. interest payments will eventually pass national security spending offered an "element of truth" that warranted a slightly better rating. The harsh ruling reflected how deceptive the statement was in comparing budget figures separated by a decade without revealing that math to his audience.[31]

In some cases the ruling statement must be tweaked or trimmed to achieve consensus. For instance, in a television interview in early 2011, Minnesota Republican and Tea Party favorite Michele Bachmann decried the latest over-reach of big government: "To think that government has to go out and buy my breast pump for my babies? You want to talk about the nanny state? I think you just got a new definition of the nanny state."[32] Her charge stemmed from an Internal Revenue Service rule change classifying breast pumps as medical expenses, meaning they could now be purchased with special tax-free health savings accounts. Clearly, Bachmann turned a misleading phrase in equating the new tax status with state-bought breast pumps. But was her claim "False," or did it contain a large enough grain of truth to be "Barely True"? (That rating had not yet been changed to "Mostly False.") PolitiFact's editors debated the question briefly. Refocusing the ruling statement on Bachmann's actual choice of words—that the government would *"go out* and buy" breast pumps, which seemed to rule out a tax-free purchase—helped to build a consensus around "False."[33]

The most controversial star chamber session I witnessed involved what promised to be a straightforward ruling on unemployment figures. In a speech to the Conservative Political Action Conference, Republican presidential hopeful Mitt Romney came up with a dramatic way to depict the state of the U.S. labor market: "Today there are more men and women out of work in America than there are people working in Canada."[34] This proved surprisingly difficult to parse because of the many different ways of calculating unemployment and underemployment. Economists interviewed suggested that it was possible to make Romney's math add up but not by the standard U.S. unemployment figure nor even by an expanded government definition that includes workers who are "marginally attached" to the labor force. Meanwhile, as backup, Romney's staff offered a larger measure that counts Americans forced to settle for part-time work.[35]

The lack of a clear standard left room for a heated disagreement among editors who convened to review the item. Those arguing for a "False" invoked the PolitiFact principle that "words matter." Romney had said "out of work" and therefore clearly did not mean to count underemployed, part-time workers.

(This is the same logic FactCheck.org used to debunk the claim in a pithy analysis that simply compared official labor statistics from the United States and Canada.[36]) However, extending that argument further, "out of work" Americans might include happily retired persons or even children—in which case his statement would be literally true, but nonsensical, some staff pointed out. That is, "words matter" in a very bounded way. Even literal interpretation follows established conventions for talking about economic data.[37]

Another major argument for finding the claim "False" relied on "triangulating the truth." Economists interviewed from the left (the Brookings Institution) and the right (the Heritage Foundation) disputed Romney's claim. More than that, both economists said the comparison was somewhat arbitrary. "Frankly, I don't see that Romney's comparison makes much sense, whether it can be backed up or not. No doubt the total number of people out of work in the United States exceeds the total workforce of Luxembourg," the conservative economist was quoted as saying. "The U.S. and Canada have similar land masses and languages, but otherwise, the comparison strikes me as, let's be diplomatic, ill-chosen." In others words, even if the claim were defensible by some standard, it seemed designed to create a misleading impression. This wasn't direct evidence against Romney, but it cast the inadequacy of the evidence his staff supplied in a worse light.[38]

The case for Romney was equally revealing. One PolitiFact editor felt strongly that U.S. unemployment statistics tend to understate the problem by excluding underemployed workers and, especially, people who have given up looking for a job altogether. Every journalist in the meeting understood this well-established critique. The article draft even pointed out that counting all Americans who have left the work force involuntarily might make Romney's comparison work; however, no reliable, official count of such former workers exists, and this was not how Romney's staff had justified the claim. Still, the objecting editor felt a rating of "Barely True" or even "Half True" would better "tell the story" of the unemployed. Politics had intruded here, but not binary party politics. The editor was invoking a normative claim about what the role of journalism is and whose story it should tell. Another editor in the review panel chided, "Don't let your personal bias against unemployment cloud your judgment." Ultimately, the objecting editor was mollified somewhat by the writer's promise to "beef up the empathy" while preserving the "False" ruling, and several sentences were added to the piece.[39]

The Truth-O-Meter manual urges journalists to think like judges. But PolitiFact's "star chamber" doesn't rule on a fixed document. Both the claim being assessed and the write-up of it may shift or evolve in the interests of achieving consensus. In this case, the process broke down. Editors were forced to reconvene twice, and an indecisive panelist had to be replaced before a ruling of "False" could be reached. Having three panelists vote did not yield a clean majority because of the strong preference for unanimity and perhaps because of a reluctance to ignore the writer's firm objection to a softer rating. (In roughly 90 percent of cases, the writer's original ruling survives the process, I heard.) The Truth-O-Meter methodology is not bulletproof. It operates best as a flexible device for achieving consensus in routine cases, and participants had to defy standard procedures to handle a situation in which consensus was difficult to achieve.[40]

In my observation, PolitiFact journalists share a sense that, while the Truth-O-Meter is not a scientific instrument, treating it like one reminds reporters that this is "a different kind of journalism" and helps them to practice it. "At the end of the day, the 'star chamber' is three people who are trained in journalism but are putting their judgment into the Truth-O-Meter," editor Angie Drobnic Holan told me, emphasizing that the difference between adjacent rulings can turn on values.[41] It matters less that the mechanism operate perfectly than that it operate routinely, by embodying a commitment and orienting a set of activities that may vary in particular cases. The fictional Truth-O-Meter objectifies the process of deciding what's true and the epistemological questions that attend that fraught enterprise. This makes it easier for journalists to talk about these challenges and thus to critique and adjust their own methods—to "tune" the Truth-O-Meter, as one editor's note put it.[42] It makes it possible to acknowledge their own imperfection as arbiters of truth without relinquishing their faith in and commitment to objectivity. The Truth-O-Meter is not scientific, but it encourages the humans who use it to proceed more scientifically.

Checking Glenn Beck

A close review of a PolitiFact item I wrote as a participant-observer will illustrate the day-to-day work of operating the Truth-O-Meter. My main visit to the Washington-based fact-checking group coincided with the popular uprisings in Egypt in early 2011. This was a topic of obvious interest and importance. PolitiFact's "buffet" of possible claims to check quickly filled with statements about Egypt, and the group would publish five related Truth-O-Meter items during the uprisings.

Assigned to research and write a Truth-O-Meter article, I searched through transcripts of political talk shows on MSNBC and the Fox News Channel and found a handful of claims related to the uprisings that seemed worth checking.[43] A business analyst on Fox offered the surprising statistic that Egyptians spend more than half of their income on food while Americans spend only 6 percent. Rachel Maddow, the liberal MSNBC host, likened the uprisings to the collapse of the Berlin Wall in that "nobody really saw it coming"; I wondered whether this bit of conventional historical wisdom was really true. But Fox News host Glenn Beck (who has since left the network) made an alarming claim about Egypt's Muslim Brotherhood that seemed the best candidate for the Truth-O-Meter. On a broadcast the previous week, Beck explained the following to his listeners: "We told you this week how if Mubarak does step down, however, the Muslim Brotherhood would be the most likely group to seize power. They've openly stated they want to declare war on Israel and they would end the peace agreement with Israel and they would work towards instituting something we told you about, a caliphate."[44]

Truth-O-Meter items render a verdict on a single claim, usually a verbatim quote, known as the "ruling statement." With an editor's approval, I began researching the claim that the Muslim Brotherhood had "openly stated they want to declare war on Israel." I tried to put aside my general misgivings about Beck's program and engage the question with an open mind; I knew little about the Islamic political organization and it seemed entirely possible that the claim would turn out to be at least partly true. In fact, the initial evidence pointed in that direction: On a broadcast three days earlier, Beck quoted a "top official" in the Muslim Brotherhood as declaring that "the people should be prepared for war against Israel."[45] If true, that sounded like fairly damning testimony. The first step was to find out who that official was and confirm the rhetoric Beck attributed to him.

Translations and Evaluations

PolitiFact instructs fact-checkers to begin by trying to contact the author of a suspect claim. As noted earlier, this is seen as fair but also expedient: backup information from the source helps to orient the investigation and, because it's so often taken out of context, can offer powerful ammunition to defend a "False" ruling. I began by trying to reach, by e-mail and phone, the press contact listed on the website for Glenn Beck's program. PolitiFact had investigated several statements by Beck in the past, and other reporters told me his staff would not reply; this case was no exception. So I set about trying to trace the origin of the phrase the conservative pundit had quoted. Not realizing yet that the website for Beck's show published a source list for his broadcasts, I searched Google for the words "The people should be prepared for war against Israel." More than twenty thousand results appeared, all of which seemed to be from the previous two weeks.[46]

Documenting the precise origin of the words proved tricky. The earliest reference I could find was on the website of the English-language *Jerusalem Post* in a brief February 1 article that began this way: "A leading member of the Muslim Brotherhood in Egypt told the Arabic-language Iranian news network Al-Alam on Monday that he would like to see the Egyptian people prepare for war against Israel, according to the Hebrew-language business newspaper Calcalist."[47] The piece also mentioned a name, "Muhammad Ghannem." But neither that article nor any of the subsequent English-language coverage linked to the *Calcalist*, nor to any stories on Al-Alam. I began trying to find a reference to the original report on the Iranian network's website and eventually hit on a strategy that worked. Translating the name "Ghannem" into Arabic and pasting that into Al-Alam's search box brought up a January 31 article that, rendered into English by Google Translate, appeared to report on a news interview with Ghannem the day before on the subject of U.S. support for the Egyptian military. Halfway down, it included a sentence paraphrasing Ghannem's call for civil disobedience demonstrating "the willingness of people to war against Israel, until the world realizes that the Egyptian people are ready for everything . . . to get rid of this system."[48]

Consider the media trajectory this suggests. The inflammatory words were vocalized on the air, in Arabic, in an Al-Alam interview on January 30.

Somehow they came to the attention of a Hebrew-language business paper; perhaps the *Calcalist* routinely monitors Iranian media, or some reader alerted the paper to the broadcast. Then the *Jerusalem Post* ran its web item in English, attributed entirely to the other newspaper. The new piece was only three paragraphs long but featured an arresting title that gave the phrase a new author: "Muslim Brotherhood: 'Prepare Egyptians for War with Israel.'"

Several kinds of translation come into play here. First, Arabic words have been translated into Hebrew and then into English, more or less faithfully. People might disagree about both the literal meaning of the words or the sense in which they should be taken, depending on context, rhetorical practice, social and political norms, and so on. I would eventually see translations from four different sources, each slightly different.[49] One political scientist I interviewed pointed to earlier instances of "meaningless rhetoric" from members of the Muslim Brotherhood, stressing that these should not be confused with official policy. Another expert stressed that the reference to preparing for war had followed Ghannem's call for civil disobedience. The point, he claimed, was to demonstrate that the regime of Hosni Mubarak did not represent the Egyptian people, not to start a war.

But other translations are at work as well.[50] First, a person's speech has been attributed to an organization. As we shall see, the question of whether Ghannem could legitimately speak for the group became crucial to the analysis. And then text has been translated from one material, documentary context to another. A phrase buried in a lengthy discussion of U.S. ties to Egypt's military has become the subject of its own news report, with a shocking headline about a declaration of war. Now a nodal document existed to anchor Ghannem's violent rhetoric in online discourse—a textual artifact in English with its own URL and from an established journalistic source. Variants of the phrase propagated rapidly across blogs, discussion groups, news sites, and cable television.[51] The day the *Jerusalem Post* article appeared, Beck repeated the quote on his Fox show:

> How do they feel about Israel? Well, a top official in the Muslim Brotherhood has just said that—he said this while expressing support for the Egyptian protesters. And this is critical that you remember this. "The people should be prepared for war against Israel." . . .

You don't believe me? I don't really care. Do your own homework. Don't trust me on anything. Do your own homework. Go to GlennBeck .com and look all of it up. If you don't believe our research, go find it yourself.

The next day, February 2, the phrase appeared on the website of Illinois senator Mark Kirk, in a press release with the text of his floor speech calling on the White House to "heed growing warnings about the Muslim Brotherhood, their leaders and plans for taking Egypt back to the 13th century."[52] That day the words also turned up in opinion pieces at the *Washington Times*, the *New York Post*, and *Investors Business Daily*, and in comments at the *Business Insider*. These reports all identified the phrase's author as a "leader" or "leading member" of the Muslim Brotherhood, with no explanation of that status.[53] Subtle rhetorical elisions gave Ghannem's words more authority in standing for the aims of the Muslim Brotherhood as a whole. The *Washington Times* declared matter-of-factly that the group's "foreign policy was *succinctly summed up* by brotherhood leader Muhammad Ghannem."[54] But was that succinct summing up a fact, an argument, or merely a clever turn of phrase? Meanwhile, Beck skirted the question entirely with an ambiguous pronoun: "They've openly stated they want to declare war on Israel."

The circuit traveled by Ghannem's words offers a window on how news travels across media networks via a process of translation and recontextualization. Fact-checkers in their daily work are students of this process. Tracing the spread of the claim about the Muslim Brotherhood was part of the work of evaluating it. Reasonably or not, the shape of the phrase's network footprint began to color my judgment. If Ghannem's declaration was so important, why weren't elite U.S. news outlets covering it? And why hadn't the White House responded? In fact, as my published Truth-O-Meter item would point out, CNN and NPR and the news wires were carrying official reassurances about the peace treaty from Brotherhood spokesmen.

Who Was Muhammad Ghannem?

With the source of Glenn Beck's claim established, the question became what to make of it. This was impossible to research without relying on experts. Assuming Muhammad Ghannem's words had been accurately quoted, the ruling seemed to turn on one question: whether they reflected Muslim Brotherhood policy. But how to know what the official policy was or whether it was sincere? I found any number of news articles and scholarly reports that seemed to bear on these questions. But my confidence that I was reading the evidence correctly came from having scholars agree it was ludicrous to say the Brotherhood planned to declare war on Israel.

To seek context for Ghannem's interview on Al-Alam, I began by sending e-mails to Middle East experts at the Brookings Institution, the Council on Foreign Relations, and the Carnegie Endowment for International Peace. (Two of these groups had been cited in a Truth-O-Meter item weighing an earlier claim by Glenn Beck about the Muslim Brotherhood's alleged ties to al-Qaeda.[55]) I was mindful that this is the foreign policy elite that journalists have been criticized for relying on so unquestioningly but saw no other strategy for finding unbiased sources. Only one of these academics wrote back, directing me to four additional scholars, political scientists at George Washington University, Georgetown University, Kent State University, and the University of Texas–Austin.[56]

The four political scientists all responded. Three of them confirmed, crucially, that Muhammad Ghannem was not a member of the Muslim Brotherhood's sixteen-member Guidance Office. "I have never heard of him," one expert on Egyptian politics told me. The consensus in these interviews was that the sprawling movement included many divergent views, but that Glenn Beck had grossly mischaracterized its aims; one scholar called his statement "propaganda." The Brotherhood's official policy toward Israel had been "a bit ambiguous," another expert conceded, but had never come close to calling for war. These scholars stressed that rhetoric vis-a-vis Israel could not always be taken at face value, and placed Ghannem's comments in the wider historical context of Egyptian views about the 1979 peace treaty with Israel and the way it was achieved.[57] As one explained by e-mail,

> The MB is a massive organization with many many different ideological trends within it. I have never heard anyone on or off the record say they "wish to declare war on Israel." I have heard people in the MB rail against Zionism (equating it as imperialism). They almost always talk about the U.S. and Israel and double-standards. I have also read in the

papers Mohamad Akif say that the treaty could be put up for a popular referendum. But no one ever said anything about war.

Couple things: This is not a an [sic] usual position in Egypt. Many feel like the treaty was signed unilaterally and does not serve their interests (due to how it was signed and implemented). Many of the democratic protesters in Tahrir sq (who are secular, nationalist, progressive, and atheists) would make similar claims re Israel and the treaty.[58]

The evidence after two days of research appeared fairly unambiguous. Other than various conservative accounts all pointing to the same *Jerusalem Post* item as proof, I had not uncovered any support for Beck's contention that the Muslim Brotherhood had "openly stated they want to declare war on Israel." My argument seemed like it should convince a reasonable observer. But the case was not unassailable. Several basic objections would be raised that were impossible to dispel in any decisive way: that I was biased against Glenn Beck; that the experts I quoted were biased; and that the item ignored evidence that told a different story, putting too much faith in the official pronouncements of hard-line Islamists whose oft-stated view was, after all, that Israel should not exist. It is only fair to note that at this point in the uprisings Muslim Brotherhood spokesmen also had officially disavowed any presidential aspirations—a position the group would soon abandon.

This underscores the uncertainty that attends fact-checking work. I set out to verify whether the Muslim Brotherhood had *said* it wanted war. But this led—inevitably, given the tricky question of who could speak for the Brothers—into evaluating whether they really *intended* to declare war. Even the basic "facts" of who Muhammad Ghannem was and what he had said were not stable starting points for analysis; they could be made or unmade by the comparison to other statements from the Brotherhood, to the group's history, and so on. If Ghannem's statements varied wildly from official policy, that in itself could be seen as evidence that he was not a reliable spokesperson or that his rhetoric shouldn't be read the way conservatives in the United States and Israel read it.[59] Conversely, one can imagine an expert making the case that the true goals of the Brotherhood could only be read by taking the temperature of its members on the "Arab street."

The testimony from experts on the Muslim Brotherhood seemed to offer the clarity of a logical syllogism built on the premise that only officials can speak authoritatively for organizations. As the published piece would conclude, "some members of the Muslim Brotherhood may be calling for war. But the ones who say that don't speak for the group; and the ones who do speak for the group, don't say that." However, the premises of that argument depended ultimately on the sense that it is *unreasonable* to think the Brotherhood intended to make war on Egypt's powerful neighbor across the Sinai. If history took an unexpected turn, in hindsight the logic of dismissing statements by people such as Muhammad Ghannem would be open to question. Future events could cast the facts in a very different light.[60]

Glenn Beck Responds

Based largely on the testimony from experts on the Middle East, I gave Beck's claim a provisional rating of "False"; in a "star chamber" session, three PolitiFact editors agreed unanimously. The Truth-O-Meter item went live shortly after 11 A.M. on February 15, 2011.[61] A condensed data box bearing Glenn Beck's picture, his claim, and the verdict appeared at the top of PolitiFact's news feed; links also went out on Twitter and Facebook. Clicking on the ruling brought up the full 1,100-word analysis, including a list of eighteen different sources used.[62] Adding the item to PolitiFact's content management system automatically registered one more "False" rating on Glenn Beck's official record at the site. With the new data point, his tally covered twenty-one statements, only seven of which were rated "Half True" or better.[63]

The new "False" ruling immediately began to carve a trail through media-political networks as allies and opponents of Glenn Beck responded. The day the item went live, Media Matters turned it into a headline: "PolitiFact Gives 'False' Rating to Beck Claim That Muslim Brotherhood Wants to Declare War on Israel."[64] That post linked back to PolitiFact and reproduced the bulk of the original article; other progressive bloggers in turn linked to the Media Matters item. The ruling could be recruited into progressive networks in much the same way that the striking *Jerusalem Post* headline had been cited by conservatives. Reducing lengthy analyses to a single, decisive data point invites citation and helps to make PolitiFact's work highly portable.

The Truth-O-Meter ruling also came to the attention of Glenn Beck's staff. Two days after the item was posted, Stu Burguiere, then the in-house blogger at GlennBeck.com, ran a point-by-point refutation under a mock-up of PolitiFact's Truth-O-Meter graphic, with the needle pointing to "UTTER-FAIL."[65] PolitiFact had conceded that Beck accurately quoted the *Jerusalem Post*, Burguiere noted; shouldn't that make his claim true by definition? Wasn't the newspaper the right target for this fact check? (This is a complaint fact-checkers hear often; PolitiFact's policy holds people responsible for the accuracy of the sources they use.) Burguiere also took aim at one of the experts consulted, from a research center at George Washington University, by way of an in-joke regarding Beck's long-running crusade against the legacy of President Woodrow Wilson: "They go, without irony, to quite possibly the least trustworthy source imaginable when dealing with Glenn Beck: The Woodrow Wilson Center. I'm not kidding." (Interestingly, the first comments on the Media Matters item had predicted this line of attack.) The "Stu Blog" post summed up: "So, the FALSE rating comes from Glenn accurately quoting a newspaper, accurately quoting a Muslim Brotherhood member, who apparently doesn't rise high enough on the Muslim Brotherhood popularity list for the Woodrow Wilson Center. What a devastating case."

As further proof, Burguiere cited violent anti-Israel rhetoric from a popular cleric, Youssef al-Qaradawi, whom the German weekly *Der Speigel* had identified as an intellectual leader of the Brotherhood. According to the magazine, the Islamic televangelist had praised the Holocaust and in one sermon "asked God 'to kill the Jewish Zionists, every last one of them.'"[66] Later that day, Beck picked up this line of reasoning on his television program: "PolitiFact says that my statement about the Muslim Brotherhood wanting to war with Israel is false despite the fact that we showed you the words of Yusuf al-Qaradawi. Oh, that guy, he's rated the ninth-most influential Muslim on earth with an audience of 60 million people a week."[67]

I also received several personal e-mails from fans of Glenn Beck, taking issue with my analysis and directing me to the evidence compiled on his website as well as by PBS, *Der Spiegel*, and other news outlets. These e-mails were civil but blunt. "Dear Mr. Graves," one began, "What is the difference between 'declaring war on Israel' and praying to Allah 'to kill all the Zionist Jews'? The goal is the same even if the words used to attain that goal are not." Another declared, "I have to say, this and a couple of other ratings you guys are posting is putting a crack in my trust in you guys. . . . Night after night Beck shows video of MB members calling for the destruction of Israel."[68] One engaged very closely with the key argument:

> Several figures within the Muslim Brotherhood have in fact stated this. The Jerusalem Post incorrectly reported that the particular man Glenn Beck was quoting was an important figure in the Muslim Brotherhood, but no less other members of the organization have said much to the same effect.
>
> I suggest you change your 'truth-o-meter' to reflect the accuracy of Glenn's statement, and perhaps consider reprimanding the Jerusalem Post instead of Glenn Beck.
>
> For further reference, there's a well laid out argument found at glennbeck.com.
>
> I suspect you don't care and simply want to bash Glenn Beck.[69]

Both my analysis and the refutation at Glenn Beck's website would continue to be recruited into online political debates in the weeks to come. The episode resurfaced months later during a mediated confrontation between Fox News, PolitiFact, and Jon Stewart's *Daily Show*. In a mid-June interview on Fox News, Stewart had declared that polls found the network's audience to be the "most consistently misinformed media viewers"; PolitiFact analyzed his claim and rated it "False."[70] (Viewers of particular Fox Shows performed quite well in knowledge surveys, sometimes better than Stewart's own audience.) In response, on his own show two days later Stewart declared, with mock seriousness, "I defer to their judgment and I apologize for my mistake. . . . To not do so . . . would undermine the very integrity and credibility that I work so hard to pretend to care about."[71] He then launched into a four-minute review of the abysmal PolitiFact record compiled by various Fox News personalities. As Stewart narrated, twenty-one "False" and "Pants on Fire" statements from Fox filled the screen until the comedian's face was barely visible. Here the Truth-O-Meter was being used in precisely the way the database envisions, as a data point to be cited in ongoing arguments. PolitiFact responded eagerly to the attention from the comedian, with an editor's letter offering the "annotated edition" of Stewart's broadcast: a summary of all of the rulings he referred to, in the order cited.[72]

"Objectivity in Shirtsleeves"

Did the Muslim Brotherhood state the intent to declare war on Israel? The question sounds straightforward, and arriving at a convincing factual answer was not, in hindsight, very difficult. What proves trickier is understanding exactly how the answer was "factual" and what made it convincing. The case shows once again how the day-to-day work of checking facts differs from what we might casually imagine. My investigation of Beck's claim was objective in the sense of being driven by evidence and reason. The available facts constrained the analysis; if members of the Guidance Office had endorsed Ghannem's rhetoric, for instance, I would have been pushed toward a different result. But the analysis was not objective if that means reaching an indisputable conclusion based on a God's-eye view of the facts, free of any trace of judgment or interpretation. To follow professional fact-checkers at work is to watch what Lorraine Daston and Peter Galison, in reference to the history of science, call "objectivity in shirt sleeves": objectivity as "the gestures, techniques, habits, and temperament ingrained by training and daily repetition."[73] John Nerone observes that this is also a good description of objective practice in journalism, though it does not produce the certainty we crave: "So what counts for truth among journalists . . . is what they recognize as produced in the responsible way. . . . Although it is the best answer right now for the problem of truth, objectivity in shirtsleeves is neither convincing as an epistemology (because it is not an epistemology), nor reliable as a way of policing falsehoods and manipulations."[74]

Like every other fact check reviewed in these pages, the investigation of Beck's claim turned on institutional facts—facts produced within the agreed-upon institutional reality humans inhabit. I suggest in chapter 2 that these facts are in practice much less stable than we might suppose. Institutional facts depend on standards or definitions—of unemployment, for instance—that often turn out to be uncertain or understood in more than one way. These definitional differences don't always matter very much in day-to-day institutional life, and may in fact ease it.[75] They surface in moments of controversy, when someone seeks to justify a claim—whether material or rhetorical—by invoking an authoritative standard. Disputes over institutional facts raise the question of who is a legitimate spokesperson for an organization or arrangement or idea.[76]

The instability of institutional facts can be easily seen when it comes to an organization, like the Muslim Brotherhood, without its own legitimating institutional ties in the U.S. political context. The usual deference to an organization's self-definition did not apply in this case. To people who saw the Brotherhood as fundamentally illegitimate and untrustworthy, the idea of using its official pronouncements as evidence of its stance toward Israel was ludicrous. A case that reveals similar dynamics is the question of the extent of al-Qaeda today, raised, for instance, after the 2012 attack on the U.S. diplomatic compound in Benghazi, Libya. Is al-Qaeda a tightly knit organization, a loose network, or a broad ideology? Because the group has no institutional purchase in the United States, officials have had wide latitude to define its boundaries (for instance, to justify military action in Africa, Southeast Asia, and elsewhere).[77]

The question of how to weigh Muhammad Ghannem's anti-Israel rhetoric highlights an epistemological dilemma at the center of fact-checking. Should the cleric's words be tested against official Brotherhood policy and dismissed if they don't match, or instead do they offer evidence that official policy is not a reliable standard? This is a version of what laboratory studies call the "experimenter's regress." As sociologist Harry Collins describes the dilemma, scientists unable to reproduce another lab's experimental results can't know whether they've disproven that result or simply failed to run the experiment properly.[78] Collins and others argue that replication does not—in fact, cannot—play the straightforwardly dispositive role it assumes in naïve accounts of how science works. This underscores the role of tacit knowledge in both conducting an experiment and interpreting the result. It points to the importance of trust, as embedded in social relations and institutional arrangements, in the making of scientific facts. Scientists must trust an entire network of facts—related to their instruments, their supplies, and so on—in order to test any particular fact, as suggested by the improbable string of tests a truly skeptical scientist would need to conduct for even a simple lab procedure.[79] This has a clear echo in everyday reporting routines, as Gaye Tuchman illustrated with her famous example of what a truly skeptical news article would look like: "Robert Jones and his alleged wife, Fay Smith Jones, yesterday held what they described as a cocktail party at their supposed home."[80]

PolitiFact and other fact-checkers rely on official data and established standards whenever possible. Even well-established institutional mechanisms for certifying public facts are always open to question, as illustrated by the debate among PolitiFact editors over how to assess Mitt Romney's claims about joblessness. Researching that claim forced the fact-checkers to consider whether the figure used most often in the United States failed to capture the realities of employment. In this respect, Romney's argument represented a provisional, incremental unmaking of the conventional unemployment standard, aligning the candidate in that political instant with other voices (such as progressive economists) arguing for a more expansive definition. Romney's staff did not in the event defend his statistic by making a principled argument for a new unemployment measure, but they might have—and others could now point to his attack to make such a case. PolitiFact's write-up also left the institutional fact of the unemployment rate a tiny bit less stable: It underscored that there really *is* no unemployment rate but rather a number of competing measures, none of which fully captures the number of people who have involuntarily left the workforce.

Standards have to be maintained. They come to seem universal or abstract by virtue of being honored in each instance: reproduced in newspaper articles or legal arguments or scientific calculations, and encoded into intellectual technologies from algorithms and textbooks to mnemonic devices. Sociologist Bruno Latour argues that the circulation of standards, including loosely defined ones, naturalizes the categories we take as inherently social and then use to understand ourselves, to conduct research, to implement public policies, and so on. "How would one identify oneself as 'upper middle class,' 'yuppy,' or 'preppy' without reading the newspapers?" he asks.[81] That is to say in different terms that the messy, historically specific circulation of particular standards and "quasi-standards" is the basis for institutional facts.

Fact-checkers confront standards far hazier than unemployment rates. News judgment draws these journalists to sensational or surprising claims and into areas of political controversy. It draws them precisely to those regions where definitions are in flux and institutional facts are at risk of coming apart. Crucially, it is in acts of justification that a standard will be invoked or challenged. To make a case or defend a position, we draw lines from the specific to the general, the local to the universal, in a way that potentially changes both. The *Jerusalem Post* had equated "Muhammad Ghannem" to "Muslim Brotherhood." The references that quickly followed from Glenn Beck and other conservative voices both drew strength from and reinforced that association (a dual action caught in Latour's idea of "enrolling" allies[82]). They tied the link into a network of evidence and arguments attesting to the danger posed by the Muslim Brotherhood: "You don't believe me? . . . Do your own homework. Go to GlennBeck.com and look all of it up." Challenged by PolitiFact's ruling, Glenn Beck and his defenders appealed to common sense and began to articulate the standards to justify his position: "Night after night Beck shows video of MB members calling for the destruction of Israel"; "we showed you the words of Yusuf al-Qaradawi"; what counts are *these* words from violent Islamists, not *those* analyses by liberal experts.

Looking for "Goodness of Fit"

Having to navigate unstable factual terrain invites a comparison between professional fact-checkers and investigative journalists, as I've suggested earlier. These two styles of journalism deal with stories in which the facts are not simply unknown, in the sense of being as-yet unreported, but actively contested or in doubt. Both require the journalist to not only report but adjudicate between competing accounts of reality. Both therefore presume that reporters will when necessary question official claims and the procedures or standards those claims rest on. In their study of investigative journalism, James Ettema and Ted Glasser give the example of a *Washington Post* reporter who investigated an alleged epidemic of rape in a detention center in the Maryland suburbs. She obviously could not rely on official sources and statistics; the organizing premise of the story was that such rapes are systematically underreported. But neither could the reporter simply take the accounts of inmates at face value or verify their separate stories in any straightforward way. Instead of direct corroboration, arriving at the truth in cases like this means looking for "goodness of fit" among multiple inconsistent pieces of testimony and other evidence, weighed and woven together in light of "a value-loaded conceptual scheme that renders them both morally ordered and true"—the journalist's evolving sense of what the larger story is and why it matters.[83] Corroboration is thus a matter of "tacit knowledge of the journalistic craft" and always structured by values. The oft-used metaphor of putting together the pieces of a puzzle doesn't do justice to these kinds of investigations, Ettema and Glasser insist, because the "set of facts that seems to interlock so convincingly into the story has been shaped by that story in the first place, just as the story has been shaped by a moral order."[84]

The notion of "goodness of fit," borrowed from philosopher Hilary Putnam, also nicely describes the way fact-checkers reason past disjunctures in the institutional reality they must navigate. Fact-checkers don't directly challenge the institutional order as investigative reporters do. But they do have to find ways to resolve its contradictions to reach a verdict, and to achieve this they look for coherence across inconsistent accounts and from a range of experts. The ambiguity of Muhammad Ghannem's words, his uncertain status within the Muslim Brotherhood, the group's official reassurances about the peace treaty, and the seeming illogic of a declaration of war on Israel all cohered to support the "False" ruling for Beck's claim. Of course, that reasoning reflected any number of unspoken convictions about the world. Most notably it assumed that, contrary to some portrayals, the Muslim Brotherhood was more like than unlike the other kinds of political groups reporters normally write about and that it would behave as rationally and self-interestedly as any long-established organization.

On balance, Beck's alarmist rhetoric seemed unreasonable. This is a standard that comes up often among fact-checkers, one that leaves room for moral as well as logical judgments, underscoring what Ettema and Glasser call "the intimate interdependence of fact and value."[85] The talk show host's claim was unreasonable because it flew in the face of significant evidence to the contrary but also because it seemed to deliberately take words out of context to exaggerate their threat. As is so often the case, PolitiFact's refutation rested partly on mapping the media-political geography of the claim in question—in this case, tracing the anti-Israel rhetoric back to its source and showing how it spread to conservative media outlets and the floor of the U.S. Senate.

Judgments of fairness and accuracy become deeply entwined here. In PolitiFact's methodology and its rating system, evidence of deceit and of falsehood are considered together. Of course, it is possible for a perfectly accurate claim to be advanced unfairly, by using evidence that has been taken out of context, for instance. PolitiFact endeavors to rate claims against the best available evidence or expertise. In practice, however, factual inaccuracy and disregard for the truth often go together, and the latter helps to build a case for the former. Crucially, it was not necessary to offer an affirmative definition of Muhammad Ghannem's status or of Brotherhood policy in order to show that Beck and others had taken liberties with those details. Assessments of the fairness of an argument help to close the gap when evidence is unclear or standards are uncertain. But that is only to say that the values always bound up in the mechanisms we rely on to certify institutional facts become visible when those mechanisms break down.

Fact-checking captures with unusual clarity a paradox at the center of objective reporting, one understood by many professional journalists: that separating fact from value is both necessary and impossible.[86] The ways in which values structure reporting routines emerge most visibly in styles of newswork, like fact-checking and investigative reporting, where institutional mechanisms for certifying facts are in doubt. At the same time, adhering to a thoughtful set of procedures for investigating factual claims yields, in most cases, a reasonable and consensually validated picture of the world. To say we don't have unmediated access to reality or that there is no universal, Archimedean vantage from which to establish indisputable facts is not to argue that one view is as good as any other. It is only to defer to what has been called a "more realistic realism"—to recognize that truth claims grounded in reality are also bounded by meaning-making context.[87]

The conflict between PolitiFact and Glenn Beck draws our attention once again to the medium fact-checkers work in. It underscores the open-ended nature of online discourse and the difficulty of resolving factual debates in a permanent way. Such episodes bring to mind the image, nicely drawn by Bruno Latour, of a skeptical scientist, "the dissenter," confronting a cluster of citations that must be untangled if a scientific claim is to be challenged. What was the Muslim Brotherhood's *real* stance toward Israel? Beck had his list of links, and I had my own. Latour writes of scientific literature in *Science in Action*:

A paper that does not have references is like a child without an escort walking at night in a big city it does not know; isolated, lost, anything may happen to it. On the contrary, attacking a paper heavy with footnotes means that the dissenter has to weaken each of the other papers, or will at least be threatened with having to do so. . . . The difference at this point between technical and non-technical literature is not that one is about fact and the other about fiction, but that *the latter gathers a few resources to hand, and the former a lot of resources, even from far away in time and space.*[88]

In this material sense the debate over facts online becomes quite technical. Of course, it is not really just a question of who has the longer list of citations—sources come with varying levels of authority, and they may be deployed more or less reasonably to build a case. But making these assessments takes real work; it is a matter of judgment, not self-evident fact; and the results are always vulnerable to challenge. The fact-checkers operate in media-political networks whose contours shape their reasoning as well as the impact it has the world. The next section turns to the fact-checkers' relationship with three key constituencies—readers, politicians, and other journalists—and raises the difficult question of who their work is for and what it is meant to accomplish.

PART III

THE EFFECTS

OF FACT-CHECKING

"Say Anything"

ONE OF THE MOST CLOSELY WATCHED RACES OF 2014 WAS THE FIGHT for the U.S. Senate seat held for thirty years by Kentucky's Mitch McConnell. With anti-incumbent feeling strong across the country, the powerful Republican faced a surprisingly vigorous challenge from Alison Lundergan Grimes, Kentucky's Democratic secretary of state. The contest featured a string of vicious negative ads from both campaigns. With a month left in the race, hurt by charges that she was in league with forces bent on destroying the state's coal industry, Grimes fought back with an ad charging that McConnell and his wife "personally took $600,000 from anticoal groups, including New York City mayor Michael Bloomberg's anticoal foundation." To make the point, the commercial juxtaposed cutouts of Bloomberg and of McConnell and his wife, the men clad in matching tuxedos, against the iconic New York skyline. The ominous closing shot positioned the famous billionaire mayor behind and slightly above a scowling McConnell, as if directing him.

Fact-checkers eviscerated the commercial. To back it up, the Grimes campaign pointed to compensation received by McConnell's wife, former labor secretary Elaine Chao, for serving on the boards of Bloomberg

Philanthropies and of Wells Fargo bank. But spokespeople for both organizations explained that board members had nothing to do with setting investment policy. The philanthropy, which had supported an environmental initiative called "Beyond Coal," paid Chao less than $10,000 a year. She earned a great deal more from the bank, but it hardly qualified as an "anticoal group": despite a pledge to curtail investment in mountaintop-removal operations, Wells Fargo remained a major backer of the coal industry and in fact had been singled out by environmentalists for financing coal-fired power plants. The *Washington Post*'s Fact Checker pointed out that Grimes's "misleading and flimsy ad" was never posted to YouTube—"often a sign that a campaign wants to slip something under the radar"—and gave it four Pinocchios, the site's worst rating.[1] A day later PolitiFact issued its own verdict, "False," in a detailed analysis citing more than twenty sources, including its rival.[2]

The Grimes campaign paid close attention to fact-checkers. "If we put something on the air that is factually incorrect we have done a huge disservice to the campaign," declared a top consultant for Grimes at a postmortem in late 2014. Being fact-checked can do serious damage, he explained: "Most campaigns are only about one thing, and that is do I believe the sonofabitch or not, that's what it comes down to. We are desperately trying to say we won't lie to you."[3] Staffers fielded dozens of queries from fact-checking outlets over the course of the election. The candidate trumpeted rulings that went against McConnell in mailings and advertisements. One Grimes spot, called "Say Anything," cited FactCheck.org, PolitiFact, the Fact Checker, and other "independent fact-checkers" to make the case that her opponent could not be trusted.[4] Nevertheless, the sharp rebuke from these same fact-checkers did not force Grimes to back down. On the contrary, just two weeks before Election Day a new spot had the candidate herself standing in front of a partly shuttered power plant, again accusing McConnell of taking $600,000 from "enemies of coal." The *Washington Post*'s Glenn Kessler gave the new effort another four Pinocchios, calling it "likely the worst ad of a nasty campaign year" and concluding that "Grimes should be ashamed of herself."[5] The harsh verdict hurt Grimes at least a bit: it triggered a tough article in the *Lexington Herald-Leader* and was made into a frightening mailer by the McConnell campaign.[6] To fact-checkers, it only confirmed the depths politicians will sink to in a desperate campaign. As Kessler would later explain:

What was striking was that Grimes herself stood in front of the camera and personally repeated this claim, even though she had already been told that it was false, which was a pretty good indication of the deep hole she found herself in. . . . Grimes ended up being the first Democratic Senate candidate in Kentucky history to lose every coal county, which again indicates why she was so desperate to keep making this charge.[7]

Professional fact-checkers often point to episodes like this one to disabuse anyone of the idea that their work will somehow cleanse American politics of deception and distortion. No episode makes the point more clearly than the debate over health care reform in 2009.[8] President Obama's ambitious reform plan was the first major policy initiative to unfold in the contemporary fact-checking landscape. The issue dominated the national media for more than as year and hinged on precisely the sort of detailed and complex questions fact-checkers specialize in.

As the debate took shape, veteran journalist James Fallows made a bold prediction about the salutary effect online fact-checking would have. Fallows had chronicled the collapse of President Bill Clinton's health care reform initiative in the 1990s, paying special attention to misinformation that circulated freely on talk radio as well as in the elite media. The most damaging charge came from Betsy McCaughey, a future lieutenant governor of New York, who authored an influential analysis in the *New Republic* suggesting the plan would all but outlaw private health care.[9] This interpretation was explicitly contravened by one of the first provisions of the Clinton bill.[10] Nevertheless, claims about its sharp restrictions and draconian punishments spread widely. As repeated by George Will in *Newsweek* in early 1994,

> Escaping government control to choose your own doctor or buy other care would be virtually impossible. Doctors could be paid only by government-approved plans, at rates set by the government. It would be illegal for doctors to accept money from patients, and there would be 15-year jail terms for people driven to bribery for care they feel they need but the government does not deem necessary.[11]

In contrast, today's "ecology of news and opinion" would be much less hospitable to such malicious distortions, Fallows declared on the radio in May and again in July of 2009. The "instant feedback" provided by fact-checkers would deflate the most egregious falsehoods before they could gain traction, whereas "in those days something that was plainly false, and provably false, could not be knocked down because there was not an alternative machine to deal with it." Fallows pointed to a promising example: a new falsehood from Betsy McCaughey, about restrictions on medical care supposedly hidden in a 2009 stimulus bill, had been picked up by Rush Limbaugh and the *Wall Street Journal* but then seemed to lose traction after being debunked online.[12]

Then came "death panels." The idea that new health care rules would save money by requiring seniors to undergo counseling on "how to end their life sooner," as McCaughey put it on the radio show of former Republican senator Fred Thompson, had been percolating among conservative pundits for months. But a media frenzy ensued after Sarah Palin picked up this line of argument in an incendiary Facebook post: "The America I know and love is not one in which my parents or my baby with Down Syndrome will have to stand in front of Obama's 'death panel' so his bureaucrats can decide, based on a subjective judgment of their 'level of productivity in society,' whether they are worthy of health care."

In one sense Fallows's prediction was accurate: Palin's claim was immediately and widely debunked, not just by fact-checkers but by many TV and print reporters, in state and local outlets as well as national ones. Some journalists challenged rhetoric about "death panels" in their own voice rather than by quoting an outside authority.[13] FactCheck.org, PolitiFact, and Media Matters refuted the charge unequivocally; the claim became PolitiFact's inaugural "Lie of the Year."[14] A front-page *New York Times* headline declared, "False 'Death Panel' Rumor Has Some Familiar Roots," drawing attention to McCaughey's role in the latest distortions.[15] But these interventions did little to promote more reasonable public discourse about health care. Even as fact-checkers issued their verdicts, conservative lawmakers, candidates, and pundits repeated the charge. Crowds took it up at town hall meetings across the country, producing dramatic footage for the nightly news and presaging major losses for Democrats in the 2010 midterm elections. Within a week of Palin's Facebook post, Fallows officially reversed course in his blog at the *Atlantic*: "I said two weeks ago that I thought today's communications system had caught up with people who invented facts. I was wrong."[16]

Professional fact-checkers are asked all of the time if the work they do makes a difference.[17] The question comes up in conferences and panel discussions and on-air interviews. Trend pieces about this new brand of journalism wonder whether it really manages to persuade anybody or to inhibit political lying—and if not, "why bother spending all of this time holding politicians accountable?"[18] Any number of critiques from journalists and scholars have focused on whether fact-checking "works" and how it might work better.[19] "For the fact checkers who police political ads, debates and speeches, it's an article of faith that factually accurate information is something voters want and need," announced a *USA Today* article on the movement. "What they can't seem to do is get politicians to stop saying things that aren't true."[20] At the close of the 2012 campaigns, the late, influential *New York Times* media columnist David Carr dismissed the efforts that produced "the most fact-checked election in history":

> At any given moment during the last 18 months, there were so many truth squadrons in the air that mid-air collisions seemed a genuine possibility.
>
> But as the campaign draws to a close, it's clear that it was the truth that ended up as a smoldering wreck. Without getting into a long tick-tock of untruthfulness, a pattern emerged over the summer and fall: both candidates' campaigns laid out a number of whoppers, got clobbered for doing so, and then kept right on saying them."[21]

Fact-checking can potentially "work" in three different ways, on three distinct audiences.[22] First, it may provide factual information that disabuses readers of mistaken beliefs or inoculates them against deceptive claims—and, perhaps, changes their thinking about political issues or leads them to vote a different way. Second, fact-checkers may, either as a direct resource or by way of example, encourage other journalists to challenge falsehoods and adjudicate factual debates rather than just reporting competing views. And finally, fact-checking may, as a consequence of its effects (or perceived effects) on public opinion or press coverage, inhibit political lying by making it more costly for public figures to distort the truth.

The fact-checkers, however, make only very modest claims about their impact on the world. When asked, they have a few anecdotal responses that line up with those three models of influence. Fact-checkers often point to the popularity of the genre with readers, as reflected in traffic statistics and encouraging e-mails from the public. "Voters are hungry for fact-checking," PolitiFact's Bill Adair wrote in response to Carr's column, noting that daily traffic to the site sometimes surpassed a million page views during the election.[23] They often mention the usefulness of fact-checking as a resource for other reporters. "We do have a lot of impact on other journalists, that's the beauty of what we do," one FactCheck.org editor told a group of overseas journalists visiting the site. "We get cited a lot by newspaper reporters. . . . They turn to us to say, 'Well, these are kind of the nonpartisan arbiters of truth.'"[24]

And fact-checkers can all cite cases in which a public figure seemed to abandon a talking point once it was ruled false—while freely conceding that that political lying continues unabated and always will. An early example came during the 2008 presidential campaign, when Barack Obama often claimed to have worked his way through college and law school. FactCheck .org challenged a television ad that repeated the line, pointing out that (according to Obama's book *Dreams from My Father*) the candidate had held a few summer jobs and taken out loans to pay tuition—not the common sense of working one's way through school.[25] "Afterward Obama never said that again," Brooks Jackson recalled.[26] At a fact-checking conference, the *Washington Post*'s Glenn Kessler told the story of a Senate Republican leader who, before a major floor speech about health care, instructed his staff to read through every relevant Fact Checker column to make sure he wouldn't earn any Pinocchios. Bill Adair agreed: "I've heard the same kinds of things Glenn has about senators who tell their staff, 'I do not want to get a "Pants on Fire," I want you to vet everything that I say,' and so I think it's a really positive thing."[27]

Other politicians, though, pay no attention. Former New York mayor Rudy Giuliani is a favorite example among fact-checkers: Despite being challenged over and over, Giuliani, a prostate cancer survivor, insisted on repeating a grossly inflated statistic about mortality rates for the disease under "socialized medicine" in the United Kingdom.[28] Fact-checkers frequently trade stories of desperate or heedless candidates who see nothing to lose in repeating a debunked claim. They happily cite the now-infamous vow delivered by a Romney pollster as the candidate's prospects dimmed late in the 2012 race: "we're not going let our campaign be dictated by fact-checkers."[29] Although meant to question their objectivity, among fact-checkers, the line became shorthand for politicians' disregard for the truth. It only confirmed what they often say themselves: journalists will never force politicians to stop lying.[30] Four years later, the favored object for the same lesson became the campaign of Donald Trump. "In the 12 years of FactCheck.org's existence, we've never seen his match," that site wrote late in 2015, naming a "King of Whoppers" for the first time. "He stands out not only for the sheer number of his factually false claims, but also for his brazen refusals to admit error when proven wrong."[31]

The final section of this book takes up the question of what fact-checking is *for*. That question contains within it any number of other difficult questions: Who is the actual audience for fact-checking, and who do fact-checkers imagine they write for? What is an appropriate mission for this brand of journalism? What kinds of effects does fact-checking actually have in the world? Can fact checks be designed to have greater impact—and should they? These questions turn on the fact-checkers' relationships with three core constituencies: politicians, journalists, and the general public. Chapter 6 examines how fact-checkers relate to the public and to the press; their ties to the political world are the subject of the concluding chapter.

6

FACT-CHECKERS
AND THEIR PUBLICS

LIKE OTHER JOURNALISTS, FACT-CHECKERS WANT THEIR WORK TO make a difference in the world. They aspire to be relevant in major political debates and to have their verdicts cited by important people and believed by the general public. Every gathering of fact-checkers turns at some point to the question of whether this kind of journalism matters and how it might matter more. At London's global summit on fact-checking in 2014, the editor of the *Tampa Bay Times*, PolitiFact's parent newspaper, delivered a hopeful keynote address that underscored the nobility of the fact-checker's calling, "returning power to citizens who for too long have been at a serious disadvantage in the marketplace of political speech."[1] This invited the inevitable question: where are examples of fact checks actually having an impact, an Italian journalist wanted to know? American reporters began trading stories from the 2012 races. A few candidates seemed to abandon false claims once they were exposed. In Ohio, a Senate contender who earned a remarkable string of "False" and "Pants on Fire" rulings paid the price when voters rejected him, citing his record of dishonesty.[2] PolitiFact founder Bill Adair declared that fact-checkers needed to do a better job of recording such "anecdotes of impact":

We get asked this question a lot, I'm sure you all do, you know, "What fact checks have you done that really had impact?" . . . If you're [like] me, I'm a journalist, and so my inclination is just to go out and create more journalism, not to sing my own tune about, you know, what impact I had. And, well, we need to keep track of these because we *are* having a big impact.[3]

The question came up again six months later at a meeting of fact-checkers in Washington, DC, after the 2014 U.S. midterm elections. A series of panel discussions took up questions like why false advertising persisted despite the tremendous growth in fact-checking and what new formats or technologies might make this work more effective. At the end of the day, the event's organizer, longtime press critic and media analyst Tom Rosenstiel, argued that fact-checkers needed to be more willing to think about the real-world impact of their own work:

One of the things that is implicit here is, is there a theory of change? How are we impacting political discourse or voters? . . . I think to simply say, "I'm throwing rocks into the pond because that's my job," without any thought about what ripples does it create or not create, and are people throwing bigger rocks to wipe out my rocks—I mean, we're in a different world because we're not the only stimuli in people's news diet.[4]

But "throwing rocks into the pond" is a deliberate and deeply rooted professional stance in objective journalism. The question of their impact on politicians, on fellow reporters, and even on readers remains a fraught one for fact-checkers, no less than for their peers at conventional news outlets. For journalists, it's one thing to speak casually about the effect an article had once it was published. It is quite another to set out deliberately to modify people's beliefs or behavior. Fact-checkers seek to *inform* but not, at least formally, to persuade or to influence. When I asked Brooks Jackson of FactCheck .org whether fact-checking could "change the conversation" around important public issues, he demurred, falling back on a classic lesson of objective journalism: "What excites me is that the information we put out is getting wider dissemination. In terms of trying to change the conversation, I'm old school. I was always taught that you should report the story, not be a part of the story."[5]

This chapter explores the fact-checkers' relationships with the public and with the press, two vital constituencies for their work. These remain distinct audiences and will be treated separately. But it is important to recognize that the lines between them blur in the contemporary media environment, which turns everyday readers into a kind of communications medium while also making clearer than ever the ways that other reporters are a crucial audience for journalism. The daily routine of professional fact-checkers includes not just newswork but *media work*, designed to boost the impact of their stories and to manage the reactions they provoke. Professional fact-checkers need to write for an idealized, information-hungry citizenry—one free to disagree with their conclusions—to resolve the political and epistemological tension at the center of fact-checking. But this image of a truth-seeking democratic public clashes with the audience they encounter every day.

Other reporters are in some ways the most important audience for this new genre, and changing the culture of journalism is a defining if sometimes unacknowledged goal. The fact-checkers' unmistakable critique of conventional political reporting remains mostly implicit in their published work for two reasons: because fact-checkers' relevance and impact as niche outlets depends on their working ties to other news organizations and because operating as media (rather than political) critics would destabilize their own status as objective journalists. This account emphasizes the way in which objective status in journalism is grounded not only in particular newsroom practices but in a network of professional, organizational, and institutional relationships that reproduce journalistic authority across the field.

"The Way You Talk Is Not How Journalists Actually Think"

Fact-checking exposes the tensions implicit in the practice of objective journalism precisely because it flirts so openly with reformist ambitions and rhetoric. The possibility of making a difference by cleaning up public discourse leads inevitably to a new set of questions that are attractive to activists and social scientists but very awkward for journalists: How should fact checks be modified for maximum impact? If research shows they don't always convince the reader, how can they be made more persuasive? Why do politicians heed fact-checkers in some instances but not others? How can other journalists be encouraged to take up this style of reporting?

All of these questions came up at the fact-checking conference I helped to organize in Washington, DC, at the end of 2011.[6] The meeting included professional fact-checkers and other journalists as well as political scientists, communications scholars, policy advocates, and foundation officials involved in media and political reform. A constant motif was the incompatibility of the journalists' and the other participants' sense of what fact-checking is *for*. When the discussion turned to how journalists might better "shame" politicians into telling the truth, Michael Dobbs, the *Washington Post*'s original fact-checker, interjected:

> Can I respond very briefly to that? You're talking about all these sort of highfaluting missions for journalists. I mean, most journalists are rather more modest in their ambitions. We're not sort of talking about changing the world or changing political discourse. We're talking about, you know, just reporting things honestly and truly. It's a much more—the way you talk is not how journalists actually think.[7]

At another point the discussion focused on making fact checks more convincing to readers. Many experimental studies have shown that people prove surprisingly resistant to new information that cuts against their political views and may cling even more tightly to false beliefs after reading a correction, a so-called backfire effect.[8] In advance of the meeting, two political scientists prepared a report that summarized this research and suggested ways to make fact checks more persuasive (by avoiding confusing negations, using charts to convey facts, and so on).[9] In the discussion, these scholars were at pains to stress that well-educated and politically engaged readers— the sort who presumably visit fact-checking sites—are not necessarily more receptive to new information. On the contrary, as Brendan Nyhan explained, "those are precisely the folks who are very good at weeding out the information that contradicts their previous positions and coming up with reasons to stick to what they already believe."[10]

Journalists in the room seemed unfazed by the grim picture painted by research about their real-world influence, however. Glenn Kessler, the

Washington Post's current fact-checker, pointed to a "hunger" for this brand of explanatory journalism he noticed with his very first effort at fact-checking, covering a presidential debate in 1996: "The reader response was just amazing. I mean, they just loved it." PolitiFact's Bill Adair agreed. "I have a theory of American politics that's basically a pie with three slices," he explained, arguing that fact-checkers are a valuable resource for voters between the two political extremes.[11] Brooks Jackson suggested that journalists have long lived with the fact that some people will believe whatever they want to believe, regardless of the evidence. He gave the famous example of doomsday cults whose faith only grows stronger after the prophesied Armageddon fails to arrive.[12] "That's the human animal that we're up against," Jackson said, continuing: "So I have limited expectations of what we can accomplish. I think that it's good what we do, I'm glad to see there's more of it. I take it on faith that doing more of it will have a positive effect on democracy. I would love some evidence if that's true. If you have any that it's not, I'm not going to pay any attention to it."[13]

Although offered with a dose of humor, that response suggests a belief that journalists only serve democracy by being blind to the particular effects of their work. The problem of being persuasive troubles professional journalism's claim to objectivity, at least beyond the op-ed page. Fact-checkers don't want to be responsible for amplifying public distortions and have been receptive to research that helps to avoid this risk.[14] But they also don't want to be held responsible for persuading people to adopt a certain view. "We're not here to change people's minds, we're here to give voters the information they need," Angie Drobnic Holan, then PolitiFact's second in command, told me in an interview. "What we do has intrinsic value."[15] As seen in part 2 of this book, these journalists aim for definitive truth—and believe that on the whole they reach it—but also insist that readers are free to disagree with any of their conclusions. "I guess our goal is we don't want people to continue having misconceptions about things, but again, I'm not a propagandist, I am a journalist," Adair explained at a panel discussion in 2012.[16]

Fact-checkers likewise reject the responsibility to change political behavior, a role reserved for the democratic public to whom they address their work. During the same panel discussion, a journalist in the audience asked, "There has to be some sort of line where people know they're being watched and they just can't lie any more. Are you seeing any effect from that?" Adair gave the usual examples of public figures who pay attention to the fact-checkers and others who don't—including the surprise that Fox News host Bill O'Reilly once apologized after being called out by PolitiFact. But then he turned the question around:

> My goal is not to get politicians to stop lying. I am a journalist and my goal is to empower democracy. And then you, democracy, can decide what you want to do with the information I provide. You may decide that you agree with it and that you're going to hold this elected official account-able in ways and not vote for him or her or whatever, or you may decide in some cases you disagree. You might disagree about "Lie of the Year," you may disagree about any particular ruling we make. But my goal isn't to get politicians to stop lying. My goal is to give you the information you need to be a better citizen. And I think that's the role of the journal-ist. And when we get into this role of, well, we want them to stop lying, I think we sort of get out of the bounds of what is a journalist.[17]

Distancing remarks like these capture the effort to define the mission of fact-checking in a way appropriate to objective journalism. They elevate an informational model of citizenship, reflecting perfectly what sociologist Herb Gans calls U.S. journalism's "theory of democracy," centered on the idea that the data the news media provide to voters drives the democratic process.[18] Like investigative reporters, fact-checkers participate in an unusually naked way in public discourse. They contradict and endorse political speech rather than simply transmitting it to the public. Their work makes direct interven-tions that often provoke an immediate response from a public figure. But in terms of professional self-understanding, only a reasoning democratic public can make fact-checkers' work meaningful. "To be sure, fact-checkers do not necessarily expect to change [the] behavior of politicians," Glenn Kessler explained in an article about the global fact-checking movement for *Foreign Affairs*. "Instead, their goal is to educate citizens about critical policy issues. If people are better informed, the thinking goes, they will make better choices."[19]

At the same time, these distancing remarks belie a powerful countervail-ing desire to be relevant, to matter, to make a difference. Fact-checkers want to be trusted by readers and by fellow journalists, and respected or even feared by the politicians they cover. Like other journalists (and like doctors, college professors, restaurant workers, and so on) they understand their public in multiple and sometimes contradictory ways. For fact-checkers, moving across these different registers is a way to respond to the daily exigencies and instrumental demands of the job while maintaining the formal distance their practice of objectivity requires.

The Audience for Fact-Checking

Like many journalists today, fact-checkers experience their audience most immediately in the form of online traffic statistics and a daily torrent of e-mails and comments. It is a well-established trope in newsroom research that reporters historically have known, and cared to know, surprisingly little about their readers and viewers. Gans observed of the elite journalists he studied at CBS, NBC, *Time*, and *Newsweek* in the 1970s, "I was surprised to find . . . that they had little knowledge about the actual audience and rejected feedback from it."[20] Layers of administration shielded journalists from audience information and feedback, such as letters of complaint. Meanwhile, reporters and editors found it useful to imagine an abstract public of democratic citizens—what Gans called an "audience image"—that was presumed to share their class and educational background and to need the information they provided.

Exactly how much the accuracy of that picture has improved remains open to question.[21] But there is no doubt that journalists today have much more routine exposure to feedback from, and information about, their audience than was the case two decades ago.[22] Even reporters low on the masthead commonly know how well their site is doing overall and which articles are drawing the most interest. Although policies about sharing "metrics" or "analytics" internally still vary, such data is available from multiple sources and highly contagious in the newsroom.[23] Major news sites display their own index of which pieces are being viewed, e-mailed, tweeted, or blogged about the most. And of course journalists are avid media users who can see what people are saying about their work online. It would be difficult for reporters to operate in the isolation from their audience that was typical through the last century.

Fact-checkers are no exception. They closely follow the traces their work leaves across the digital media landscape. And yet they remain no less invested in an idealized audience image than earlier generations of journalists. (This echoes a wider finding that "dominant occupational values" continue to guide news judgment even in the face of contradictory information about what audiences prefer.)[24] Fact-checkers address their audience in very different ways depending on the context: as an abstract public of informed citizens making democratic choices but also as online traffic that ebbs and flows in response to their work and as a rabid, partisan "crowd" that is a crucial vector in the spread of political misinformation.

Media Work: Promoting Stories and Cultivating Attention Online

The three elite fact-checking organizations are awash in information about their audience. Top editors always know which stories are "performing" on any given day. In interviews, they volunteered statistics like their typical traffic figures, the number of people on their mailing lists (tens of thousands), and the amount of e-mail they receive (hundreds and sometimes thousands of messages each week). During my fieldwork, FactCheck.org used Google Analytics to measure activity on its site, while PolitiFact and the *Washington Post*'s Fact Checker received daily traffic reports from Omniture. At PolitiFact I was shown this report, which tabulated hour-by-hour traffic to the site as a whole as well as the top twenty-five articles by page views, unique visitors, and average time spent. The report also showed how well the site was doing in the twenty-five largest U.S. metro areas, the top "referring domains," and the search keywords bringing traffic in.[25] This information was hardly kept secret. At least once a day during my visits, office conversation turned to site performance: which fact checks were being tweeted or blogged about and by whom, how well the various state PolitiFact sites were doing, and whether it was a "good traffic day" or a "good traffic week" for PolitiFact overall.[26]

Editors and reporters not only have access to this information, they develop a sense for the ebbs and flows of online attention, and actively try to shape it in order to attract new readers and make overall traffic as high and consistent as possible. In this respect the audience becomes an instrumental traffic-driving resource. Only sizable numbers of people can move the needle of traffic statistics at the major fact-checking sites, which receive millions of page views and hundreds of thousands of unique visitors per month. But overall traffic is taken to be a function of interest from a much smaller circle of influence, reflected in Twitter activity, inbound links from well-read blogs and news sites, and interviews or citations on major broadcast networks, sometimes called "media hits." In my observation, fact-checkers pay close attention to these various signs of digital attention and have a finely honed feeling for the actual or potential "buzz" around particular stories. Day to day, this is the most convenient proxy for their success or impact as journalists.

Cultivating attention and traffic begins with writing headlines and tags that perform well on search engines. "We write headlines for one reader—Google," Bill Adair told a class of journalism students. This acts as a brake on cleverness or puns; search-engine optimization requires first of all clear and descriptive headlines using mostly proper nouns. (Only FactCheck.org deviates from this formula, sometimes running clever headlines such as "Cheney's Tortured Logic.") Searches programmed into Twitter and Google show who in the media and political world is talking about which items. Editors try to release new fact checks in a way that will drive consistent traffic to their sites; if two items are ready at the same time, one may be posted and promoted later in the day in order to spread traffic out, giving each item the chance to generate as much buzz as possible. Fact-checkers see high-profile events, like debates and major speeches, as a chance to draw in new readers and build their regular audience. As noted in chapter 3, the sites often bring together multiple fact checks under a topical story keyed to current events (and may post a story "shell" before the event even takes place, to rank more highly on Google).[27]

Drawing audiences also means promoting new articles by e-mail and on social media. Reporters and editors at the three fact-checking outlets promote their work (and sometimes that of their rivals) assiduously on Facebook and Twitter. Twitter especially is seen as a primary traffic driver; new items go out on each site's official Twitter account and under reporters' individual Twitter handles. A surprising amount of thought goes into devising a smart approach to social media, a topic that claimed a lively panel at the 2014 meeting of fact-checkers from around the world. Social media are also a frequent topic of office conversation and in training sessions for new fact-checkers. While I was at PolitiFact, an editor lamented that staff had forgotten to tweet a promising fact check, meaning the site missed out on "four hours of prime traffic time." Later in the day, the staff convened to develop a consistent strat-egy for "who is tweeting when," discussing questions like the best time of day to tweet a new item, how often to retweet it, and whether the process could be automated. One fact-checker felt uncomfortable with such online self-promotion. But the consensus was that competition in the fact-checking landscape made Twitter all the more important for PolitiFact and that, in general, social media had become more valuable than search engines in driv-ing traffic.[28]

This routine promotional labor by journalists can be called "media work" to distinguish it from the traditional newswork of reporting, writing, and editing stories.[29] Media work appears to be increasingly basic to the profes-sion and figures prominently in the relationship between fact-checkers and other journalists, discussed later in this chapter. However, its importance of-ten goes unacknowledged, and its success relies on informal organizational resources and a degree of tacit knowledge.[30] Media work online collapses together the distinct audiences for fact-checking. Politicians, journalists, ac-ademics, bloggers, and everyday readers all become potential drivers of atten-tion and interest. All become a kind of media. Likewise, the detailed traffic measurements afforded by online publishing, at least as they are commonly used and discussed, do little to distinguish between these audiences.

Real and Imagined Audiences

Despite the intense attention they receive, audience metrics and traffic sta-tistics do not seem to color the fact-checkers' editorial sense of whom they are writing for. They work with an abstract image of their democratic public in mind. The ideal reader of the fact-checking sites seeks to stay informed about public issues but lacks the time or the expertise to sort through all of the competing claims. The ideal reader wants to make well-reasoned choices on election day but is overwhelmed by a torrent of political misinformation. Most of all, the ideal reader may have political preferences but will not ig-nore factual information that cuts against those preferences.[31]

The fact-checkers receive hundreds of reader e-mails every week and of-ten highlight the few that bear out that image. "What I love are the letters I get from readers—and it comes once, twice, three times a week—from read-ers that say, you know, 'I was really thinking this, but you've convinced me otherwise,'" the *Washington Post*'s Glenn Kessler said at a fact-checking conference. FactCheck.org's Brooks Jackson agreed:

> I know there are people who are genuinely . . . perplexed by all of the political malarkey that they hear, especially when candidates contradict each other. They're looking for a trusted source of information, and those are the ones we're here for. And sometimes we even get messages from people, like a guy will say, "Well I'm a Democrat, but I appreciate what you do because I want to know when my guys are lying to me." And there are people out there like that.[32]

This image of an engaged but politically inexpert public is clearly reflected in the journalism the fact-checkers produce. Although their tone of voice differs somewhat, all three outlets write for a lay public. They strive to cut through technical jargon and political rhetoric and to present complex issues in terms the everyday reader can understand. "There was a hunger that I noticed from readers for basic information," Kessler has said. "Because the problem is, politicians speak in code."[33] The fact-checkers see themselves as providing the substantive coverage of issues that voters need—even if they don't always realize it—and which conventional "horse race" stories fail to deliver. As PolitiFact's Bill Adair told an interviewer:

> I would say one other flaw [of conventional reporting] is that there's too much emphasis on the politics, on who's up and who's down, who's winning and who's losing and not enough on the substance of what the things would really mean for voters. PolitiFact is really a creative way of covering issues and public policy. I think of it like getting people to eat their vegetables. They don't want to eat their vegetables but if you can make the vegetables tasty they will eat them.[34]

In keeping with this "eat your vegetables" approach, PolitiFact trainees were instructed that the site prizes "fresh, clear, writing." "And the key word there is clear," an editor stressed. "We put a lot of emphasis in PolitiFact on clarity. It's not a place for flowery anecdotal leads." As noted in chapter 3, editors sometimes invoke a hypothetical middle-income reader far from the Beltway, "Mabel," to choose among possible stories. Fact-checkers also try to inject humor into their work. This is especially true at PolitiFact, which, as the Truth-O-Meter training manual instructs, has a slightly irreverent voice that "doesn't take this stuff too seriously" and tries to make politics accessible to people who aren't "political junkies."[35] (For instance, one "birther" fact check began this way: "With all this health care debate dominating our time for the last few weeks, can we please get back to the issues that matter? Like, what's up with Obama's Kenyan birth certificate?"[36]) But the public always gets to be in on the joke. The fact-checking sites avoid the insider language and snarky humor of professional media or political hubs such as Gawker and Politico.

Most of their actual audience, however, does not match the idealized reader-image fact-checkers cater to. Even more than peers at traditional news outlets, these journalists are inundated in hostile and sometimes unhinged communication from their readers. This is a theme fact-checkers bring up often in private conversation and at public forums; it is an aspect of the job every new fact-checker has to get used to and part of the camaraderie that binds them together. On the first day of their training, FactCheck.org interns learned how to respond to the roughly two hundred e-mails the group receives every day. An editor urged them to be respectful no matter how ridiculous the question—everyone tittered at the more outlandish examples— and warned about partisans looking to pick a fight: "Don't engage in any back and forth. You can just send [the information] along. If they say, 'You're full of it,' or 'I don't believe it,' just let it go. It's just not worth it."[37]

Likewise, trainees at PolitiFact learned that they would need a thick skin to do this kind of work. After my PolitiFact item on Glenn Beck began to draw personal e-mail from unhappy readers, I was encouraged to reply to polite objections but not "hate mail" and to remember that anything written in an e-mail response might be used against me. I remarked on how unsettling direct criticism can feel. "That's the reaction the first thousand times," I was told; soon one learns to scan for factual objections and ignore the vitriol. FactCheck.org and PolitiFact regularly publish selections from reader e-mail, including some scathing assessments of their work, balanced to show that both liberal and conservative readers find fault with them. However, only the Fact Checker allows readers to post comments directly on published articles (a standard feature of the *Washington Post* website). FactCheck .org and PolitiFact relegate comments to their Facebook pages. One reason for this is that Facebook does not permit anonymity, which may promote more civil discourse. Even so, I was told, partisans dominate the comments and as a result the discussion is not very worthwhile.[38]

Day in and day out, these patterns of public reaction become routine and predictable. Fact-checkers develop a strong sense for the charged partisan dynamics of online political discourse. They anticipate which pieces will produce an unusually furious reaction from readers on the left or the right, especially once a well-known pundit takes note. (At both PolitiFact and FactCheck.org I heard that a few unkind words from liberal MSNBC host Rachel Maddow will precipitate a flood of angry e-mails from what one editor called the "sheep" who blindly follow her.[39]) Angry letters to journalists are hardly a new phenomenon, of course.[40] Online, however, this kind of feedback is more immediate, more voluminous, and more visible—to journalists and to the rest of their audience. Ironically, an audience of rabid partisans is probably preferable, in terms of site performance, to the thoughtful information-seekers fact-checkers like to envision. However, I did not hear these journalists talk about controversies over fact-checking instrumentally, as a source of traffic. On the contrary, fact-checkers gave me the clear impression of wishing their work would not be received so polemically.

"The Crowd Is the Extremists"

This predictable, patterned hostility only reinforces the fact-checkers' anchoring conviction that public discourse is distorted by partisan extremism on "both sides" of the spectrum. It also gives them a mixed view of their audience's role as a journalistic resource.[41] All three elite outlets emphasize the value readers offer in suggesting items to be checked and in critiquing their work. "I get thousands of letters every day from readers loving or hating what I write, and actually I learn a lot from some of those readers who make very thoughtful responses to what I've written, and it informs my thinking," Glenn Kessler said in a radio interview.[42] As noted earlier, PolitiFact reconfigured the Truth-O-Meter (changing "Barely True" to "Mostly False") based on public feedback and in a handful of cases has altered rulings after readers objected: "when enough people tell you you're wrong, sometimes it's not partisan," I was told. Editors have discussed adding a feature that would let readers rate claims themselves, and publishing the result alongside the official Truth-O-Meter ruling. FactCheck.org also solicits story ideas and comments from readers and dedicates real effort to responding to reader queries. Asked by a visiting journalist whether fact-checking can be "crowd-sourced," an editor replied that readers sometimes spot factual errors in FactCheck.org's work and said a major project for the coming year was to increase public involvement in the site.[43]

Still, although fact-checkers sometimes gesture toward the rhetoric of crowd-sourcing, in my observation they were very skeptical of the idea that this work could be reliably performed by some self-organizing online public. The challenge of trying to institutionalize the reader's role in fact-checking is to keep partisan impulses at bay, fact-checkers say. In the words of Michael Dobbs, the *Washington Post*'s original fact-checker, "readers are an extraordinary source of knowledge and good sense, if we can find ways to showcase real expertise, rather than inciting more partisan mudslinging."[44] Or, as I heard at PolitiFact, "you need enough of a crowd to overwhelm the partisanship."[45] While several overseas sites rely on some form of crowd-sourcing, the most ambitious U.S. effort in this vein was NewsTrust's "Truthsquad," a short-lived pilot program launched in mid-2010 with foundation support. Truthsquad let readers rate claims on a slider from "True" to "False" and tabulated the results.[46] I made a point of asking professional fact-checkers what they thought of the venture. Although FactCheck.org was an official partner, Brooks Jackson doubted the effort held promise for real fact-checking: "I wish there were a way to harness crowd-sourcing to do actual fact-checking, but it's tough. You don't determine facts by voting on them, and at its heart that's what crowd-sourcing is."[47] PolitiFact's Bill Adair was equally skeptical:

It's an intriguing idea, and I'm open to it, but so far I haven't seen that the crowd is willing to do all that homework. . . . There are a lot of nuances in this stuff. . . . At this point I just think professional journalists do the best fact-checking. And the problem with the crowd in politics is it's just so polarized, you don't get neutral people coming to this. The crowd is the extremists.[48]

It is easy to see these responses as boundary-drawing by members of a profession under siege. But the skepticism about crowd-sourcing underscores a much deeper ambivalence regarding new media technologies and their effect on public discourse. At lunch with one of PolitiFact's fact-checkers, I asked for an opinion about the fairly meteoric rise of political fact-checking—why now? Does the Internet have something to do with it? Yes, came the immediate answer: the network has made it easier than ever for lies and distortions to spread unchecked and unchallenged. This is the default view among professional fact-checkers, who recognize that the Internet makes their work possible but also insist that it makes that work necessary. "That's the paradox of new media," Adair told a class of journalism students. "It's easier than ever to get unbiased facts, but people don't."[49]

Fact-checkers do celebrate the "Internet revolution" for greatly easing access to original data and research.[50] But these reporters openly lament the decline of journalism's "gatekeeper" status, which media and political reformers so often paint as a positive development. As Adair explained to one interviewer, "in the 1960s in any country there were a few television networks and probably some large newspapers and they were the filters that decided what information people needed to read or to hear." He continued:

> What's happened in the internet age is that those filters, the legacy media, are not as important any more because you may get information from your newspaper or your television network still, but you probably also get information from blogs and internet news sources and even emails that are forwarded to you by your crazy uncle who has various conspiracy theories. And so it's important for us as journalists, particularly as fact checkers, to realize the filter is gone.[51]

To fact-checkers, this shift—"the filter is gone"—offers the most urgent rationale for their new genre. In a 2007 book about political misinformation, Brooks Jackson and Kathleen Hall Jamieson emphasized the harmful impact of media-system changes on public discourse and understanding, pointing to cable news as well as the Internet—a "potent new weapon of deception."[52] In an interview, Jackson gave me the example of the controversy over President Obama's birth certificate; two decades ago journalists would not have had to debunk such absurd rumors, which could be denied publicity altogether. "It used to be that professional reporters and editors served a gatekeeper function," he explained:

Those days are gone and now every human being on the planet practically is subjected to all the wild tips, leads, rumors, malicious lies and bullshit that we used to as journalists sort out and keep out of the public discourse. . . . There is no gatekeeping function any more because there are no gates, there are no fences. There's just a constant wash of information, and mostly misinformation.[53]

In the existential narrative of the fact-checking movement, a rising tide of digital-age misinformation has prompted a shift in journalism's basic orientation toward the political sphere. No longer able to play the role of deciding what's news, reporters must take up the trickier task of deciding what's true. But it is important to recognize that their ambivalence toward the Internet is really ambivalence toward the public that animates the network, an often hostile and unreasoning audience that reporters know more intimately than ever. This makes it all the more striking that, in editorial discussions and in their published work, fact-checkers hew so closely to the idealized audience of democratic citizens envisioned by traditional journalistic values.

Fact-Checkers and Other Journalists

Fact-checkers are very reluctant press critics. Consider "Muffingate," a minor scandal that occupied the national news media for a week in the fall of 2011: among other instances of "extravagant spending," the U.S. Justice Department was billed $16 for every muffin served to attendees at a law enforcement conference in a Washington hotel, according to a report by the department's inspector general. Politicians and pundits seized on the damning statistic, as did news outlets across the country. One analysis found that in the eight days after the report came out, 223 stories mentioned "$16 muffins" or some variation; more than 4 out of 5 repeated the figure uncritically, with no effort to challenge or explain it.[54] The overpriced pastries offered an irresistible lead for newspaper reports. A page-one article in the *Washington Post* opened this way:

Where does a muffin cost more than $16?
At a government conference, it turns out.
They may run just over $2 at your average coffee shop, but the Justice Department paid seven to eight times as much at a gathering it held at

the Capital Hilton in Washington. And on Tuesday, the muffins seemed well on their way to joining the Pentagon's $600 toilet seat as symbols of wasteful spending.[55]

The story was, of course, "too good to be true," as a sharply worded critique by the *Post*'s own ombudsman noted the following week. The inspector general's report did cite the $16 figure several times, based on the way the hotel itemized expenses. But a closer reading—or "a visit to the Capital Hilton's restaurant, which is a few hundred feet from The Post"—would have shown the bill covered more than muffins.[56] In fact the government had spent a fairly thrifty $15 per person per day on food, which included a continental breakfast of fruit and pastries, an afternoon snack, and coffee and other beverages. Both the hotel chain and the Justice Department corrected the record within a few days.

In this case, newspaper and TV reporters did at least as much as politicians to popularize the distorted figure. Critiques quickly appeared in outlets from Media Matters to the *Wall Street Journal*, taking journalists to task for failing to report the story thoroughly or to correct it prominently once new information came to light.[57] PolitiFact also analyzed the $16 muffin claim, as repeated by conservative pundit Bill O'Reilly on Jon Stewart's *Daily Show*. O'Reilly earned a "Mostly False." PolitiFact linked to stern assessments of journalism's role in the affair, but itself offered only the mildest rebuke: "Media reports summarized the inspector general's overall negative findings, but couldn't resist starting with the $16 muffin. In fairness, it was a verbatim quote from the report."[58]

Among the elite fact-checking outlets, that counts as an unusually direct bit of press criticism. Professional fact-checkers have a fascinating and conflicted relationship with their fellow journalists. Fact-checking is assembled from the news, fills absences in the news, and arguably has its biggest impact through the news. Fact-checkers cite other journalists constantly and strive to be cited and quoted by them. The genre offers a strikingly clear example of journalism's turn toward collaboration between news organizations.[59] At the same time, the existence of dedicated fact-checking outlets stands as an indictment of the failures conventional political reporting. A reformist critique of their own profession surfaces constantly in the fact-checker's daily work and, sometimes, in broad public remarks. But this critique remains at best implicit in their published articles.

"This Is What We Should Have Been Doing All Along"

A common refrain when fact-checkers have to explain what they do, whether in casual conversation or a formal interview, is that it's what every good reporter should be doing. I heard this from nearly every fact-checker I spoke to, but moments of controversy can put a sharper edge on the critique. In an NPR interview, Bill Adair accounted for the widespread backlash against PolitiFact's 2011 "Lie of the Year" selection this way:

> We have disrupted the protocol in a lot of ways. We have come in and said we're not just going to pass along what the politicians are saying any-more. . . . That has shaken the establishment. I think people are not accustomed to the press doing this, and I think that's a reflection that the press has been, has fallen down on the job. *This is what we should have been doing all along.*[60]

As reviewed in chapter 2, fact-checkers often describe their genre as a re-sponse to the failures of traditional journalism. Asked this question at a conference, the founders of the three elite fact-checking sites all agreed; Brooks Jackson called himself a "recovering 'he said, she said' reporter," while Adair insisted that PolitiFact "grew out of my own guilt."[61] Certain profes-sional debacles come up over and over in the wider fact-checking milieu, like the failure to challenge White House claims before the 2003 invasion of Iraq.[62] "I think the media really abdicated its role in the early part of this decade, in the run-up to the war in Iraq," ABC News correspondent Jake Tap-per told Stephen Colbert when he and Adair appeared on the *Colbert Report* to announce a new partnership between PolitiFact and ABC's *This Week*.[63] Fact-checkers see themselves as leading by the example of a reporting practice they consider more demanding, more honest, and truer to the profession's founding ideals. As Michael Dobbs has written:

> In suggesting a "Fact Checker" feature to the editors of the *Washington Post* in the summer of 2007, I was motivated in large part by a sense that Washington reporting had strayed away from the truth-seeking tradi-tion. While there is a place for horse race reporting . . . I felt that we had been snookered by the political class into ignoring, or at least playing

down, larger, more important questions. . . . Truth-seeking and truth-telling were relegated to the sidelines of journalism, rather than assuming their rightful place, at the center.[64]

This sense of mission was palpable during my visits to FactCheck.org and PolitiFact. I heard criticisms of "he said, she said" reporting and "horse race" coverage not just from the founders of these organizations but also from almost everyone on staff, even part-time employees. PolitiFact's sales pitch to potential franchisees, who pay tens of thousands of dollars to license the group's methodology, was fairly bold in inviting these news organizations to embrace a higher journalistic standard than they currently practice. The Truth-O-Meter training manual echoed this sense of a higher calling: "The bar is higher for PolitiFact stories than for many other stories we publish in the newspaper. For a typical newspaper story, we lay out the facts on each side and let readers decide how they feel. But for PolitiFact, we dig deeper, examine more sources and draw a conclusion about what's right."[65]

As noted, fact-checkers constantly emphasize that their genre requires more time and effort than the typical campaign story. They sometimes excuse the absence of fact-checking in routine coverage as a matter of meeting tight deadlines and writing for fit. "When I was a political reporter . . . doing the day-to-day campaign coverage . . . I would try to fact-check," Glenn Kessler has explained. "But often I didn't have enough space or that was cut for space, because . . . the details got a little too complicated for the narrative."[66] In an interview, CNN's resident media critic asked Bill Adair why more newspapers don't do fact-checking. "It takes a lot of resources, it takes a real commitment," Adair responded. "They have to be willing to commit reporters and editors to journalism that takes longer, because this is not something that you can do quickly."[67]

Fact-checkers sometimes offer a more critical account, though, which holds that political reporters are afraid to contradict officials for fear of losing "access." "Some reporters favor access over accuracy," FactCheck.org's Brooks Jackson told me bluntly.[68] With this in mind, PolitiFact encourages its state partners to dedicate a number of reporters to fact-checking full time rather than having a larger pool rotate in from other beats. The fear is that journalists who need to be on good terms with political figures will be afraid to produce hard-hitting Truth-O-Meter items. "Fact-checking journalism is the most liberating journalism because you never care about access," Adair told me. He continued:

> You hope the beat reporter would have no more reluctance [to challenge an official's facts] than they would to say the mayor got a DUI, or whatever. And yet I just think it's inherent. . . . What an official holds over a beat reporter is that they can cut off that reporter's access if they want. And I never have to worry about that. To the extent there's any resistance to this idea that we should be calling [politicians] out, I think often it comes from beat reporters.[69]

Despite this well-developed critique, the major fact-checking outlets take great care not to sound like media critics in their journalism. Most of the statements fact-checkers investigate appeared first in a news report. Fact-checkers cite those sources but almost never fault them for certifying a deceptive claim. Remarkably, this holds even when a falsehood originated in flawed or sensationalistic reporting. One example came up during a training session at PolitiFact: the site had given a "Pants on Fire" to Florida Democrats for a press release claiming the state's Republican attorney general said the subprime mortgage crisis was not "a big deal."[70] As the analysis made clear, the error resulted from accurately quoting a local newspaper report that mistakenly put someone else's words in the mouth of the attorney general. "The transcript differs with the news account in two critical ways," the item noted mildly. Despite the newspaper's blunder, Democrats received PolitiFact's worst rating.

Similarly, PolitiFact and FactCheck.org have several times refuted the claim that Phoenix is a global kidnapping capital, repeated by Sen. John McCain, among others.[71] The fact-checkers both traced the origin of this dubious statistic to an ABC News segment that the network has, despite multiple requests, never substantiated. They noted that the figure had been widely repeated in newspaper and TV reports. But they reserved their criticism for political figures. "Keeping up with this one is a bit like playing Whac-A-Mole. You knock down one politician for saying it, and another one pops up saying it somewhere else," PolitiFact wrote.[72] As in the "Muffingate" controversy, though, news organizations did as much as politicians to propagate the sensational statistic. "The media played a game of Whisper Down The Lane, and it led to this insane distortion that Phoenix was the number-two place in the world to get yourself kidnapped," argued a critic at the *Huffington Post*.[73]

Being seen to stray into the terrain of media criticism clearly makes fact-checkers uncomfortable. In his first year as the *Washington Post*'s fact-checker, Glenn Kessler weighed in on a debate about whether Vice President Joe Biden had likened Tea Party activists to "terrorists" during closed-door negotiations over raising the U.S. debt ceiling. The accusation originated in a report on the Washington news site Politico, and Kessler took issue with "dubious" reporting in that piece and in others that repeated the claim, which the vice president denied.[74] Politico responded harshly: "Wait a second. Either he said it, or he didn't. That's the fact to check here. The way to check it is to report it out, not to attack the people who did report it out."[75] In a year-in-review article, Kessler called his own piece a "clunker" and all but apologized to Politico and to his readers: *"We never intended to be journalism critics, and we will try to keep our focus on the politicians in this election season."*[76]

That response points to one reason for the fact-checkers' reluctance, in their published work, to criticize other news organizations. Professional journalism draws a bright line between news reporting and media criticism, and the fact-checkers place themselves squarely in the former camp. "The point is to get the truth out," a star intern at FactCheck.org told me; to tweak other reporters would be "gossipy" and "petty." At PolitiFact, the case of Florida's Democrats being led into a "Pants on Fire" by a faulty newspaper article was used during a training session to make the point that fact-checkers should always go back to the original transcript. "The paper was incorrect," an editor stressed. And did PolitiFact call out the reporting error, one trainee wanted to know? "No, because we weren't fact-checking the paper," came the response: "I don't even know of the paper is aware of this. And sometimes I wrestle with this. Like, how much do I want to call up my colleagues in the news media and say, 'Hey, you screwed this up?' That's not what I do. *I'm not here to correct the news press.*"[77]

Criticizing their peers in the press is awkward and cuts against the fact-checkers' sense of their own place in journalism's truth-seeking tradition. These organizations wear their reporting honors proudly.[78] They were founded by veteran journalists with long reporting careers and deep professional networks. They are staffed by experienced political reporters who attend exclusive events like the White House Correspondents' Dinner. They see themselves as standard-bearers for objectivity—nothing like the partisan media watchdogs who are the most vocal press critics in U.S. political discourse. As noted in chapter 1, media criticism mostly comes with a political taint in the fact-checking world.

Media Work: Building Ties to Other Newsrooms

Professional fact-checking outlets operate in a kind of symbiosis with the conventional news organizations who so often promote their work. Fact-checkers acknowledge this part of the job but often try to put it in perspective. Both Brooks Jackson and Bill Adair told me that being cited and interviewed by other outlets is not a primary objective.[79] "I'm still a journalist first, my goal is to do great journalism," Adair said. "It's nice if it gets picked up and mentioned on network television or in the *New York Times*, and that happens a lot, but I don't ever think of that as our goal." The day-to-day reality is more complicated, though. In my observation, "hits" in high-profile media outlets were a vital source of validation that fact-checking matters—as when the *Times*, in a profile of Minnesota's Michele Bachmann, dedicated long sidebar to her abysmal performance on the Truth-O-Meter. At a training session for new fact-checkers, an editor pointed to that coverage to show how PolitiFact's work mattered in the campaigns: "This is valuable. This is important. We accurately captured that she had a real problem with accuracy."[80] Such cases came up often at both PolitiFact and FactCheck.org. Both sites often post articles alerting their readers to interviews or citations in prominent media venues.[81] Attention from major media outlets helps to draw bigger audiences, and fact-checkers often note traffic spikes after a major media "hit."[82] But it also brings greater professional recognition, shows the acceptance of fact-checking as a legitimate form of journalism, and offers tangible evidence that it can have a meaningful impact on public affairs.

At an organizational level, substantial work and attention go into the fact-checkers' relationships with other media outlets. Fact-checking as a genre adapts happily to—and is arguably a product of—professional journalism's turn toward collaboration and partnership between newsrooms and across media platforms.[83] PolitiFact's unusual franchise model illustrates this dramatically. The licensing contracts with state media partners cover syndication and revenue sharing but also training in a new journalistic methodology. Remarkably, these partnerships subject reporters in one newsroom to the editorial standards of editors working for another company, in a separate newsroom, in a different city.[84] Fact-checking sites also strike formal and informal alliances with a shifting array of news outlets in print, broadcast, and online. The appeal of the new genre as a convenient source of political news programming became clear as soon as FactCheck.org went live to cover the 2004 presidential race. Right away, media outlets began citing the group's work and inviting Brooks Jackson on the air to deliver pithy assessments of campaign claims. Jackson gave on-air fact checks dozens of times during that race, appearing on NPR, CNN, NBC, ABC, and PBS, among other venues. When they launched in 2007, PolitiFact and the *Washington Post*'s Fact Checker quickly joined the media circuit; Bill Adair was especially ubiquitous, making more than two hundred on-air guest appearances during PolitiFact's first year alone.[85] Journalists lower on the masthead at both FactCheck.org and PolitiFact (including the latter's state franchises) are also called on by newspapers and broadcast outlets, though not as often.[86]

These ad hoc relationships may yield longer-term distribution agreements, often pegged to an election season. Thus, in 2012, FactCheck.org coproduced weekly fact-checking segments on WCBS radio—called "FactCheck Friday"— and with a network of NBC television stations. (An NBC producer worked on-site at FactCheck.org's headquarters in the Annenberg Center to create the highly polished video segments.) The site allows its work to be reproduced free of charge and has struck informal agreements with a range of print and online news outlets, including *USA Today*, the *Philadelphia Inquirer*, *Huffington Post*, and *Yahoo News*. In an interview, the site's incoming director, Eugene Kiely, emphasized that expanding such partnerships is a priority.[87] Although based at a high-circulation national newspaper, the *Washington Post*'s Glenn Kessler has also pursued media engagements avidly. During the 2012 races Kessler offered on-air fact checks on a range of networks, from PBS and NPR to MSNBC and Fox; with 2016 in view, a goal was to establish a "regular gig" for that election cycle.[88]

PolitiFact has set the pace in media partnerships. In 2010, the year it launched its network of state media franchises, the site also joined with ABC's *This Week* to package weekly fact checks of the show's guests. (The results appeared on Wednesdays, promoted by both sites.) For the 2012 presidential races, PolitiFact produced an election-coverage feature with NPR called "Message Machine" and at different points had agreements with both CNN and MSNBC, where its fact-checkers appeared scores of times during election season. The organization has also partnered with local TV stations, and in 2012 and 2014 Hearst Television paid to carry PolitiFact segments on local affiliates around the country. PunditFact began seeking similar distribution deals as soon as it launched; media visibility is one of the metrics used by the site's nonprofit backers to gage its success. In 2014 PunditFact struck a deal for its wrap-ups of the Sunday political shows to appear each week on the *Daily Beast*, which pays a fee for the stories. However, the focus on media figures and outlets—PunditFact keeps running "scorecards" of the five major TV news networks—may limit the site's appeal to potential partners.[89]

The appeal of fact-checking for broadcast outlets is particularly striking. "The Truth-O-Meter makes for great television because it is both lively and substantive," Adair told a TV industry reporter.[90] Fact-checking also makes "great television" because it is timely programming that, when lifted from a dedicated site, is very inexpensive to produce. Typically, no money changes hands in deals with broadcast outlets; the media outlet gains material to fill the daily news hole while fact-checkers win a wider audience for themselves and for the genre.[91] "Being stolen or plagiarized is fine with us," Brooks Jackson told me.[92] From the start, relying on material from dedicated fact-checkers helped other newsrooms to embrace the practice. At a 2007 conference a political reporter for San Francisco's KGO-TV joked about how his station began running fact checks during the 2004 presidential race: "What we were doing was ripping off FactCheck.org. . . . We got Brooks to go to the ABC bureau and do an interview with us and explain to us what he was doing and get him to agree to let us take his stories, basically, and put them on the air."[93]

The fact-checkers produce a kind of journalism that wedges very neatly into the modular programming economy of radio and television news, still the primary source of news for most Americans.[94] Published fact checks assemble easily into three- to five-minute segments for either live broadcasts or edited, magazine-style pieces. These segments have a highly standardized format, dictated by the need to be balanced. Most run about four minutes and include three or four distinct fact checks, challenging both contenders in an electoral race, or testing claims from several candidates in a primary debate, for instance. The basic narrative and the research to support it have been supplied by the fact-checking site; all that's needed is to drop in video or audio clips of politicians making claims. An interview with one of the professional fact-checkers provides context, often in live banter with the host that moves the segment from one claim the next. (See figure 6.1.)

Observing some of the behind-the-scenes work involved in arranging and executing these media appearances only reinforced how well adapted the genre is to today's media landscape. Broadcast fact-checking segments come together very quickly. One case I witnessed at PolitiFact yielded a five-minute live interview with Adair on MSNBC's *Daily Rundown* pegged to ongoing budget debates in Washington. A brief e-mail exchange just the day before the interview decided the three Truth-O-Meter items to be featured, on statements by President Obama, House Speaker John Boehner, and presidential contender Donald Trump. The TV network produced a simple, one-page outline listing, in the order they would be discussed, the three speakers, the exact wording of their claims, and PolitiFact's ruling in each case. This was shared with PolitiFact to make sure the details were accurate and then used to assemble the graphical elements that would be layered on-screen during Adair's appearance. "We're going to get to the bottom of 'numberpalooza' with Bill Adair," host Chuck Todd said to open the interview. As the segment ran, text overlays highlighted the statements being questioned, and an animated Truth-O-Meter—accompanied by a loud buzzer for "False" rulings and siren for "Pants on Fire"—registered each verdict as Adair delivered it. "The Truth-O-Meter is equal opportunity, if nothing else," cohost Savannah Guthrie intoned to mark the transition from the president to his Republican antagonists.[95]

As noted earlier, this kind of media work depends greatly on informal resources—especially personal relationships with other media professionals—and on tacit knowledge.[96] Media work by fact-checkers and other journalists involves know-how that usually is not formally seen as part of the job. No page in the Truth-O-Meter training manual deals with giving a good TV interview, choosing an appropriate media partner, or weathering the outrage over a controversial fact check. But these skills, perhaps always more relevant to journalism than has been acknowledged, become increasingly important in a world characterized by freelancing, by cross-media partnerships, and by specialized news organizations that rely on other outlets to

FIGURE 6.1 Fact-checking articles translate easily into three- to five-minute broadcast segments. Here PolitiFact's Bill Adair visits CNN to check several claims from a 2011 primary debate; video clips and animated Truth-O-Meter graphics enliven the segment. *Source: "American Morning," CNN, October 19, 2011.*

reach a meaningful audience. (Another contemporary example can be found in investigative news nonprofits, which similarly seek media partners and give their work away to mainstream news outlets.[97])

Thus, knowing one's way around a television studio, both on-camera and off, is vital for fact-checkers to participate in daily news discourse. As I observed on a pair of studio visits, frequent guests are recognized by security (and may even have a visitor's badge from their last visit). They can trade jokes with other guests about which network has the best "green room." They know how early to leave for the studio—you don't want a media appearance to eat up the whole morning, but you absolutely can't be late. In this sense, going on TV is both serious and not. For a veteran, the experience of live television may become quite casual, but the consequences of error are not. The programming economy of television and radio news rewards trusted guests who have the studio experience to participate in assembling stories and segments—often live segments—on the fly. Most important, of course, is on-screen behavior: the ability to feel comfortable in an empty soundstage talking into a camera; to speak clearly and in short, punchy sound bites; to be well-prepared while seeming natural, with a joke or two at the ready; and to take cues from the anchors. "I know how to hit my lines," Bill Adair told me.[98]

Intermedia Ties and Objective Status

A vital resource in establishing this upstart genre has been the fact-checkers' relationships with other journalists and media executives, built up over long careers. Fact-checkers are embedded in personal and professional networks that reproduce their status as objective journalists, entrusted by other objective journalists to perform the tricky business of adjudicating factual disputes. As noted earlier, fact-checkers assume the role of testifiers in these media appearances—"Jackson says President Obama was born where he says he was." These scripts take pains to emphasize that the testimony comes from experienced professional journalists without partisan commitments: "That's Brooks Jackson, a former senior investigative reporter for the *Wall Street Journal* and for CNN itself. He now runs FactCheck.org, a nonpartisan outfit associated with the University of Pennsylvania's Annenberg Center."[99] Journalists who cite or quote them reflexively attach the label "nonpartisan" to the fact-checkers. A few examples will illustrate this consistent journalistic genuflection:

> The nonpartisan FactCheck.org turned up congressional testimony from just two years ago in which the former speaker said he would still support cap and trade for major polluters.[100]

> Bill Adair is editor of the nonpartisan fact-checking site PolitiFact, and he joins me in the studio to talk about the film.[101]

> According to [Viveca Novak of] the nonpartisan FactCheck.org, none of Obama's votes would have raised taxes on families making $42,000.[102]

> We are joined now by Angie Drobnic Holan. She is the Florida editor for PolitiFact.com, which is a nonpartisan fact-checking website.[103]

> But who would have won that bet between Romney and Perry? The nonpartisan group FactCheck.org says—*Eugene Kiely, FactCheck.org*: "Rick Perry would have been wrong."[104]

> PolitiFact, which is nonpartisan—both sides tend to agree with its nonpartisan analysis—looked at the very issue of interest on the debt, and they said that if the President's budget passes, annual spending minus interest will equal annual revenue in 2017.[105]

That final excerpt comes from an episode also mentioned in chapter 3. President Obama had given a press conference promising that his new budget would, within a few years, stop adding to the national debt; just hours later PolitiFact ran a 1,200-word Truth-O-Meter item ruling the statement "False."[106] When the new White House press secretary repeated the claim at a briefing the next morning, ABC's White House correspondent, Jake Tapper, openly contradicted him. Tapper pressed the point, invoking PolitiFact's nonpartisan status like a talisman: "This White House is still going to continue to make the claim that you're not adding to the debt, even when nonpartisan people have looked at it and said you actually are?"[107]

Tapper is a declared ally of the fact-checking movement. He staffed ABC's "Just the Facts" desk during the 2004 election and has run numerous on-air fact checks featuring Brooks Jackson or Bill Adair; as interim host of ABC's *This Week*, he instituted that show's partnership with PolitiFact. He has joined fact-checkers in conferences and panel discussions about the movement. But it was essential in the moment of confrontation to invoke PolitiFact's objective status, to insist that "both sides tend to agree with its nonpartisan analysis." (More precisely, each "side" agrees with some of its analyses, and rarely the same ones.) It goes without saying that he would not have cited—that no correspondent for an elite news outlet would cite—an openly political source such as Media Matters or the Media Research Center to contradict something the president said.

This was a rare coup, the clearest example I witnessed of fact-checking work being deployed—face-to-face, at the White House no less—to undercut a public claim at the very moment of utterance. When news of the exchange reached PolitiFact, the office was fairly jubilant. Work broke off for a few moments. Somebody suggested publishing a note about the episode, as both PolitiFact and FactCheck.org have done on similar occasions, but this time the idea was dismissed as too self-congratulatory. A staffer joked that it would sound a little desperate, like declaring, "Look! We matter!" But the professional fact-checkers *do* want to matter, and the most tangible evidence that they do comes in being cited and quoted and interviewed by prominent media outlets.[108]

The ability to matter in this way depends on the fact-checkers' status as objective journalists. This status is reflected in *and shaped by* their media profile; that is, in the network of places and people who cite and link to them. It is a matter of formal declarations and mission statements; of peer recognition in the form of professional awards, media partnerships, and so on; but also of countless individual endorsements and affirmations. "The nonpartisan group, FactCheck.org, says . . . ." These status-affirming patterns of influence are visible in new ways today but have a long history, of course. Consider Herb Gans's much-quoted observation that if the *New York Times* did not exist, "it would probably have to be invented."[109] A competitive but deeply consensus-driven field like journalism *needs* editorial standard-bearers and agenda-setters. Taking editorial cues from a leader like the *Times* offers a kind of protection to other news outlets, even as it increases the authority of journalistic elites and ratifies particular sets of reporting practices and news judgments.

The elite fact-checkers actively cultivate their own media profiles through conscious choices as well as automatic or unthinking ones. Just as they avoid partisan sources (except certain establishment think tanks) in their own research, the fact-checkers seek exposure in outlets that will burnish their own claim to objectivity. They boast about a "hit" in the *Times* but care little for traffic from Media Matters, which routinely promotes work by the fact-checking sites. They prefer interviews at CNN and the three traditional broadcast networks to Fox News and MSNBC, which have partisan profiles. One fact-checker told me it was acceptable to do the "daytime" news shows at the last two networks, but not the evening "political" programs hosted by pundits such as Bill O'Reilly and Rachel Maddow. I also heard that in choosing broadcast partners, concerns about political identification may trump even strong preferences in terms of production values and technical expertise. That is, producing the best fact-checking segments or even having the largest audience does not always make a network the best campaign partner if it is tainted by partisan ties.[110]

Finally, it should be stressed that these concerns and preferences—of the fact-checkers as well as the news outlets that cite them—color their *actual* media profiles in dramatic fashion. This is immediately and intuitively clear, I think, to anyone who pays attention to the fact-checking milieu: the kinds of media people that talk to or about particular fact-checking outlets differ sharply along political lines. Simply put, the elite, nonpartisan fact-checkers are mentioned most often by their professional peers. Meanwhile partisan media venues pay disproportionate attention to partisan fact-checking sites—although not only to like-minded ones.

These differences show up unmistakably in comparing the media footprints of different fact-checkers in broadcast news programming. A simple but revealing analysis is to tally news broadcasts that interview or talk about the three elite fact-checkers or their most vocal partisan counterparts: the left-identified Media Matters and the conservative Media Research Center or its site NewsBusters.[111] Aggregating results for 2008 through 2014 for news programming on eight major networks demonstrates, first, that the fact-checkers are all familiar names in the broadcast news universe. All but the *Washington Post*'s Fact Checker appear hundreds of times; Media Matters tops

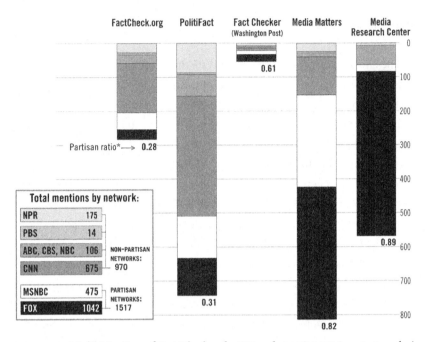

FIGURE 6.2 Media Mentions of Fact-Checkers by Network, 2008–2014 A content analysis reveals differences in the broadcast media footprint of fact-checkers according to their political profile. Partisan fact-checkers are cited mainly by the partisan networks Fox and MSNBC while the three elite fact-checking organizations appear most often on networks such as CNN, PBS, and NPR. Analysis by Lucas Graves and Patrice Kohl. *Credit: Chart by Janice Olson.*

the list with mentions on more than 800 broadcasts, followed by PolitiFact with nearly 750.[112] (See figure 6.2.)

However, differences in media profile were striking. FactCheck.org and PolitiFact each received the lion's share of their attention from networks that position themselves as nonpartisan, especially CNN and NPR. In each case, fewer than a third of their program mentions came on Fox News or MSNBC, self-identified as conservative and liberal, respectively. (The *Washington Post*'s Fact Checker is a notable exception; Glenn Kessler gave frequent interviews in daytime news programming on both Fox News and MSNBC in 2012.)

The pattern was reversed for the two partisan media-criticism sites. The conservative Media Research Center received nearly 90 percent of its attention from the partisan news networks, the lion's share from Fox News. The effect was nearly as dramatic for the progressive Media Matters, with 80 percent of its program mentions on either Fox News or MSNBC. Interestingly, Media Matters received even more attention from the conservative network than the liberal one. Fox News accounted for nearly a half of all mentions—assuredly negative ones—of the liberal media critics, who dedicate most of their effort to debunking misinformation presented on Fox News.[113]

Studying the relationships professional fact-checkers have with their key audiences begins to reveal the contradictions at the heart of this emergent practice. As we have seen, fact-checkers insist that the only appropriate mission for journalists is to provide information to a reasoning public hungry for facts—although they understand as well as anyone how small that public is and care a great deal about their impact on real-world political debates. In practice, fact-checkers matter in public discourse mainly through their status-reproducing relationships with other journalists, which magnify the impact of fact-checking while affirming its legitimacy. These vital tensions in audience and mission help to illuminate the epistemological paradox fact-checkers face in trying to reform the practice of objective journalism. Their project demands that they speak the language of hard facts and offer decisive rulings. But fact-checkers also need to be able to disclaim their own work, offering it up to the judgment of readers who are free to disagree with their conclusions. The final chapter examines the nature and limits of the fact-checkers' political critique.

7

THE LIMITS OF
FACT-CHECKING

EVERY FACT CHECK IS AN EVALUATIVE FOOTNOTE ATTACHED TO A
public claim, a kind of annotation that tells the world whether to trust it or
not. Fact-checkers take pride in their willingness to confront political deception head on, taking sides in factual disputes and exposing political dishonesty. As I heard many times, this is what reporters have to get used to if
they want to work for one of the new fact-checking operations. "PolitiFact is
different. And it can feel awkward at first," incoming fact-checkers were
warned at the start of their Truth-O-Meter training. "You have to decide
which side is right. And I have to say, the first time I wrote the words, 'President Obama exaggerated' . . . it made me feel really uncomfortable."[1]

Still, certain kinds of evaluations remain too uncomfortable for the new
professional fact-checkers to make. Theirs is a very narrow political critique.
Fact-checkers draw conclusions in their articles, but only immediate ones.
They focus very deliberately on discrete claims and individual political
actors. Despite having a unique vantage on the political world, fact-checkers
carefully avoid any analysis that would assign blame to one party for major
controversies or for the state of public discourse as a whole. This chapter
explores the sharp limits of the political intervention made by these journalists, limits that often see them accused of the same false balance they

always condemn. A more nuanced and interesting view emerges from close study of the day-to-day routines of fact-checking and its practice and understanding of objectivity.

"Readers Are Going to Have to Make Those Decisions for Themselves"

A clear illustration of the limits of fact-checking came during the tense Washington debate over a deficit-reduction plan in the summer of 2011, set off when Republican lawmakers refused to raise the congressionally sanctioned federal debt ceiling unless it was offset by trillions of dollars cut from government spending. Fact-checkers weighed in more than a dozen times during what was widely described as a political crisis that could, in the worst case, lead to the first-ever U.S. default on its debt obligations.[2] They refuted the Republican argument that the White House was asking for a "blank check" to run up new debt. (Lifting the debt limit was necessary to repay money that had already been spent.) They confirmed that the ceiling had been raised under every modern president but contradicted Democratic claims that the current showdown was unprecedented. (Democrats themselves had engaged in debt-limit brinksmanship under president George W. Bush.) They offered mostly inconclusive assessments of whether, as the White House had warned, Social Security checks really would stop going out if Congress failed to act by the deadline.[3]

But professional fact-checkers did not address the most hotly contested political question: Who was at fault here? Which party was behaving badly? While Democratic and Republican leaders blamed one another, a great deal of analysis in the media focused on the terms being negotiated and the willingness of each side to deal in good faith. An establishment consensus emerged that (at least in public negotiations) the White House had given more ground, agreeing to "historic" spending cuts that would anger many Democratic voters.[4] Some moderate conservatives urged Republicans to abandon their categorical opposition to new taxes, accepting a modest increase to secure a large deficit-reduction deal.[5] When a FactCheck.org editor appeared on the radio program *On the Media* to discuss the controversy, her interviewer pressed the question of which party was at fault. The exchange (as transcribed by the show) is worth quoting at length:

BROOKE GLADSTONE: Who's to blame for the crisis?

LORI ROBERTSON: It takes two to create an impasse. So both parties are to blame here for failing to come to an agreement.

BROOKE GLADSTONE: Is it true, though, that most of the compromise has been made by the President?

LORI ROBERTSON: Well, I mean, I think that's a matter of opinion. And—

BROOKE GLADSTONE: Explain to me how that's a matter of opinion. Obama has been willing to cut a huge chunk of the money going out for a smaller percentage of money coming in. The only thing that the Republicans have supported is cutting the money going out, right?

LORI ROBERTSON: Yeah, I guess—I guess that that's [LAUGHS] correct. You know, it's hard for us to say, oh somebody's blocking this more than the other. We're—you know, we're really—we're not privy to these meetings, either.

BROOKE GLADSTONE: I didn't mean to back you against the wall but I have to say if you guys aren't going to be un-mealymouthed about this, then who will be?

LORI ROBERTSON: Well, it's not that we're being mealy-mouthed. [LAUGHS] I mean, we just say constantly in our stories that we don't take an opinion one way or the other.

You know, a lot of people, particularly during the presidential campaigns will ask us, well, who lies more and can't you give me a ranking on—you know, who's the most truthful politician. And first off, we don't want to look like we're endorsing someone, so we don't wanna do that. So we're gonna tell you what we found, and if we found it to be horribly misleading, maybe you didn't, but we're gonna lay it there and—readers are gonna have to make those decisions for themselves.

BROOKE GLADSTONE: Lori, thank you very much.

LORI ROBERTSON: Thank you.[6]

This is a typical reflex. Questioned about any categorical distinction between the two major political parties, or any consistent pattern of distortion in U.S. public life, professional fact-checkers invoke the narrowest version of their mission: We provide information, not political commentary. Citizens must "make those decisions for themselves." This is not to discredit the defense the fact-checker supplied. Good reasons existed to say assigning blame for the debt-ceiling crisis was a matter of viewpoint. People disagree about what constitutes a "historic" concession on spending, or a "modest" tax increase. Depending on their views, people interpreted the drama of the unfolding crisis very differently, focusing on particular events and not others. "Facts can be subjective," the *Washington Post*'s Glenn Kessler told me. "Depending on your opinion, you look at the facts in a different way."[7] But observers had also disagreed, for similar reasons, about what counted as a "government takeover" of health care or as "ending" Medicare, questions FactCheck.org and its peers addressed decisively. As seen in the preceding chapters, critics constantly accuse the fact-checkers of straying into the realm of opinion and ideology, where objective factual analysis is not possible.

The inconsistency itself is less interesting than the question of what makes certain politically controversial judgments *look* like a "matter of opinion" to professional fact-checkers. Their understanding and practice of objectivity in these cases is shaped by several mutually reinforcing factors: first, a formal commitment to approach questions with an open mind, which militates against certain kinds of systemic analysis; second, a day-to-day, lived work experience that defies broad, partisan critiques placing the blame with one party or the other; and finally, a constant attention to their own position in U.S. media-political networks, as manifest in professional status and relationships but also in where they are cited, quoted, interviewed, linked to, and talked about.[8] As discussed in the last chapter, this network position reproduces the fact-checkers status as objective journalists and offers their most tangible evidence of doing worthwhile reporting that makes a difference in public affairs. It also informs their working sense of what constitutes a fair and reasonable fact check.

Opinion, Argument, and Political Critique

The episodes reviewed in the preceding chapters invite another look at what sets fact-checking apart from conventional political reporting. It is an unusually provocative kind of journalism. Fact-checkers pluck a statement from the news, analyze it, and turn the result into a new news story—one that judges the statement and, at least implicitly, its speaker. These journalists never call anyone a liar. (That would require knowing someone's heart, fact-checkers say. The word "lie" characterizes a speaker, not just a statement.⁹) But all three sites flirt with the accusation, awarding "Pinocchios" and "Pants on Fire" verdicts, and compiling annual lists of the biggest "whoppers." "If you give them a 'Pants on Fire,' you are essentially saying they are a liar," I heard at a training session. "It'll take some getting used to."[10]

Although playful, these designations underscore the willingness to *criticize* that fact-checking shares with articles on the op-ed page, and which sets the genre apart from conventional political reporting. Outsiders tend to treat the difference between reporters and editorialists or opinion writers as a simple question of subject matter: The former present hard facts while the latter ply a murkier trade, dispensing something less stable. Everyday usage likens "opinion" to conjecture, speculation, or even taste—the opposite of reliable data about the world. But this is a poor description of the work produced by many opinion journalists, which often involves more factual investigation and "shoe-leather" reporting than everyday dispatches from the campaign trail.[11]

Members of the profession treat the distinction differently. Opinion in journalism's actual division of labor means something closer to argument or to critique—a factual treatment invoking normative values.[12] Many articles on the op-ed page gather facts in service of building a case, evaluating a policy, making an endorsement, or dispensing political criticism. In this sense, paradoxically, fact-checking has been seen as a kind of opinion journalism (although practitioners reject that label).[13] In 2012 the public editor of the *New York Times* used this logic to ask readers whether the newspaper should become what he called a "truth-vigilante" and challenge misleading claims even in straight news.[14] As an example he pointed to a recent piece of fact-checking by a prominent *Times* columnist (about a claim the full-time fact-checkers also debunked):

> On the campaign trail, Mitt Romney often says President Obama has made speeches "apologizing for America," a phrase to which Paul Krugman objected in a December 23 column arguing that politics has advanced to the "post-truth" stage.
>
> As an Op-Ed columnist, Mr. Krugman clearly has the freedom to call out what he thinks is a lie. My question for readers is: should news

reporters do the same? . . . And if so, how can The Times do this in a way that is objective and fair?

The question made no sense to many of the *Times* readers who responded. They wanted to see more fact-checking but objected to the premise that testing facts is the natural province of opinion writers.[15] "Mr. Brisbane's view of the job of op-ed columnist vs that of reporters seems skewed," one wrote. "It is the job of columnist to present opinion and viewpoint, and to persuade. It is the job of reporters to present facts, as best as they can determine them." By this commonsense view, being objective consists precisely in adjudicating factual debates and declaring who has the facts on their side. As another respondent wrote, "Objective sometimes isn't fair."

But objectivity as conventionally practiced resists making factual challenges to official claims.[16] It resists argument, even factual argument, about controversial issues that are the subject of active debate. Fact-checking troubles journalistic objectivity because it criticizes in a way that seems to take sides. Consider again the *New York Times*'s rationale, reviewed in chapter 2, for refusing to describe waterboarding as torture only after the United States took up the practice: "When using a word amounts to taking sides in a political dispute, our general practice is to supply the readers with the information to decide for themselves."[17] People did disagree about whether the label applied. But the revealing point is that such questions weren't raised when American journalists applied the word, uncontroversially, to waterboarding by foreign governments. Protestations from the Khmer Rouge, say, wouldn't count as a "political dispute" in the same way. Reporters rely on real and specific political contexts to distinguish between statements that are self-evidently true, those that must be supported by evidence, and those that are inherently matters of political opinion or ideology.[18] In a follow-up article about fact-checking, the *Times*'s public editor came out in favor of including more of it in the newspaper but called for moderation: "Ubiquitous *argument* in straight news articles is not the way to go." He quoted then-executive editor Jill Abramson, who worried that if the paper fact-checked too routinely, "our readers would find the Times was being tendentious" and see it "as a *combatant*, not as an arbiter of what the facts were."[19] Objectivity here becomes a matter not just of truth but of neutrality.

These concerns help to illuminate the tenuous, straddling position occupied by professional fact-checkers, accused daily of being combatants and not neutral arbiters of fact. They see themselves as objective reporters and are increasingly treated that way by other journalists. But their work is controversial in a way that straight news reporting usually isn't. Someone unschooled in these distinctions, looking only at the position fact-checkers occupy in political discourse—at the patterns of conversation around their work—could be forgiven for grouping them with columnists, bloggers, and other opinion journalists. As shown in case after case, fact-checking provokes heated reactions from political actors. Some of this happens behind the scenes, with a phone call from a campaign staffer or press officer.[20] But to a much greater extent than would have been the case a decade ago, this critical discourse takes place in the open. The back-and-forth between fact-checkers and their critics is archived in a tangle of links across news sites, political blogs, comments, and tweets.[21] These mediated controversies sometimes become news facts in their own right, worthy of analysis pieces—"Political Fact-Checking Under Fire"—in elite news outlets such as NPR and the *New York Times*.[22]

To criticize publicly is to invite a response and thus to risk becoming engaged in a political argument. One way to understand fact-checking is as a journalism adapted to taking sides—to dispensing political critique and weathering the reactions it provokes. Many of the specific practices that set these organizations apart from other news outlets can be read through this lens. Professional fact-checkers practice a kind of slow news, staying at least a beat behind the news cycle. They do their best to find claims to check from "both sides" of U.S. politics. They use only public sources of information. And they devote thousands of words to analyzing even simple claims, showing all of their work, in order to be able to issue the fact-checkers' standard disclaimer: "even if you don't agree with every call we make, our research and analysis helps you sort out what's true in political discourse."[23]

A Balancing Frame

Fact-checkers anticipate political criticism and develop reflexes for trying to defuse it. "We're going to make the best calls we can, in a pretty gutsy form of journalism," Bill Adair told NPR. "And when we do, I think it's natural that the people on one side or the other of this very partisan world we live in are going to be unhappy."[24] One strategy is responding only minimally or in carefully chosen venues, and always asserting their balance, often by showing the criticism they receive from the other side of the spectrum. Fact-checkers make this point constantly. "There are people that write . . . 'what is this radical conservative doing writing a fact-check column for the *Washington Post?*'" Glenn Kessler said in TV interview. "And then there are things like Power Line or the *Weekly Standard* that say I'm part of some liberal agenda to dominate the political discourse."

Fact-checkers see the world through the lens of two political parties that subscribe to incompatible ideologies. In interviews or public forums, they almost always follow an example involving one party with an example from the other side, or at least a reflexive disclaimer: "and I should note that both sides do this."[25] This balancing frame applies even to the egregious distortions that have become enshrined in fact-checking's origin narrative (discussed in chapter 2). It is impossible not to notice that the signal cases, mentioned over and over in articles and at conferences about fact-checking, come mainly from the Republican side: the "Tank" and "Weekend Passes" (a.k.a. Willie Horton) ads by the Bush campaign in 1988; the "Swift Boat" attacks against John Kerry in 2004; Zell Miller's speech at the Republican National Convention that year; and any number of outlandish claims from 2008 and beyond, like "birther" rumors about President Obama or Sarah Palin's rhetoric about "death panels."

As noted, fact-checkers often point to the "Swift Boat" attacks as a turning point for political journalism.[26] Attendees at the first major conference on "media fact-checking," in 2007, were treated to video clips of ABC's Jake Tapper investigating the Vietnam era–rumors. Tapper talked about the challenges of debunking the attacks—and then quickly pivoted to an example of an exaggeration by the Kerry campaign.[27] Zell Miller's convention speech the same year, full of distortions about Kerry's voting record, offered another sign that political reporting needed to become more aggressive. "I actually went to the editors and said, 'This is crazy stuff, let me write a big front page story,'" the *Washington Post*'s Glenn Kessler recalled at a 2011 meeting. He continued: "But then I got like a screaming phone call from the campaign manager for Bush, [who] said, "Why the hell did you assholes [not] do this for Kerry?" Which was a very good question, you know, because Kerry was just as bad as the Republicans."[28]

But did the two parties distort the truth equally during what was called the "Year of the Fact Check"?[29] Was Kerry "just as bad as the Republicans?" One prominent Washington journalist drew sharp criticism that year for an internal memo, leaked to the conservative Drudge Report, arguing that the press should not pretend the Democrats had been as nasty or deceptive as their opponents.[30] The question came up directly in a PBS roundtable about fact-checking at the peak of the presidential race. "What do you do . . . if in fact one side has been much more egregious in its distortions or exaggerations or misstatements than the other?" a *NewsHour* host wanted to know. "Do you achieve some sort of balance and, if so, is it an artificial balance?" "Well, that's a complicated question," Tapper responded, arguing that if Republican attacks were worse initially that year, the Democrats had quickly caught up. He continued, "It's not necessarily 'he said, she said.' You don't want to be equating a minor misstatement that one candidate says with a huge whopper that another makes, but if both candidates are saying falsehoods, which is generally the case, you try to provide a balance, a balanced look."[31]

FactCheck.org founder Brooks Jackson, also on the roundtable, weighed in on the same question. "I think the balance has to come in the standards you bring to each individual factual claim," he explained. "We're going to criticize the misstatements that we find. And if one candidate's telling the truth all the time and the other candidate isn't, it's going to be pretty one-sided, but so far that hasn't happened."[32]

A Well-Known Liberal Bias?

These questions came to a head in striking fashion during my fieldwork with PolitiFact. As noted, the fact-checking site places real emphasis on its historical database, which allows readers to look up the overall Truth-O-Meter scorecard for various politicians, pundits, and political groups. As a matter of policy, the site does not aggregate results by political party—but these calculations are easy for outsiders to make. In early 2011 a political scientist at the University of Minnesota, on his blog, tallied all of the more than five hundred Truth-O-Meter rulings issued during the previous thirteen months.[33] The analysis found that PolitiFact checked statements by Republicans and Democrats at roughly the same rate. But Republican politicians fared far worse in the results, earning "False" and "Pants on Fire" rulings more than three times as often; 39 percent of Republican statements fell into the two lowest categories, compared to just 12 percent for Democrats. In all, the GOP accounted for three-quarters of "False" and "Pants on Fire" verdicts issued to current and former officeholders.

The post fairly exploded across the web and was the subject of immediate concern in PolitiFact's office. Two possible explanations existed for statistics inclined so dramatically against one party. One interpretation, offered by the political scientist who performed the analysis and quickly taken up by conservative media critics, was that PolitiFact must be biased in choosing claims to check. "These findings beg the central unanswered question, and that is what is the process by which PolitiFact selects the statements that it ultimately grades?" the post asked. It concluded, "by levying 23 Pants on Fire ratings to Republicans over the past year compared to just 4 to Democrats, it appears the sport of choice is game hunting—and the game is elephants." Outlets from the conservative *Weekly Standard* to the *New York Times* have cited the study as evidence of a possible fact-checking tilt against Republicans.[34]

The other explanation, of course, was that the results revealed an *actual* bias in political behavior—that members of the two major U.S. political parties do not always lie at the same rate or in the same way. Although the political scientist barely acknowledged this possibility, other observers took the results as clear evidence that Republicans are worse offenders when it comes to political deception and exaggeration. An article by Chris Mooney in the *Nation* argued, "after all, there is another possibility: the left just might be right more often (or the right, wrong more often), and the fact-checkers simply too competent not to reflect this—at least over long periods."[35] The author, a well-known liberal observer of the fact-checking scene, conducted a parallel analysis of "Pinocchios" issued by the *Washington Post*'s Fact Checker. He found that Republicans fared worse on average and, notably, that they received "four-Pinocchio" ratings—reserved for the most egregious falsehoods—at twice the rate of Democrats. The piece concluded, "I don't expect the fact-checkers to stop trying to be bipartisan—or to stop calling out Democrats when they deserve it. Still, the real message of their work may best be captured in a line by Stephen Colbert: 'Reality has a well-known liberal bias.'"

However, the fact-checkers themselves have strenuously avoided this interpretation. Glenn Kessler's own year-end analysis of "Pinocchios" awarded in 2011 found that Democrats did better by a small margin, a difference he attributed to the Republican presidential primaries. ("We are looking at you, Rep. Bachmann," he wrote.)[36] But Kessler has stressed repeatedly that he sees no consistent difference based on party. "I pay little attention to whether I am rating Democrats or Republicans, believing the numbers average out over time," he told Mooney. "My own experience, after three decades of covering Washington politicians, is that both sides will spin the facts if they think it will give them a political advantage."[37] In another interview Kessler gave me a very precise formulation:

> What I believe is that both parties are equal in terms of willingness to manipulate statistics if they believe it will advance their political interests. Now, like I said, *I'm not making a judgment as to whether or not one party does it more than the other*—it's just a question of, when faced with the decision of whether they should manipulate the statistics or not, they will do it in equal measure. . . .
>
> The only difference I see is that the Democrats seem to get more angry when you question their willingness to do this than Republicans, which I attribute to the fact that Democrats kind of believe reporters should be more on their side, and Republicans believe the mainstream media is just against them all the time, so they don't have that expectation.[38]

PolitiFact has been very reluctant to weigh in on the debate over its own statistics. The political scientist's analysis caused a real stir in the office the day it was posted. PolitiFact's basic methodology was being thrown into question, and everybody understood that critics would seize upon the results. Staffers joked that the previous week the site was under assault from liberals, angered by a series of rulings in favor of Wisconsin's combative Republican governor; now conservatives would join the fray. PolitiFact's staff clearly felt confident in their procedures and did not take the analysis to reveal any pervasive selection bias. At the same time, in my observation at least, the fact-checkers did not gravitate to the other interpretation—although it validated their work.[39] Adair has frankly acknowledged the stark choice framed by the debate as it played out online: "That prompted a really interesting discussion in the blogosphere: Either we're biased or Republicans lie more, depending on your point of view. But I want, as much as possible, to stay out of that analysis business and focus on giving others the data points that they can use to make those sort of sweeping interpretations."[40]

Controversies over the aggregate data compiled by PolitiFact and its state partners have continued to surface. In the summer of 2012 the Virginia GOP published an eighty-six-page report, billed as an "open letter to the Commonwealth," purporting to document anti-Republican bias at PolitiFact Virginia, an affiliate based in the *Richmond Times-Dispatch*. The report found that Republican claims were checked more often and received more negative ratings. "We cannot continue to stand by while this bias persists, unfairly influencing Virginia voters' perceptions of key state officials and potentially skewing election coverage and results," the authors declared.[41] Soon after, a conservative media watchdog group released an analysis finding that registered Democrats outnumbered Republicans four to one on the staff of PolitiFact Ohio. And then, in 2013, the Center for Media and Public Affairs at George Mason University announced the finding that Republicans received PolitiFact's two worst ratings 33 percent of the time, compared to just 11 percent for Democrats. More than half of statements by Democrats were ruled at least "Mostly True," compared to fewer than one-fifth by Republicans, according to the center.[42] This time PolitiFact did issue a direct response. An editor's note pointed out that the group selects claims based on "news judgment," and then carefully skirted the underlying question: "PolitiFact rates the factual accuracy of specific claims; we do not seek to measure which party tells more falsehoods."[43]

Why not? Editors have been asked more than once why PolitiFact refuses to sort Truth-O-Meter statistics by party, although the site aggregates data for readers in other ways—by speaker, by topic, and so on. The responses to such questions always invoke the group's role as an objective observer. "People crunch our data various ways. They find what they want to find," Bill Adair told a class of journalism students, arguing that PolitiFact, as umpire, should stay out of those debates: "You don't ask an umpire for commentary on the Rays-Yankees game. . . . You want the umpire focused on making calls." He developed that metaphor further at a fact-checking conference:

> The question of trends is tricky for us. . . . People will ask, you know, who lies more, Republicans or Democrats, and I say, that's like asking an umpire who's out at home more, the Yankees or the Red Sox—well,

you know, it just depends on the play. So I think as fact-checkers, as journalists, I think our fundamental role is to make the determination on an individual claim—is it true, is it false, is it somewhere in between—and so we don't engage too much in that sort of speculation.[44]

It has been easy for critics to read the fact-checkers' tentative approach to these questions as another case of artificial balance and misplaced objectivity among professional journalists.[45] One liberal observer coined a new term, "he lied/she lied," to describe "false equivalence" in the world of fact-checking.[46] That is a crude analysis but not an altogether incorrect one in this sense: the same concerns that generally inhibit political argument and criticism in traditional news reports also restrain *particular* arguments and *certain* kinds of critique by fact-checkers. That this is true despite fact-checkers' deliberate and, I think, very sincere commitment to a journalism that rejects a false practice of objectivity tells us something important.

The Question of Trends

Fact-checking groups have developed and gradually refined both a professional discourse and a set of concrete journalistic practices adapted to the task of adjudicating politically contested facts. They dispense political critique in every article they publish. Nevertheless, they resist, to the point of awkwardness, what might be called "meta" critique, even when that emerges from their own work: "the question of trends is tricky for us." As suggested at the outset of this chapter, the fact-checkers' practice of objectivity is shaped and constrained by three related factors that sharply limit their political critique.

The first factor is a formal commitment to approach factual questions with an open mind and to avoid analyses—even factual ones—that might interfere with that mission. Fact-checkers take seriously the need to treat each statement they investigate in isolation, following the same procedures regardless of who the speaker is and what his or her record looks like. Even student interns at FactCheck.org were told they must "be able to think independently and set aside any partisan biases." Despite their commitment to facts, these journalists also often say that "the truth is not black and white," that "facts can be subjective," and that people can reasonably disagree with their factual conclusions. That is to say, as suggested in chapter 2, fact-checkers have an unusually strong sense of how slippery facts can be. They see daily how political framing shapes factual interpretation. This day-to-day work only reinforces their own sensitivity to staking general positions that may color their own analysis of individual claims.

This is one way the "question of trends" is tricky. If Republicans (or Democrats) mislead more often or more egregiously, over some period of time or in general, fact-checkers would prefer not to know that, not to think about it, and certainly not to make tracking the party differential their primary mission, which could affect not only how they are perceived but also how they approach their work. "We don't keep score by party because we want our selection to be based on what's timely and relevant to our readers—not on false balance that tries to make sure each side gets an equal number of Pants on Fire ratings," Bill Adair has said.[47] By this view, paradoxically, it is precisely because fact-checkers don't pay attention to how the parties fare overall that we can place a measure of trust in their aggregate data. Fact-checkers admit that their work is not truly scientific. But they nevertheless adopt the language of experimental method and try to model it roughly in their work. This includes the notion that certain knowledge can corrupt, that certain positions are out of bounds for the neutral observer. Glenn Kessler told me, "In the position I'm in, I don't feel comfortable trying to make a judgment there. . . . I just can't be in a position to say one side or the other is more keenly willing to ignore facts, particularly when I'm confronted with many examples of both sides being willing to ignore facts."[48]

That response also hints at a second factor: how their day-to-day participation in a contentious media-political discourse shapes the fact-checkers' practice of objectivity. This is true in two respects. First, their daily experience provides abundant real-world models of what they consider to be politically framed fact-checking. Being objective means, in one basic sense, behaving differently than people or groups with stated agendas—especially the partisan media watchdogs whom professional fact-checkers take such care to distinguish themselves from. Organizations like Media Matters and the Media Research Center specialize in looking at the big picture, with reports meant to reveal large patterns of bias in American media. They celebrate fact checks that support their views and reject any that don't. Their own fact-checking is framed in terms of a broad political critique. Professional fact-checkers reinforce their own sense of what counts as tendentious, one-sided analysis through the examples they see every day. Their aversion to this ideological style of critique is only reinforced by the vehement reactions their own work provokes among politicians, pundits, and everyday readers.

More than that, the immediate experience of political fact-checking may defy the observation that one party lies more or more egregiously. Trends are tricky because fact-checkers encounter absurd claims day in and day out, from well-known politicians and unknown ones, in presidential contests and state primary races. As shown in chapters 4 and 5, statements are assessed not in arid isolation but in their actual, mediated political context—as vulgar, fear-mongering television advertisements or as bald stump-speech distortions repeated over and over until they no longer yield political advantage. At this textural level, the more meaningful observation to professional fact-checkers is not that Republicans average more Pinocchios but that politicians as a rule lie and distort grossly. This of course may not jibe with the views of political professionals who believe deeply in their candidates and their message. At a postmortem on the 2014 races, a campaign consultant worried that fact-checking can obscure the "larger truths" of important political arguments. The same consultant complained:

> I think it is the accepted wisdom that corrupt politicians want to pull a fast one over people and they're going to put these ads on the air, they'll lie, cheat, and steal, and just want to win. . . . I guess it's sometimes true. In a lot of cases it isn't true. But I would posit to you that that is the lens through which a lot of fact-checkers and the public approach political ads, and it becomes something of self-fulfilling prophecy.[49]

As we have seen, fact-checkers cultivate a familiar journalistic cynicism and have low expectations for political behavior or for their own impact on it. This is a very comfortable cynicism. It jibes well with the sense that journalists shouldn't try to change political behavior, efforts seen as possibly inappropriate and probably futile as well. Analyzing broad patterns of lying in American politics would raise new and difficult questions about how the fact-checkers do their work—for instance, if one party distorts the discourse more, why not focus on it? Systemic analysis invites new ways of understanding the mission of fact-checking. At the same conference in 2014, one observer asked whether fact-checkers might have the greatest effect on public discourse by agreeing to vet political ads for campaigns *before* they air. Journalists in the room objected strenuously. "I don't think it's our role to pre-approve messages at all. I think that's a very dangerous place," PolitiFact's Angie Drobnic Holan argued:

> When you're giving preapproval you're becoming an advocate and an actor in a way that—I think it's a slippery slope. Where we can stand firm as journalists is as truth-tellers. But when we get into this role of working with political actors, we start to have stakes in the outcome. . . . For us coming out of a tradition of independent journalism where we don't take sides, any role advising political actors is not something we should be doing.[50]

Finally, fact-checkers' practice of objectivity reflects a constant, reflexive attention to their own position in U.S. media-political networks. Although they are accused daily—as they always point out—of being partisans for the left or the right, these novel news outlets enjoy real purchase in elite political discourse. They have the attention of national politicians in the White House and on Capitol Hill. Their work appears in newspapers and news broadcasts around the country, including the most respected national news sources. They win top professional honors for leading what is often called a bold new movement in journalism. The "question of trends" is tricky because the fact-checkers' purchase in public discourse depends on protecting their nonpartisan status. Fact-checking organizations resist systemic political critiques—assigning blame to one party or simply characterizing discourse on the left and the right as significantly different—in part because such critiques can erode the professional status that allows them to issue individual factual judgments. They acknowledge this more or less directly; as Glenn Kessler told me, "If I were to suddenly make a judgment and say, 'Aha, this side is just totally off their rocker,' then it completely undercuts my credibility in terms of being what I try to be, which is a really neutral arbiter."[51]

What a journalist describes as a question of credibility with readers can also be seen in terms of network position, where that is understood in the broad sense described in chapter 6: as the fabric of individual and institutional relationships, involved in daily routines of both newswork and media work, which manifest and reproduce professional status. The language journalists use to talk about these questions underscores that being objective and being *seen* as objective are not distinct problems in the way an outsider might suppose. Fact-checkers do worry that declaring one party is less honest will invite accusations of bias. But they also believe it would be inappropriate, biasing their own judgment and producing work that their peers would not recognize as fair and impartial analysis. In the context of day-to-day journalistic work, concerns about professional status and about correct journalistic practice define and reinforce each other.

The notion that routines of objectivity are embedded in real-world relations—business, political, professional, and so on—is not new. What counts as evidence varies in practice depending on the political context and especially on the status or power of the people being reported on. As noted earlier, a classic illustration of this is the unusually strict "two sources" rule which the *Washington Post* supposedly enforced during the Watergate investigation. Although apocryphal, that story illustrates the point that standards of verification are defined with respect to the subject.[52] We may speak in principle of abstract rules of evidence, but these must always be applied to a specific case. It makes sense intuitively to journalists, as to scientists, lawyers, and so on, that certain investigations demand more care than others, and certain claims can be taken on faith while others must be meticulously verified.

In journalism, this perspective highlights the essentially defensive nature of the claim to objectivity and of the specific practices that constitute it. These always to a degree reflect potential threats to reporters and the organizations they work for: lawsuits, loss of advertising, and so on. That is, crudely, what journalists do to establish facts and the kinds of things that qualify as reportable fact depend partly on what external actors can do to them in response.[53] The objectivity norm as it developed in American journalism during the early part of the twentieth century has been seen as defensive in a second way as well. Michael Schudson and others read objectivity, in a longer historical-cultural register, as a kind of epistemological fall-back position—a professional accommodation to a rising distrust of public reason and "naive realism."[54] It is vital to see that these two views of the objectivity norm are deeply linked. Defensive habits like reporting "both sides" of every story or avoiding direct political critique are ways that reporters deal with *both* political and epistemological uncertainty.

This defensive frame applies to fact-checkers' understanding and practice of objectivity but with differences that reflect the unusual kind of journalism they produce as well as broader changes in the media system. Fact-checkers matter in public life, to the extent they do, in a very particular way. They affect the political realm not through Watergate-style exposés but via thousands of small factual interventions that percolate across a news environment increasingly characterized by what scholars call "intermedia" ties and effects.[55] Their journalism propagates by partnerships and interviews and countless individual acts of annotation, appropriation, and promotion. What has to some extent always been the case in the field is more visibly and immediately true for these journalists: success, both for individual stories and as news organizations, depends on what other media and political voices do with their work. Like many of their peers today, fact-checkers' status is reflected in the network traces their work leaves—traces they and others observe on a daily basis.

In this politically charged, deeply interconnected media environment, fact-checkers manifest their objectivity in the sources and methods they use in their own work but also in the news outlets they link to, the interviews they give, the partnerships they form, the attacks they choose to respond to. If the defining risks in traditional newsrooms were legal and economic, for the organizations leading the fact-checking movement over the last decade, the most immediate danger has been a loss of purchase in elite media and political networks. In trying to establish the journalistic legitimacy and the political relevance of fact-checking, these journalists have faced the real possibility that some controversy would finally prove too great—that it would unwind their status-affirming relationships, alter their media profile, and push them into a new network equilibrium, into a role that mirrors the partisan political and media critics they define themselves against. That this outcome seems unlikely today speaks to fact-checkers' success in institutionalizing a new practice of objectivity.

EPILOGUE

FACT-CHECKING IS TIGHTLY WOVEN INTO THE INSTITUTIONAL
fabric of American politics. It has become part of the daily thrum of political life in Washington, treated as routine and legitimate by not just journalists but most of the politicians they cover. One notable sign of this came on
the Thursday in October 2015 when Hillary Clinton finally appeared before
the House Select Committee on Benghazi, which for eighteen months had
been looking into the attack on a U.S. diplomatic compound in Libya that
left four Americans dead. All eyes were on the confrontation between the
Democratic front-runner and her Republican opponents, whose widening
investigation into Clinton's tenure as secretary of state had the potential to
seriously damage her presidential campaign. Over a day of questioning, her
Democratic allies on the committee cited independent fact-checking four
times to deflect Republican accusations. "Well, when the Washington Post
Fact Checker examined this claim, they gave it four Pinocchios," the senior
Democrat declared at one point, to rebut the charge that Clinton had personally denied requests for additional security. "They called it a whopper."[1]

This was nothing unusual. It is increasingly common for lawmakers on
both sides of the aisle to cite fact checks in floor speeches and committee debates, often reading published pieces into the *Congressional Record*.[2] The

month before Clinton's appearance, Republican leaders drew on research from fact-checkers to defend an antiabortion bill and to challenge the president's nuclear deal with Iran. PolitiFact's Lie of the Year for 2013, awarded to President Obama for the promise that "if you like your health care plan, you can keep it," became a badge of the movement to overturn the health law. Opponents of the law on Capitol Hill turned the award into posters and trophies. "Obamacare is a broken law filled with broken promises," the Senate majority leader declared, citing PolitiFact, when the chamber finally passed legislation to repeal the health law at the end of 2015.[3]

As I write this in early 2016, it seems certain the ongoing presidential contest will set a new high-water mark for fact-checking by American journalists. Already almost every major candidate has faced questions about honesty that dominated the news cycle for a day or two. News outlets reported widely that Hillary Clinton was downplaying her previous enthusiasm for the Trans-Pacific Partnership, that Ben Carson embellished various details of his life story, and that Carly Fiorina misrepresented what she saw in a disturbing antiabortion video, a point she was bluntly challenged about even on Fox News.[4] Donald Trump has drawn fire across the news media for a string of inflammatory falsehoods, including made-up statistics about black-on-white crime, wild exaggerations of the number of Syrian refugees the White House planned to admit to the country, and the baseless rumor that thousands of U.S. Muslims celebrated in the streets of New Jersey after the World Trade Center fell. On *Meet the Press*, often criticized as a forum where political figures pay no price for stretching the truth, Trump's insistence that he personally saw video of cheering Muslims earned a sharp rebuke: "You're running for President of the United States. Your words matter. Truthfulness matters. Fact-based stuff matters."[5]

Major national newsrooms have invested heavily in fact-checking for the race. NPR unveiled a new campaign feature, "Break It Down," which unites fact checks and explanatory reporting "to add a layer of analysis to fast-paced political coverage."[6] CNN is producing weekly video fact checks based on research by FactCheck.org and has devised its own truth meter to rate campaign claims, a first for the network. The five-point scale runs from true to false; the middle setting is "It's Complicated." NBC News struck a partnership with PolitiFact to build fact checks into its political news programming, beginning with *Meet the Press*. Under the arrangement, the network's journalists can commission exclusive research by the fact-checkers. Meanwhile the *New York Times* assigned a "chief fact checker" for the 2016 races and for the first time is collecting all of its fact checks on a dedicated page online. The paper has even taken a small step toward rating claims, stamping its fact checks with colored labels—red, yellow, or green—bearing ad hoc rulings like "kind of" and "overstated." These capsule verdicts can then be embedded into related news reports.[7]

Each debate brings a deluge of fact-checking by news outlets of all kinds. This election season major networks and newspapers have been joined by specialized politics and policy venues like Vox, FiveThirtyEight, and Politico, which debuted a new "Wrongometer" to cover the debates. (Despite the name, Politico's fact checks don't use a rating system.) Fox News introduced a bold visual device to analyze Republican primary debates: a large, animated stamp that brands the word "True" or "False" across clips of candidates making questionable statements.[8] Meanwhile, *The Daily Show* has dissected the debates in a recurring segment, "What the actual fact?," which marries earnest research to a gentle send-up of the genre; claims earn ratings like "wrong but adorable" and "true but meaningless, kind of like how Hitler was nice to dogs."[9]

The full-time fact-checking outlets have not been idle. In 2015 FactCheck .org launched SciCheck, a permanent feature funded by the Stanton Foundation, to debunk "false and misleading scientific claims that are made by partisans to influence public policy"; the site has weighed in on campaign rhetoric about climate change, vaccine risks, and even the laws of thermodynamics, mangled by candidate Ben Carson. In addition to its CNN partnership, FactCheck.org also has election-year distribution deals in place with *USA Today* and NBC Universal, and its campaign coverage appears on MSN. com, the *Huffington Post*, and other high-traffic outlets. Meanwhile, PolitiFact's network of state franchises appears resurgent after several difficult years. In the fall of 2015 the site launched an Iowa edition, in partnership with the *Des Moines Register*, and another for California, working with California Public Radio. A deal with media company E. W. Scripps is bringing PolitiFact affiliates to TV stations in Ohio, Colorado, Arizona, and Nevada. Four more state sites, seeded by a large grant from the Democracy Fund, are expected to go live before the summer. And the election-year partnership with NBC News will help to pay for PolitiFact's research and give it broad exposure across NBC and MSNBC.

Various joint initiatives promise to make fact-checking still more visible. The nonprofit Internet Archive has a grant to build fact-checking into its 2016 Political Ad Tracker, a database of political ads culled from local television stations around the country. The site marries data about donors and spending for each commercial to research by PolitiFact, FactCheck.org, the *Washington Post*'s Fact Checker, the Center for Public Integrity, and others. More significant in the long term is a project led by the Reporters Lab at Duke University to develop a system of invisible web codes journalists can use to label the different parts of their fact checks: the claim being investigated, the person who uttered it, the final verdict, and so on. Once implemented, the new standard will make it easier for search engines to identify fact-checking and for news sites or apps to automatically attach corrections to political claims reported in the news.

In this way, a kind of journalism that barely existed fifteen years ago has become impossible to miss. It would be hard to argue that this has diminished political lying in absolute terms, even if such a thing could be measured. On the contrary, the consensus seems to be that, at least in the primaries, the 2016 presidential race marks a new low for reasonable, fact-based political discourse, worse even than recent contests dominated by wild claims about death panels and birth certificates.[10] A mounting chorus of journalists and academics has read the success of populist outsiders like Donald Trump, named the "post-truth" candidate, as evidence of a dangerous public indifference to falsehood.[11] The national fact-checkers all singled out the celebrity billionaire as exhibiting an exceptional disregard for facts even in an unusually mendacious season. "It's been a banner year for political whoppers—and for one teller of tall tales in particular," FactCheck.org wrote at the end of 2015.[12]

Paradoxically, the visibility of political deception represents a kind of victory for fact-checking. Journalists may not be able to inhibit lying in politics, but they undoubtedly draw our attention to it, wiring the now-reflexive focus on questions of fact in political discourse. If the primary goal of the "ink-stained fact-checkers" who came together for the first time in 2007 was to establish a role for their new kind of journalism, they have emphatically succeeded. The ethical and practical vocabulary of professional journalism has widened to accommodate them. The excesses of the ongoing race have only fueled calls for more aggressive campaign reporting, and the influence of the fact-checking movement can be felt across the field. Late in 2015, for instance, the *New York Times* debuted a new kind of campaign story: a computer-driven analysis of 95,000 words worth of Donald Trump's public statements, highlighting his oratorical affinity to "demagogues of the past century."[13] This extraordinary scrutiny shared the critical spirit of fact-checking; it also suggested the view, anchored by the work of professional fact-checkers, that Trump's singular record of dishonesty warranted the use of uncommon journalistic tools.

Where does this leave the fact-checking movement? A main argument of this book has been that fact-checkers should be understood above all as journalistic reformers. Their unifying mission has not been to clean up politics—seen as obviously futile and possibly inappropriate—but rather to change journalism. A shared critique of conventional political reporting is what the fact-checkers leading the movement had in common from the start, more than organizational arrangements or even reporting style. That critique supplied the overarching theme of their evolving professional discourse and has been instrumental in recruiting media partners, training new recruits, and explaining themselves to fellow journalists. It lent narrative coherence and moral force to the institutional history of fact-checking that took hold among practitioners, helping to define the movement and place it in the story of American journalism.

That professional discourse continues to evolve. With the legitimacy of the genre no longer seriously in question, fact-checkers may be gaining greater freedom to assert its distinct possibilities. First, the taboo against drawing comparisons by party shows some signs of fading. Late in 2015 the new editor of PolitiFact, Angie Drobnic Holan, penned an op-ed for the *New York Times* examining the Truth-O-Meter records of current and former presidential contenders.[14] After the usual caveat that fact-checkers' methods are journalistic, not scientific, the piece made a simple case, summed up in the headline: "All Politicians Lie. Some Lie More Than Others." The accompanying chart ranked seventeen politicians according to how often they earned rulings of "Mostly False" or worse. What was left unsaid but impossible to miss is that the list split almost perfectly according to party. All of the candidates who received the worst ratings a third of the time or more came from the right, led by stunningly bad records for three of the 2016 presidential contenders. As one newspaper editorial observed in response, "There's no way to sugarcoat the Republican–Democratic divide among PolitiFact's statistics."[15]

It is risky to read too much into ongoing events, but the leaders of the fact-checking movement in the United States seem bolder about describing their mission in interventionist language—as not only to provide information to an abstract democratic public but also to actively shape political debates. "From governors to U.S. senators, American politicians . . . are clearly changing their behavior because of us," PolitiFact founder Bill Adair declared in the opening remarks at the second global summit of fact-checkers, held in London in July 2015.[16] The journalistic attitude of "throwing rocks into the pond," discussed in chapter 6, appears to be fading, at least in settings that bring fact-checkers together to discuss the future of their movement. Every new meeting raises more urgently the question of how to measure, and how to maximize, the effects fact-checking has in the political sphere. This is the major topic of conversation across an increasingly active global mailing list, where fact-checkers trade "anecdotes of impact," review academic research about their work, and consider how new technologies may boost their influence on real-world debates. "Measuring the impact of fact-checkers" is one of the four core themes of the online hub for the International Fact-Checking Network launched in late 2015 by the Poynter Institute.[17]

Of course fact-checkers have always wanted their work to make a difference. As we've seen, these journalists seize happily on any sign that they can change public discourse or alter political behavior while insisting in other moments that this is not the goal. Like members of any occupational field, they think and talk about their work in different ways depending on the context. And this is perhaps the best way to understand how the field is changing today. As the leading U.S. fact-checkers increasingly inhabit their own well-defined professional networks with strong, persistent ties to the non-profit and academic worlds, they find themselves more often in contexts where an interventionist mission is appropriate: seeking a new grant from a foundation, reporting on achievements to a current funder, discussing best practices with fact-checkers from other countries, and so on. The growing international fact-checking movement includes outlets from partisan media traditions, like the United Kingdom's *Guardian* or France's *Libération*, as well as many activist and good-government groups with open missions of political reform. In these settings U.S. journalism's broad injunction against "being part of the story"—the notion that reporters should seek only to inform, never to influence—loses some of its force.[18]

None of this is to say professional fact-checkers are casting off the language and conventions of objective reporting.[19] On the contrary, it will surely make more sense in hindsight to see the movement as an affirmation of the objectivity norm in American journalism. But the way reporters understand that norm and related ideas like accuracy and fairness will be different. The field's center of gravity shifts, incrementally but meaningfully, with the institutionalization of new reporting practices and the professional values they enact. Ultimately, the most lasting impact of the fact-checking movement may be in giving political reporters new license to embrace the muckraking, reformist impulse that is both so vital and so tenuous in professional journalism.

NOTES

Introduction

1. Mitt Romney, "Let Detroit Go Bankrupt," *New York Times*, November 18, 2008.

2. Paul Bedard, "Jeep, an Obama Favorite, Looks to Shift Production to China," *Washington Examiner*, October 25, 2012, http://washingtonexaminer.com/jeep-an-obama -favorite-looks-to-shift-production-to-china/article/2511703.

3. Craig Trudell, "Fiat Says Jeep Output May Return to China as Demand Rises," *Bloomberg Business*, October 22, 2012, http://www.bloomberg.com/news/2012-10-21/fiat-says-china -may-build-all-jeep-models-as-suv-demand-climbs.html.

4. Nathan Bomey and Brent Snavely, "Romney Repeats False Claim of Jeep Outsourcing to China; Chrysler Refutes Story," *Detroit Free Press*, October 26, 2012, http://www .freep.com/article/20121026/BUSINESS01/121026036/Obama-Chrysler-Romney-s -claim-of-Jeep-outsourcing-to-China-is-false; and Tom Troy, "Romney Worries about Jeep Going to China," *Toledo Blade*, October 26, 2012, http://www.toledoblade.com /Politics/2012/10/26/Romney-worries-about-Jeep-going-to-China.html.

5. Jill Lawrence, "Romney Ad Wrongly Implies Chrysler Is Sending U.S. Jobs to China," *National Journal*, October 28, 2012; see also Todd Spangler, "Romney's Latest Ad Claims He Will Do More for the Auto Industry than Obama," *Detroit Free Press*, October 28, 2012, http://www.freep.com/article/20121028/NEWS15/121028024/Romney-s-latest -ad-claims-he-will-do-more-for-the-auto-industry-than-Obama.

6. Greg Sargent, "The Morning Plum: Romney's Jeep-to-China Lie Earns Brutal Headlines in Ohio," *Plum Line* (blog), *Washington Post*, October 30, 2012, http://www.washing tonpost.com/blogs/plum-line/post/the-morning-plum-romneys-jeep-to-china-lie

-earns-brutal-headlines-in-ohio/2012/10/30/6ca63574-227e-11e2-ac85-e669876
c6a24_blog.html.

7. "Remarks by the President at a Campaign Event—Hilliard, OH," Office of the Press
   Secretary, the White House, November 2, 2012, http://www.whitehouse.gov/the-press
   -office/2012/11/02/remarks-president-campaign-event-hilliard-oh.

8. "This ad is cynical campaign politics at its worst," a GM spokesman complained after
   the firm was mentioned in a companion radio commercial. Jim Rutenberg and Jeremy
   W. Peters, "Two American Automakers Rebut Claims by Romney," *New York Times*,
   October 31, 2012.

9. Jim Rutenberg and Jeremy W. Peters, "G.O.P. Turns Fire on Obama Pillar, the Auto
   Bailout," *New York Times*, October 30, 2012.

10. "In Context: Mitt Romney, Ohio, and the Auto Bailout," *All Things Considered*, National
    Public Radio, October 31, 2012.

11. Jon Greenberg, "Mitt Romney Says Obama's Chrysler Deal Undermined U.S. Work-
    ers," PolitiFact, October 30, 2012, http://www.politifact.com/truth-o-meter/statements
    /2012/oct/30/mitt-romney/mitt-romney-obama-chrysler-sold-italians-china-ame/;
    Glenn Kessler, "4 Pinocchios for Mitt Romney's Misleading Ad on Chrysler and
    China," Fact Checker, *Washington Post*, October 30, 2012, http://www.washington
    post.com/blogs/fact-checker/post/4-pinocchios-for-mitt-romneys-misleading-ad-on
    -chrysler-and-china/2012/10/29/2a153a04-21d7-11e2-ac85-e669876c6a24_blog.html;
    and Eugene Kiely, "Romney Distorts Facts on Jeep, Auto Bailout," FactCheck.org,
    October 29, 2012, http://www.factcheck.org/2012/10/romney-distorts-facts-on-jeep
    -auto-bailout/.

12. Angie Drobnic Holan, "Lie of the Year: The Romney Campaign's Ad on Jeeps Made in
    China," PolitiFact, December 12, 2012, http://www.politifact.com/truth-o-meter/arti
    cle/2012/dec/12/lie-year-2012-Romney-Jeeps-China/.

13. Quoted in Lois Romano, "10 Most Delusional Campaign Moments," Politico, December
    6, 2012, http://www.politico.com/story/2012/12/10-most-delusional-campaign
    -moments-84670.html; David Axelrod quoted in Drobnic Holan, "Lie of the Year."

14. A tally in early 2015 by the Reporters Lab at Duke University found eighty-nine fact-
    checking sites around the world, thirty of them in North America. See Joshua Benton,
    "Fact-Checking Sites Continue to Grow in Number Around the World," *Nieman Lab* (blog),
    January 20, 2015, http://www.niemanlab.org/2015/01/fact-checking-sites-continue
    -to-grow-in-number-around-the-world/.

15. According to the *Oxford English Dictionary*, the first use of "proofreader" is in 1803; of
    "copy editor," in 1899; and of "fact-checker," in 1938, the last in reference to *Time* mag-
    azine's research department.

16. Christian Lorentzen, "Short Cuts," *London Review of Books*, April 5, 2012; and Craig
    Silverman, *Regret the Error: How Media Mistakes Pollute the Press and Imperil Free Speech*
    (New York: Union Square Press, 2007).

17. An early instance is Frank Scully, "Scully's Scrapbook," *Variety*, March 1, 1944.

18. See, e.g., Craig Silverman, "Newsweek Ditched Its Fact-checkers in 1996, then Made a Major Error," Poynter.org, August 21, 2012, http://www.poynter.org/news/media wire/185899/the-story-of-when-newsweek-ditched-its-fact-checkers-then-made-a -major-error/.

19. Ta-Nehisi Coates, "In Praise of Fact-Checkers," *Atlantic*, August 21, 2012, http:// www.theatlantic.com/national/archive/2012/08/in-praise-of-fact-checkers/261368/.

20. Peter Canby, interview by author, e-mail, February 26, 2012; Madeleine Elfenbein, interview by author, telephone, August 11, 2011; and Justin Vogt, interview by author, August 24, 2011.

21. John McPhee, "Checkpoints," in *Silk Parachute* (New York: Farrar, Straus and Giroux, 2010), 165–96.

22. Author's field notes, February 9 and 17, 2011.

23. Author's field notes, June 9, 2014. See Neil Brown, "Five 'Essential Understandings' of the Fact-Checking Movement," PolitiFact, June 18, 2014, http://www.politifact.com/truth-o -meter/article/2014/jun/18/5-essential-understandings-fact-checking-movement/.

24. Within the profession, the award was taken as validation of a claim often made by Politi-Fact itself: that fact-checking constitutes "a new form of journalism," reinventing the watchdog tradition for a digital age. See, e.g., Jack McElroy, "PolitiFact Is Most Important Pulitzer This Year," *Knoxville News Sentinel*, April 21, 2009, http://knoxblogs .com/editor/2009/04/21/politifact_is_most_important_p/.

25. Craig Silverman, "AP Grows Fact Checking Beyond Politics to Breaking News, Beat Reporting," Poynter.org, January 9, 2012, http://www.poynter.org/news/mediawire /158337/ap-grows-fact-checking-beyond-politics-to-breaking-news-beat-reporting/.

26. The *Wall Street Journal*'s editorials and columnists have repeatedly decried political fact-checking as a form of opinion journalism. See, e.g., James Taranto, "The Pinocchio Press," *Wall Street Journal*, September 4, 2012; and James Taranto, "Factitious 'Fact Checking,'" *Wall Street Journal*, September 21, 2015, sec. Opinion.

27. I heard variations of this many times in my fieldwork, and it is a point fact-checkers also make publicly. See, e.g., Bill Adair, "Inside the Meters: Responding to a George Mason University Press Release About Our Work," PolitiFact, May 29, 2013, http:// www.politifact.com/truth-o-meter/blog/2013/may/29/responding-george-mason -university-press-release-a/.

28. Walter Lippmann made this argument as early as 1922 in *Public Opinion* (1922; New York: Free Press, 1997). The sociological study of news production arguably begins with White's canonical study of "gatekeeping." See David M. White, "The 'Gatekeeper': A Case Study in the Selection of News," *Journalism Quarterly* 27, no. 1 (1950): 383–96. See also Stephen D. Reese and Jane Ballinger, "The Roots of a Sociology of News: Remembering Mr. Gates and Social Control in the Newsroom," *Journalism and Mass Communication Quarterly* 78, no. 4 (2001): 641–58.

29. In addition to Gans's *Deciding What's News: A Study of "CBS Evening News," "NBC Nightly News," "Newsweek," and "Time"* (1979; repr. Evanston, IL: Northwestern University Press, 2004), foundational studies of the structural influences and biases in news production in the United States include Mark Fishman, *Manufacturing the News* (Austin: University of Texas Press, 1980); Todd Gitlin, *The Whole World Is Watching: Mass Media in the Making and Unmaking of the New Left* (Berkeley: University of California Press, 2003); Daniel C. Hallin, *The Uncensored War: The Media and Vietnam* (Berkeley: University of California Press, 1989); Leon V. Sigal, *Reporters and Officials: The Organization and Politics of Newsmaking* (Lexington, MA: D. C. Heath, 1973); and Gaye Tuchman, *Making News: A Study in the Construction of Reality* (New York: Free Press, 1978).

30. Michael Schudson, *Why Democracies Need an Unlovable Press* (Cambridge: Polity Press), 88.

31. C. W. Anderson, *Rebuilding the News: Metropolitan Journalism in the Digital Age* (Philadelphia: Temple University Press, 2013), 6.

32. Notable books in this vein include Anderson, *Rebuilding the News*; Pablo J. Boczkowski, *Digitizing the News: Innovation in Online Newspapers* (Cambridge, MA: MIT Press, 2005); Pablo J. Boczkowski, *News at Work: Imitation in an Age of Information Abundance* (Chicago: University of Chicago Press, 2010); Emma Hemmingway, *Into the Newsroom: Exploring the Digital Production of Regional Television News* (London: Routledge, 2008); and Nikki Usher, *Making News at the* New York Times (Ann Arbor: University of Michigan Press, 2014).

33. Michael Schudson, "The Objectivity Norm in American Journalism," *Journalism* 2, no. 2 (August 1, 2001): 150, doi:10.1177/146488490100200201. This element of deliberate elaboration and codification in new institutional forums (like journalism schools and professional societies) is the argument for locating the origins of the objectivity norm in the 1920s rather than in the complex of reporting practices that took hold over the previous half-century.

34. Although this phrase has come into vogue in the last several years, the idea is an old one; see, e.g., Barbie Zelizer, "Journalists as Interpretive Communities," *Critical Studies in Mass Communication* 10, no. 3 (1993): 223-24, doi:10.1080/15295039309366865.

35. Although the objectivity norm gained institutional acceptance through the interwar period (and was grounded in reporting practices that took hold in the late 1800s), the ideal of professional, objective journalism arguably did not become paradigmatic until after World War II. For a thoughtful discussion, see Silvio R. Waisbord, *Reinventing Professionalism: Journalism and News in Global Perspective* (Cambridge: Polity Press, 2013), 29-31.

36. This evolution is discussed at length in chapter 2; a good overview is Kevin G. Barnhurst, "The Interpretive Turn in News," in *Journalism and Technological Change: Historical Perspectives, Contemporary Trends*, ed. Clemens Zimmermann and Martin Schreiber (Chicago: University of Chicago Press, 2014), 111-41.

37. These shifts inform nearly all contemporary scholarship about the media and politics at some level. They receive sustained attention in different ways in, for instance, Ronald

N. Jacobs and Eleanor R. Townsley, *The Space of Opinion: Media Intellectuals and the Public Sphere* (New York: Oxford University Press, 2011); Markus Prior, *Post-Broadcast Democracy: How Media Choice Increases Inequality in Political Involvement and Polarizes Elections* (New York: Cambridge University Press, 2007); and Bruce A. Williams and Michael X. Delli Carpini, *After Broadcast News: Media Regimes, Democracy, and the New Information Environment*, Communication, Society, and Politics (New York: Cambridge University Press, 2011).

38. I discuss "intermedia" relationships and the literature on them in two articles: Lucas Graves, "Blogging Back Then: Annotative Journalism in I. F. Stone's Weekly and Talking Points Memo," *Journalism* 16, no. 1 (January 2014): 99–118, doi:10.1177/1464884914545740; and Lucas Graves and Magda Konieczna, "Sharing the News: Journalistic Collaboration as Field Repair," *International Journal of Communication* 9 (June 2015): 1966–84, http://ijoc.org/index.php/ijoc/article/view/3381/1412. Key studies focused directly on intermedia links and effects include Boczkowski, *News at Work*; Pablo J. Boczkowski, "Technology, Monitoring, and Imitation in Contemporary News Work," *Communication, Culture, and Critique* 2, no. 1 (2009): 39–59, doi:10.1111/j.1753-9137.2008.01028.x; Stephen D. Reese and Lucig H. Danielian, "Intermedia Influence and the Drug Issue: Converging on Cocaine," in *Communication Campaigns About Drugs: Government, Media, and the Public*, ed. Pamela J. Shoemaker (Hillsdale, NJ: L. Erlbaum Associates, 1989), 29–46; Carsten Reinemann, "Routine Reliance Revisited: Exploring Media Importance for German Political Journalists," *Journalism and Mass Communication Quarterly* 81, no. 4 (December 2004): 857–76, doi:10.1177/107769900408100409; and Daron R. Shaw and Bartholomew H. Sparrow, "From the Inner Ring Out: News Congruence, Cue-Taking, and Campaign Coverage," *Political Research Quarterly* 52, no. 2 (June 1999): 323–51, doi:10.1177/106591299905200204.

39. See, e.g., Matt Hadro, "Pants on Fire? Despite Media Outcry, Romney's 'Lie of the Year' Was True," *NewsBusters*, January 18, 2013, http://newsbusters.org/blogs/matt-hadro/2013/01/18/pants-fire-despite-media-outcry-romneys-lie-year-was-true; and Kyle Drennen, "NBC's Lauer: 'Swift and Unanimous' Agreement Romney Ohio Ad 'Campaign Politics at Its Cynical Worst,'" *Media Research Center*, November 6, 2012, http://www.mrc.org/biasalerts/nbcs-lauer-swift-and-unanimous-agreement-romney-ohio-ad-campaign-politics-its-cynical-wor.

40. See Hannah Groch-Begley, "Fox Airs Misleading Fact Check of Romney Jeep Ad," Media Matters for America, November 2, 2012, http://mediamatters.org/blog/2012/11/02/foxs-airs-misleading-fact-check-of-romney-jeep/191106; and "Fox's Varney Declares That Romney's Misleading Claim About Jeep Production in China Is 'Flat-Out Accurate,'" Media Matters for America, November 1, 2012, http://mediamatters.org/video/2012/11/01/foxs-varney-declares-that-romneys-misleading-cl/191061.

41. The Fact-Checking in the News conference took place December 14, 2011, at the headquarters of the New America Foundation (NAF) in Washington, DC. I organized the event with Tom Glaisyer, a graduate-school colleague who was then a media policy fellow

at NAF; we selected major themes for the meeting, recruited all attendees, programmed the day's four panels, and commissioned original research to spur the discussion. We also coauthored one of the reports presented at the conference, "The Fact-Checking Universe in Spring 2012: An Overview" (NAF, February 2012). Attendees included the founders of PolitiFact and FactCheck.org and the *Washington Post*'s two Fact Checker columnists.

42. The first Global Fact-Checking Summit, discussed in more detail in chapter 2, took place in London, June 9–10, 2014. The U.S.-based Poynter Institute hosted the event with support from the Ford Foundation, the National Endowment for Democracy, the Omidyar Network, and Craigconnents. PolitiFact's founder and former top editor, Bill Adair, who joined the journalism faculty at Duke University in 2013, planned the conference; I was one of several people asked to help devise the agenda and individual panels. I also analyzed and presented data gathered by the Duke Reporters' Lab on overseas fact-checking. I received travel support from the Poynter Institute to attend the conference.

43. Christopher M. Kelty, *Two Bits: The Cultural Significance of Free Software* (Durham, NC: Duke University Press, 2008), 18, 263–64. Kelty's research with projects extending the free-software ethic into new arenas offers useful parallels to studying the fact-checking milieu. In the periods under study both were emerging areas where practices remained open and unsettled (hence the "figuring out") and in which, partly for that reason, academic researchers were invited to participate to an unusual degree *as* academics (by organizing conferences, sharing findings with informants, etc.).

44. Even academic research produced for the meeting exposed the tensions that run through the fact-checking world. One scholar's report draft featured a prominent example of a false belief held widely on the left, about the danger of childhood vaccines, to counter the assumption that conservatives have a monopoly on misinformation. An event backer objected vocally to this as an instance of "false balance," though the case remained in the published report.

45. The idea that hidden social structures and processes surface in moments of change, controversy, or anomaly—that the normal is made visible in the unusual—runs through qualitative social science. Moments of unsettlement or poor fit give access to Howard Becker's "worlds" and to Bruno Latour's actor-networks. ("New topics, that's what you need ANT for," he writes.) The same notion underlies Harold Garfinkel's notion of "breaching" experiments. See Howard Becker, *Art Worlds* (Berkeley: University of California Press, 1982); Geoffrey C. Bowker and Susan Leigh Star, *Sorting Things Out: Classification and Its Consequences* (Cambridge, MA: MIT Press, 1999); Harold Garfinkel, *Studies in Ethnomethodology* (Cambridge: Polity Press, 1984); and Bruno Latour, *Reassembling the Social: An Introduction to Actor-Network-Theory*, Clarendon Lectures in Management Studies (Oxford: Oxford University Press, 2005), 142.

46. Such criticism is a constant refrain in the fact-checking world; many examples appear in chapters 4, 5, and 6.

47. I am indebted to an anonymous reviewer for pushing me to raise clearly the question of the ideology of the fact-checkers and whether it substantially challenges the U.S. media-political mainstream. Rasmus Kleis Nielsen, who read a draft of this manuscript, made the important and counterintuitive point that, given the pressures they face, we might be amazed at how *little* politicians lie. Politicians and campaign strategists argue that they go to great lengths to vet their own work and complain that fact-checkers seize on trivial details while ignoring larger truths; examples can be found in chapter 4 and throughout the final section of the book.

1. Ink-Stained Fact-Checkers

1. The event was the Global Fact-Checking Summit, hosted by the Poynter Institute, June 9–10, 2014. Data about fact-checkers are from a survey of attendees conducted by Poynter and a study of worldwide fact-checking sites by the Reporter's Lab of the DeWitt Wallace Center for Media and Democracy at Duke University. Data were analyzed together with PolitiFact founder Bill Adair, now a journalism professor at Duke, and with research associate Shannon Beckham.

2. Author's field notes, June 9, 2014. For two accounts of the summit from attendees, see Bill Adair, "Lessons from London: Fact-Checkers Have Passion, but Need More Checks," Poynter.org, June 13, 2014, http://www.poynter.org/how-tos/journalism-education/255806/lessons-from-london-fact-checkers-have-passion-but-need-more-checks/; and Glenn Kessler, "The Global Boom in Political Fact Checking," Fact Checker, *Washington Post*, June 13, 2014, http://www.washingtonpost.com/blogs/fact-checker/wp/2014/06/13/the-global-boom-in-fact-checking/.

3. Author's field notes, June 9, 2014. Speakers noted were Govindraj Ethiraj of Fact-Checker.in, Amr Sobhy of MorsiMeter, Margo Gontar of StopFake, Matteo Agnoletto of Il Politicometro, and Juliette Jowit of the *Guardian*.

4. PolitiFact founder Bill Adair organized the summit from his new position as a journalism professor at Duke University. The event grew out of a research project to identify fact-checking initiatives around the world; a primarily goal was to launch an international association of fact-checkers. Since 2010 Adair, Brooks Jackson, and Glenn Kessler have advised fact-checking ventures in Africa, Australia, Europe, and South America.

5. Comment by Michael Dobbs at Pants on Fire: Political Mendacity and the Rise of Media Fact-Checkers, a conference at the Annenberg Public Policy Center, Washington, DC, November 9, 2007.

6. Margaret Sullivan, "Facts, Truth . . . and May the Best Man Win," *Public Editor's Journal* (blog), *New York Times*, September 4, 2012, http://publiceditor.blogs.nytimes.com/2012/09/04/facts-truth-and-may-the-best-man-win/. In an interview, Sullivan called explicitly for the *Times* to be a "truth vigilante," answering the question raised by her predecessor: see Joe Strupp, "Incoming *New York Times* Public Editor: 'Newspapers Must

Be Truth Vigilantes,'" *Media Matters for America* (blog), July 16, 2012, http://mediamatters.org/blog/2012/07/16/incoming-new-york-times-public-editor-newspaper/187159. On concerns over fact-checking in straight news reports, see Arthur S. Brisbane, "Should the Times Be a Truth Vigilante?" *Public Editor's Journal* (blog), *New York Times*, January 12, 2012, http://publiceditor.blogs.nytimes.com/2012/01/12/should-the-times-be-a-truth-vigilante/. I discuss Brisbane's argument and the responses to it in Lucas Graves, "Digging Deeper into the New York Times' Fact-Checking Faux Pas," *NiemanLab*, January 18, 2012, http://www.niemanlab.org/2012/01/digging-deeper-into-the-new-york-times-fact-checking-faux-pas/.

7. Ken Layne, "More Funny Fisk, from Sept. 19," *KenLayne.com* (blog), December 9, 2001, http:/kenlayne.com/2000/2001_12_09_logarc.html#7775149 (accessed via archive.org). The object of this attack was Robert Fisk, a veteran Middle East correspondent for London's *Independent*, perhaps best known as one of the few Western journalists to interview Osama bin Laden. Layne and other so-called war-bloggers dismantled Fisk's dispatches so regularly that "to fisk" became a verb. This episode has been widely reviewed by scholars and journalists; a detailed account is in Scott Rosenberg, *Say Everything: How Blogging Began, What It's Becoming, and Why It Matters* (New York: Crown, 2009), 131–64.

8. Nicholas Lemann, "Amateur Hour: Journalism Without Journalists," *New Yorker*, August 7, 2006.

9. Mark Gongloff, "Fact-Checking Walmart's Fact-Check of the New York Times," *Huffington Post*, June 24, 2014, http://www.huffingtonpost.com/2014/06/24/walmart-fact-check-new-york-times_n_5525588.html; Ari Rabin-Havt, "Wal-Mart Flunks Its Fact-Check: The Truth Behind Its Sarcastic Response to the Times," *Salon*, http://www.salon.com/2014/06/25/walmart_flunks_its_fact_check_the_truth_behind_its_sarcastic_response_to_the_times/; and David Tovar, "Fact Check: The New York Times 'The Corporate Daddy,'" *Walmart TODAY*, June 20, 2014, http://blog.walmart.com/opportunity/20140620/fact-check-the-new-york-times-the-corporate-daddy.

10. "Fact Check: Why What Speaker Boehner Just Said Is Completely Wrong," Nancy Pelosi: Democratic Leader, September 30, 2013, http://www.democraticleader.gov/newsroom/fact-check-why-what-speaker-boehner-just-said-is-completely-wrong/.

11. Don Seymour, "#SOTUGOP: House Republicans Host Digital Fact Check & Social Q&A on GOP.gov/SOTU," Office of the Speaker of the House, January 24, 2012, http://www.speaker.gov/video/sotugop-house-republicans-host-digital-fact-check-social-qa-gopgovsotu; and Jake Sherman, "GOP Launching SOTU Website," Politico, February 12, 2013, http://www.politico.com/story/2013/02/gop-launching-website-for-sotu-87481.html.

12. See, e.g., "Clinton's Hard Choices: Facts Vs. Fiction Volume 1," GOP.com, June 10, 2014, http://www.gop.com/news/research/clintons-hard-choices-facts-vs-fiction-volume-1/.

13. Karen Tumulty, "Will Obama's Anti-Rumor Plan Work?" *Time*, June 12, 2008; and Marisa Taylor, "White House Launches Health-Care Response Site 'Reality Check,'" *Wall*

Street Journal Blogs, August 11, 2009, http://blogs.wsj.com/digits/2009/08/11/white -house-launches-health-care-response-site-reality-check/.

14. As is often the case, that rumor contained a grain of truth. According to the fact check, a bust loaned to President George W. Bush while the White House's original bust was being worked on had been returned to the British Embassy at the end of his presidency. Dan Pfeiffer, "Fact Check: The Bust of Winston Churchill," *White House Blog*, July 27, 2012, http://www.whitehouse.gov/blog/2012/07/27/fact-check-bust-winston -churchill. See also Dan Pfeiffer, "Fact Checking the Fact Checker," *White House Blog*, June 7, 2011, http://www.whitehouse.gov/blog/2011/06/07/fact-checking-fact-checker.

15. Elizabeth Flock, "Attack Watch, New Obama Campaign Site to 'Fight Smears,' Becomes Laughing Stock of Conservatives," *Washington Post*, September 16, 2011, https://www .washingtonpost.com/blogs/blogpost/post/attack-watch-new-obama-campaign-site -to-fight-smears-becomes-laughing-stock-of-the-internet/2011/09/14/gIQAspHDSK _blog.html.

16. One way to talk about the changing relationship between political and media institutions is through the language of Bourdieusian field theory. In a recent analysis, for instance, Monica Krause identifies four distinct eras of U.S. journalism based on the relative strength of the field-specific, "autonomous" pole of the journalistic field as against the "heteronomous" pole of economic and state power. "The power of field-specific capital to organize practices in the media has varied," Kraus writes. She argues that since the 1970s increased economic pressures and diminished regulation (among other factors) have yielded a decline in "active newsgathering" and in the autonomy of the journalistic field. Monika Krause, "Reporting and the Transformations of the Journalistic Field: U.S. News Media, 1890–2000," *Media, Culture, and Society* 33, no. 1 (2011): 100, doi:10.1177/0163443710385502. For a broadly parallel argument, see Erik Neveu, "Four Generations of Political Journalism," in *Political Journalism: New Challenges, New Practices*, ed. Raymond Kuhn and Erik Neveu, ECPR Studies in European Political Science (London: Routledge, 2002). At the same time, such developments may offer "a more visible target for professional journalistic critique and opposition," inviting greater assertiveness in some parts of the field; see Rodney Benson, "News Media as a Journalistic Field: What Bourdieu Adds to New Institutionalism, and Vice Versa," *Political Communication* 23, no. 2 (2006): 193, doi:10.1080/10584600600629802.

17. Of course, journalism and politics are always intertwined in ways both obvious and subtle. Daniel Hallin defines U.S. journalism's "high modernism" as the midcentury period when the professional claim to independence *seemed* mostly unproblematic— precisely because of the shared ideology of media and political elites. Daniel C. Hallin, "The Passing of the 'High Modernism' of American Journalism," *Journal of Communication* 42, no. 3 (September 1992): 14–25, doi:10.1111/j.1460-2466.1992.tb00794.x.

18. Jay G. Blumler and Dennis Kavanagh, "The Third Age of Political Communication: Influences and Features," *Political Communication* 16, no. 3 (July 1, 1999): 218, doi:10.1080 /105846099198596. Looking mainly at the United States and the United Kingdom, the

authors argued on the eve of the new century that greater competitive pressure for news outlets and the media generally was altering the relationship between politicians and political journalists in several important ways, promoting, for instance, more mutual animosity, a shift toward tabloid coverage and "infotainment," and so on.

19. Ronald N. Jacobs and Eleanor R. Townsley, *The Space of Opinion: Media Intellectuals and the Public Sphere* (New York: Oxford University Press, 2011), 12. On the expanding space of opinion, see pp. 10, 35–53.

20. David Hochman, "Rumor Detectives: True Story or Online Hoax?" *Reader's Digest*, April 2009, http://www.rd.com/home/rumor-detectives-true-story-or-online-hoax/; David Pogue, "At Snopes.com, Rumors Are Held Up to the Light," *New York Times*, July 15, 2010, http://www.nytimes.com/2010/07/15/technology/personaltech/15pogue-email.html; and Brian Stelter, "Debunkers of Fictions Sift the Net," *New York Times*, April 4, 2010.

21. The site maintains dedicated pages for a dozen well-known politicians, including recent presidential candidates. But these political figures feature mainly as targets rather than purveyors of falsehoods.

22. "About snopes.com," Snopes.com, http://www.snopes.com/info/aboutus.asp.

23. "About Spinsanity," Spinsanity, http://www.spinsanity.org/about/. The site took aim at pundits, politicians from both major parties, and other well-known political voices.

24. *The Daily Show*, Comedy Central (New York: August 12, 2004).

25. Under the auspices of the New America Foundation and the American Press Institute, I have worked closely with Nyhan on several research projects designed to measure the increase in, and possible effects of, political fact-checking.

26. In the language preferred by some observers, they engaged in "acts of news" or "acts of journalism." See, e.g., Sue Robinson, "The Active Citizen's Information Media Repertoire: An Exploration of Community News Habits During the Digital Age," *Mass Communication and Society* 17, no. 4 (March 17, 2014): 509–30, doi:10.1080/15205436.2013. 816745; and Josh Stearns, "A New Call to Protect Acts of Journalism," *Free Press* (blog), October 17, 2013, http://www.freepress.net/blog/2013/10/17/new-call-pro tect-acts-journalism.

27. Herbert J. Gans, *Democracy and the News* (New York: Oxford University Press, 2003).

28. The original mission statement was accessed via the Internet Archive. As of mid-2015, it remains unchanged; see "Our Mission," FactCheck.org, http://www.factcheck.org /about/our-mission/.

29. Brooks Jackson, interview with the author, Washington, DC, December 3, 2012; Eugene Kiely, interview with the author, Philadelphia, PA, March 17, 2011; Cary Spivak, "The Fact-Checking Explosion," *American Journalism Review* 32 (2010); and "Slip by Dick Cheney regarding FactCheck.org," *All Things Considered*, NPR (Washington, DC: October 6, 2004).

30. Between fiscal years 2010 and 2015, Annenberg support averaged $734,000 per year, according to the site's public disclosures. See "Our Funding," FactCheck.org, http:// www.factcheck.org/our-funding/.

31. "Our Mission," FactCheck.org, http://www.factcheck.org/about/our-mission/; and Brooks Jackson, interview with the author, Washington, DC, December 3, 2010.

32. Brooks Jackson, interview with the author, Washington, DC, December 3, 2010; and Eugene Kiely, e-mail interview, March 24, 2014. See also Lucas Graves and Magda Konieczna, "Sharing the News: Journalistic Collaboration as Field Repair," *International Journal of Communication* 9 (June 2015): 1966–84, http://ijoc.org/index.php/ijoc /article/view/3381/1412.

33. Author's field notes, March 17, 2011, and June 8, 2011. The cohort of student interns I observed was decidedly more interested in politics than in journalism, with only one of four expressing any interest in a career in the news.

34. Bill Adair, interview with the author, Washington, DC, December 2, 2010; and author's field notes, February 7, 2011.

35. PolitiFact's site for July 12, 2007, accessed through the Internet Archive.

36. Bill Adair, interview by author, Washington, DC, December 2, 2012; Steve Myers, "PolitiFact Takes Lesson from Fast-Food Industry as It Franchises Fact Checking," Poynter.org, May 3, 2010, http://www.poynter.org/latest-news/top-stories/102422 /politifact-takes-lesson-from-fast-food-industry-as-it-franchises-fact-checking/; Spivak, "The Fact-Checking Explosion"; and author's field notes, February 7, 9, and 17, 2011.

37. The defections underscore the tensions implicit in these unusual journalistic partnerships, discussed in Graves and Konieczna, "Sharing the News." Accounts of one departure, by the *Cleveland Plain-Dealer*, cited staff cuts and unhappiness with the "arbitrary categories" of PolitiFact's Truth-O-Meter; the newspaper came up with its own ten-point rating system. See Ted Diadiun, "Coming: Truth Squad Reporting without the Gimmicks," Cleveland.com, http://www.cleveland.com/readers/index.ssf/2014/01 /coming_truth_squad_reporting_w.html; and Anna Clark, "The Plain Dealer Drops PolitiFact, but Keeps on Factchecking," *Columbia Journalism Review*, June 17, 2014, http://www.cjr.org/united_states_project/cleveland_plain_dealer_politifact_fact checking.php.

38. Myers, "PolitiFact Takes Lesson."

39. Andrew Beaujon, "New PolitiFact Service Will Fact-Check Pundits," Poynter.org, October 10, 2013, http://www.poynter.org/latest-news/mediawire/225595/new -politifact-service-will-fact-check-pundits/; Rem Rieder, "Rieder: PunditFact Will Keep the Pundits Honest," Gannett News Service, October 14, 2013; and "Who We Invest In: PolitiFact and PunditFact," Democracy Fund, http://www.democracyfund.org /portfolio/entry/politifact-and-punditfact.

40. A web page on the Democracy Fund's site explained the rationale: "We are hopeful that this initiative will demonstrate the valuable role that fact checking can play in holding opinion leaders accountable and influence other media organizations to adopt similar practices." See http://www.democracyfund.org/portfolio/entry/pundit-fact.

41. Discussed in part 3 of this book and in Graves and Konieczna, "Sharing the News."

42. Comments by Michael Dobbs at the Pants on Fire: Political Mendacity and the Rise of Media Fact-Checkers conference. See also Jack Shafer, "Lie Detectors," *Slate*, September 20, 2007, http://www.slate.com/articles/news_and_politics/press_box/2007/09/lie _detectors.html.

43. Michael Dobbs, *The Rise of Political Fact-Checking* (Washington, DC: New America Foundation, February 2012), 7.

44. Michael Dobbs, "True but False," Fact Checker, *Washington Post*, December 19, 2007, http://voices.washingtonpost.com/fact-checker/2007/12/true_but_false_1.html.

45. Dobbs, *Rise of Political Fact-Checking*, 9.

46. Comments by Glenn Kessler at Fact-Checking in the News, a meeting hosted by the New America Foundation (NAF), Washington, DC, December 14, 2011; Glenn Kessler, interview with the author, telephone, April 18, 2012; and comments by Glenn Kessler at Global Fact-Checking Summit.

47. Glenn Kessler, "About the Fact Checker," Fact Checker, *Washington Post*, September 11, 2013, http://www.washingtonpost.com/blogs/fact-checker/about-the-fact -checker/.

48. Gregory Ferenstein, "Realtime Political Fact-Checking Becomes A Reality with WaPo's 'Truth Teller,'" TechCrunch, January 29, 2014, http://techcrunch.com/2013/01 /29/realtime-political-fact-checking-becomes-a-reality-with-wapos-truth-teller/; Craig Silverman, "Washington Post's TruthTeller Project Hopes to Birth Real-Time Fact-Checking," Poynter.org, August 8, 2012, http://www.poynter.org/latest-news/regret -the-error/183774/washington-posts-truthteller-project-hopes-to-birth-real-time-fact -checking/; and Craig Silverman, "Washington Post Expands Fact-Checking Project— and Not Just to Movie Trailers," Poynter.org, February 28, 2014, http://www.poynter .org/latest-news/top-stories/241474/washington-post-expands-fact-checking-project -and-not-just-to-movie-trailers/.

49. Author's field notes, June 10, 2014.

50. Rem Rieder, "A Busy Season for Political Fact-Checkers," *American Journalism Review* 34 (June 2012).

51. Author's field notes, June 15, 2011.

52. Comment by Michael Dobbs at Pants on Fire: Political Mendacity and the Rise of Media Fact-Checkers conference.

53. Author's field notes, February 15, 2011.

54. "Q&A with Glenn Kessler," *Q&A*, C-SPAN (Washington, DC: January 15, 2012); see transcript at http://www.c-spanvideo.org/program/303324-1.

55. The phrase "he said, she said" has been used to indicate hard-to-adjudicate factual disputes since at least Anita Hill's Senate testimony at the 1991 confirmation hearings for Supreme Court Justice Clarence Thomas; William Safire, "On Language," *New York Times*, April 12, 1998. As early as 2003, it became a label for reporting that fails to adjudicate factual disputes even when clear evidence does exist: see, e.g., Brent Cunningham, "Re-Thinking Objectivity," *Columbia Journalism Review* 42, no. 2 (August 200):

24–32; and Jay Rosen, "He Said, She Said, We Said," *PressThink* (blog), June 4, 2004, http://archive.pressthink.org/2004/06/04/ruten_milbank.html.

56. Comment by Brooks Jackson at Fact-Checking in the News.

57. Barbie Zelizer, "Journalists as Interpretive Communities," *Critical Studies in Mass Communication* 10, no. 3 (1993): 224, doi:10.1080/15295039309366865. The key reference for thinking through the role of metadiscourse in shaping journalistic practice and self-understanding is Barbie Zelizer, *Covering the Body: The Kennedy Assassination, the Media, and the Shaping of Collective Memory* (Chicago: University of Chicago Press, 1992). For a recent conceptual overview, see Matt Carlson, " 'Where Once Stood Titans': Second-Order Paradigm Repair and the Vanishing U.S. Newspaper," *Journalism* 13, no. 3 (2012): 267–83, doi:10.1177/1464884911421574.

58. Fact-checking organizations have been remarkably welcoming to academic researchers for a number of reasons, including genuine excitement about outsiders taking an interest in their work. Scholarly attention may also yield more direct benefits, helping to garner press attention for fact-checkers, to validate their public-service mission, and, crucially, to encourage support from the nonprofit sector.

59. The concept of "field repair" is developed in Graves and Konieczna, "Sharing the News."

60. Dominique Marchetti has argued that particular subfields of journalism vary in terms of both economic and political autonomy from the fields they cover—sports, medicine, etc.—which "control to a greater or lesser extent the process of their own mediatization." In these Bourdieusian terms fact-checking appears to be quite autonomous from the field (politicians) it covers; however, fact-checkers rely on ties to other neighboring fields, like academia and the nonprofit sector, to shore up that autonomy. See Dominique Marchetti, "Subfields of Specialized Journalism," in *Bourdieu and the Journalistic Field*, ed. Rodney Benson and Erik Neveu (Cambridge: Polity, 2005), 77.

61. Ben Smith, "The Facts About the Fact Checkers," Politico, November 1, 2011, http://www.politico.com/news/stories/1011/67175.html; and Brooks Jackson, interview with the author, Washington, DC, December 3, 2010.

62. This sort of "media work" is discussed in detail in chapter 6. Spivak, "The Fact-Checking Explosion"; see also, e.g., Diana Marszalek, "PolitiFact Aims to Boost Local TV Presence," *TVNewsCheck*, February 28, 2012, http://www.tvnewscheck.com/article/57723/politifact-aims-to-boost-local-tv-presence.

63. Comments by Bill Adair at Global Fact-Checking Summit; Bill Adair, interview with the author, Washington, DC, December 2, 2012; Hannah Vinter, "Bill Adair, Editor of Politifact: 'Readers Love This Kind of Accountability Journalism,' " World Association of Newspapers and News Publishers, August 18, 2011, http://www.wan-ifra.org/articles/2011/08/18/bill-adair-editor-of-politifact-readers-love-this-kind-of-accountability-journal; and Jackie Ogburn, "Bill Adair: Creating New Forms of Journalism," Sanford School of Public Policy, Duke University, September 26, 2013, http://news.sanford.duke.edu/news-type/news/2013/bill-adair-creating-new-forms-journalism.

64. Comment by Jim Drinkard at the "Fact Checking the 2012 Presidential Candidates" panel discussion, National Press Club, Washington, DC, September 26, 2012. See also Michael Scherer, "Fact Checking and the False Equivalence Dilemma," *Time*, October 9, 2012, http://swampland.time.com/2012/10/09/fact-checking-and-the-false-equiv alence-dilemma/.

65. As of late 2014, meters were in use by all but eleven of seventy-one active fact-checking sites in a global database compiled by the Duke Reporter's Lab. (The database counts each U.S. PolitiFact franchise separately.) Those using meters ranged from long-established media outlets in print and broadcast to sites based in pro-democracy groups, universities, and think tanks.

66. Brooks Jackson, interview with the author, telephone, August 18, 2011; and Matt Schwartz, "Truth Police: The Man Behind Factcheck.org," *Huffington Post*, March 28, 2008, http://www.huffingtonpost.com/good-magazine/truth-police-the-man-behi_b_88654.html.

67. Comment by Brooks Jackson at Fact-Checking in the News; Brooks Jackson, interview with the author, Washington, DC, December 3, 2010; and Eugene Kiely, interview with the author, e-mail, March 24, 2014.

68. Glenn Kessler, "Pinocchio Tracker: Fact-Checking the Presidential Candidates," Fact Checker, *Washington Post*, December 14, 2011, http://www.washingtonpost.com /blogs/fact-checker/post/pinocchio-tracker-fact-checking-the-presidential-candi dates/2011/12/13/gIQABntttO_blog.html.

69. A useful framework for understanding such convergence is what Paul DiMaggio and Walter Powell call "institutional isomorphism," which they attribute to the need for organizations to deal with uncertainty within structured organizational fields. See Paul J. DiMaggio and Walter W. Powell, "The Iron Cage Revisited: Institutional Iso-morphism and Collective Rationality in Organizational Fields," *American Sociological Review* 48, no. 2 (April 1, 1983): 147–60, doi:10.2307/2095101.

70. Brooks Jackson, "Firefighters, Fact-Checking and American Journalism," FactCheck. org, December 21, 2012, http://www.factcheck.org/2012/12/firefighters-fact-checking -and-american-journalism/.

71. Comments by Neil Brown at Global Fact-Checking Summit.

72. Referring to Eugene Kiely and to the cofounder of FactCheck.org, communications scholar Kathleen Hall Jamieson, Adair said, "And, by the end, Eugene is going to walk out of here and he's going to be on his cell phone to Kathleen and he's going to be like, 'Oh my god, you've been so wrong all these years, Kathleen!'" Comments by Bill Adair at Global Fact-Checking Summit.

73. Author's field notes, June 9–10, 2014. Comments by Bill Adair and Will Moy at Global Fact-Checking Summit.

74. Author's field notes, June 9–10, 2014. This principle did not exclude any of the groups invited to the global summit.

75. Gaye Tuchman has captured better than anyone the essentially strategic and defensive cast of many of the routines of objective reporting, and offered one of the earliest

scholarly descriptions of what would be called "he said, she said" reporting. Gaye Tuchman, "Objectivity as Strategic Ritual: An Examination of Newsmen's Notions of Objectivity," *American Journal of Sociology* 77 (1972): 660–79.

76. Gianpietro Mazzoleni and Winfried Schulz, "'Mediatization' of Politics: A Challenge for Democracy?," *Political Communication* 16, no. 3 (1999): 247–61, doi:10.1080/10584609919861₃; and Jesper Strömbäck, "Four Phases of Mediatization: An Analysis of the Mediatization of Politics," *International Journal of Press/Politics* 13, no. 3 (2008): 228–46, doi:10.1177/1940161208319097.

77. The social theorist Manuel Castells argues that to a still greater extent than in the era of mass media, in today's network society "the media are not the holders of power, but they constitute by and large the space where power is decided." Manuel Castells, "Communication, Power and Counter-Power in the Network Society," *International Journal of Communication* 1 (2007): 242, http://ijoc.org/index.php/ijoc/article/view/46/35.

78. "Frustration in the White House Press Corps," narrated by Brooke Gladstone and Bob Garfield, *On the Media*, NPR (Washington, DC: March 1, 2013), http://www.onthemedia.org/story/272841-frustration_white_house_press_corps/.

79. An important challenge to the strong version of the "mediatization" hypothesis can be found in Rasmus Kleis Nielsen, *Ground Wars: Personalized Communication in Political Campaigns* (Princeton, NJ: Princeton University Press, 2012). See also David Deacon and James Stanyer, "Mediatization: Key Concept or Conceptual Bandwagon?" *Media, Culture and Society* 36, no. 7 (October 1, 2014): 1032–44, doi:10.1177/0163443714542218.

80. Lori Robertson, "Campaign Trail Veterans for Truth," *American Journalism Review*, 26 (December/January 2005): 38–43; Spivak, "The Fact-Checking Explosion."

81. "Campaign Desk: CJR's Desk for Politics, Policy, and the Press," *Columbia Journalism Review*, http://www.cjr.org/press_room/_resources/pdf/Campaign_Desk_One_Sheet.pdf.

82. Thomas Medvetz, *Think Tanks in America* (Chicago: University of Chicago Press, 2012).

83. "About PolitiFact Bias/FAQ," PolitiFact Bias, http://www.politifactbias.com/p/about-politifact-bias.html.

84. "Our Mission," Accuracy in Media, http://www.aim.org/about/mission-statement/.

85. Arthur S. Hayes, *Press Critics Are the Fifth Estate: Media Watchdogs in America* (Westport, CT: Praeger, 2008), 21–34; and Mike Hoyt, "Defining Bias Downward: Holding Political Power to Account Is Not Some Liberal Plot," *Columbia Journalism Review* 43 (January 2005), http://www.cjr.org/behind_the_news/defining_bias_downward_holding.php.

86. Roger Aronoff and Bethany Stotts, "New York Times Attempts to Blur Benghazi Scandal," *AIM Report*, January 1, 2014, 1, 3.

87. Rich Noyes, phone interview, February 25, 2011; and Rich Noyes, "Hillary Shot at in '96? No Media Mention of Bosnia 'Sniper Fire,'" *NewsBusters* (blog), March 18, 2008, http://newsbusters.org/blogs/rich-noyes/2008/03/18/hillary-shot-96-no-media-mention-bosnia-sniper-fire.

88. Jeff Cohen, "What's FAIR?," *Extra!*, June 1, 1987.

89. Hayes, *Press Critics Are the Fifth Estate*, 76. See also Constance L. Hays, "Making It Work; FAIR or Not?," *New York Times*, May 19, 1996.

90. Jim Naureckas, "Dems Didn't Start Social Security—and Other False Factchecks from Factcheck.org," *FAIR Blog*, September 5, 2012, http://fair.org/blog/2012/09/05/dems-didnt-start-social-security-and-other-false-factchecks-from-factcheck-org/.

91. Peter Hart, "AP's Mostly Factless Factcheck," *FAIR Blog*, September 6, 2012, http://www.fair.org/blog/2012/09/06/aps-factless-fact-check/.

92. "About Us," Media Matters for America, http://mediamatters.org/p/about_us/.

93. Charles Clark, "Media Matters Stakes Claim as High-Volume Watchdog," *National Journal*, September 4, 2010.

94. Author's field notes, October 15, 2010.

95. Tate Williams, interview with the author, Washington, DC, October 15, 2010.

96. This point is developed in chapters 3 and 4. A prominent example comes from the first Fact Checker columnist at the *Washington Post*, who wrote: "If you criticize only one side (in the manner of the left-leaning Media Matters, for example), you are no longer a fact checker. You are a tool in a political campaign." Dobbs, *Rise of Political Fact-Checking*, 13.

97. Comments by Glen Kessler at Fact-Checking in the News.

98. In the original reference, Thomas Gieryn described boundary work in science as "an ideological style found in scientists' attempts to create a public image for science by contrasting it favorably to non-scientific intellectual or technical activities." He noted that scientists stressed different and inconsistent aspects of scientific work as being the source of its authority depending on the context. See Thomas Gieryn, "Boundary-Work and the Demarcation of Science from Non-Science: Strains and Interests in Professional Ideologies of Scientists," *American Sociological Review* 48 (1983): 781.

99. On "boundary work" in the context of professional journalism, see Ronald Bishop, "From behind the Walls: Boundary Work by News Organizations in Their Coverage of Princess Diana's Death," *Journal of Communication Inquiry* 23, no. 1 (January 1999): 90–112, doi:10.1177/0196859999023001005; Mark Coddington, "Defending a Paradigm by Patrolling a Boundary: Two Global Newspapers' Approach to WikiLeaks," *Journalism & Mass Communication Quarterly* 89, no. 3 (2012): 377–96, doi:10.1177/1077699012447918; Seth C. Lewis, "The Tension Between Professional Control and Open Participation," *Information, Communication & Society* 15, no. 6 (2012): 836–66, doi:10.1080/1369118X.2012.674150; and Matthias Revers, "Journalistic Professionalism as Performance and Boundary Work: Source Relations at the State House," *Journalism* 15, no. 1 (2014): 37–52, doi:10.1177/1464884913480459.

100. Rob Tornoe, "'Pants On Fire,'" *Media Matters for America* (blog), December 22, 2011, http://mediamatters.org/blog/2011/12/22/pants-on-fire/162174.

101. Jeffrey Meyer, "Tampa Bay Times Slams Michelle Bachmann for 'Lying' According to Liberal 'PolitiFact,'" *NewsBusters* (blog), May 30, 2013, http://newsbusters.org/blogs/jeffrey-meyer/2013/05/30/tampa-bay-times-slams-michelle-bachmann-lying-according-liberal-polit.

102. Jack Coleman, "Maddow Heaves NY Times Under the Bus in Ongoing Feud with Politi-Fact," *NewsBusters* (blog), June 11, 2014, http://newsbusters.org/blogs/jack-coleman/2014/06/11/maddow-heaves-ny-times-under-bus-ongoing-feud-politifact.

103. Bill Adair, "The Value of Fact-Checking in the 2012 Campaign," PolitiFact, November 8, 2012, http://www.politifact.com/truth-o-meter/article/2012/nov/08/value-fact-checking-2012-campaign/; and Jackson, "Firefighters, Fact-Checking and American Journalism."

104. Justin Bank, "Palin vs. Obama: Death Panels," FactCheck.org, August 14, 2009, http://www.factcheck.org/2009/08/palin-vs-obama-death-panels/; Angie Drobnic Holan, "Sarah Palin Falsely Claims Barack Obama Runs a 'Death Panel,'" PolitiFact, August 10, 2009, http://www.politifact.com/truth-o-meter/statements/2009/aug/10/sarah-palin/sarah-palin-barack-obama-death-panel/; "Fox News Personalities Advance Palin's 'Death Panel' Claim," Media Matters for America, August 10, 2009, http://mediamatters.org/research/200908100054; "Trudy Lieberman on Healthcare Reform, Gary Schwitzer on Health News Study," *CounterSpin*, August 14, 2009, http://fair.org/counterspin-radio/trudy-lieberman-on-healthcare-reform-gary-schwitzer-on-health-news-study/; and Gabriel Voiles, "How 'Death Panels' Became a 'Justifiable Political Claim,'" *FAIR Blog*, August 19, 2009, http://www.fair.org/blog/2009/08/19/how-death-panels-became-a-justifiable-political-claim/.

105. This parallels a central argument in Susan Herbst, *Reading Public Opinion: How Political Actors View the Democratic Process* (Chicago: University of Chicago Press, 1998). Herbst notes that political actors including congressional staff and partisan activists rely on the media for representations of public opinion. Thanks to Rasmus Kleis Nielsen for this point.

106. Michael Schudson, *Discovering the News: A Social History of American Newspapers* (New York: Basic Books, 1978), 188–89.

2. Objectivity, Truth Seeking, and Institutional Facts

1. Hannah Arendt, "Lying in Politics: Reflections on the Pentagon Papers," *New York Review of Books*, November 18, 1971, http://www.nybooks.com/articles/archives/1971/nov/18/lying-in-politics-reflections-on-the-pentagon-pape/.

2. A useful overview of the reasoning is in Glenn Kessler, "Reaffirmed: 4 Pinocchios for a Misleading Mitt Romney Ad on Chrysler and China," Fact Checker, *Washington Post*, January 24, 2013, http://www.washingtonpost.com/blogs/fact-checker/post/reaffirmed-4-pinocchios-for-a-misleading-mitt-romney-ad-on-chrysler-and-china/2013/01/24/095964a8-667d-11e2-9e1b-07db1d2ccd5b_blog.html.

3. These cases are discussed in chapter 4 and in Lucas Graves, "In Defense of Factchecking," *Columbia Journalism Review*, August 9, 2013, http://www.cjr.org/united_states_project/in_defense_of_factchecking.php.

4. See, e.g., Andrew McCarthy, "Palin Was Right on the 'Death Panels'—A Dissent from Today's NRO Editorial," *National Review Online*, August 17, 2009, http://www.nation

alreview.com/corner/185755/palin-was-right-death-panels-dissent-todays-nro-edito rial-and-andrew-c-mccarthy. Meanwhile, some supporters of "Obamacare" agreed that death panels were real and run by the private insurance industry: e.g., Froma Harrop, "There Are Death Panels: The Insurance Industry Runs Them," *Seattle Times*, August 18, 2009; and Mike Madden, "The 'Death Panels' Are Already Here," *Salon*, August 11, 2009, http://www.salon.com/2009/08/11/denial_of_care/.

5. This is a key point: The way we talk about facts in everyday life (though not the way we actually reason with them) reflects aspects of what William James called "rationalism," the view that imagines a unified, logically coherent scheme of abstract truths that transcend and explain the reality we experience. There is a practical sense in this; the usefulness of "facts" as a category lies in precisely their assertion, in the claim they make on permanence and universality. But the difference in how we imagine facts and how we use or make them goes a long way toward explaining controversies around fact-checking. William James, *Pragmatism and Other Writings* (New York: Penguin Books, 2000).

6. Jelani Cobb, "Last Battles," *New Yorker*, July 6, 2015, 27. See also Ta-Nehisi Coates, "What This Cruel War Was Over," *Atlantic*, June 22, 2015, http://www.theatlantic.com/poli tics/archive/2015/06/what-this-cruel-war-was-over/396482/; and Jon Greenberg, "In Defense of Confederate Flag, Frequent Fox News Guest Claims Civil War Wasn't About Slavery," PolitiFact, June 25, 2015, http://www.politifact.com/punditfact/state ments/2015/jun/25/gavin-mcinnes/tweet-civil-war-was-about-secession-not-slavery/.

7. Jon Greenberg, "George Will Says a Sneeze or Cough Could Spread Ebola," Pundit-Fact, October 19, 2014, http://www.politifact.com/punditfact/statements/2014/oct/19 /george-will/george-will-claims-sneeze-cough-spread-ebola/.

8. Perspectives on and examples of such "metajournalistic discourse" are usefully reviewed in Matt Carlson, " 'Where Once Stood Titans': Second-Order Paradigm Repair and the Vanishing U.S. Newspaper," *Journalism* 13, no. 3 (April 2012): 268–69, doi:10.1177/1464884911421574. Two prominent metajournalistic critiques that helped lay the groundwork for the contemporary fact-checking movement were Brent Cunningham, "Re-Thinking Objectivity," *Columbia Journalism Review* 42, no. 2 (August 2003): 24–32; and Jay Rosen, "The View from Nowhere," *PressThink* (blog), September 18, 2003, http://archive.pressthink.org/2003/09/18/jennings.html.

9. Lucas Graves, "Blogging Back Then: Annotative Journalism in I. F. Stone's Weekly and Talking Points Memo," *Journalism* 16, no. 1 (2015): 99–118, doi:10.1177/1464884 914545740.

10. Houston Waring, quoted in Ronald May, "Is the Press Unfair to McCarthy?" *New Republic*, April 1953.

11. Ibid. See discussion in Barbie Zelizer, "Journalists as Interpretive Communities," *Critical Studies in Mass Communication* 10, no. 3 (1993): 230–33, doi:10.1080/152950 39309366865.

12. Looking back from the vantage point of 1981, for instance, one reporter who had covered McCarthy argued that it took "a performance as spectacular as his to move the

guardians of objectivity to admit that the meaning of an event is as important as the facts." Edwin R. Bayley, *Joe McCarthy and the Press* (Madison: University of Wisconsin Press, 1981), 85. Discussed in Zelizer, "Journalists as Interpretive Communities," 232.

13. Michael Schudson (with Elliot King) argues that the myth of Reagan's unshakable connection to the American people resulted from efforts on the part of reporters to reconcile his policy success with their own impressions of him, and from conventional wisdom about the "television age." Michael Schudson, *The Power of News* (Cambridge, MA: Harvard University Press, 1995), 137.

14. Lou Cannon, *Governor Reagan: His Rise to Power* (New York: Public Affairs, 2003), 470. See, e.g., "Ronald Reagan and the Facts," *Argus-Press*, June 3, 1980; and Lou Cannon, "Winging It: What the President Really Meant to Say," *Washington Post*, January 24, 1982.

15. Christopher Hanson (under pseudo. William Boot), "Iranscam: When the Cheering Stopped," *Columbia Journalism Review*, March/April 1987, 20. Discussed in Schudson, *Power of News*, 130.

16. Howard Kurtz, "15 Years Later, the Remaking of a President," *Washington Post*, June 7, 2004.

17. Michael Dobbs, *The Rise of Political Fact-Checking* (Washington, DC: New America Foundation, February 2012).

18. David Hoffman, "Press Conference by Reagan Follows Familiar Pattern," *Washington Post*, September 30, 1982, A20.

19. Lou Cannon, "Reagan Calls South Africa 'Reformist'; White House Later Modifies President's Praise for Regime," *Washington Post*, August 27, 1985; and Glenn Frankel, "Reagan's South Africa," *Washington Post*, August 27, 1985.

20. Dobbs, *Rise of Political Fact-Checking*, 4–5.

21. "Buying the War," *Bill Moyers Journal*, PBS, April 25, 2007; and Dobbs, *Rise of Political Fact-Checking*.

22. See, e.g., Lori Robertson, "Campaign Trail Veterans for Truth," *American Journalism Review*, December/January 2005, http://www.ajr.org/article.asp?id=3784.

23. Kathleen Hall Jamieson, quoted in Lloyd Grove, "Campaign Ads Play Fast and Loose with the Truth," *Washington Post*, October 21, 1988, A1. A piercing treatment of the race and its coverage is in Joan Didion, "Insider Baseball," *New York Review of Books* 35, no. 16 (October 27, 1988).

24. Tom Rosenstiel, "Policing Political TV Ads," *Los Angeles Times*, October 4, 1990.

25. See Bill Adair and Angie Drobnic Holan, "Remembering David Broder and His Passion for Fact-Checking," PolitiFact, March 11, 2011, http://www.politifact.com/truth-o-meter/article/2011/mar/11/remembering-david-broder/; Dobbs, *Rise of Political Fact-Checking*; and Mark Stencel, "Broder's Shift Key: An Unlikely Online Makeover," NPR, March 10, 2011, http://www.npr.org/2011/03/10/134421511/broders-shift-key-an-unlikely-online-makeover.

26. See David Broder, "Should the Media Police the Accuracy of Political Ads?" *Washington Post*, January 19, 1989, A22; David Broder, "Five Ways to Put Some Sanity Back in

Elections," *Washington Post*, January 14, 1990, B1; David Broder, "Put Sanity Back into Our Elections," *Washington Post*, February 25, 1990, B7; and David Broder, "Sick of Issueless Campaigns," *Washington Post*, March 28, 1990, A23.

27. Broder, "Five Ways to Put Some Sanity Back in Elections."

28. Broder, "Should the Media Police the Accuracy of Political Ads?"

29. Grove, "Campaign Ads Play Fast and Loose with the Truth." Discussed in Broder, "Should the Media Police the Accuracy of Political Ads?"

30. Comments by Richard Threlkeld at "Media Analysis of Political Ads," panel discussion hosted by the Annenberg School for Communication, Washington, DC, February 26, 1992. See also Bob Collins, "Death of a Fact-Checker," *NewsCut* (blog), January 13, 2012, http://blogs.mprnews.org/newscut/2012/01/death_of_a_fact-checker/.

31. The origins of the adwatch trend are discussed in Debra Gersh Hernandez, "Improving Election Reporting," *Editor & Publisher* 129, no. 40 (October 5, 1996): 16. According to this account, the format first appeared at the *Los Angeles Times* in 1986.

32. David Broder, "Sick of Issueless Campaigns."

33. Emphasis added. Rosenstiel, "Policing Political TV Ads." See also Adair and Holan, "Remembering David Broder."

34. Justin Bank, *Newspaper Adwatch Stories: Coming Back Strong* (Philadelphia, PA: Annenberg Public Policy Center, November 9, 2007), which examined the largest newspapers with full text available for searching. On the growth of adwatches in the 1990s, see also Courtney Bennett, "Assessing the Impact of Ad Watches on the Strategic Decision-Making Process: A Comparative Analysis of Ad Watches in the 1992 and 1996 Presidential Elections," *American Behavioral Scientist* 40, no. 8 (August 1997): 1,161–82, doi:10.1177/0002764297040008014; Stephen Frantzich, "Watching the Watchers: The Nature and Content of Campaign Ad Watches," *Harvard International Journal of Press/Politics* 7, no. 2 (Spring 2002): 34–57, doi:10.1177/1081180X0200700204; and Chris Glowaki, Thomas J. Johnson, and Kristine E. Kranenburg, "Use of Newspaper Political Adwatches from 1988–2000," *Newspaper Research Journal* 25, no. 4 (Fall 2004): 40–54.

35. Brooks Jackson, interview with the author, Washington, DC, December 3, 2012; "Media & The Campaign: Better This Year?" *All Things Considered*, NPR, May 26, 1992; and Edwin Diamond, "Getting It Right," *New York*, November 2, 1992.

36. Bob Papper, *TV Adwatch Stories: On the Rise* (Philadelphia, PA: Annenberg Public Policy Center, November 9, 2007).

37. Brooks Jackson, interview with the author, Washington, DC, December 3, 2012.

38. See, e.g., Joseph N. Cappella and Kathleen Hall Jamieson, "Broadcast Adwatch Effects: A Field Experiment," *Communication Research* 21, no. 3 (June 1994): 342–56, doi:10.1177/009365094021003006; and Kathleen Hall Jamieson and Joseph N. Cappella, "Setting the Record Straight: Do Ad Watches Help or Hurt?" *Harvard International Journal of Press/Politics* 2, no. 1 (January 1997): 13–22, doi:10.1177/1081180X97002001003. This research led to the technique of setting the ad under review off at an angle rather

than letting it fill the screen. Discussed in Bennett, "Assessing the Impact of Ad Watches"; Brooks Jackson and Kathleen Hall Jamieson, *UnSpun: Finding Facts in a World of Disinformation* (New York: Random House, 2007); and Robertson, "Campaign Trail Veterans for Truth."

39. "Not So Fast," *On the Media*, WYNC, January 16, 2004, http://www.onthemedia.org /2004/jan/16/not-so-fast/.

40. Robertson, "Campaign Trail Veterans for Truth"; see also "Fact Checking the 2004 Presidential Debates," *NewsHour*, PBS, October 21, 2004.

41. Comments by Jake Tapper at Pants on Fire: Political Mendacity and the Rise of Media Fact-Checkers, a conference at the Annenberg Public Policy Center, Washington, DC, November 9, 2007.

42. See Bennett, "Assessing the Impact of Ad Watches"; Frantzich, "Watching the Watchers"; and Glowaki, Johnson, and Kranenburg, "Use of Newspaper Political Adwatches."

43. Bill Adair, interview with the author, Washington, DC, December 2, 2010; see also Adair's comments at Pants on Fire: Political Mendacity and the Rise of Media Fact-Checkers conference; Gabrielle Gorder, "Just the Facts: An Interview with Bill Adair, Founder and Editor of PolitiFact," *NPF Newsbag* (blog), National Press Foundation, October 3, 2011, https://web.archive.org/web/20150603095125/http://national press.org/blogs/newsbag/just-the-facts-an-interview-with-bill-adair-founder-and -editor-of-politifac/.

44. Miller was challenged in interviews following the speech; see "Interview with Senator Zell Miller," *Live Event/Special*, CNN, September 1, 2004; and *Hardball with Chris Matthews*, MSNBC, September 1, 2004.

45. Comments by Bill Adair at Fact-Checking in the News, a meeting hosted by the New America Foundation, Washington, DC, December 14, 2011.

46. Comments by Bill Adair at "The Facts of Political Life," panel discussion at the New America Foundation, Washington, DC, February 28, 2012.

47. Comments by Michael Dobbs at Pants on Fire: Political Mendacity and the Rise of Media Fact-Checkers; and Dobbs, *Rise of Political Fact-Checking*, 4.

48. Glenn Kessler and Dan Morgan, "GOP Prism Distorts Some Kerry Positions," *Washington Post*, September 3, 2004.

49. Kessler, quoted in Thomas Lang, "Glenn Kessler on Fact-Checking Candidates, Getting off the Bus, and Reporters Who Are Ahead of the Curve," *Columbia Journalism Review*, September 17, 2004, http://www.cjr.org/the_water_cooler/glenn_kessler_on_factchecking .php.

50. Glenn Kessler, interview with the author, telephone, April 18, 2012; see also "Q&A with Glenn Kessler," *Q&A*, C-SPAN, January 15, 2012, http://www.c-spanvideo.org /program/303324-1.

51. Comments by Michael Dobbs at Pants on Fire: Political Mendacity and the Rise of Media Fact-Checkers.

52. This argument is developed, for instance, in Michael Schudson, *Watergate in American Memory: How We Remember, Forget, and Reconstruct the Past* (New York: Basic Books, 1992); and Barbie Zelizer, *Covering the Body: The Kennedy Assassination, the Media, and the Shaping of Collective Memory* (Chicago: University of Chicago Press, 1992).

53. Zelizer, "Journalists as Interpretive Communities," 223–24.

54. See, e.g., Dobbs, *Rise of Political Fact-Checking*, 5–6; and discussion at Pants on Fire: Political Mendacity and the Rise of Media Fact-Checkers.

55. Dobbs, *Rise of Political Fact-Checking*, 8. See also, e.g., comments by Jake Tapper in "Sunday Morning Fact-Checking," *Colbert Report*, Comedy Central, April 14, 2010, http://www.cc.com/episodes/6r394e/the-colbert-report-april-14-2010-david-shields -season-6-ep-06051; and comments by Walter Pincus in "Buying the War," *Bill Moyers Journal*, PBS, April 25, 2007.

56. Professional fact-checkers rely exclusively on public documents and sources. Some suggestive evidence of the flimsiness of the Bush administration's case against Iraq could be found in public reports, such as those by UN weapons inspectors. But the best skeptical reporting before the U.S. invasion (such as much-lauded coverage by Knight Ridder's Washington bureau) was based on anonymous dissenting experts within the defense and intelligence establishments. See Michael Massing, "Now They Tell Us," *New York Review of Books*, February 26, 2004.

57. Kevin G. Barnhurst, *Seeing the Newspaper* (New York: St. Martin's Press, 1994).

58. See, e.g., Michael Schudson, *Discovering the News: A Social History of American Newspapers* (New York: Basic Books, 1978), 160–64, 183–94.

59. Kevin G. Barnhurst, "The Interpretive Turn in News," in *Journalism and Technological Change: Historical Perspectives, Contemporary Trends*, ed. Clemens Zimmermann and Martin Schreiber, 111–41 (Chicago: University of Chicago Press, 2014).

60. See, e.g., Kevin Barnhurst and Diana Mutz, "American Journalism and the Decline in Event-Centered Reporting," *Journal of Communication* 47, no. 4 (December 1997): 27–53, doi:10.1111/j.1460-2466.1997.tb02724.x; Thomas E. Patterson, *Out of Order* (New York: A. Knopf, 1993); Michael Schudson, "The Politics of Narrative Form: The Emergence of News Conventions in Print and Television," *Daedalus* 111, no. 4 (1982): 97–112; and Carl Sessions Stepp, "The State of the American Newspaper: Then and Now," *American Journalism Review* 14 (1999): 60–76.

61. Katherine Fink and Michael Schudson, "The Rise of Contextual Journalism, 1950s–2000s," *Journalism* 15, no. 1 (2014): 11, doi:10.1177/1464884913479015.

62. The editor of the *New York Times* Upshot series explained its mission this way in mid-2014: "We will not hesitate to make analytical judgments about why something has happened and what is likely to happen in the future. We'll tell you how we came to those judgments—and invite you to come to your own conclusions." David Leonhardt, "Navigating the News with the Upshot," Facebook, April 21, 2014, https://www.face book.com/notes/the-new-york-times-the-upshot/navigating-the-news-with-the-up shot/1453536644883143.

63. Margaret Sullivan, "'Just the Facts, Ma'am' No More," *New York Times*, January 25, 2014, http://www.nytimes.com/2014/01/26/public-editor/just-the-facts-maam-no-more.html.

64. A recent analysis is in Erik P. Bucy and Maria Elizabeth Grabe, "Taking Television Seriously: A Sound and Image Bite Analysis of Presidential Campaign Coverage, 1992–2004," *Journal of Communication* 57, no. 4 (2007): 652–75, doi:10.1111/j.1460-2466.2007.00362.x. See also Kevin G. Barnhurst and Catherine A. Steele, "Image-Bite News: The Visual Coverage of Elections on U.S. Television, 1968–1992," *Harvard International Journal of Press/Politics* 2, no. 1 (1997): 40–58, doi:10.1177/1081180X97002001005; and Daniel C. Hallin, "Sound Bite News: Television Coverage of Elections, 1968–1988," *Journal of Communication* 42, no. 2 (1992): 5–24, doi:10.1111/j.1460-2466.1992.tb00775.x.

65. Kevin G. Barnhurst, "The Makers of Meaning: National Public Radio and the New Long Journalism, 1980–2000," *Political Communication* 20, no. 1 (2003): 9, doi:10.1080/10584600390172374.

66. Barnhurst and Mutz, "American Journalism"; and Michael Schudson, "Political Observatories, Databases & News in the Emerging Ecology of Public Information," *Daedalus* 139, no. 2 (2010): 100–109.

67. Walter Lippmann, *Public Opinion* (1922; repr. New York: Free Press Paperbacks, 1997).

68. Michael Schudson, "Political Observatories, Databases & News."

69. Schudson, *Discovering the News*, 173, 176–82.

70. Stepp, "The State of the American Newspaper," 65; discussed in Fink and Schudson, "Rise of Contextual Journalism," 7.

71. Daniel C. Hallin, "The Passing of the 'High Modernism' of American Journalism," *Journal of Communication* 42, no. 3 (1992): 14–25.

72. The Progressive critique of politics and confidence in science provided the "discursive framework to anchor claims to authority and respectability" for journalism; see Sylvio Waisbord, *Reinventing Professionalism: Journalism and News in Global Perspective* (Cambridge, U.K.: Polity Press, 2013), 28.

73. Barnhurst and Mutz, "American Journalism," 49; and Fink and Schudson, "Rise of Contextual Journalism."

74. James Fallows, *Breaking the News: How the Media Undermine American Democracy* (New York: Vintage Books, 1997), 116–26.

75. Alicia C. Shepard, "Celebrity Journalists," *American Journalism Review*, September 1997, http://ajrarchive.org/article.asp?id=247.

76. See discussion at Lucas Graves, "Digging Deeper into The *New York Times*' Fact-Checking Faux Pas," Nieman Journalism Lab, January 18, 2012, http://www.niemanlab.org/2012/01/digging-deeper-into-the-new-york-times-fact-checking-faux-pas/.

77. Comments by Brooks Jackson and Glenn Kessler at "Fact-Checking in the News."

78. In fact, alongside stories about political strategy, Hallin's much-cited 1992 essay points to an early fact-check as an example of journalistic mediation; see Hallin, "Passing of the 'High Modernism' of American Journalism," 19.

79. A useful review of this literature is Toril Aalberg, Jesper Strömbäck, and Claes H. de Vreese, "The Framing of Politics as Strategy and Game: A Review of Concepts, Operationalizations and Key Findings," *Journalism* 13, no. 2 (February 1, 2012): 162–78, doi:10.1177/1464884911427799.

80. Press scholar Jay Rosen has made this point memorably with his notion of "savviness" as the "professional religion" of the political press. See Jay Rosen, "Why Political Coverage Is Broken," PressThink, August 26, 2011, http://pressthink.org/2011/08/why -political-coverage-is-broken/; and Jay Rosen, "Karl Rove and the Religion of the Washington Press," PressThink, August 14, 2007, http://archive.pressthink.org/2007 /08/14/rove_and_press.html.

81. On strategic frames and cynicism, see Joseph N. Cappella and Kathleen Hall Jamieson, *Spiral of Cynicism: The Press and the Public Good* (New York: Oxford University Press, 1997). See also Rosen, "Why Political Coverage Is Broken."

82. For instance, the fear of being seen as un-American generated a memo at CNN requiring coverage of civilian casualties in Afghanistan to be balanced with reminders of American dead. Similar fears led MSNBC to dismiss host Phil Donahue for airing skeptical views of the U.S. case for invading Iraq; an internal memo explained that he presented a "difficult public face for NBC in a time of war"; see Matt Wells, "CNN to Carry Reminders of U.S. Attacks," *Guardian*, November 1, 2001; see also "Buying the War."

83. Charles Hanley, interviewed in "Buying the War."

84. Gaye Tuchman, *Making News: A Study in the Construction of Reality* (New York: Free Press, 1978), 87n4.

85. "It Pays to Advertise? Using Advertising to Convince Americans of the Need to Go to War with Iraq," *60 Minutes*, CBS, December 8, 2002.

86. Bob Simon, interviewed in "Buying the War."

87. Comparisons between fact-checking and scientific work come up often among fact-checkers (as discussed in the next section) as well as their critics. See, e.g., Joseph E. Uscinski and Ryden W. Butler, "The Epistemology of Fact Checking," *Critical Review* 25, no. 2 (June 2013): 164–65, 178, doi:10.1080/08913811.2013.843872.

88. This is the idea that beliefs or statements are truth-bearing or not in definite relation to truth-making facts of reality. In analytic philosophy, key advocates of this definition are Bertrand Russell and G. E. Moore, although it is sometimes traced to Aristotle. In *Metaphysics*, Aristotle writes, "To say of what is that it is not, or of what is not that it is, is false, while to say of what is that it is, and of what is not that it is not, is true."

89. This notion is elaborated first in Edmund Husserl's *Ideas* (1913); see discussion in Steven Shapin, *A Social History of Truth: Civility and Science in Seventeenth-Century England* (Chicago: University of Chicago Press, 1994), 29–32.

90. Author's field notes, February 16, 2011.

91. This point has been made best through Ludwig Wittgenstein's notion of "family resemblances" in language. He saw this imprecision as a meaning-making asset of language,

not a flaw. Ludwig Wittgenstein, *Philosophical Investigations*, 4th ed. (Chichester, West Sussex, U.K.: Wiley-Blackwell, 2009), 36e–41e (para. 67–77).

92. Greenberg, "George Will Says a Sneeze"; and Aaron Sharockman, "A Few Words to Those Who Think George Will Was Right about Ebola Going Airborne Through a Sneeze," PunditFact, October 20, 2014, http://www.politifact.com/punditfact/arti cle/2014/oct/20/few-words-those-who-think-george-will-was-right-ab/.

93. John R. Searle, *The Construction of Social Reality* (New York: Free Press, 1995); and John R. Searle, *Speech Acts: An Essay in the Philosophy of Language* (London: Cambridge University Press, 1969).

94. Searle develops the attack on relativist or "antirealist" views in *Construction of Social Reality*, 149–176. See also John R. Searle, "Why Should You Believe It?" *New York Review of Books*, September 24, 2009.

95. Searle, *Construction of Social Reality*, 28. A constitutive rule observes the simple formula "X counts as Y in context C."

96. Searle argues that institutional facts arise from a human capacity for "collective intentionality," which allows us to assign a particular status function to, for instance, a boundary marker, or to a rectangle of green paper made in a certain way and bearing certain markings. Searle, *Construction of Social Reality*, 47–51.

97. This is nicely documented in, for instance, Neal Desai, Andre Pineda, Majken Runquist, Mark Andrew Fusunyan, Katy Glenn, Gabrielle Kathryn Gould, Michelle Rachel Katz, et al., *Torture at the* Times: *Waterboarding in the Media* (Cambridge, MA: Joan Shorenstein Center on the Press, Politics, and Public Policy, 2010), http://dash.harvard .edu/handle/1/4420886.

98. See, for instance, discussion of "experimenter's regress" in Harry M. Collins, "Tacit Knowledge, Trust and the Q of Sapphire," *Social Studies of Science* 31, no. 1 (February 2001): 71–85.

99. Even these facts have been contested; for instance, in a 2014 television appearance former vice president Dick Cheney challenged the common understanding that Japanese soldiers were tried for the crime in the United States. See Glenn Kessler, "Cheney's Claim That the U.S. Did Not Prosecute Japanese Soldiers for Waterboarding," Fact Checker, *Washington Post*, December 16, 2014, http://www.washingtonpost.com/blogs/fact-checker/wp/2014/12/16 /cheneys-claim-that-the-u-s-did-not-prosecute-japanese-soldiers-for-waterboarding/.

100. Brian Stelter, "Study of Waterboarding Coverage Prompts a Debate in the Press," *Media Decoder* (blog), *New York Times*, July 2, 2010, http://mediadecoder.blogs.nytimes.com /2010/07/02/study-of-waterboarding-coverage-prompts-a-debate-in-the-press/. See discussion in Graves, "Digging Deeper."

101. Dean Baquet, "The Executive Editor on the Word 'Torture,'" *New York Times*, August 7, 2014, http://www.nytimes.com/times-insider/2014/08/07/the-executive-editor-on-the -word-torture/.

102. Latour associates this view with positivism, but it arguably reflects our commonsense notion of facts. Bruno Latour, *Reassembling the Social: An Introduction to Actor-Network-Theory* (Oxford: Oxford University Press, 2005), 112.

103. See, e.g., Searle, "Why Should You Believe It?" Searle here appears to misunderstand "social constructivism" as either a kind of radical nominalism or the position that no material reality exists independent of our understanding. In various places, Latour has explicitly rejected these views as well as the label of "social construction" precisely for reifying a view of the "social" as something nonmaterial and outside of "nature"; see, e.g., Latour, *Reassembling the Social*, 88–106. But the smartest and pithiest reply to this common misunderstanding may come from John Durham Peters: "Latour is not the foe of science: he is its lover, and therefore prefers to see it naked." See John Durham Peters, *The Marvelous Clouds: Toward a Philosophy of Elemental Media* (Chicago: University of Chicago Press, 2015), 40. For a direct challenge to Searle, see also Howard S. Becker, "Book Review: John R. Searle *Making the Social World: The Structure of Human Civilization*; Paul A. Boghossian *Fear of Knowledge: Against Relativism and Constructivism*," *Science, Technology & Human Values* 36, no. 2 (March 1, 2011): 273–79, doi:10.1177/0162243910378070.

104. Michel Callon, "Some Elements of a Sociology of Translation: Domestication of the Scallops and the Fishermen of St Brieuc Bay," in *The Science Studies Reader*, ed. Mario Biagioli, 67–83 (New York: Routledge, 1999); Bruno Latour, *Science in Action: How to Follow Scientists and Engineers Through Society* (Cambridge, MA: Harvard University Press, 1987); and Susan Leigh Star and James R. Griesemer, "Institutional Ecology, 'Translations' and Boundary Objects: Amateurs and Professionals in Berkeley's Museum of Vertebrate Zoology, 1907–39," *Social Studies of Science* 19, no. 3 (August 1989): 387–420, doi:10.1177/030631289019003001.

105. Star and Griesemer, "Institutional Ecology," 388.

106. Jürgen Habermas's reasoning public was wider than the aristocracy but culturally and socially proximate to it. He argues explicitly that the "bourgeois avant-garde of the educated middle class learned the art of critical-rational public debate through its contact with the 'elegant world.'" And he concedes that the new public did not speak for everyone; rather, it is the utopian aspiration to do so that represents the "transcendent legacy" of the bourgeois public sphere. Jürgen Habermas, *The Structural Transformation of the Public Sphere: An Inquiry into a Category of Bourgeois Society* (Cambridge, MA: MIT Press, 1989), 29.

107. The tension between an ideal of publicness and one of rational-critical debate runs through Habermas's account. It is a simplification but not an unfair one to say he blames greater democratic inclusivity for the degradation of public discourse and the disappearance of the reasoning public sphere. Habermas, *Structural Transformation*, 127. See also Craig J. Calhoun, ed., "Introduction: Habermas and the Public Sphere," in *Habermas and the Public Sphere* (Cambridge, MA: MIT Press, 1992).

108. Shapin argues that the culture of courtly society permeated scientific practice in seventeenth-century England, visible in the personal and family networks linking gentleman scientists; in the discursive conventions that took shape around scientific communication and argumentation; and in a formal ideal of objectivity based more or less explicitly in the personal virtues and capacity for "free action" associated with men of noble birth. Shapin, *Social History of Truth*.

109. This perspective highlights the social character of scientific knowledge, replacing an image of the solitary, skeptical scientist with a focus on the "morally textured relations" between people doing scientific work. Ibid., 19, 27.

110. Ibid., 36.

111. Civility linked to social or professional status has real bite, not to be confused with the wan, hopeful appeals we often hear in open public settings. It is worth noting that civility is one of the "five pillars" of Wikipedia, the collaborative online encyclopedia; see "Wikipedia: Five Pillars," Wikipedia, http://en.wikipedia.org/wiki/Wikipedia:Five _pillars.

112. See, e.g., Jay Rosen, "My Simple Fix for the Messed Up Sunday Shows," *Jay Rosen: Public Notebook*, December 27, 2009, https://publicnotebook.wordpress.com/2009 /12/28/my-simple-fix-for-the-messed-up-sunday-shows/. The useful notion "professional communicators" as a category that includes politicians and media figures is from Benjamin I. Page, *Who Deliberates? Mass Media in Modern Democracy*, American Politics and Political Economy (Chicago: University of Chicago Press, 1996).

113. Both scholars and media critics complain that the economic and cultural logic of television, in particular, discourages careful factual arguments, rewarding instead what sociologist Pierre Bourdieu has called "fast thinkers" who rely on received wisdom and well-established analytical frames. Pierre Bourdieu, *On Television* (New York: New Press, 1998); see also, e.g., Fallows, *Breaking the News*.

114. A fascinating and revealing discussion of the question of differentiating between inaccurate and misleading statements can be found in the official adjudication, by the Financial Times editorial complaints commissioner, of a complaint brought about an article by economist Niall Ferguson. See Greg Callus, "Adjudication," Financial Times Ltd., May 27, 2015, http://aboutus.ft.com/files/2010/09/Ferguson-Adjudication-with -PS.pdf.

115. On "interpretive communities" as structuring common readings of a text, see Stanley Fish, *Is There a Text in This Class? The Authority of Interpretive Communities* (Cambridge, MA: Harvard University Press, 1980). Discussed also in Zelizer, "Journalists as Interpretive Communities."

116. Thomas S. Kuhn, *The Structure of Scientific Revolutions*, 4th ed. (Chicago: University of Chicago Press, 2012). An antecedent of the scientific paradigm is Ludwik Fleck's notion of "thoughtstyles"; Ludwik Fleck, *Genesis and Development of a Scientific Fact* (Chicago: University of Chicago Press, 1981).

117. For instance, Karin Knorr-Cetina contrasts high-energy physicists and molecular biologists in *Epistemic Cultures: How the Sciences Make Knowledge* (Cambridge, MA: Harvard University Press, 1999). Peter Galison compares three classes of physicists in "Trading Zone: Coordinating Action and Belief," in *The Science Studies Reader*, ed. Mario Biagioli, 137–60 (New York: Routledge, 1999).

118. Knorr-Cetina defines epistemic cultures as "those sets of practices, arrangements and mechanisms bound together by necessity, affinity and historical coincidence which, in

a given area of professional expertise, make up how we know what we know." Karin Knorr Cetina, "Culture in Global Knowledge Societies: Knowledge Cultures and Epistemic Cultures," in *The Blackwell Companion to the Sociology of Culture*, ed. Mark D. Jacobs and Nancy Weiss Hanrahan (Malden, MA: Blackwell, 2005), 67.

119. Schudson, *Discovering the News*, 9; and Waisbord, *Reinventing Professionalism*. This point is also developed in chapter 4.

120. Tuchman, *Making News*, 85–88. On sourcing practices during Watergate, see Barry Sussman, "Watergate, Twenty-Five Years Later: Myths and Collusion," Watergate.info, http://watergate.info/1997/06/17/watergate-25-years-later-barry-sussman.html; and Bonnie Brennen, "Book Review: Sweat Not Melodrama: Reading the Structure of Feeling in *All the President's Men*," *Journalism* 4, no. 1 (February 2003): 113–31, doi:10.1177/14648849030 04001444.

121. Steven Epstein, "The Construction of Lay Expertise: AIDS Activism and the Forging of Credibility in the Reform of Clinical Trials," *Science, Technology, and Human Values* 20, no. 4 (1995): 408, doi:10.1177/016224399502000402. The activists' main concern was with the conduct of clinical trials: what scientists viewed only as a research tool they saw as opportunities for life-saving treatment.

122. Ibid., 418.

123. Original italics; Greg Marx, "What the Fact-Checkers Get Wrong," *Columbia Journalism Review*, January 5, 2012, http://www.cjr.org/campaign_desk/what_the_fact-checkers _get_wro.php. See also Jay Rosen, "Politifact Chose the Vice of the Year but They Called It a Lie. That Was Dumb." *PressThink*, December 22, 2011, http://pressthink.org/2011 /12/politifact-chose-the-vice-of-the-year-and-called-it-a-lie/.

124. This is a defining feature of Enlightenment thought, marking the decisive break from what we now see as religiously grounded traditions like medieval Scholasticism. Separating the "true" from the "good" would have been profoundly alien to Plato and Aristotle. Plato's *Republic*, for instance, defines branches of knowledge as promoting the well-being of their respective domains. In the famous allegory of the cave, Plato writes that "what gives truth to things known and the power to know to the knower is the form of the good." This is why classical Greek philosophy could be appropriated by Christian thinkers like St. Augustine and St. Aquinas, and by medieval Islamic and Jewish thought. Plato, *The Republic*, 2nd rev. ed. (London: Penguin, 2007), 342d, 508e.

125. Perhaps the most direct challenge has come from pragmatists like William James, John Dewey, and (in their later work) Richard Rorty and Hilary Putnam. "Truth is one species of good, and not, as is usually supposed, a category distinct from good, and co-ordinate with it," James argues in *Pragmatism and Other Writings*, 38. Meanwhile much social theory points to the political projects implicit in ostensibly neutral knowledge-building, and to the way language and culture always frame factual reasoning. Two iconic examples are Michel Foucault, *Discipline and Punish: The Birth of the Prison*, 2nd ed. (New York: Vintage Books, 1995); and Edward W. Said, *Orientalism*, rev. ed. (London: Penguin, 2003).

126. See, e.g., Shapin, *Social History of Truth*. This purging can be understood as one component of what Bruno Latour calls the work of "purification" necessary to sustain the modernist divide between nature and society. Bruno Latour, *We Have Never Been Modern* (Cambridge, MA: Harvard University Press, 1993).

127. In this sense they apply what Habermas called "discourse ethics," as developed in, e.g., *Moral Consciousness and Communicative Action* (Cambridge, MA: MIT Press, 1990). What is interesting for the present discussion is the central argument that rational discourse presupposes ethical discourse, in the sense that participants are committed in good faith to rules that allow the best argument to carry the day.

128. James S. Ettema and Theodore L. Glasser, *Custodians of Conscience: Investigative Journalism and Public Virtue* (New York: Columbia University Press, 1998), 11.

129. Ibid., 12.

130. Ibid., 152.

Part II. The Work of Fact-Checking

1. Quoted in Dylan Stableford, " 'Born in Kenya': Obama's Literary Agent Misidentified His Birthplace in 1991," Yahoo News, May 18, 2012, http://news.yahoo.com/blogs /ticket/born-kenya-obama-literary-agent-misidentified-birthplace-1991-214423507 .html.

2. Ben Smith and Byron Tau, "Birtherism: Where It All Began," Politico, April 22, 2011, http://www.politico.com/news/stories/0411/53563.html.

3. Amy Hollyfield, "Obama's Birth Certificate: Final Chapter," PolitiFact, June 27, 2008, http://www.politifact.com/truth-o-meter/article/2008/jun/27/obamas-birth -certificate-part-ii/.

4. Ibid. Under the title "Perspective: For True Disbelievers, the Facts Are Just Not Enough," Hollyfield's article was among the articles cited when PolitiFact won a Pulitzer Prize for national reporting in 2009; see http://www.pulitzer.org/winners/7086.

5. Brooks Jackson, interview with the author, telephone, May 22, 2012.

6. Jess Henig, "Born in the U.S.A.," FactCheck.org, August 21, 2008, http://factcheck .org/2008/08/born-in-the-usa/.

7. Robert Farley, " 'Birthers' Claim Gibbs Lied When He Said Obama's Birth Certificate Is Posted on the Internet," PolitiFact, July 28, 2009, http://www.politifact.com/truth-o -meter/statements/2009/jul/28/worldnetdaily/birthers-claim-gibbs-lied-when -he-said-obamas-birt/.

8. Glenn Kessler, "More 'Birther' Nonsense from Donald Trump and Sarah Palin," Fact Checker, *Washington Post*, April 12, 2011, http://www.washingtonpost.com/blogs /fact-checker/post/the-donald-has-a-memory-lapse/2011/04/14/AFrme2MD_blog .html.

9. "Dobbs' Focus On Obama Birth Draws Fire to CNN," *Morning Edition*, NPR, July 31, 2009.

10. *The Situation Room*, CNN, May 31, 2012.

11. Angie Drobnic Holan, interview with the author, telephone, February 25, 2011.

12. Author's field notes, June 8, 2011.

13. Jeff Zeleny, "Barbour Slams Obama on Economy and Energy," *The Caucus* (blog), *New York Times*, March 14, 2011, http://thecaucus.blogs.nytimes.com/2011/03/14/barbour-slams-obama-on-economy-and-energy/.

14. Author's field notes, June 8, 2011.

15. Herbert J. Gans, *Democracy and the News* (New York: Oxford University Press, 2003).

16. Bill Adair, "Does PolitiFact Seek 'the Comfort of the Middle Ground'?" PolitiFact, July 12, 2010, http://www.politifact.com/truth-o-meter/article/2010/jul/12/does-politifact-seek-comfort-middle-ground/.

17. Lauren Hitt, "Barbour Inflates Obama's Job Losses," FactCheck.org, March 15, 2011, http://www.factcheck.org/2011/03/barbour-inflates-obamas-job-losses/.

18. The relationship between fact-checkers and other journalists is developed more fully in chapter 6.

3. Choosing Facts to Check

1. Comments by Lori Robertson and Nathaniel Herz at Truth in Politics 2014: A Status Report on Fact-Checking Journalism meeting, American Press Institute, Arlington, VA, December 10, 2014.

2. Benjamin Page develops the useful idea of "professional communicators," a category spanning not just politicians but also journalists, pundits, interest groups, and other actors who routinely participate in public political deliberation through the media. Benjamin I. Page, *Who Deliberates? Mass Media in Modern Democracy*, American Politics and Political Economy (Chicago: University of Chicago Press, 1996).

3. See, e.g., Eric Ostermeier, "Selection Bias? PolitiFact Rates Republican Statements as False at 3 Times the Rate of Democrats," *Smart Politics* (blog), February 10, 2011, http://blog.lib.umn.edu/cspg/smartpolitics/2011/02/selection_bias_politifact_rate.php; and Joseph E. Uscinski and Ryden W. Butler, "The Epistemology of Fact Checking," *Critical Review* 25, no. 2 (2013): 162–80, doi:10.1080/08913811.2013.843872.

4. Bill Adair, "Inside the Meters: Responding to a George Mason University Press Release About Our Work," PolitiFact, May 29, 2013, http://www.politifact.com/truth-o-meter/blog/2013/may/29/responding-george-mason-university-press-release-a/.

5. Author's field notes, October 3, 2011. Adair has made the declaration elsewhere; see, e.g., Abby Brownback, "Facing the Truth-O-Meter," *American Journalism Review*, March 2010, http://www.ajr.org/article.asp?id=4868.

6. Brooks Jackson, interview with the author, Washington, DC, December 3, 2010.

7. PolitiFact founder Bill Adair has used this analogy: "I think of it as like the back of a baseball card. You know—that it's sort of someone's career statistics." See *Washington Journal*, C-SPAN, August 4, 2009.

8. Glenn Kessler, "About the Fact Checker," Fact Checker, *Washington Post*, September 11, 2013, http://www.washingtonpost.com/blogs/fact-checker/about-the-fact-checker/. The

site also asks for tips on errors committed by the media but in practice does not target other journalists.

9.   Brooks Jackson, interview with the author, Washington, DC, December 3, 2010.

10. Author's field notes, June 6, 2011.

11. "About PolitiFact," PolitiFact, http://www.politifact.com/about/. However, the bulk of Truth-O-Meter items target officeholders and candidates; see, e.g., analysis in Oster-meier, "Selection Bias?"

12. Angie Drobnic Holan, "Obama a Muslim? No He's Not. The Evidence Has Not Changed," PolitiFact, August 26, 2010, http://www.politifact.com/truth-o-meter/statements/2010/aug/26/18-percent-american-public/obama-muslim-no-hes-not-evidence-has-not-changed/.

13. Louis Jacobson, "Doonesbury Strip Says 270,000 Americans Have Been Killed by Guns Since 9/11," PolitiFact, February 14, 2011, http://www.politifact.com/truth-o-meter/statements/2011/feb/14/doonesbury/doonesbury-strip-says-270000-americans-have-been-k/.

14. Author's field notes, June 15, 2011, and February 10, 2015.

15. Eugene Kiely, interview with the author, Philadelphia, PA, March 17, 2011.

16. Author's field notes, June 7, 2011.

17. Ibid.

18. Ibid., June 15, 2011.

19. Ibid., February 9 and 17, 2011.

20. Angie Drobnic Holan, interview with the author, telephone, February 25, 2011; and author's field notes, February 7 and 9, 2011.

21. CTV News, "Obama Campaign Mum on NAFTA Contact with Canada," February 29, 2008, http://www.ctvnews.ca/obama-campaign-mum-on-nafta-contact-with-canada-1.279448. Both the Obama campaign and the Canadian government denied the report.

22. Author's field notes, June 15, 2011.

23. Ibid., February 9 and 17, 2011.

24. Ibid., June 7, 2011.

25. Comment by Brooks Jackson at Fact-Checking in the News, meeting hosted by the New America Foundation, Washington, DC, December 14, 2011.

26. PolitiFact statistics on total Truth-O-Meter rulings through mid-2015 yielded the following distribution: True, 16 percent; Mostly True, 18 percent; Half True, 22 percent; Mostly False, 16 percent; False, 19 percent; Pants on Fire, 9 percent. (Percentages don't add to 100 due to rounding.)

27. The site's iPhone app features a "Truth Index," modeled on stock-market indices, meant to capture overall political mendacity day by day. One version also offered subject-specific tallies that showed, for instance, a disproportionate level of deception in the health care debate.

28. Author's field notes, October 3, 2011.

29. "Q&A with Glenn Kessler," *Q&A*, C-SPAN, January 15, 2012, http://www.c-spanvideo
.org/program/303324-1.

30. See discussion of journalism's "fundamental biases" in Jack Fuller, *News Values: Ideas for an Information Age* (Chicago: University of Chicago Press, 1996), 7–10.

31. Author's field notes, October 3, 2011.

32. "Political Fact-Checking Under Fire," *Talk of the Nation*, NPR, January 10, 2012.

33. Author's field notes, June 7, 2011.

34. Ibid., February 9, 2011, and June 8 and 15, 2011; and comments at Fact-Checking in the News.

35. Willoughby Mariano, "Metro Atlanta Groundhog Boasts More Accuracy than Punxsutawney Phil," PolitiFact Georgia, February 4, 2011, http://www.politifact.com/georgia
/statements/2011/feb/04/general-beauregard-beau-lee/metro-atlanta-groundhog
-boasts-more-accuracy-punxs/.

36. Louis Jacobson, "Joe Biden Says that Closing Amtrak's Northeast Corridor Would Force I-95 to Expand by Seven Lanes," PolitiFact, February 11, 2011, http://www
.politifact.com/truth-o-meter/statements/2011/feb/11/joe-biden/joe-biden-says-closing
-northeast-corridor-would-fo/.

37. Author's field notes, February 11, 2011.

38. Ibid., June 15, 2011.

39. Angie Drobnic Holan, "Did Herman Cain Turn Around Godfather's Pizza?" PolitiFact, June 10, 2011, http://www.politifact.com/truth-o-meter/statements/2011/jun/10/herman
-cain/herman-cain-godfathers-pizza-turn-around/.

40. Brooks Jackson, interview by author, Washington, DC, December 3, 2010.

41. Author's field notes, June 7, 2011.

42. Ibid., June 8, 2011.

43. Ibid., June 15, 2011.

44. The amount of overlap in claims investigated by the fact-checkers is difficult to measure, especially as the same claim may surface in different forms or from more than one speaker. But direct citations of one another's work offer a good proxy. As of late 2015, for instance, PolitiFact and FactCheck.org had each directly cited the other more than one hundred times as evidence to support their own fact checks.

45. Comment by Glenn Kessler at Fact-Checking in the News.

46. Brooks Jackson et al., "False Claims in Final Debate," FactCheck.org, October 23, 2012, http://www.factcheck.org/2012/10/false-claims-in-final-debate/.

47. Author's field notes, June 9, 2014. Comments by Angie Drobnic Holan and Glenn Kessler at the Global Fact-Checking Summit hosted by the Poynter Institute, London, June 9-10, 2014.

48. Angie Drobnic Holan, "7 Steps to Better Fact-Checking," PolitiFact, August 20, 2014, http://www.politifact.com/truth-o-meter/article/2014/aug/20/7-steps-better-fact
-checking/.

49. On consistency among U.S. fact-checkers, see Michelle A. Amazeen, "Revisiting the Epistemology of Fact Checking," *Critical Review* 27, no. 1 (2015): 1–22, doi:10.1080/0891 3811.2014.993890.

50. "Q&A with Glenn Kessler," *Q&A*, C-SPAN, January 15, 2012.

51. Angie Drobnic Holan, "When Fact-Checkers Disagree," PolitiFact, October 21, 2011, http://www.politifact.com/truth-o-meter/article/2011/oct/21/when-fact-checkers -disagree/.

52. See, e.g., Lori Robertson, "Democrats' 'End Medicare' Whopper, Again," FactCheck.org, March 6, 2012, http://www.factcheck.org/2012/03/democrats-end-medicare-whopper -again/.

53. Comment by Brooks Jackson at Fact-Checking in the News.

54. Author's field notes, February 17, 2011.

55. Robert Farley, "Obama Wanted Higher Gasoline Prices?" FactCheck.org, March 23, 2012, http://www.factcheck.org/2012/03/obama-wanted-higher-gasoline-prices/; Glenn Kessler, "Gassy Rhetoric on Gasoline Prices," Fact Checker, *Washington Post*, February 27, 2012, http://www.washingtonpost.com/blogs/fact-checker/post/gassy-rhetoric-on-gaso line-prices/2012/02/26/gIQAqPAXdR_blog.html; and Molly Moorhead, "Gasoline Price Blame Game: 2012 Edition," PolitiFact, March 22, 2012, http://www.politifact.com /truth-o-meter/article/2012/mar/22/gas-price-blame-game-2012-edition/.

56. Comments by Glenn Kessler at Truth in Politics 2014.

57. Author's field notes, February 7, 2011; June 15, 2011; and June 10, 2014.

58. Louis Jacobson, "Barack Obama Says White House Budget Would Not Add to the Debt Within a Few Years," PolitiFact, February 15, 2011, http://www.politifact.com/truth -o-meter/statements/2011/feb/15/barack-obama/barack-obama-says-white-house -budget-would-not-add/.

59. White House, "Press Briefing by Press Secretary Jay Carney," February 16, 2011, http://www.whitehouse.gov/the-press-office/2011/02/16/press-briefing-press-secretary -jay-carney-2162011.

60. Comment by Bill Adair at "The Facts of Political Life."

61. Author's field notes, June 6, 2011.

62. Lucas Graves, "Mitch Daniels Says Interest on Debt Will Soon Exceed Security Spending," PolitiFact, February 17, 2011, http://www.politifact.com/truth-o-meter/statements /2011/feb/17/mitch-daniels/mitch-daniels-says-interest-debt-will-soon-exceed-/.

63. Author's field notes, February 17, 2011.

64. Louis Jacobson, "Fact-Checking CPAC," PolitiFact, February 11, 2011, http://www .politifact.com/truth-o-meter/article/2011/feb/11/fact-checking-cpac/; and Louis Jacobson, "Let the Budget Battling Begin," PolitiFact, February 15, 2011, http://www.politifact .com/truth-o-meter/article/2011/feb/15/let-budget-battling-begin/.

65. Author's field notes, February 17, 2011.

66. Michael Dobbs, *Rise of Political Fact-Checking* (Washington, DC: New America Foundation, February 2012).

67. Brooks Jackson, interview with the author, Washington, DC, December 3, 2010.

68. See "Beyond the Truth-O-Meter," PolitiFact, at http://www.politifact.com/curation/national/archive/.

69. "Political Fact-Checking Under Fire."

70. Comment by Glenn Kessler at Fact-Checking in the News.

71. Author's field notes, June 15, 2011.

72. Ostermeier, "Selection Bias?"

73. Author's field notes, February 10, 2011.

74. Gabrielle Gorder, "Just the Facts: An Interview with Bill Adair, Founder and Editor of PolitiFact," *NPF Newsbag*, National Press Foundation, October 3, 2011, https://web.archive.org/web/20150603095125/http://nationalpress.org/blogs/newsbag/just-the-facts-an-interview-with-bill-adair-founder-and-editor-of-politifac/.

75. At PolitiFact, I heard that outside reporters will sometimes tweet a suspicious claim from one of the politicians they cover, followed by the instruction, "PolitiFact?" Author's field notes, June 15, 2011.

76. Eugene Kiely, interview with the author, March 17, 2011.

77. Author's field notes, June 6, 2011.

78. Ibid.

79. Ibid.

80. Ibid., June 7, 2011.

81. Eugene Kiely, interview with the author, March 17, 2011; author's field notes, June 6 and 7, 2011.

82. Author's field notes, February 7–21, 2011, and June 15, 2011.

83. See Angie Drobnic Holan, "Fact-Checking Bill O'Reilly's Interview with President Barack Obama," PolitiFact, February 7, 2011, http://www.politifact.com/truth-o-meter/article/2011/feb/07/fact-checking-bill-oreillys-interview-barack-obama/.

84. Author's field notes, February 7–21, 2011.

85. Ibid., February 7–8, 2011.

86. Ibid.

87. William Kristol, "Stand for Freedom," *Weekly Standard*, February 14, 2011, 7–8.

88. See Fox News Network, *Glenn Beck*, March 31, 2011, and February 1, 2011. For instance, on his February 1 show the host argued: "The radicals here in America that are operating as Marxists and communists that are in support of this, their goals include the transformation of America into an Islamic state, the destruction of the western world. There's a strange alliance between the left and the Islamists that we're seeing. I think it's all part of the coming insurrection. You can call it a new world order or a caliphate, but the world right now is being divvied up. And the uber left and the Islamists, and the global elites are moving in the same direction. I'm not saying they are plotting together. The Islamists and the uber left are. And they share some commonalities. I mean, honestly, I can't tell the difference between extreme leftists and radical Islamists."

89. I finally settled on Beck's claim that the Muslim Brotherhood openly advocated war against Israel, reviewed in chapter 5.

90. *Rachel Maddow Show*, MSNBC, February 4, 2011. See also *Ed Schultz Show*, MSNBC, February 7, 2011; and *Hardball with Chris Matthews*, MSNBC, February 4 and 7, 2011.

91. Author's field notes, February 7–8, 2011.

92. Aaron Sharockman, "Florida Dems Say Bill McCollum Out of Touch on Subprime Mortgage Crisis," PolitiFact Florida, May 11, 2010, http://www.politifact.com/florida /statements/2010/may/11/florida-democratic-party/florida-dems-bill-mccollum-sub prime-mortgage/.

93. Author's field notes, June 7, 2011.

94. Ibid., February 7–21, 2011, June 6–10, 2011, and June 15–18, 2011.

95. Emily Lenzner, interview with the author, telephone, November 2, 2009.

96. The notion of "annotative journalism" is explored in Lucas Graves, "Blogging Back Then: Annotative Journalism in I. F. Stone's Weekly and Talking Points Memo," *Journalism* 16, no. 1 (2015): 99–118, doi:10.1177/1464884914545740.

97. Author's field notes, June 9, 2014. This approach may reflect the fact that Demagog, which launched its Slovak site in 2010 and a Czech edition in 2012, was founded by university students with no journalism background. The founders have acknowledged that their system entailed verifying many unimportant statements.

98. Tom Rosenstiel, Truth in Politics 2014.

4. Deciding What's True

1. See Lucas Graves and Tom Glaisyer, *The Fact-Checking Universe in Spring 2012: An Overview* (Washington, DC: New America Foundation, February 2012); and Brendan Nyhan, "Why the 'Death Panel' Myth Wouldn't Die: Misinformation in the Health Care Reform Debate," *Forum* 8, no. 1 (2010), doi:10.2202/1540-8884.1354.

2. Michael Schudson, *Discovering the News* (New York: Basic Books, 1978).

3. Michael Lewis, "J-School Confidential," *New Republic*, April 19, 1993, 20–27.

4. See Michael Schudson, *Watergate in American Memory: How We Remember, Forget, and Reconstruct the Past* (New York: Basic Books, 1992). It bears mentioning that neither Bob Woodward nor Carl Bernstein studied journalism. In a reflection of the field's shifting status, Bernstein began in newspapers as a copyboy at age sixteen and never finished college while Woodward went from Yale to the Army to the *Washington Post*.

5. Robert Darnton, "Writing News and Telling Stories," *Daedalus* 104 (1975): 175–94.

6. Schudson, *Discovering the News*, 9.

7. Glenn Kessler, interview with the author, telephone, April 18, 2012.

8. Tacit knowledge refers to skills necessary to accomplish some task that are acquired by experience and difficult to articulate. A classic example is the ability to ride a bike; the controversial insight has been that this kind of knowledge also informs scientific inquiry. The concept originates in Michael Polanyi, *Personal Knowledge: Towards a Post-Critical Philosophy* (London: Routledge, 1998). It has been further developed by

Harry M. Collins, who offered the powerful example (among others) of scientists unable to reproduce a laser design without face-to-face contact; see Harry M. Collins, *Changing Order: Replication and Induction in Scientific Practice* (Chicago: University of Chicago Press, 1992).

9. Lauren Hitt, "Barbour Inflates Obama's Job Losses," FactCheck.org, March 15, 2011, http://www.factcheck.org/2011/03/barbour-inflates-obamas-job-losses/.

10. Bill Adair, "Principles of PolitiFact and the Truth-O-Meter," PolitiFact, February 21, 2011, http://www.politifact.com/truth-o-meter/article/2011/feb/21/principles-truth-o-meter/.

11. Author's field notes, February 9 and 17, 2011, and June 15, 2011.

12. Ibid., June 8, 2011.

13. Ibid., June 15, 2011.

14. Glenn Kessler, "President Obama: Quoting Reagan Out of Context," Fact Checker, *Washington Post*, April 12, 2012, http://www.washingtonpost.com/blogs/fact-checker/post/president-obama-quoting-reagan-out-of-context/2012/04/11/gIQAaOsZBT_blog.html.

15. Glenn Kessler, interview with the author, telephone, April 18, 2012.

16. Michelle Malkin, "PolitiFact to 'Debunk' My Gwen Moore/Abortion Post," *Michelle Malkin* (blog), February 22, 2011, http://michellemalkin.com/2011/02/22/politifact-to-debunk-my-gwen-mooreabortion-post/.

17. Author's field notes, June 15, 2011.

18. Author's field notes, June 7 and June 15, 2011.

19. Ibid., June 6–8, 2012, and June 15, 2012.

20. Brooks Jackson, interview with the author, e-mail, May 4, 2012; author's field notes, June 6–8, 2012, and June 15, 2012.

21. Comments by Ladonna Lee at Pants On Fire: Political Mendacity and the Rise of Media Fact-Checkers, conference hosted by the Annenberg Public Policy Center, Washington, DC, November 9, 2007.

22. Bill Adair, "Defense Cuts Had GOP Support, Too," PolitiFact, October 21, 2007, http://www.politifact.com/truth-o-meter/statements/2007/oct/22/mitt-romney/defense-cuts-had-gop-support-too/; and author's field notes, February 17, 2011, June 8, 2011, and June 15, 2011.

23. Lucas Graves, "Mitch Daniels Says Interest on Debt Will Soon Exceed Security Spending," PolitiFact, February 17, 2011, http://www.politifact.com/truth-o-meter/statements/2011/feb/17/mitch-daniels/mitch-daniels-says-interest-debt-will-soon-exceed-/.

24. Author's field notes, February 14–15, 2011.

25. Ibid., June 8, 2011.

26. Eugene Kiely, "Halter's Ad: Misleading Senior Voters," Factcheck.org, June 4, 2010, http://www.factcheck.org/2010/06/halters-ad-misleading-senior-voters/; and Eugene Kiely, "Halter Questioned On Misleading TV Ad," FactCheck.org, June 8, 2010, http://www.factcheck.org/2010/06/halter-questioned-on-misleading-tv-ad/.

27. Stephen Koff, "NRCC Says Rep. Betty Sutton's 'Spending Spree' Maxed Out Federal Debt," PolitiFact, May 31, 2011, http://www.politifact.com/ohio/statements/2011/may/31/national-republican-congressional-committee/nrcc-says-rep-betty-suttons-spending-spree-maxed-o/.

28. Stephen Koff, "We Said What? NRCC Claims PolitiFact Ohio Confirmed Claim that Rep. Betty Sutton 'Maxed out Federal Debt,' " PolitiFact Ohio, June 1, 2011, http://www.politifact.com/ohio/statements/2011/jun/01/national-republican-congressional-committee/we-said-what-nrcc-claims-politifact-ohio-confirmed/.

29. Mark Stencel, *"Fact Check This": How U.S. Politics Adapts to Media Scrutiny*, American Press Institute, May 13, 2015, http://www.americanpressinstitute.org/fact-checking-project/fact-checking-research/u-s-politics-adapts-media-scrutiny/.

30. Bob Papper, *TV Adwatch Stories: On The Rise* (Philadelphia, PA: Annenberg Public Policy Center, November 9, 2007).

31. Josh Grossfield, interview with the author, telephone, November 10, 2011; Mike Rice, interview with the author, telephone, November 11, 2011; and Richard Schlackman, interview with the author, telephone, November 10, 2011. See also Stencel, *"Fact Check This."*

32. Author's field notes, June 16, 2011.

33. Jake Barry, "Michele Bachmann Says Food Prices for Barbecues up 29 Percent Because of Barack Obama," PolitiFact, June 27, 2011, http://www.politifact.com/truth-o-meter/statements/2011/jun/27/michele-bachmann/michele-bachmann-says-food-prices-barbecues-29-per/.

34. Glenn Kessler, interview with the author, telephone, April 18, 2012.

35. Glenn Kessler, "John Boehner's Misfire on Pending Federal Regulations," Fact Checker, *Washington Post*, September 16, 2011, http://www.washingtonpost.com/blogs/fact-checker/post/john-boehners-misfire-on-pending-federal-regulations/2011/09/15/gIQAufuhVK_blog.html.

36. Lara Seligman, "Trip to Mumbai," FactCheck.org, November 3, 2010, http://www.factcheck.org/2010/11/ask-factcheck-trip-to-mumbai/.

37. Robert Farley, "Rep. Michele Bachmann Claims Obama's Trip to India Will Cost the Taxpayers $200 Million a Day," PolitiFact, November 3, 2010, http://www.politifact.com/truth-o-meter/statements/2010/nov/04/michele-bachmann/rep-michele-bachmann-claims-obamas-trip-india-will/.

38. Author's field notes, June 7, 2011.

39. Author's field notes, June 15, 2011.

40. Author's field notes, February 9, 2011.

41. Ibid., February 9, 2011, and June 7, 8, and 15, 2011.

42. Lucas Graves, "Glenn Beck Says Muslim Brotherhood Wants to Declare War on Israel," PolitiFact, February 15, 2011, http://www.politifact.com/truth-o-meter/statements/2011/feb/15/glenn-beck/glenn-beck-says-muslim-brotherhood-wants-declare-w/.

43. Angie Drobnic Holan, interview with the author, telephone, February 25, 2011; and author's field notes, February 9 and 17, 2011, and June 15–17, 2011.

44. Brooks Jackson, interview with the author, e-mail, May 8, 2011.

45. Author's field notes, February 9 and 17, 2011, and June 15, 2011.

46. Graves, "Mitch Daniels Says Interest."

47. Author's field notes, February 14–15, 2011.

48. Author's field notes, February 9, 2011, and June 7 and 15, 2011.

49. Author's field notes, February 9, 2011, and June 15, 2011. This is especially true on the left, I was told, with groups like the Brookings Institution and the Urban Institute complaining about being called "liberal" or "left-leaning."

50. Molly Moorhead, "Romney Campaign Says Women Were Hit Hard by Job Losses Under Obama," PolitiFact, April 6, 2012, http://www.politifact.com/truth-o-meter /statements/2012/apr/10/mitt-romney/romney-campaign-says-women-were-hit -hard-job-losse/.

51. Ibid.

52. Louis Jacobson, "Mitt Romney Says U.S. Navy Is Smallest Since 1917, Air Force Is Smallest Since 1947," PolitiFact, January 18, 2012, http://www.politifact.com/truth-o -meter/statements/2012/jan/18/mitt-romney/mitt-romney-says-us-navy-smallest-1917 -air-force-s/.

53. Thomas Bruscino, "A PolitiFact Example," *Big Tent* (blog), January 18, 2012, http:// bigtent.blogspot.com/2012/01/politifact-example.html.

54. Bill Adair, "'There's a Fair Chance PolitiFact Spoke to Other Experts'—Yes, 13 Others," PolitiFact, January 19, 2012, http://www.politifact.com/truth-o-meter/blog/2012/jan /19/theres-fair-chance-politifact-spoke-other-experts-/.

55. Author's field notes, February 9, 2011, and June 15, 2011.

56. Lori Robertson, "Supply-Side Spin," FactCheck.org, June 11, 2007, https://web.archive .org/web/20121116165753/http://www.factcheck.org/taxes/supply-side_spin.html; and Lori Robertson, "The Impact of Tax Cuts," *FactCheck.org*, January 16, 2008, http:// factcheck.org/2008/01/the-impact-of-tax-cuts/.

57. Glenn Kessler, interview with the author, telephone, April 18, 2012.

58. Glenn Kessler, "Are Obama's Job Policies Hurting Women?" Fact Checker, *Washington Post*, April 10, 2012, http://www.washingtonpost.com/blogs/fact-checker/post/are -obamas-job-policies-hurting-women/2012/04/09/gIQAGz3q6S_blog.html.

59. Media Matters appears in a few dozen items at FactCheck.org and PolitiFact, almost always identified as a liberal media watchdog. Most of these mentions come in the course of reconstructing some online controversy, although a small handful of items appear to cite Media Matters' research in an authoritative way.

60. Rich Noyes, interview with the author, telephone, February 25, 2011; and Rich Noyes, "Hillary Shot at in '96? No Media Mention of Bosnia 'Sniper Fire,'" *NewsBusters* (blog), March 18, 2008, http://newsbusters.org/blogs/rich-noyes/2008/03/18/hillary-shot -96-no-media-mention-bosnia-sniper-fire.

61. Michael Dobbs, "Sniper Fire, and Holes in Clinton's Recollection," *Post Politics* (blog), *Washington Post*, March 22, 2008, http://www.washingtonpost.com/wp-dyn/content /article/2008/03/21/AR2008032102989.html; and Angie Drobnic Holan, "Video Shows Tarmac Welcome, No Snipers," PolitiFact, March 25, 2008, http://www.politifact.com /truth-o-meter/statements/2008/mar/25/hillary-clinton/video-shows-tarmac-welcome -no-snipers/.

62. NB Staff, "CBS Reporter: NewsBusters Prompted Story on Bosnia 'Sniper Fire,'" *NewsBusters* (blog), April 9, 2008, http://newsbusters.org/blogs/nb-staff/2008/04/09 /cbs-reporter-newsbusters-prompted-story-bosnia-sniper-fire.

63. Tim Graham, "WaPo Awards 'Four Pinocchios, to Hillary on Sniper-Fire Fable," *News-Busters* (blog), March 22, 2008, http://newsbusters.org/blogs/tim-graham/2008/03/22 /wapo-awards-four-pinocchios-hillary-sniper-fire-fable; see also Noel Sheppard, "CBS Reports Clinton's Bosnia Gaffe Six Days After NewsBusters," *NewsBusters* (blog), March 25, 2008, http://newsbusters.org/blogs/noel-sheppard/2008/03/25/cbs-exposes-clintons -bosnia-gaffe-nb-reported-six-days-ago.

64. Author's field notes, June 6, 2011.

65. I asked this question, as did several other participants; the meeting was framed in part as a discussion of the fact-checking landscape.

66. Comments by Bill Adair at Fact-Checking in the News, meeting hosted by the New America Foundation, Washington, DC, December 14, 2011.

67. Comments by Glen Kessler at Fact-Checking in the News.

68. Maryalice Gill, "Democrats Say Republican Presidential Candidates Did Not Mention Middle Class or Education in Debate," FactCheck.org, June 24, 2011, http://www .politifact.com/truth-o-meter/statements/2011/jun/24/jay-carney/democrats-say -republican-presidential-candidates-d/.

69. Author's field notes, June 16, 2011.

70. Ibid., June 6–7, 2011; and Eugene Kiely, "Chrysler Paid in Full?" FactCheck.org, June 6, 2011, http://www.factcheck.org/2011/06/chrysler-paid-in-full/.

71. Glenn Kessler, interview with the author, telephone, April 18, 2012; and Glenn Kessler, "Hyping Stats About the 'Buffett Rule,'" Fact Checker, *Washington Post*, April 18, 2012, http://www.washingtonpost.com/blogs/fact-checker/post/hyping-stats-about-the -buffett-rule/2012/04/17/gIQABtPnOT_blog.html.

72. Glenn Kessler, "Hyping Stats About the 'Buffett Rule.'"

73. Ibid.

74. Brooks Jackson, interview with author, Washington, DC, December 3, 2010; see also Ben Smith, "The Facts About the Fact Checkers," Politico, November 1, 2011, http:// www.politico.com/news/stories/1011/67175.html.

75. Robert Farley, "Obama's 'War on Women'?" FactCheck.org, April 12, 2012, http:// www.factcheck.org/2012/04/obamas-war-on-women/.

76. Kessler, "Are Obama's Job Policies Hurting Women?"; and Brent Baker, "Stephanopou-los Agrees 92% Women Job Losses Statistic 'Accurate' After ABC's World News Called

It 'Mostly False,'" *NewsBusters* (blog), April 16, 2012, http://newsbusters.org/blogs/brent
-baker/2012/04/16/stephanopoulos-agrees-92-women-job-losses-statistic-accurate
-after-abc-#ixzz1v9yl2e2b.

77. Moorhead, "Romney Campaign."

78. Anna Althouse, "Romney Campaign Says 92.3% of the Jobs Lost Under Obama Were
Women's Jobs," *Althouse* (blog), April 11, 2012, http://althouse.blogspot.com/2012/04
/romney-campaign-says-923-of-jobs-lost.html.

79. Glenn Kessler, interview with author, telephone, April 18, 2012; see also "Q&A with
Glenn Kessler," *Q&A*, CSPAN, January 15, 2012, http://www.c-spanvideo.org/program
/303324-1; and Smith, "The Facts About the Fact Checkers."

80. C. Eugene Emery Jr., "Cicilline Says Providence's Crime Rate Is the Lowest in 30
Years," PolitiFact Rhode Island, July 19, 2010, http://www.politifact.com/rhode
-island/statements/2010/jul/19/david-cicilline/cicilline-says-providence-crime-rate
-lowest-30-yea/.

81. Author's field notes, February 9, 2011, and June 15–16, 2011; and Bill Adair, interview
with the author, e-mail, January 25, 2014.

82. Bill Adair, "Tuning the Truth-O-Meter," PolitiFact, January 25, 2012, http://www.politi
fact.com/truth-o-meter/article/2012/jan/25/tuning-truth-o-meter/.

83. Author's field notes, February 9, 2011, and June 15–16, 2011.

84. Louis Jacobson, "Have Private-Sector Jobs Grown by 3 Million in 22 Months, with the
Best Annual Totals Since 2005?" PolitiFact, January 25, 2011, http://www.politifact
.com/truth-o-meter/statements/2012/jan/25/barack-obama/have-private-sector-jobs
-grown-22-months-best-annu/.

85. "Original Version of PolitiFact's Fact-Check on Obama Jobs Claim from State of the
Union 2012," PolitiFact, n.d., http://www.politifact.com/obamajobs/.

86. Adjusting a ruling once published is extremely rare. Such changes always merit an
editor's note and sometimes a longer account; this episode produced the letter explaining the problem of implied blame or credit. See Adair, "Tuning the Truth-O-Meter."

87. See Eric Dolan, "Maddow: PolitiFact Is Undermining the Word 'Fact,'" Raw Story,
January 25, 2012, http://www.rawstory.com/rs/2012/01/25/maddow-politifact-is-un
dermining-the-word-fact/.

88. FactCheck.org has challenged the claim at least four times; Fact Checker investigated
it twice; and PolitiFact and its state franchises published nine related Truth-O-Meter
items in 2011.

89. See, e.g., Angie Drobnic Holan and Louis Jacobson, "Throw-Granny-from-the-Cliff
Ad Asks What the U.S. Would Be 'Without Medicare,'" PolitiFact, May 17, 2011,
http://www.politifact.com/truth-o-meter/statements/2011/may/25/agenda-project
/throw-granny-cliff-asks-what-country-would-be-with/; Brooks Jackson, "Test Market for Spin," FactCheck.org, May 19, 2011, http://www.factcheck.org/2011/05/test
-market-for-spin/; and Glenn Kessler, "Mediscare Redux: Is McConnell Holding Debt
Ceiling Hike Hostage to Ryan Medicare Plan?" Fact Checker, *Washington Post*, June 13,

2011, http://www.washingtonpost.com/blogs/fact-checker/post/mediscare-redux-is
-mcconnell-holdingdebt-ceiling-hike-hostage-to-ryan-medicare-plan/2011/06/11
/AGrG5jQH_blog.html.

90. One summary is Greg Sargent, "Dems Brush Off PolitiFact Finding," *Plum Line* (blog),
Washington Post, December 20, 2011, http://www.washingtonpost.com/blogs/plum
-line/post/dems-brush-off-politifact-finding/2011/12/20/gIQA1zkg7O_blog.html.

91. Bill Adair and Angie Drobnic Holan, "Lie of the Year 2011: 'Republicans Voted to End
Medicare,'" PolitiFact, December 20, 2011, http://www.politifact.com/truth-o-meter
/article/2011/dec/20/lie-year-democrats-claims-republicans-voted-end-me/.

92. Brooks Jackson, "The Whoppers of 2011," FactCheck.org, December 20, 2011, http://
www.factcheck.org/2011/12/the-whoppers-of-2011/; and Glenn Kessler, "The Biggest
Pinocchios of 2011," Fact Checker, *Washington Post*, December 22, 2011, http://www
.washingtonpost.com/blogs/fact-checker/post/the-biggest-pinocchios-of-2011
/2011/12/21/gIQAzbzFAP_blog.html.

93. Paul Krugman, "PolitiFact, R.I.P.," *Conscience of a Liberal* (blog), *New York Times*, December 20, 2011, http://krugman.blogs.nytimes.com/2011/12/20/politifact-r-i-p/.

94. Dan Froomkin, "What Politifact Should Do Now," *Watchdog Blog*, December 21, 2011,
http://blog.niemanwatchdog.org/2011/12/what-politifact-should-do-now/. Liberal observers had predicted a surrender to "false equivalence," since PolitiFact's first two "Lie of the
Year" awards went to Republican claims. See, e.g., Paul Waldman, "He Lied/She Lied,"
American Prospect, December 6, 2011, http://prospect.org/article/he-liedshe-lied.

95. Jamison Foser, "Politifact's Flawed 'Lie of The Year' Selection Only Encourages More
Lying," *Media Matters* (blog), December 20, 2011, http://mediamatters.org/blog/2011/12/20
/politifacts-flawed-lie-of-the-year-selection-on/185549.

96. Jim Newell, "PolitiFact Is Bad for You," Gawker, December 20, 2011, http://gawker
.com/5869817/politifact-is-bad-for-you.

97. Igor Volsky, "PolitiFact's Finalist for 2011 Lie of the Year Is 100 Percent True," *Think-
Progress* (blog), December 2, 2011, http://thinkprogress.org/health/2011/12/02/381180
/politifacts-finalist-for-2011-lie-of-the-year-is-100-percent-true/.

98. Steve Benen, "PolitiFact Ought to Be Ashamed of Itself," *Political Animal* (blog), *Washington Monthly*, December 20, 2011, http://www.washingtonmonthly.com/political-animal
/2011_12/politifact_ought_to_be_ashamed034211.php.

99. See, e.g., Dan Kennedy, "PolitiFact and the Limits of Fact-Checking," *Huffington Post*,
December 13, 2011, http://www.huffingtonpost.com/dan-kennedy/politifact-and
-the-limits_b_1144876.html.

100. Jonathan Chait, "The Trouble with PolitiFact," *Daily Intel* (blog), *New York Magazine*,
December 20, 2011, http://nymag.com/daily/intel/2011/12/trouble-with-politifact.html.

101. "PolitiFiction," *Wall Street Journal*, December 23, 2010, http://www.wsj.com/articles
/SB10001424052748703886904576031630593433102.

102. Brooks Jackson, "'Government-Run' Nonsense," FactCheck.org, November 21, 2011,
http://www.factcheck.org/2011/11/government-run-nonsense/.

103. One liberal dissenter made a version of this argument in PolitiFact's defense; see Kevin Drum, "Ending Medicare," *Mother Jones*, December 20, 2011, http://www.motherjones .com/kevin-drum/2011/12/ending-medicare.

104. An observer at the *Columbia Journalism Review* put this argument especially well during the "end Medicare" controversy, noting that fact-checkers stray into "patrolling public discourse": they deliver judgments "not only about truth, but about what attacks are fair, what arguments are reasonable, what language is appropriate." Greg Marx, "What the Fact-Checkers Get Wrong," *Campaign Desk* (blog), *Columbia Journalism Review*, January 5, 2012, http://www.cjr.org/campaign_desk/what_the_fact-checkers _get_wro.php.

105. Brooks Jackson and Kathleen Hall Jamieson, *UnSpun: Finding Facts in a World of Disinformation* (New York: Random House, 2007), ix.

106. "Q&A with Glenn Kessler."

107. Lori Robertson, "Democrats' 'End Medicare' Whopper, Again," FactCheck.org, March 6, 2012, http://www.factcheck.org/2012/03/democrats-end-medicare-whopper-again/.

108. Comment by Bill Adair at "The Facts of Political Life," panel discussion at the New America Foundation, Washington, DC, February 28, 2012.

5. Operating the Truth-O-Meter

1. See, e.g., Eric Ostermeier, "Selection Bias? PolitiFact Rates Republican Statements as False at 3 Times the Rate of Democrats," *Smart Politics* (blog), February 10, 2011, http:// blog.lib.umn.edu/cspg/smartpolitics/2011/02/selection_bias_politifact_rate.php; and Joseph E. Uscinski and Ryden W. Butler, "The Epistemology of Fact Checking," *Critical Review* 25, no. 2 (2013): 162–80, doi:10.1080/08913811.2013.843872.

2. Bill Adair, "Inside the Meters: Responding to a George Mason University Press Release about Our Work," PolitiFact, May 29, 2013, http://www.politifact.com/truth-o-me ter/blog/2013/may/29/responding-george-mason-university-press-release-a/.

3. Lauren Carroll, "Hillary Clinton's Truth-O-Meter Record," PolitiFact, June 11, 2015, http://www.politifact.com/truth-o-meter/article/2015/jun/11/hillary-clintons -truth-o-meter-record/. In a "report card" on the 2012 presidential field, PolitiFact argued that "the tallies are not scientific, but they provide interesting insights into a candidate's overall record for accuracy." See Bill Adair, "The PolitiFact Report Card on the Presidential Candidates," PolitiFact, December 30, 2011, http://www.politi fact.com/truth-o-meter/article/2011/dec/30/how-candidates-fared-truth-o-meter -Iowa11/.

4. Author's field notes, June 15, 2011. Discussed in Lucas Graves, "What We Can Learn from the Factcheckers' Ratings," *United States Project* (blog), *Columbia Journalism Review*, June 4, 2013, http://www.cjr.org/united_states_project/what_we_can_learn_from _the_factcheckers_ratings.php.

5. See, e.g., "PolitiFiction," *Wall Street Journal*, December 23, 2010; and Greg Marx, "What the Fact-Checkers Get Wrong," *Campaign Desk* (blog), *Columbia Journalism Review*,

January 5, 2012, http://www.cjr.org/campaign_desk/what_the_fact-checkers_get
_wro.php.

6. Brendan Nyhan, "That's Not a Factcheck!" *United States Project* (blog), *Columbia Journalism Review*, March 12, 2013, http://www.cjr.org/united_states_project/thats_not_a
_factcheck.php.

7. The authors hold that this naive view, which they ascribe to journalism in general, leads fact-checkers to rely on "dubious" methods in the attempt to offer factual certainty where none is possible. The result is that the fact-checking project "ignores the most important objective reality of politics: namely, that all the facts discussed in politics are ambiguous enough to make for legitimate doubt." Uscinski and Butler, "Epistemology of Fact Checking," 162, 172.

8. Glenn Kessler, interview with the author, telephone, April 18, 2012.

9. Schudson argues that this fairly sophisticated understanding of objectivity, which informed critical discussions of journalism, drew on the prevailing view of objectivity in the sciences. "Facts here are not aspects of the world, but consensually validated statements about it," he writes. Michael Schudson, *Discovering the News: A Social History of American Newspapers* (New York: Basic Books, 1978), 7, 122, 195n6.

10. For instance, in 2014 the *Cleveland Plain-Dealer* defected from the PolitiFact network, citing, in part, methodological differences. Ted Diadiun, "Coming: Truth Squad Reporting without the Gimmicks," Cleveland.com, January 30, 2014, http://www.cleveland.com/readers/index.ssf/2014/01/coming_truth_squad_reporting_w.html. See also Anna Clark, "*The Plain Dealer* Drops PolitiFact, but Keeps on Factchecking," *Columbia Journalism Review*, June 17, 2014, http://www.cjr.org/united_states_project/cleveland
_plain_dealer_politifact_factchecking.php.

11. Author's field notes, February 9 and 17, 2011. See, e.g., Bill Adair, "Principles of PolitiFact and the Truth-O-Meter," PolitiFact, February 21, 2011, http://www.politifact.com/truth
-o-meter/article/2011/feb/21/principles-truth-o-meter/.

12. Author's field notes, February 9–11, 2011, and June 15, 2011; see also Steve Myers, "PolitiFact Takes Lesson from Fast-Food Industry as It Franchises Fact Checking," Poynter.org, May 3, 2011, http://www.poynter.org/latest-news/top-stories/102422
/politifact-takes-lesson-from-fast-food-industry-as-it-franchises-fact-checking/.

13. Discussed in Lucas Graves and Magda Konieczna, "Sharing the News: Journalistic Collaboration as Field Repair," *International Journal of Communication* 9 (June 2015): 1966–84, http://ijoc.org/index.php/ijoc/article/view/3381.

14. Bill Adair and Angie Drobnic Holan, "The Principles of PolitiFact, PunditFact and the Truth-O-Meter," PolitiFact, November 1, 2013, http://www.politifact.com/truth-o
-meter/article/2013/nov/01/principles-politifact-punditfact-and-truth-o-meter/.

15. PolitiFact polled readers before finalizing the switch; an editor's letter claimed, "We got hundreds of messages through Twitter, more than 1,000 posts on Facebook and more than 850 e-mails. At least 95 percent of them supported the change." Bill Adair, "A Change in the Meter: Barely True Is Now Mostly False," PolitiFact, July 27, 2011,

http://www.politifact.com/truth-o-meter/article/2011/jul/27/-barely-true-mostly -false/; see also Hannah Vinter, "Bill Adair, Editor of Politifact: 'Readers Love this Kind of Accountability Journalism,'" *Editors Weblog*, World Association of Newspapers and News Publishers, August 22, 2011, http://www.editorsweblog.org/2011/08/22/bill -adair-editor-of-politifact-readers-love-this-kind-of-accountability-journalism.

16. See, e.g., Maryalice Gill, "Democrats Say Republican Presidential Candidates Did Not Mention Middle Class or Education in Debate," PolitiFact, June 24, 2011, http://www .politifact.com/truth-o-meter/statements/2011/jun/24/jay-carney/democrats-say -republican-presidential-candidates-d/.

17. Author's field notes, February 9 and 17, 2011.

18. Adair, "Principles of PolitiFact and the Truth-O-Meter."

19. Author's field notes, June 15–16, 2011.

20. Bill Adair, "Numbers Game," PolitiFact, April 15, 2008, http://www.politifact.com /truth-o-meter/article/2008/apr/15/numbers-game/.

21. Author's field notes, February 7, 10, 11, 16, and 17, 2011.

22. Ibid., February 9 and 17, 2011.

23. Ibid., February 9 and 17, 2011, and June 15, 2011.

24. For instance, a brisk 2015 item used "we" and related words eight times in debunking a pundit who claimed the Civil War wasn't "about" slavery; see Jon Greenberg, "In Defense of Confederate Flag, Frequent Fox News Guest Claims Civil War Wasn't About Slavery," PolitiFact, June 25, 2015, http://www.politifact.com/punditfact /statements/2015/jun/25/gavin-mcinnes/tweet-civil-war-was-about-secession-not -slavery/.

25. Author's field notes, February 9 and 17, 2011, and June 16, 2011.

26. Adair and Holan, "Principles of PolitiFact, PunditFact and the Truth-O-Meter"; see also Adair, "Principles of PolitiFact and the Truth-O-Meter."

27. Author's field notes, December 3, 2010; February 7–18, 2011; and June 16–17, 2011.

28. An editor's note during PolitiFact's first year discussed the surprising difficulty of checking statistical claims; see Adair, "Numbers Game."

29. Jody Kyle, "Fatality Count Isn't That High," PolitiFact, September 9, 2007, http:// www.politifact.com/truth-o-meter/statements/2007/sep/09/ron-paul/fatality -count-isnt-that-high-/.

30. Lucas Graves, "Mitch Daniels Says Interest on Debt Will Soon Exceed Security Spending," PolitiFact, February 17, 2011, http://www.politifact.com/truth-o-meter/statements /2011/feb/17/mitch-daniels/mitch-daniels-says-interest-debt-will-soon-exceed-/.

31. Author's field notes, February 9, 16, and 17, 2011.

32. Angie Drobnic Holan, "Michele Bachmann Says the Government Will Buy You a Breast Pump for Your Baby," PolitiFact, February 18, 2011, http://www.politifact.com/truth-o -meter/statements/2011/feb/18/michele-bachmann/michele-bachmann-says -government-will-buy-you-brea/.

33. Author's field notes, February 18, 2011.

34. Louis Jacobson, "Mitt Romney Tells CPAC that More Are out of Work in U.S. than Employed in Canada," PolitiFact, February 11, 2011, http://www.politifact.com/truth -o-meter/statements/2011/feb/11/mitt-romney/mitt-romney-tells-cpac-more-are-out -work-us-employ/.

35. Author's field notes, February 11, 2011.

36. D'Angelo Gore, Brooks Jackson, Michael Morse, and Eugene Kiely, "FactChecking Republicans at CPAC," FactCheck.org, February 14, 2011, http://www.factcheck .org/2011/02/factchecking-republicans-at-cpac/.

37. Sociologist Bruno Latour describes well the often unrecognized role that journalists play in maintaining the standards and "quasi-standards" that are a basis for collective fact-making. See Bruno Latour, *Reassembling the Social: An Introduction to Actor-Network-Theory* (Oxford: Oxford University Press, 2005), 230.

38. Author's field notes, February 11, 2011.

39. Ibid.

40. Ibid.

41. Angie Drobnic Holan, interview with the author, telephone, February 25, 2011.

42. Bill Adair, "Tuning the Truth-O-Meter," PolitiFact, January 25, 2012, http://www .politifact.com/truth-o-meter/article/2012/jan/25/tuning-truth-o-meter/.

43. Author's field notes, February 7–8, 2011.

44. *Glenn Beck*, Fox News Network, February 4, 2011.

45. Ibid., February 1, 2011.

46. Author's field notes, February 8–11, 2011.

47. Yaakov Lappin, "Muslim Brotherhood: 'Prepare Egyptians for war with Israel,'" *Jerusalem Post*, February 1, 2011, http://www.jpost.com/Breaking-News/Muslim-Broth erhood-Prepare-Egyptians-for-war-with-Israel.

48. Ibid. This sentence appeared to be paraphrased by the reporter, though using Google Translate I could not be entirely certain. Later I found a direct transcript of the interview.

49. Even a transcript from a conservative, U.S.-based, media monitoring group made Ghannem's words seem a bit less threatening than the *Jerusalem Post*'s present-tense command: "I am absolutely certain that this revolution will not die, and that the next step must be one of civil disobedience. . . . This disobedience must include halting passage through the Suez Canal, stopping the supply of petroleum and natural gas to Israel, and preparing for war with Israel." See "Muhammad Ghanem, Muslim Brotherhood Representative in London, Calls for Civil Disobedience, Including 'Halting Passage through the Suez Canal . . . and Preparing for War with Israel,'" *Middle East Media Research Institute*, January 30, 2011, http://www.memritv.org/clip/en/2787.htm.

50. The work done by such "translations" is a central concern of actor-network theory (ANT), sometimes described as a "sociology of translation." ANT draws attention to efforts, both rhetorical and material, to associate one entity or concept with another (and in turn with the latter's network of associations). A basic strategy of translation is

to tie actors' interests together—to make one *stand for* another or become its "spokesperson." Latour draws on both the linguistic and geometric meanings of translation in arguing that "translating interests means at once offering new interpretations of these interests and channeling people in different direction." Bruno Latour, *Science in Action* (Cambridge, MA: Harvard University Press, 1987), 117. See also Latour, *Reassembling the Social*, 106–9; and Michel Callon, "Some Elements of a Sociology of Translation: Domestication of the Scallops and the Fishermen of St Brieuc Bay," in *The Science Studies Reader*, ed. Mario Biagioli (New York: Routledge, 1999), 67–83.

51. Ghannem's name appeared with various spellings in English, including "Ghannam" and "Ghanem"; here I use what appeared to be the most common.

52. "Senator Kirk Statement on Muslim Brotherhood," Office of Senator Mark Kirk, February 2, 2011, http://www.kirk.senate.gov/record.cfm?id=330818&.

53. Author's field notes, February 8–11, 2011. In fact, I never determined Ghannem's relationship to the group beyond establishing that he was not in its official leadership body; one conservative research institute described him as a Brotherhood "representative in London." See *Middle East Media Research Institute*, http://www.memritv.org/clip /en/2787.htm.

54. "Editorial: Egypt's Blood on Obama's Hands?" *Washington Times*, February 2, 2011, http://www.washingtontimes.com/news/2011/feb/2/egypts-blood-obamas-hands/, emphasis added.

55. Beck earned a "Half True" for linking the "9/11 conspirators" to the Muslim Brotherhood. Robert Farley, "Glenn Beck on Al-Qaida Links to Muslim Brotherhood," PolitiFact, February 4, 2011, http://www.politifact.com/truth-o-meter/statements/2011/feb/04 /glenn-beck/glenn-beck-al-qaeda-links-muslim-brotherhood/.

56. Author's field notes, February 8–11, 2011.

57. Ibid.

58. E-mail to author, February 9, 2011.

59. This evokes the notion Gaye Tuchman called a "web of facticity." As she wrote, "to flesh out any one supposed fact one amasses a host of supposed facts that, when taken together, present themselves as both individually and collectively self-validating." Gaye Tuchman, *Making News: A Study in the Construction of Reality* (New York: Free Press, 1978), 86.

60. This is what sociologist Bruno Latour means by the "collective fate of fact-making." As he writes, "By itself a given sentence is neither a fact nor a fiction; it is made so by others, later on." See Latour, *Science in Action*, 25. This approach finds an antecedent in the Pragmatist critique of truth as an "inert static relation"; on the contrary, William James argues, "Truth *happens* to an idea. It *becomes* true, is *made* true by events." William James, *Pragmatism and Other Writings* (New York: Penguin Books, 2000), 88.

61. Lucas Graves, "Glenn Beck Says Muslim Brotherhood Wants to Declare War on Israel," PolitiFact, February 15, 2011, http://www.politifact.com/truth-o-meter/statements/2011 /feb/15/glenn-beck/glenn-beck-says-muslim-brotherhood-wants-declare-w/.

62. These included two Glenn Beck transcripts and a posting on his website; an article on the Muslim Brotherhood's website; seven news articles or editorials; two policy reports; a congressional press release; an earlier Truth-O-Meter item; and the four expert interviews.

63. Author's field notes, February 15, 2011.

64. Media Matters staff, "PolitiFact Gives 'False' Rating to Beck Claim that Muslim Brotherhood Wants to Declare War on Israel," Media Matters, February 15, 2011, http:// mediamatters.org/blog/201102150034.

65. Stu Burguiere, "Politifail. Factchecking Politifact's Claims about the Muslim Brotherhood and Glenn Beck," The Stu Blog, February 17, 2011, http://www.glennbeck.com/content /blog/stu/politifail-factchecking-politifact%e2%80%99s-claims-about-the-muslim-broth erhood-and-glenn-beck/.

66. Alexander Smoltczyk, "Islam's Spiritual 'Dear Abby': The Voice of Egypt's Muslim Brotherhood," Der Spiegel, February 15, 2011, http://www.spiegel.de/international /world/islam-s-spiritual-dear-abby-the-voice-of-egypt-s-muslim-brotherhood-a-745526 .html.

67. Glenn Beck, Fox News Network, February 17, 2011.

68. E-mails to author, February 22 and 24, 2011.

69. E-mail to author, February 19, 2011.

70. Louis Jacobson, "Jon Stewart Says Those Who Watch Fox News Are the 'Most Consistently Misinformed Media Viewers,'" PolitiFact, June 20, 2011, http://www.politifact .com/truth-o-meter/statements/2011/jun/20/jon-stewart/jon-stewart-says-those -who-watch-fox-news-are-most/.

71. "Fox News' False Statements," Daily Show with Jon Stewart, June 21, 2011, http://the dailyshow.cc.com/videos/lkmdal/fox-news-false-statements.

72. Louis Jacobson, "Jon Stewart's Politifact Segment: The Annotated Edition," PolitiFact, June 22, 2011, http://www.politifact.com/truth-o-meter/article/2011/jun/22/jon -stewarts-politifact-segment-annotated-edition/.

73. Lorraine Daston and Peter Galison, Objectivity (New York: Zone Books, 2007), 52.

74. John Nerone, "History, Journalism, and the Problem of Truth," in Assessing Evidence in a Postmodern World, ed. Bonnie Brennen, Diederich Studies in Media and Communication, no. 3 (Milwaukee, WI: Marquette University Press, 2013), 26.

75. As discussed in chapter 2, the idea that different views of common objects or people or ideas may facilitate scientific inquiry, engineering, and so on is a central insight of science and technology studies. See, e.g., Geoffrey C. Bowker and Susan Leigh Star, Sorting Things Out: Classification and Its Consequences, Inside Technology (Cambridge, MA: MIT Press, 1999); and David Stark, The Sense of Dissonance: Accounts of Worth in Economic Life (Princeton, NJ: Princeton University Press, 2011).

76. See discussion of "spokespersons" in Latour, Science in Action, 71–73. This is a recurring question in science and technology studies. Classic examples are Callon, "Some Elements of a Sociology of Translation"; and Michel Callon, "Society in the Making:

The Study of Technology as a Tool for Sociological Analysis," in *The Social Construction of Technological Systems: New Directions in the Sociology and History of Technology*, ed. Wiebe E. Bijker, Thomas Parke Hughes, and T. J. Pinch, 83–103 (Cambridge, MA: MIT Press, 1989).

77. See discussion in "No End in Sight," *On the Media*, WNYC, January 3, 2014, http://www.onthemedia.org/story/no-end-sight/.

78. Harry M. Collins, "Tacit Knowledge, Trust and the Q of Sapphire," *Social Studies of Science* 31, no. 1 (2001): 71–85.

79. Steven Shapin, *A Social History of Truth: Civility and Science in Seventeenth-Century England* (Chicago: University of Chicago Press, 1994), 17–19.

80. Tuchman, *Making News*, 84–85. Tuchman uses this example to highlight what she calls "webs of facticity" in reporting work.

81. Latour, *Reassembling the Social*, 230. Latour argues that "the circulation of quasi-standards allow anonymous and isolated agencies to slowly become, layer after layer, comparable and commensurable—which is surely a large part of what we mean by being human."

82. Latour, *Science in Action*, 109–10. As Latour writes, "the easiest means to enroll people in the construction of facts is to let oneself be enrolled by them!"

83. James S. Ettema and Theodore Lewis Glasser, *Custodians of Conscience: Investigative Journalism and Public Virtue* (New York: Columbia University Press, 1998), 135–36.

84. Ibid., 142, 145.

85. Ibid., 131.

86. The question of how critical working journalists are in their understanding of objectivity is taken up in Schudson, *Discovering the News*, 155, and in Ettema and Glasser, *Custodians of Conscience*, 9–11. The latter argue that "belief in the 'purest usage' of objectivity has faltered (if it ever really existed), but . . . the notion of 'disinterested' knowledge continues to shape the news as a form of discourse and also to shape journalists' discourse about the news."

87. Bruno Latour, *Pandora's Hope: Essays on the Reality of Science Studies* (Cambridge, MA: Harvard University Press, 1999), 15. Latour argues here and elsewhere for letting go of the false binary which opposes the naturally "real" to the socially or humanly "constructed," one he traces to the ontological divide between subject and object established by Enlightenment thinkers such as Kant and Decartes. Latour argues for the "relative certainty"—in the sense of relativity, not relativism—of a mind once again embedded in the world.

88. Latour, *Science in Action*, 33, emphasis added.

Part III. The Effects of Fact-Checking

1. Glenn Kessler, "4 Pinocchios for a Misguided 'Big Money' Coal Attack by Alison Grimes," Fact Checker, *Washington Post*, October 7, 2014, https://www.washingtonpost.com/news/fact-checker/wp/2014/10/07/4-pinocchios-for-a-misguided-big-money-coal-attack-by-alison-grimes/.

2. Steve Contorno, "Alison Lundergan Grimes Says Mitch McConnell, Not She, Is Taking Money from Anti-Coal Groups," PolitiFact, October 8, 2014, http://www.politifact .com/truth-o-meter/statements/2014/oct/08/alison-lundergan-grimes/alison-lunder gan-grimes-says-mitch-mcconnell-not-s/.

3. Comments by Jim Duffy at Truth in Politics 2014: A Status Report on Fact-Checking Journalism, American Press Institute, Arlington, VA, December 10, 2014.

4. Greg Sargent, "A Blistering Attack on Mitch McConnell," *Plum Line* (blog), *Washington Post*, October 22, 2014, http://www.washingtonpost.com/blogs/plum-line/wp/2014/10 /22/a-blistering-attack-on-mitch-mcconnell/.

5. Glenn Kessler, "Alison Grimes Doubles Down on a 4-Pinocchio Claim," Fact Checker, *Washington Post*, October 23, 2014, http://www.washingtonpost.com/blogs/fact-checker /wp/2014/10/23/alison-grimes-doubles-down-on-a-4-pinocchio-claim/.

6. Sam Youngman, "Washington Post Fact-Checker Says 'Grimes Should Be Ashamed of Herself,' " *Lexington Herald-Leader*, October 24, 2014, http://www.kentucky.com /news/politics-government/election-results/article44517492.html; and Glenn Kessler, "How Not to Cite a Fact Check," Fact Checker, *Washington Post*, October 31, 2014, http:// www.washingtonpost.com/blogs/fact-checker/wp/2014/10/31/how-not-to-cite-a-fact -check/.

7. Comments by Glenn Kessler Truth in Politics 2014.

8. A version of this health care case, written by the author, appears in Lucas Graves and Tom Glaisyer, *The Fact-Checking Universe in Spring 2012: An Overview* (Washington, DC: New America Foundation, February 2012).

9. Elizabeth McCaughey, "No Exit: What the Clinton Plan Will Do for You," *New Republic*, February 7, 1994, 21–25.

10. The bill specified, "Nothing in this Act shall be construed as prohibiting the following: (1) An individual from purchasing any health care services." See Theodore R. Marmor and Jerry L. Mashaw, "Cassandra's Law," *New Republic*, February 14, 1994, 20; and James Fallows, "A Triumph of Misinformation," *Atlantic*, January 1995, 26–37.

11. George Will, "The Clintons' Lethal Paternalism," *Newsweek*, February 7, 1994.

12. James Fallows interviewed in "Rewrite," *On the Media*, WYNC, May 22, 2009; and in "The Origin of Rumors," *On the Media*, WYNC, July 31, 2009.

13. Regina G. Lawrence and Matthew L. Schafer, "Debunking Sarah Palin: Mainstream News Coverage of 'Death Panels,' " *Journalism* 13, no. 6 (August 2011): 766–82, doi:10.1177/1464884911431389; and Brendan Nyhan, "Why the 'Death Panel' Myth Wouldn't Die: Misinformation in the Health Care Reform Debate," *Forum* 8, no. 1 (2010), doi:10.2202/1540-8884.1354.

14. Justin Bank, "Palin vs. Obama: Death Panels," FactCheck.org, August 14, 2009, http://www.factcheck.org/2009/08/palin-vs-obama-death-panels/; Angie Drobnic Holan, "Sarah Palin Falsely Claims Barack Obama Runs a 'Death Panel,' " PolitiFact, August 10, 2009, http://www.politifact.com/truth-o-meter/statements/2009/aug/10 /sarah-palin/sarah-palin-barack-obama-death-panel/; and Hannah Dreier, "Fox News

Personalities Advance Palin's 'Death Panel' Claim," Media Matters for America, August 10, 2009, http://mediamatters.org/research/200908100054.

15. Jim Rutenberg and Jackie Calmes, "False 'Death Panel' Rumor Has Some Familiar Roots," *New York Times*, August 14, 2009.

16. James Fallows, "I Was Wrong," *Atlantic*, August 13, 2009, http://www.theatlantic.com/technology/archive/2009/08/i-was-wrong/23254/.

17. I should emphasize that I asked every fact-checker I spoke to whether and how their work has an impact; this is also the first question people have when they hear I do research on the movement.

18. Cary Spivak, "The Fact-Checking Explosion," *American Journalism Review* 32 (2010): 38–43.

19. See, e.g., Brendan Nyhan, "Does Fact-Checking Work? False Statements Are Wrong Metric," *United States Project* (blog), *Columbia Journalism Review*, March 30, 2012, http://www.cjr.org/swing_states_project/does_fact-checking_work_false.php; and Paul Waldman, "Does Fact-Checking Work?" *American Prospect*, November 1, 2011, http://prospect.org/article/does-fact-checking-work.

20. Martha T. Moore, "Fact Checkers Help Sort Through Political Claims," *USA Today*, March 21, 2012, http://www.usatoday.com/news/politics/story/2012-03-21/fact-checkers-politicians/53693798/1.

21. David Carr, "A Last Fact Check: It Didn't Work," *Media Decoder* (blog), *New York Times*, November 6, 2012, http://mediadecoder.blogs.nytimes.com/2012/11/06/a-last-fact-check-it-didnt-work/.

22. See discussion in Graves and Glaisyer, *Fact-Checking Universe*.

23. Bill Adair, "The Value of Fact-Checking in the 2012 Campaign," PolitiFact, November 8, 2012, http://www.politifact.com/truth-o-meter/article/2012/nov/08/value-fact-checking-2012-campaign/. See also, e.g., Hanna Vinter, "Bill Adair, Editor of Politi-Fact: 'Readers Love This Kind of Accountability Journalism,'" *Editors Weblog*, World Association of Newspapers and News Publishers, August 22, 2011, http://www.editorsweblog.org/2011/08/22/bill-adair-editor-of-politifact-readers-love-this-kind-of-accountability-journalism.

24. Author's field notes, June 8, 2011.

25. Viveka Novak, "Obama's Work Claim," FactCheck.org, July 2, 2008, http://www.factcheck.org/2008/07/obamas-work-claim/.

26. Brooks Jackson, interview with the author, Washington, DC, December 3, 2010. A subsequent Obama campaign ad softened the language: "through student loans and hard work, he graduated from college." See Novak, "Obama's Work Claim."

27. Comments by Bill Adair and Glenn Kessler at Fact-Checking in the News meeting hosted by the New America Foundation, Washington, DC, December 14, 2011.

28. Author's field notes, December 14, 2011; see also Michael Dobbs, *The Rise of Political Fact-Checking* (Washington, DC: New America Foundation, February 2012).

29. Michael Cooper, "Fact-Checkers Howl, but Campaigns Seem Attached to Dishonest Ads," *New York Times*, September 1, 2012.

30. Author's field notes, June 10 and December 10, 2014. Also see, e.g., Adair, "The Value of Fact-Checking"; and Brooks Jackson, "Firefighters, Fact-Checking and American Journalism," FactCheck.org, December 21, 2012, http://www.factcheck.org/2012/12/firefighters-fact-checking-and-american-journalism/.

31. Brooks Jackson, Eugene Kiely, Lori Robertson, Robert Farley, and D'Angelo Gore, "The 'King of Whoppers': Donald Trump," FactCheck.org, December 21, 2015, http://www.factcheck.org/2015/12/the-king-of-whoppers-donald-trump/. Among many other examples, see also Jack Schafer, "The Limits of Fact-Checking," *Politico Magazine*, December 24, 2015, http://www.politico.com/magazine/story/2015/12/the-limits-of-the-fact-checker-213461.

6. Fact-Checkers and Their Publics

1. Comments by Neil Brown at Global Fact-Checking Summit conference hosted by the Poynter Institute, London, June 9, 2014. An edited version of the speech can be found at Neil Brown, "5 'Essential Understandings' of the Fact-Checking Movement," PolitiFact, June 18, 2014, http://www.politifact.com/truth-o-meter/article/2014/jun/18/5-essential-understandings-fact-checking-movement/.

2. Author's field notes, June 9, 2014. The Ohio candidate was Republican Josh Mandel, challenging incumbent Democratic senator Sherrod Brown. Mandel received five "False" and six "Pants on Fire" rulings from PolitiFact Ohio over the course of the race.

3. Comments by Bill Adair at Global Fact-Checking Summit.

4. Comments by Tom Rosenstiel at Truth in Politics 2014: A Status Report on Fact-Checking Journalism, American Press Institute, Arlington, VA, December 10, 2014.

5. Brooks Jackson, interview with the author, telephone, August 18, 2011.

6. The one-day conference, called Fact-Checking in the News, took place December 14, 2011, in Washington, DC. As discussed in the introduction, I helped to program the event as a fellow at the New America Foundation.

7. Comment by Michael Dobbs at Fact-Checking in the News.

8. See, e.g., Brendan Nyhan and Jason Reifler, "When Corrections Fail: The Persistence of Political Misperceptions," *Political Behavior* 32, no. 2 (June 2010): 303–30, doi:10.1007/s11109-010-9112-2.

9. Brendan Nyhan and Jason Reifler, *Misinformation and Fact-Checking: Research Findings from Social Science* (Washington, DC: New America Foundation, February, 2012).

10. Comment by Brendan Nyhan at Fact-Checking in the News.

11. Comments by Glenn Kessler and Bill Adair at Fact-Checking in the News.

12. Social psychologist Leon Festinger's research with a 1950s UFO cult is discussed in Brooks Jackson and Kathleen Hall Jamieson, *UnSpun: Finding Facts in a World of Disinformation* (New York: Random House, 2007), 55–56.

13. Comment by Brooks Jackson Fact-Checking in the News.

14. For instance, as noted in chapter 2, research by Kathleen Hall Jamieson and others aided in redesigning adwatch segments in the 1990s in order to avoid reinforcing the political messages they set out to debunk.

15. Angie Drobnic Holan, interview with the author, telephone, February 25, 2011.

16. Comment by Bill Adair at "The Facts of Political Life," panel discussion at the New America Foundation, Washington, DC, February 28, 2012.

17. Ibid.

18. Herbert J. Gans, *Democracy and the News* (Oxford: Oxford University Press, 2003). This view hews closely to the "informed citizen" ideal described in Michael Schudson, *The Good Citizen: A History of American Civic Life* (New York: Martin Kessler Books, 1999).

19. Glenn Kessler, "Just the Facts," *Foreign Affairs*, December 26, 2014, http://www.for eignaffairs.com/articles/142741/glenn-kessler/just-the-facts.

20. Herb Gans, *Deciding What's News: A Study of "CBS Evening News," "NBC Nightly News," "Newsweek," and "Time"* (1979; repr. Evanston, IL: Northwestern University Press, 2004), 230. On "audience-image," see 238–40.

21. Questions about the accuracy of online audience measurement are reviewed in Lucas Graves, "Traffic Jam," *Columbia Journalism Review*, September/October 2010, 17–18.

22. See discussion in C. W. Anderson, "Between Creative and Quantified Audiences: Web Metrics and Changing Patterns of Newswork in Local U.S. Newsrooms," *Journalism* 12, no. 5 (July 2011): 550–66, doi:10.1177/1464884911402451; and Angela M. Lee, Seth C. Lewis, and Matthew Powers, "Audience Clicks and News Placement: A Study of Time-Lagged Influence in Online Journalism," *Communication Research* 41, no. 4 (June 2014): 505–30, doi:10.1177/0093650212467031.

23. For a discussion of shifting norms with regard to sharing data with reporters, see Mary Clare Fischer, "No Analytics for You: News Sites Grapple with Who Can See Data," *American Journalism Review*, March 19, 2014, http://ajr.org/2014/03/19/analytics -news-sites-grapple-can-see-data/.

24. Pablo J. Boczkowski, *News at Work: Imitation in an Age of Information Abundance* (Chicago: University of Chicago Press, 2010), 153. However, Anderson offers contradictory evidence from the Philadelphia newsrooms he studied, arguing that "website traffic often appeared to be the primary ingredient in . . . news judgment"; see also C. W. Anderson, "Between Creative and Quantified Audiences," 561.

25. On the report I saw, the main referring sites were Google, Fox News, and Facebook. Top search terms included "obama birth certificate" and "glenn beck."

26. Author's field notes, February 7, 9, 10, 11, 15, and 16, 2011; June 8 and 15, 2011; and February 10, 2015. Bill Adair, interview with the author, Washington, DC, December 2, 2010; Brooks Jackson, interview with the author, Washington, DC, December 3, 2010; and Eugene Kiely, interview with the author, Philadelphia, PA, March 17, 2011.

27. Author's field notes, February 9, 11, 15, and 16, 2011; June 15, 2011; October 3, 2011; October 3, 2013; and June 9–10, 2014.

28. Ibid., February 9, 11, 15, and 16, 2011; June 15, 2011; October 3, 2013; June 10, 2014; and February 10, 2015.

29. Mark Deuze has used this term more generally to refer to professional work across the media industries; see, e.g., Mark Deuze, *Media Work* (Cambridge: Polity, 2007).

30. As noted earlier, this term is used in the sense that Michael Polanyi applied to suggest the craft-like aspects of scientific work, whose success often depends on skills that are difficult to articulate. See Michael Polanyi, *Personal Knowledge: Towards a Post-Critical Philosophy* (London: Routledge, 1998), 52–53. See also Harry M. Collins, "Tacit Knowledge, Trust and the Q of Sapphire," *Social Studies of Science* 31, no. 1 (February 2001): 71–85, http://www.jstor.org/stable/285818.

31. In its general contours, this mirrors the "audience-image" Gans saw professional journalists subscribing to: sufficiently like the journalists in economic and educational profile to be interested in their work and to understand and benefit from it. Gans, *Deciding What's News*, 238–40.

32. Comments by Brooks Jackson and Glenn Kessler at Fact-Checking in the News.

33. Comments by Glenn Kessler at "Fact-Checking and the News."

34. Hannah Vinter, "Bill Adair, Editor of Politifact: 'Readers Love this Kind of Accountability Journalism,'" *Editors Weblog*, World Association of Newspapers and News Publishers, August 22, 2011, http://www.editorsweblog.org/2011/08/22/bill-adair-editor-of-politifact-readers-love-this-kind-of-accountability-journalism.

35. Author's field notes, February 9 and 17, 2011; and June 15, 2011.

36. Robert Farley, "Alleged Obama Birth Certificate from Kenya Is a Hoax," PolitiFact, August 21, 2009, http://www.politifact.com/truth-o-meter/statements/2009/aug/21/orly-taitz/alleged-obama-birth-certificate-kenya-hoax/.

37. Author's field notes, June 6, 2011.

38. Ibid., February 14 and 19, 2011; and February 10, 2015.

39. Ibid., March 17, 2011; and June 6, 8, 15, and 16, 2011.

40. Gans found in the 1970s that elite American journalists had little interest in mail from readers and viewers due to its "predictability": "journalists expect to receive mostly critical letters, particularly from cultural and political conservatives, and their expectations are usually realized"; Gans, *Deciding What's News*, 230–31.

41. Journalism's voguish rhetoric of the "productive and generative" audience is discussed in Anderson, "Between Creative and Quantified Audiences."

42. "Political Fact-Checking Under Fire," *Talk of the Nation*, NPR, January 10, 2012, http://www.npr.org/2012/01/10/144974110/political-fact-checking-under-fire.

43. Author's field notes, June 8 and 16, 2011.

44. Michael Dobbs, *The Rise of Political Fact-Checking* (Washington, DC: New America Foundation, February 2012), 13.

45. Author's field notes, June 15, 2011.

46. The site also provided guides to relevant research and hosted discussion moderated by professional journalists. The primary goal of the project was to promote news literacy

and public engagement. Fabrice Florin, interview with the author, telephone, March 1, 2011.

47. Brooks Jackson, interview with the author, Washington, DC, December 3, 2010.

48. Bill Adair, interview with the author, Washington, DC, December 2, 2010.

49. Author's field notes, October 3, 2011.

50. See, e.g., Craig Silverman, "Conferences Raise Unanswered Questions About Fact Checking," Poynter.org, December 28, 2011, http://www.poynter.org/latest-news/re gret-the-error/157031/conferences-raise-unanswered-questions-about-fact-checking/.

51. Vinter, "Bill Adair, Editor of PolitiFact."

52. Jackson and Jamieson, *UnSpun*, x.

53. Brooks Jackson, interview with the author, Washington, DC, December 3, 2010.

54. Sam Stein, "Muffingate's Sad Story: 178 Articles Perpetuate DOJ Myth, 37 Correct It," *Huffington Post*, September 30, 2011, http://www.huffingtonpost.com/2011/09/30 /muffins-justice-department-muffingate-myth_n_988928.html. The analysis relied on LexisNexis.

55. Jerry Markon, "A $16 Muffin? Justice Dept. Audit Finds 'Wasteful' and Extravagant Spending," *Washington Post*, September 21, 2011.

56. Patrick B. Pexton, "Another Look at Justice Dept.'s $16 Muffin," *Washington Post*, September 30, 2011.

57. Rob Savillo, "Muffin-gate Update: Many Outlets Fail to Correct Half-Baked Allegation," *Media Matters* (blog), November 3, 2011, http://mediamatters.org/blog/2011/11/03 /muffin-gate-update-many-outlets-fail-to-correct/153386; Stein, "Muffingate's Sad Story"; and James Q. Wilson, "Muffingate and the Media's Big Fat Mistake," *Wall Street Journal*, December 8, 2011.

58. Angie Drobnic Holan, "$16 Muffin Included Coffee, Tea, Event Space," PolitiFact, October 4, 2011, http://www.politifact.com/truth-o-meter/statements/2011/oct/04 /bill-oreilly/16-muffin-included-coffee-tea-event-space/.

59. This collaborative turn is the subject of Lucas Graves and Magda Konieczna, "Sharing the News: Journalistic Collaboration as Field Repair," *International Journal of Communication* 9 (June 2015): 1966–84, http://ijoc.org/index.php/ijoc/article/view/3381.

60. "With 'Lie of the Year' Controversy, Fact Checking Comes Under Scrutiny," *All Things Considered*, NPR, December 22, 2011; emphasis added.

61. Comments by Bill Adair, Michael Dobbs, and Brooks Jackson at Fact-Checking in the News. Glenn Kessler was less emphatic in indicting traditional journalism.

62. See, e.g., Dobbs, *Rise of Political Fact-Checking*.

63. "Sunday Morning Fact-Checking," *Colbert Report*, Comedy Central, April 14, 2010, http://www.colbertnation.com/full-episodes/wed-april-14-2010-david-shields. The partnership between PolitiFact and *This Week* was a response to a proposal by Jay Rosen; see Rosen, "My Simple Fix for the Messed Up Sunday Shows," *Jay Rosen: Public Notebook* (blog), December 28, 2009, https://publicnotebook.wordpress.com/2009/12/28/my -simple-fix-for-the-messed-up-sunday-shows/.

64. Dobbs, *Rise of Political Fact-Checking*, 3.

65. Author's field notes, February 7, 9, 10, 11, 15, and 17, 2011; and June 6, 8, and 15, 2011.

66. Comment by Glenn Kessler at Fact-Checking in the News.

67. "PolitiFact vs. Rachel Maddow," *Reliable Sources*, CNN, February 27, 2011; see also W. Gardner Selby, "Politifact Fields Fire After Rating False a Rachel Maddow Statement," PolitiFact Texas, February 28, 2011, http://www.politifact.com/texas/article/2011 /feb/28/context-matters-politifact-check-maddow/.

68. Brooks Jackson, interview with the author, telephone, August 16, 2011.

69. Bill Adair, interview with the author, Washington, DC, February 17, 2011.

70. Aaron Sharockman, "Florida Dems Say Bill McCollum out of Touch on Subprime Mortgage Crisis," PolitiFact Florida, May 11, 2010, http://www.politifact.com/flor ida/statements/2010/may/11/florida-democratic-party/florida-dems-bill-mccollum -subprime-mortgage/.

71. Louis Jacobson and Ciara O'Rourke, "Wayne LaPierre Says Phoenix Is 'One of the Kidnapping Capitals of the World,'" PolitiFact, February 19, 2013, http://www .politifact.com/truth-o-meter/statements/2013/feb/19/wayne-lapierre/wayne -lapierre-says-phoenix-one-kidnapping-capital/; Viveca Novak, "Sunday Replay," FactCheck.org, June 28, 2010, http://www.factcheck.org/2010/06/sunday-replay-10/; and Ciara O'Rourke, "McCain Says Phoenix Is the Second Kidnapping Capital in the World," PolitiFact, June 28, 2010, http://www.politifact.com/texas/statements/2010 /jun/28/john-mccain/mccain-says-phoenix-second-kidnapping-capital-worl/.

72. Robert Farley, "Beheadings, Kidnappings and Other Immigration Distortions," PolitiFact, September 10, 2010, http://www.politifact.com/truth-o-meter/article/2010 /sep/10/fact-checking-beheadings-and-other-immigration/. PolitiFact debunked the claim in at least four separate Truth-O-Meter items.

73. Jason Linkins, "McCain Falsely Claims Phoenix Is 'Number-Two Kidnapping Capital of the World,'" *Huffington Post*, June 29, 2010, http://www.huffingtonpost.com/2010/06 /28/mccain-falsely-claims-pho_n_627605.html.

74. Glenn Kessler, "Obama's Denial that Biden Called Tea Party Activists 'Terrorists,'" Fact Checker, *Washington Post*, August 17, 2011, http://www.washingtonpost.com/blogs /fact-checker/post/obamas-denial-that-biden-called-tea-party-activists-terrorists /2011/08/16/gIQArIg3JJ_blog.html.

75. Ben Smith, "The End of Fact-Checking," Politico, August 17, 2011, http://www.polit ico.com/blogs/bensmith/0811/The_end_of_factchecking.html.

76. Glenn Kessler, "One Year of Fact Checking—an Accounting," Fact Checker, *Washington Post*, December 30, 2011, http://www.washingtonpost.com/blogs/fact-checker/post /one-year-of-fact-checking--an-accounting/2011/12/27/gIQARItaOP_blog.html. Italics added.

77. Author's field notes, June 8 and 15, 2011. Emphasis added.

78. As of mid-2015, FactCheck.org had won a Sigma Delta Chi Award from the Society of Professional Journalists, a Clarion Award from the Association for Women in

Communications, and a long string of Webby awards for online journalism. PolitiFact was awarded a Pulitzer Prize for national reporting in 2009 and has also received a Digital Edge Award from the National Newspaper Association, a pair of Knight-Batten Awards for Innovations in Journalism, and several Green Eyeshades awards from the Society of Professional Journalists.

79.   Bill Adair, interview with the author, Washington, DC, December 2, 2010; Brooks Jackson, interview with the author, Washington, DC, December 3, 2010.

80.   Author's field notes, June 15, 2011; and see Monica Davey, "Fact Checker Finds Falsehoods in Remarks," *New York Times*, October 15, 2009.

81.   See, e.g., Bill Adair, "Colbert: 'Who Are These PolitiFact Guys?'" PolitiFact, April 15, 2010, http://www.politifact.com/truth-o-meter/article/2010/apr/15/colbert-who-are-these-politifact-guys/; and Melissa Siegel, "Halter Questioned on Misleading TV Ad," FactCheck.org, June 8, 2010, http://www.factcheck.org/2010/06/halter-questioned-on-misleading-tv-ad/.

82.   For instance, PolitiFact saw dramatic traffic spikes every time Comedy Central replayed an episode of the *Daily Show* that showcased the group's work. Gabrielle Gorder, "Just the Facts: An Interview with Bill Adair, Founder and Editor of PolitiFact," *NPF Newsbag*, National Press Foundation, October 3, 2011, https://web.archive.org/web/20150603095125/http://nationalpress.org/blogs/newsbag/just-the-facts-an-interview-with-bill-adair-founder-and-editor-of-politifac/.

83.   Discussed in Graves and Konieczna, "Sharing the News."

84.   Author's field notes, February 7, 9, 14, 17, and 18, 2011; and June 15–18, 2011. The unusual lines of authority become evident when PolitiFact has to schedule supplemental training for state partners producing substandard Truth-O-Meter items or having trouble with the quota of roughly five articles per week.

85.   Cary Spivak, "The Fact-Checking Explosion," *American Journalism Review* 32 (2010): 38–43.

86.   A Lexis-Nexis search found that between June 2007 and the end of 2014, Bill Adair was interviewed or mentioned in 312 broadcast transcripts, Glenn Kessler in 148, and Brooks Jackson in 77. The two most common outlets for these broadcast citations were CNN and NPR. (This is only cursory scan; not all references were authoritative citations or necessarily have to do with fact-checking.)

87.   Eugene Kiely, e-mail to author, March 24, 2014.

88.   Glenn Kessler, e-mail to author, January 9, 2015.

89.   Author's field notes, February 7 and 16, 2011; October 3, 2013; and February 15, 2015.

90.   Diana Marszalek, "PolitiFact Aims to Boost Local TV Presence," TVNewsCheck, February 28, 2012, http://www.tvnewscheck.com/article/57723/politifact-aims-to-boost-local-tv-presence.

91.   PolitiFact has explored the possibility of selling exclusive distribution deals to national partners such as broadcasters or news wires. However, such deals are difficult to reach because of the site's existing network of state partners, who have syndication rights at the

state level, and because it targets media figures as well as politicians. In late 2015 the site negotiated a paid partnership with NBC, though detailed terms were not disclosed; see discussion in the epilogue.

92. Brooks Jackson, interview with the author, Washington, DC, December 3, 2010.

93. Comment by Mark Matthews at Pants on Fire: Political Mendacity and the Rise of Media Fact-Checkers, a conference at the Annenberg Public Policy Center, Washington, DC, November 9, 2007.

94. In a national survey by the Pew Research Center in late 2010, two-thirds of respondents named television as their primary news source; another 16 percent named radio. The Internet and newspapers came in at 41 percent and 31 percent, respectively. See *Internet Gains on Television as Public's Main News Source* (Washington, DC: Pew Research Center for the People and the Press, January 4, 2011), http://www.people-press.org /2011/01/04/internet-gains-on-television-as-publics-main-news-source/.

95. Author's field notes, February 7 and 17, 2011; and February 10, 2015.

96. Polanyi, *Personal Knowledge*, 52–53; and Collins, "Tacit Knowledge, Trust and the Q of Sapphire."

97. Author's field notes, February 7 and 14–17, 2011; and February 10, 2015. On investigative nonprofits, see Graves and Konieczna, "Sharing the News."

98. Author's field notes, October 17, 2010; and February 7 and 14–17, 2011.

99. "Dobbs' Focus On Obama Birth Draws Fire to CNN," *Morning Edition*, NPR, July 31, 2009. See also chapter 3.

100. "Republican Race Heating Up," *Anderson Cooper 360°*, CNN, December 12, 2011.

101. "PolitiFact's Adair Discusses Accuracy of Romney Film," *All Things Considered*, NPR, January 13, 2012.

102. "Reality Check," *CBS Evening News*, CBS, October 3, 2008.

103. "Fact-Checking the Florida Mudslinging," *Weekend Edition Sunday*, NPR, January 29, 2012.

104. "Fact-Checking Romney's Bet," *Situation Room*, CNN, December 12, 2011.

105. White House, "Press Briefing by Press Secretary Jay Carney," February 16, 2011, http:// www.whitehouse.gov/the-press-office/2011/02/16/press-briefing-press-secretary-jay -carney-2162011.

106. Louis Jacobson, "Barack Obama Says White House Budget Would Not Add to the Debt Within a Few Years," PolitiFact, February 15, 2011, http://www.politifact.com/truth -o-meter/statements/2011/feb/15/barack-obama/barack-obama-says-white-house -budget-would-not-add/.

107. The simile is Gaye Tuchman's: "attacked for a controversial presentation of 'facts,' newspapermen invoke their objectivity almost the way a Mediterranean peasant might wear a clove of garlic around his neck to ward off evil spirits." Gaye Tuchman, "Objectivity as Strategic Ritual: An Examination of Newsmen's Notions of Objectivity," *American Journal of Sociology* 77, no. 4 (1972): 660. In this case, the official, not the "newsman," is being attacked; but invoking objectivity is still a *defensive* strategy in the journalistically controversial move of contradicting official facts.

108. Author's field notes, February 16, 2011.

109. Gans, *Deciding What's News*, 181. See also discussion in Stephen D. Reese and Lucig H. Danielian, "Intermedia Influence and the Drug Issue: Converging on Cocaine," in *Communication Campaigns About Drugs: Government, Media, and the Public*, ed. Pamela J. Shoemaker, 29–46 (Hillsdale, NJ: Erlbaum Associates, 1989). A classic account of journalistic cue-taking on the campaign trail is Timothy Crouse, *The Boys on the Bus* (New York: Ballantine Books, 1973).

110. Author's field notes, February 14 and 16, 2011; and June 6 and 8, 2011.

111. This analysis relied on broadcast news transcripts in the LexisNexis database. Coding was carried out by Patrice Kohl under a grant from the Wisconsin Alumni Research Fund. A previous version of this analysis, carried out by the author with support from the New America Foundation, appears in Graves and Glaisyer, *Fact-Checking Universe in Spring 2012*.

112. Mentions in program transcripts consist mainly of on-air interviews but could take any form, including authoritative citations as well as cursory or even negative references by a program anchor or guest. Search terms consisted of organization names (author names also counted in the case of the *Washington Post*'s Fact Checker). All results were verified by human coding.

113. Although the analysis did not code for the valence of the citation, a scan of several dozen individual mentions of Media Matters on Fox News found that all were negative.

7. The Limits of Fact-Checking

1. Author's field notes, May 15, 2011.

2. For overviews of this coverage, see Meghan Ashford-Grooms, "Truth-O-Meter Works Hard During Federal Debt Debate," PolitiFact, July 29, 2011, http://www.politifact.com/texas/article/2011/jul/29/truth-o-meter-works-hard-during-federal-debt-debat/; and Lori Robertson, "Debt Limit Debate Roundup," FactCheck.org, July 29, 2011, http://www.factcheck.org/2011/07/debt-limit-debate-round-up/.

3. See, e.g., Glenn Kessler, "Can President Obama Keep Paying Social Security Benefits Even If the Debt Ceiling Is Reached?" Fact Checker, *Washington Post*, July 13, 2011, http://www.washingtonpost.com/blogs/fact-checker/post/can-president-obama-keep-paying-social-security-benefits-even-if-the-debt-ceiling-is-reached/2011/07/12/gIQA9myRBI_blog.html.

4. The behind-the-scenes narrative is always more complex; see Matt Bai, "Obama vs. Boehner: Who Killed the Debt Deal?" *New York Times Magazine*, March 28, 2012.

5. See, e.g., David Brooks, "The Mother of All No-Brainers," *New York Times*, July 4, 2011, sec. Opinion; and Megan McArdle, "Why Can't the GOP Get to Yes?" *Atlantic*, July 5, 2011, http://www.theatlantic.com/business/archive/2011/07/why-cant-the-gop-get-to-yes/241437/.

6. "Fact Checking the Debt Ceiling Debate," *On the Media*, WNYC, July 29, 2011, http://www.onthemedia.org/2011/jul/29/fact-checking-debt-ceiling-speeches/.

7. Glenn Kessler, interview with the author, telephone, April 18, 2012.

8. One might also say the "media-political field." I mean to emphasize a shifting, partly mediated milieu of elite media and political actors. This is distinct from (but grounded in and structured by) the field-theoretic or institutionalist sense of well-defined, partly autonomous professional fields of politics and journalism; see Rodney Benson, "News Media as a Journalistic Field: What Bourdieu Adds to New Institutionalism, and Vice Versa," *Political Communication* 23, no. 2 (2006): 187–202.

9. Brooks Jackson, interview with the author, December 3, 2010; and Glenn Kessler interviewed in "Political Fact-Checking Under Fire," *Talk of the Nation*, NPR, January 10, 2012.

10. Author's field notes, June 15, 2011.

11. Consider, for instance, the work of *New York Times* columnist Nicholas Kristof, whose 2006 Pulitzer Prize for commentary cited "his graphic, deeply reported columns that, at personal risk, focused attention on genocide in Darfur and that gave voice to the voiceless in other parts of the world." A very thoughtful take on the cultural work done by "shoe leather" discourse is Jay Rosen, "Good Old Fashioned Shoe Leather Reporting," *PressThink* (blog), April 16, 2015, http://pressthink.org/2015/04/good-old-fashioned -shoe-leather-reporting/.

12. Thus, Michael Schudson has written that the "objectivity norm guides journalists to separate facts from values, and report only the facts." See Michael Schudson, "The Objectivity Norm in American Journalism," *Journalism* 2, no. 2 (2001): 149.

13. PolitiFact founder Bill Adair, for instance, has called fact-checking "reported-conclusion journalism," arguing that this is distinct from opinion journalism. Brendan Nyhan, "Bill Adair, Setting Pants Ablaze No More," *Columbia Journalism Review*, April 8, 2013, http://www.cjr.org/united_states_project/bill_adair_setting_pants_ablaze _no_more.php.

14. Arthur Brisbane, "Should the Times Be a Truth Vigilante?" *Public Editor's Journal* (blog), *New York Times*, January 12, 2012, http://publiceditor.blogs.nytimes.com/2012/01/12 /should-the-times-be-a-truth-vigilante/.

15. See discussion in Lucas Graves, "Digging Deeper into the New York Times' Fact-Checking Faux Pas," *Nieman Journalism Lab* (blog), January 18, 2012, http://www.niemanlab .org/2012/01/digging-deeper-into-the-new-york-times-fact-checking-faux-pas/.

16. A classic example, cited by Gaye Tuchman, is national coverage of a massive 1969 oil spill off of the coast of California. Journalists faithfully relayed President Nixon's onsite declaration that a Santa Barbara beach was clean although every reporter present could see that it wasn't. See Harvey Molotch and Marilyn Lester, "Accidental News: The Great Oil Spill as Local Occurrence and National Event," *American Journal of Sociology* 81, no. 2 (1975): 235–60; and Gaye Tuchman, *Making News: A Study in the Construction of Reality* (New York: Free Press, 1978), 83.

17. Then-editor Bill Keller quoted in Brian Stelter, "Study of Waterboarding Coverage Prompts a Debate in the Press," *Media Decoder* (blog), *New York Times*, July 2, 2010,

http://mediadecoder.blogs.nytimes.com/2010/07/02/study-of-waterboarding-cover
age-prompts-a-debate-in-the-press/. See also Graves, "Digging Deeper."

18. This idea echoes Daniel Hallin's notion of three distinct "spheres" of political discourse in the ideology of professional journalism: the spheres of consensus, of legitimate controversy, and of deviance. Daniel C. Hallin, *The Uncensored War: The Media and Vietnam* (Berkeley: University of California Press, 1989).

19. Arthur Brisbane, "Keeping Them Honest," *New York Times*, January 22, 2012, sec. Opinion / Sunday Review. Italics added.

20. Glenn Kessler, interview with the author, telephone, April 18, 2012.

21. For instance, every blow in Rachel Maddow's "feud" with PolitiFact has been documented in real time by media-and-politics sites such as *Politico*, *Mediaite*, Business Insider, the *Huffington Post*, and even the *Washington Post*; the liberal pundit has her own subsection on PolitiFact's Wikipedia page. For a review, see Dylan Byers, "Why Is Maddow Obsessed with PolitiFact?" *Politico*, May 11, 2012, http://www.politico.com /blogs/media/2012/05/why-is-maddow-obsessed-with-politifact-123170.html.

22. "Political Fact-Checking Under Fire," *Talk of the Nation*; and "With 'Lie of the Year' Controversy, Fact Checking Comes Under Scrutiny," *All Things Considered*, NPR, December 22, 2011.

23. Bill Adair quoted in Dylan Byers, "PolitiFact Without the 'Truth-O-Meter,'" *Politico*, February 16, 2012, http://www.politico.com/blogs/media/2012/02/politifact-without -the-truthometer-114704.html.

24. "With 'Lie of the Year' Controversy."

25. "Q&A with Glenn Kessler," *Q&A*, C-SPAN, January 15, 2012, http://www.c-spanvideo .org/program/303324-1.

26. Lori Robertson, "Campaign Trail Veterans for Truth," *American Journalism Review*, December/January 2005, http://www.ajr.org/article.asp?id=3784.

27. Comments by Jake Tapper at Pants on Fire: Political Mendacity and the Rise of Media Fact-Checkers, a conference at the Annenberg Public Policy Center, Washington, DC, November 9, 2007.

28. Comments by Glenn Kessler at Fact-Checking in the News, a meeting hosted by the New America Foundation (NAF), Washington, DC, December 14, 2011.

29. Robertson, "Campaign Trail Veterans for Truth."

30. The journalist was Mark Halperin, then political director for ABC News. See ibid.

31. "Fact Checking in the 2004 Presidential Debates," *NewsHour*, PBS, October 21, 2004.

32. Ibid.

33. Eric Ostermeier, "Selection Bias? PolitiFact Rates Republican Statements as False at 3 Times the Rate of Democrats," *Smart Politics* (blog), February 10, 2011, http://blog.lib .umn.edu/cspg/smartpolitics/2011/02/selection_bias_politifact_rate.php.

34. Mark Hemingway, "Lies, Damned Lies, and 'Fact Checking,'" *Weekly Standard*, December 19, 2011, http://www.weeklystandard.com/articles/lies-damned-lies-and-fact-checking _611854.html; and Brisbane, "Keeping Them Honest."

35. Chris Mooney, "Reality Bites Republicans," *Nation*, June 4, 2012, http://www.the nation.com/article/167930/reality-bites-republicans#.

36. Glenn Kessler, "One Year of Fact Checking—an Accounting," Fact Checker, *Washington Post*, December 30, 2011, http://www.washingtonpost.com/blogs/fact-checker/post/one -year-of-fact-checking--an-accounting/2011/12/27/gIQARItaOP_blog.html.

37. Mooney, "Reality Bites Republicans"; see also comments by Kessler in "Political Fact-Checking Under Fire."

38. Glenn Kessler, interview with the author, telephone, April 18, 2012. Italics added.

39. Author's field notes, February 10–11, 2011; and June 15, 2011.

40. Comment by Bill Adair at Fact-Checking in the News, meeting hosted by the New America Foundation, Washington, DC, December 14, 2011.

41. PolitiFact Virginia responded by pointing out that major state offices were dominated by the GOP. Warren Fiske, "PolitiFact Virginia Responds to the State GOP," PolitiFact Virginia, July 10, 2012, http://www.politifact.com/virginia/article/2012 /jul/10/politifact-virginias-responds-state-gop/. See also Erik Wemple, "Virginia Republican Party Publishes Huge Attack Paper on PolitiFact," *Erik Wemple* (blog), *Washington Post*, July 11, 2012, http://www.washingtonpost.com/blogs/erik-wemple/post /virginia-republican-party-publishes-huge-attack-paper-on-politifact/2012/07/11 /gJQA9iuMdW_blog.html.

42. Andrew Beaujon, "Study: PolitiFact Finds Republicans 'Less Trustworthy than Democrats,'" Poynter.org, May 28, 2013, http://www.poynter.org/news/mediawire /214513/study-politifact-finds-republicans-less-trustworthy-than-democrats/.

43. Bill Adair, "Inside the Meters: Responding to a George Mason University Press Release about Our Work," PolitiFact, May 29, 2013, http://www.politifact.com/truth-o -meter/blog/2013/may/29/responding-george-mason-university-press-release-a/.

44. Comment by Bill Adair at Fact-Checking in the News.

45. See, e.g., Dylan Otto Krider, "A Fact Not Even PolitiFact Can Spin: Conservatives More Wrong, More Often," *Intersection* (blog), May 23, 2012, https://web.archive.org /web/20121225095258/http://scienceprogressaction.org/intersection/2012/05/a -fact-not-even-politifact-can-spin-conservatives-more-wrong-more-often/.

46. Paul Waldman, "He Lied/She Lied," *American Prospect*, December 6, 2011, http:// prospect.org/article/he-liedshe-lied/.

47. Quoted in Brisbane, "Keeping Them Honest."

48. Glenn Kessler, interview with the author, telephone, April 18, 2012.

49. Author's field notes, December 10, 2014. The consultant also said, "We become so concerned about how a particular fact-checker is going to interpret a piece of data that may well be ambiguous, that we dial back larger truths that people should be hearing. . . . The fact checker, I'm afraid, plays a role in obscuring larger truths that are really more meaningful than whether this vote could be read two different ways."

50. Ibid.

51. Glenn Kessler, interview with the author, telephone, April 18, 2012.

52. Tuchman, *Making News*, 85.

53. This defensive view has been advanced most fully by Gaye Tuchman, who pointed to journalists' institutional fear of drawing criticism or even lawsuits from the subjects of their stories. Gaye Tuchman, "Objectivity as Strategic Ritual: An Examination of Newsmen's Notions of Objectivity," *American Journal of Sociology* 77, no. 4 (1972): 660–79; see also Tuchman, *Making News*. Herb Gans found the threat of libel suits to be less significant in the news organizations he studied, but he also saw potential criticism as a primary factor in the application of the objectivity norm; see Herb Gans, *Deciding What's News: A Study of "CBS Evening News," "NBC Nightly News," "Newsweek," and "Time"* (1979; repr. Evanston, IL: Northwestern University Press, 2004), 185–86.

54. Michael Schudson, *Discovering the News: A Social History of American Newspapers* (New York: Basic Books, 1978).

55. Intermedia effects are discussed in the introduction. Three key studies in this literature are Pablo J. Boczkowski, "Technology, Monitoring, and Imitation in Contemporary News Work," *Communication, Culture, and Critique* 2, no. 1 (2009): 39–59, doi:10.1111 /j.1753-9137.2008.01028.x; Stephen D. Reese and Lucig H. Danielian, "Intermedia Influence and the Drug Issue: Converging on Cocaine," in *Communication Campaigns About Drugs: Government, Media, and the Public*, ed. Pamela J. Shoemaker (Hillsdale, NJ: Lawrence Erlbaum Associates, 1989), 29–46; and Carsten Reinemann, "Routine Reliance Revisited: Exploring Media Importance for German Political Journalists," *Journalism and Mass Communication Quarterly* 81, no. 4 (December 2004): 857–76, doi:10.1177 /107769900408100409.

Epilogue

1. See a transcript of the hearing at "Full Text: Clinton Testifies Before House Committee on Benghazi," *Washington Post*, October 22, 2015, https://www.washingtonpost .com/news/post-politics/wp/2015/10/22/transcript-clinton-testifies-before-house -committee-on-benghazi/.

2. A search of the *Congressional Record* yields eleven mentions of one of the three national fact-checkers in the 111th Congress, forty-three mentions in the 112th, seventy-three in the 113th, and twenty-six in the first half of the 114th. These are unverified results from the search interface of the Library of Congress's Thomas database but offer at least a preliminary view of increasing reliance on the fact-checkers in congressional rhetoric. See also the discussion in Mark Stencel, *"Fact Check This": How U.S. Politics Adapts to Media Scrutiny*, American Press Institute, May 13, 2015, http://www.american pressinstitute.org/fact-checking-project/fact-checking-research/u-s-politics-adapts -media-scrutiny/.

3. Mitch McConnell, "Promise Kept: Senate Passes Obamacare Repeal Legislation," Mitch McConnell," December 7, 2015, http://www.mcconnell.senate.gov/public/in dex.cfm?p=newsletters&ContentRecord_id=166c80b2-ee00-4add-a44b-0d349d 7c301a; see also Alex Seitz-Wald, "How Republicans Learned to Stop Worrying and

Love PolitiFact," *National Journal,* December 18, 2013, http://www.nationaljournal
.com/politics/2013/12/19/how-republicans-learned-stop-worrying-love-politifact.

4. Fox's Chris Wallace asked Fiorina, "Do you acknowledge what every fact-checker has found, that as horrific as that scene is, it was only described on the video by someone who claimed to have seen it? There is no actual footage of the incident that you just mentioned." Dahlia Lithwick, "Carly Fiorina's Big Lie," *Slate,* September 25, 2015, http://www.slate.com/articles/news_and_politics/jurisprudence/2015/09/carly_fiorina _lied_about_planned_parenthood_video_gop_debate_fact_checking.html.

5. *Meet the Press,* NBC, November 29, 2015; see also "Lies Lies, Lies," *On the Media,* NPR, December 4, 2015.

6. Benjamin Mullin, "Seeking to Bring Context to Politics, NPR Launches Fact-Checking Feature," Poynter.org, September 18, 2015, http://www.poynter.org/news/mediawire /373868/seeking-to-bring-context-to-the-news-npr-launches-fact-checking-feature/.

7. Margaret Sullivan, "A New Emphasis on Fact-Checking in Real Time," *Public Editor's Journal* (blog), *New York Times,* December 15, 2015, http://publiceditor.blogs.nytimes.com/2015/12/15 /a-new-emphasis-on-fact-checking-in-real-time/.

8. "Fact Checking GOP Candidates' Debate Claims," *Fox News,* January 15, 2016, http:// video.foxnews.com/v/4706371355001/fact-checking-gop-candidates-debate-claims/.

9. *Daily Show,* Comedy Central, November 11, 2015; *Daily Show,* Comedy Central, November 16, 2015; and Matt Wilstein, "'Daily Show' Finds Less to Fact-Check in Democratic Debate," *Daily Beast,* November 17, 2015, http://www.thedailybeast.com/articles/2015 /11/17/daily-show-finds-less-to-fact-check-in-democratic-debate.html.

10. See, e.g., Chris Cillizza, "Donald Trump Is Leading an Increasingly Fact-Free 2016 Campaign," *The Fix* (blog), *Washington Post,* November 23, 2015, https://www.washing tonpost.com/news/the-fix/wp/2015/11/23/the-2016-campaign-is-largely-fact-free -thats-a-terrible-thing-for-american-democracy/; Dave Helling, "Misleading Politics May Hit an Unprecedented High in 2016, Pundits Say," *Kansas City Star,* December 9, 2015, http://www.kansascity.com/news/government-politics/article48805775.html; Janell Ross, "Is the 2016 Election Truly Unprecedented? Sort Of," *The Fix* (blog), *Washington Post,* November 25, 2015, https://www.washingtonpost.com/news/the-fix /wp/2015/11/25/is-the-2016-election-truly-unprecedented-yes-and-no/; Editorial, "Mr. Trump's Applause Lies," *New York Times,* November 24, 2015, http://www.ny times.com/2015/11/24/opinion/mr-trumps-applause-lies.html; and Editorial, "Crazy Talk at the Republican Debate," *New York Times,* September 17, 2015, http://www .nytimes.com/2015/09/18/opinion/crazy-talk-at-the-republican-debate.html ?smtyp=cur.

11. Chuck Todd, Mark Murray, and Carrie Dann, "First Read: Donald Trump, the Post-Truth 2016 Candidate," *NBC News,* November 24, 2015, http://www.nbcnews.com /meet-the-press/first-read-donald-trump-post-truth-2016-candidate-n468111. See also Paul Farhi, "Thanks to Trump, Fringe News Enters the Mainstream," *Washington Post,* December 11, 2015, https://www.washingtonpost.com/lifestyle/style/thanks-to-trump

-fringe-news-enters-the-mainstream/2015/12/11/292e518c-a01b-11e5-8728-1af6af2 08198_story.html.

12. "The 'King of Whoppers': Donald Trump," FactCheck.org, December 21, 2015, http://www.factcheck.org/2015/12/the-king-of-whoppers-donald-trump/. See also Angie Drobnic Holan and Linda Qiu, "2015 Lie of the Year: The Campaign Misstatements of Donald Trump," PolitiFact, December 21, 2015, http://www.politifact.com/truth-o -meter/article/2015/dec/21/2015-lie-year-donald-trump-campaign-misstatements/; and Glenn Kessler, "The Biggest Pinocchios of 2015," Fact Checker, December 14, 2015, https://www.washingtonpost.com/news/fact-checker/wp/2015/12/14/the-biggest -pinocchios-of-2015/.

13. Patrick Healy and Maggie Haberman, "95,000 Words, Many of Them Ominous, from Trump's Tongue," *New York Times*, December 6, 2015, http://www.nytimes.com/2015 /12/06/us/politics/95000-words-many-of-them-ominous-from-donald-trumps -tongue.html.

14. Angie Drobnic Holan, "All Politicians Lie. Some Lie More Than Others," *New York Times*, December 13, 2015, http://www.nytimes.com/2015/12/13/opinion/campaign -stops/all-politicians-lie-some-lie-more-than-others.html.

15. Editorial, "Truth, or Lack of It, in Politics," *Anniston Star* (Alabama), December 12, 2015, http://www.annistonstar.com/opinion/editorial-truth-or-lack-of-it-in-politics /article_869e6f40-a062-11e5-b296-9b8aafc9a19c.html.

16. Author's field notes, July 23, 2015.

17. Alexios Mantzarlis, "Introducing Poynter's International Fact-Checking Network," Poynter.org, http://www.poynter.org/news/international-fact-checking/379716/fact -checkers-of-the-world-unite/.

18. See discussion in chapter 6 and, for example, "SPJ Cautions Journalists: Report the Story, Don't Become Part of It," Society of Professional Journalists, January 22, 2010, http://www.spj.org/news.asp?REF=948. Like other professional norms, this one is no less revealing for being observed selectively; investigative journalists, for instance, may embrace reformist or activist agendas in ways that would make a political reporter un-comfortable. James S. Ettema and Theodore L. Glasser, *Custodians of Conscience: Investigative Journalism and Public Virtue* (New York: Columbia University Press, 1998).

19. It is striking how reliably fact-checkers describe their role in terms of helping voters to make an informed choice, even in the midst of an unusually wild political season. See, e.g., comments in Hadas Gold, "Fact-Checking the Candidates in a 'Post-Fact' World," *Politico*, December 15, 2015, http://www.politico.com/blogs/on-media/2015/12/fact -checking-the-candidates-in-a-post-fact-world-216790; Helling, "Misleading Politics"; Holan, "All Politicians Lie."

SELECTED BIBLIOGRAPHY

Aalberg, Toril, Jesper Strömbäck, and Claes H. de Vreese. "The Framing of Politics as Strategy and Game: A Review of Concepts, Operationalizations and Key Findings." *Journalism* 13, no. 2 (February 2012): 162–78. doi:10.1177/1464884911427799.

Adair, Bill. "Lessons from London: Fact-Checkers Have Passion, but Need More Checks." Poynter.org, June 13, 2014. http://www.poynter.org/how-tos/journalism-education /255806/lessons-from-london-fact-checkers-have-passion-but-need-more-checks/.

Amazeen, Michelle A. "Revisiting the Epistemology of Fact Checking." *Critical Review* 27, no. 1 (2015): 1–22. doi:10.1080/08913811.2014.993890.

Anderson, C. W. "Between Creative and Quantified Audiences: Web Metrics and Changing Patterns of Newswork in Local US Newsrooms." *Journalism* 12, no. 5 (July 1, 2011): 550–66. doi:10.1177/1464884911402451.

——. "Journalistic Networks and the Diffusion of Local News: The Brief, Happy News Life of the 'Francisville Four.'" *Political Communication* 27, no. 3 (2010): 289–309. doi:10.1080/1 0584609.2010.496710.

——. *Rebuilding the News: Metropolitan Journalism in the Digital Age*. Philadelphia: Temple University Press, 2013.

Arendt, Hannah. "Lying in Politics: Reflections on The Pentagon Papers." *New York Review of Books*, November 18, 1971. http://www.nybooks.com/articles/archives/1971/nov /18/lying-in-politics-reflections-on-the-pentagon-pape/.

Bank, Justin. *Newspaper Adwatch Stories: Coming Back Strong*. Philadelphia, PA: Annenberg Public Policy Center, November 9, 2007.

Barnhurst, Kevin G. *Seeing the Newspaper*. New York: St. Martin's Press, 1994.

——. "The Interpretive Turn in News." In *Journalism and Technological Change: Historical Pers pectives, Contemporary Trends*, ed. Clemens Zimmermann and Martin Schreiber, 111–41. Chicago: University of Chicago Press, 2014.

——. "The Makers of Meaning: National Public Radio and the New Long Journalism, 1980–2000." *Political Communication* 20, no. 1 (2003): 1–22. doi:10.1080/10584600390172374.

Barnhurst, Kevin G., and Diana Mutz. "American Journalism and the Decline in Event-Centered Reporting." *Journal of Communication* 47, no. 4 (December 1, 1997): 27–53. doi:10.1111/j.1460-2466.1997.tb02724.x.

Barnhurst, Kevin G., and Catherine A. Steele. "Image-Bite News: The Visual Coverage of Elections on U.S. Television, 1968–1992." *Harvard International Journal of Press/Politics* 2, no. 1 (1997): 40–58. doi:10.1177/1081180X97002001005.

Bayley, Edwin R. *Joe McCarthy and the Press*. Madison: University of Wisconsin Press, 1981.

Beaujon, Andrew. "New PolitiFact Service Will Fact-Check Pundits." Poynter.org, October 10, 2013. http://www.poynter.org/latest-news/mediawire/225595/new-politifact-service -will-fact-check-pundits/.

Becker, Howard. *Art Worlds*. Berkeley: University of California Press, 1982.

——. "Book Review: John R. Searle Making the Social World: The Structure of Human Civilization Oxford: Oxford University Press, 2010. 224 Pp. $24.95. ISBN 0-195-39617-1 Paul A. Boghossian Fear of Knowledge: Against Relativism and Constructivism Oxford: Clarendon Press, 2006. 148 Pp. $24.95. ISBN 978-0-199-23041-9." *Science, Technology & Human Values* 36, no. 2 (March 1, 2011): 273–79. doi:10.1177/0162243910378070.

Bennett, Courtney. "Assessing the Impact of Ad Watches on the Strategic Decision-Making Process: A Comparative Analysis of Ad Watches in the 1992 and 1996 Presidential Elections." *American Behavioral Scientist* 40, no. 8 (August 1997): 1161–82. doi:10.1177/00027 64297040008014.

Benson, Rodney. "News Media as a Journalistic Field: What Bourdieu Adds to New Institutionalism, and Vice Versa." *Political Communication* 23, no. 2 (2006): 187–202. doi:10.1080 /10584600600629802.

Benton, Joshua. "Fact-Checking Sites Continue to Grow in Number Around the World." *Nieman Lab* (blog), January 20, 2015, http://www.niemanlab.org/2015/01/fact-checking -sites-continue-to-grow-in-number-around-the-world/.

Bishop, Ronald. "From Behind the Walls: Boundary Work by News Organizations in Their Coverage of Princess Diana's Death." *Journal of Communication Inquiry* 23, no. 1 (January 1999): 90–112. doi:10.1177/019685999923001005.

Blumler, Jay G., and Dennis Kavanagh. "The Third Age of Political Communication: Influences and Features." *Political Communication* 16, no. 3 (July 1, 1999): 209–30. doi:10.1080 /105846099198596.

Boczkowski, Pablo J. *Digitizing the News: Innovation in Online Newspapers*. Cambridge, MA: MIT Press, 2005.

——. *News at Work: Imitation in an Age of Information Abundance.* Chicago: University of Chicago Press, 2010.

——. "Technology, Monitoring, and Imitation in Contemporary News Work." *Communication, Culture, and Critique* 2, no. 1 (2009): 39–59. doi:10.1111/j.1753-9137.2008.01028.x.

Boczkowski, Pablo J., and Martin de Santos. "When More Media Equals Less News: Patterns of Content Homogenization in Argentina's Leading Print and Online Newspapers." *Political Communication* 24, no. 2 (2007): 167–80. doi:10.1080/10584600701313025.

Bourdieu, Pierre. *On Television.* New York: New Press, 1998.

Bowker, Geoffrey C., and Susan Leigh Star. *Sorting Things Out: Classification and Its Consequences.* Cambridge, MA: MIT Press, 1999.

Brennen, Bonnie. "Book Review: Sweat Not Melodrama: Reading the Structure of Feeling in All the President's Men." *Journalism* 4, no. 1 (February 2003): 113–31. doi:10.1177/146 4884903004001444.

Brown, Neil. "Five 'Essential Understandings' of the Fact-Checking Movement," PolitiFact, June 18, 2014, http://www.politifact.com/truth-o-meter/article/2014/jun/18/5-essential -understandings-fact-checking-movement/.

Brownback, Abby. "Facing the Truth-O-Meter." *American Journalism Review.* March 2010. http://www.ajr.org/article.asp?id=4868.

Bucy, Erik P., and Maria Elizabeth Grabe. "Taking Television Seriously: A Sound and Image Bite Analysis of Presidential Campaign Coverage, 1992–2004." *Journal of Communication* 57, no. 4 (December 2007): 652–75. doi:10.1111/j.1460-2466.2007.00362.x.

Calhoun, Craig J., ed. "Introduction: Habermas and the Public Sphere," in *Habermas and the Public Sphere.* Cambridge, MA: MIT Press, 1992.

Callon, Michel. "Society in the Making: The Study of Technology as a Tool for Sociological Analysis." In *The Social Construction of Technological Systems: New Directions in the Sociology and History of Technology,* ed. Wiebe E. Bijker, Thomas Parke Hughes, and T. J. Pinch, 83–103. Cambridge, MA: MIT Press, 1989.

——. "Some Elements of a Sociology of Translation: Domestication of the Scallops and the Fishermen of St Brieuc Bay." In *The Science Studies Reader,* ed. Mario Biagioli, 67–83. New York: Routledge, 1999.

"Campaign Desk: CJR's Desk for Politics, Policy, and the Press." *Columbia Journalism Review.* http://www.cjr.org/press_room/_resources/pdf/Campaign_Desk_One_Sheet.pdf.

Cannon, Lou. *Governor Reagan: His Rise to Power.* New York: Public Affairs, 2003.

Cappella, Joseph N., and Kathleen Hall Jamieson. "Broadcast Adwatch Effects: A Field Experiment." *Communication Research* 21, no. 3 (June 1994): 342–65. doi:10.1177/009365 094021003006.

——. *Spiral of Cynicism: The Press and the Public Good.* New York: Oxford University Press, 1997.

Carlson, Matt. "'Where Once Stood Titans': Second-Order Paradigm Repair and the Vanishing U.S. Newspaper." *Journalism* 13, no. 3 (April 1, 2012): 267–83. doi:10.1177/1464 884911421574.

Castells, Manuel. "Communication, Power and Counter-Power in the Network Society." *International Journal of Communication* 1 (2007): 238–266. http://ijoc.org/index.php/ijoc/article /view/46/35.

Clare Fischer, Mary. "No Analytics for You: News Sites Grapple with Who Can See Data." *American Journalism Review*, March 19, 2014. http://ajr.org/2014/03/19/analytics-news -sites-grapple-can-see-data/.

Clark, Anna. "The Plain Dealer Drops PolitiFact, but Keeps on Factchecking." *Columbia Journalism Review*, June 17, 2014. http://www.cjr.org/united_states_project/cleveland _plain_dealer_politifact_factchecking.php.

Coddington, Mark. "Defending a Paradigm by Patrolling a Boundary: Two Global Newspapers' Approach to WikiLeaks." *Journalism & Mass Communication Quarterly* 89 (2012): 377–96. doi:10.1177/1077699012447918.

Collins, Harry M. *Changing Order: Replication and Induction in Scientific Practice*. Chicago: University of Chicago Press, 1992.

——. "Tacit Knowledge, Trust and the Q of Sapphire." *Social Studies of Science* 31, no. 1 (February 2001): 71–85. http://www.jstor.org/stable/285818.

Crouse, Timothy. *The Boys on the Bus*. New York: Ballantine Books, 1973.

Cunningham, Brent. "Re-Thinking Objectivity." *Columbia Journalism Review* 42, no. 2 (August 2003): 24–32.

Darnton, Robert. "Writing News and Telling Stories." *Daedalus* 104, no. 2 (Spring 1975): 175–94.

Daston, Lorraine, and Peter Galison. *Objectivity*. New York: Cambridge, MA: Zone Books; Distributed by the MIT Press, 2007.

Deacon, David, and James Stanyer. "Mediatization: Key Concept or Conceptual Bandwagon?" *Media, Culture & Society* 36, no. 7 (October 2014): 1032–44. doi:10.1177/016 3443714542218.

Desai, Neal, Andre Pineda, Majken Runquist, Mark Andrew Fusunyan, Katy Glenn, Gabrielle Kathryn Gould, Michelle Rachel Katz, et al. *Torture at Times: Waterboarding in the Media*. Cambridge, MA: Joan Shorenstein Center on the Press, Politics, and Public Policy, 2010. http://dash.harvard.edu/handle/1/4420886.

Deuze, Mark. *Media Work*. Cambridge: Polity, 2007.

Diamond, Edwin. "Getting It Right." *New York*, November 2, 1992.

Didion, Joan. "Insider Baseball." *New York Review of Books* 35, no. 16 (October 27, 1988).

DiMaggio, Paul J., and Walter W. Powell. "The Iron Cage Revisited: Institutional Isomorphism and Collective Rationality in Organizational Fields." *American Sociological Review* 48, no. 2 (April 1983): 147–60. doi:10.2307/2095101.

Dobbs, Michael. *The Rise of Political Fact-Checking*. Washington, DC: New America Foundation, February 2012.

Epstein, Steven. "The Construction of Lay Expertise: AIDS Activism and the Forging of Credibility in the Reform of Clinical Trials." *Science, Technology & Human Values* 20, no. 4 (1995): 408–37. doi:10.1177/016224399502000402.

Ettema, James S., and Theodore L. Glasser. *Custodians of Conscience: Investigative Journalism and Public Virtue*. New York: Columbia University Press, 1998.

——. "The Irony in—and of—Journalism: A Case Study in the Moral Language of Liberal Democracy." *Journal of Communication* 44, no. 2 (June 1994): 5–28. doi:10.1111/j.1460-2466 .1994.tb00674.x.

Fallows, James M. *Breaking the News: How the Media Undermine American Democracy*. New York: Vintage Books, 1997.

Fink, Katherine, and Michael Schudson. "The Rise of Contextual Journalism, 1950s–2000s." *Journalism* 15, no. 1 (2014): 3–20. doi:10.1177/1464884913479015.

Fish, Stanley. *Is There a Text in This Class? The Authority of Interpretive Communities*. Cambridge, MA: Harvard University Press, 1980.

Fishman, Mark. *Manufacturing the News*. Austin: University of Texas Press, 1980.

Fleck, Ludwik. *Genesis and Development of a Scientific Fact*. Chicago: University of Chicago Press, 1981.

Foucault, Michel. *Discipline and Punish: The Birth of the Prison*. 2nd ed. New York: Vintage Books, 1995.

Frantzich, Stephen. "Watching the Watchers: The Nature and Content of Campaign Ad Watches." *Harvard International Journal of Press/Politics* 7, no. 2 (Spring 2002): 34–57. doi :10.1177/1081180X0200700204.

Fuller, Jack. *News Values: Ideas for an Information Age*. Chicago: University of Chicago Press, 1996.

Galison, Peter. "Trading Zone: Coordinating Action and Belief." In *The Science Studies Reader*, ed. Mario Biagioli, 137–60. New York: Routledge, 1999.

Gans, Herbert J. *Deciding What's News: A Study of "CBS Evening News," "NBC Nightly News," "Newsweek," and "Time."* 1979. Reprint, Evanston, IL: Northwestern University Press, 2004.

——. *Democracy and the News*. New York: Oxford University Press, 2003.

Garfinkel, Harold. *Studies in Ethnomethodology*. Cambridge: Polity Press, 1984.

Gersh Hernandez, Debra. "Improving Election Reporting." *Editor & Publisher* 129, no. 40 (October 5, 1996): 16–20.

Gieryn, Thomas F. "Boundary-Work and the Demarcation of Science from Non-Science: Strains and Interests in Professional Ideologies of Scientists." *American Sociological Review* 48, no. 6 (December 1983): 781–95.

Gitlin, Todd. *The Whole World Is Watching: Mass Media in the Making and Unmaking of the New Left*. Berkeley: University of California Press, 2003.

Glowaki, Chris, Thomas J. Johnson, and Kristine E. Kranenburg. "Use of Newspaper Political Adwatches from 1988–2000." *Newspaper Research Journal* 25, no. 4 (Fall 2004): 40–54.

Graves, Lucas. "Blogging Back Then: Annotative Journalism in I. F. Stone's Weekly and Talking Points Memo." *Journalism* 16, no. 1 (January 2015): 99–118. doi:10.1177/1464884914545740.

——. "Digging Deeper into the New York Times' Fact-Checking Faux Pas." *Nieman Journalism Lab*, January 18, 2012. http://www.niemanlab.org/2012/01/digging-deeper-into-the -new-york-times-fact-checking-faux-pas/.

——. "In Defense of Factchecking." *Columbia Journalism Review*, August 9, 2013. http://www
.cjr.org/united_states_project/in_defense_of_factchecking.php.

——. "Traffic Jam." *Columbia Journalism Review*, October 2010.

——. "What We Can Learn from the Factcheckers' Ratings." *United States Project* (blog).
Columbia Journalism Review, June 4, 2013. http://www.cjr.org/united_states_project/what
_we_can_learn_from_the_factcheckers_ratings.php.

Graves, Lucas, and Tom Glaisyer. *The Fact-Checking Universe in Spring 2012: An Overview.*
Washington, DC: New America Foundation, February 2012.

Graves, Lucas, and Magda Konieczna. "Sharing the News: Journalistic Collaboration as
Field Repair." *International Journal of Communication* 9 (June 2015): 1966–84. http://
ijoc.org/index.php/ijoc/article/view/3381.

Habermas, Jürgen. *Moral Consciousness and Communicative Action.* Studies in Contemporary
German Social Thought. Cambridge, MA: MIT Press, 1990.

——. *The Structural Transformation of the Public Sphere: An Inquiry into a Category of Bourgeois
Society.* Cambridge, MA: MIT Press, 1989.

Hallin, Daniel C. "Sound Bite News: Television Coverage of Elections, 1968–1988." *Journal of
Communication* 42, no. 2 (June 1992): 5–24. doi:10.1111/j.1460-2466.1992.tb00775.x.

——. "The Passing of the 'High Modernism' of American Journalism." *Journal of Communication* 42, no. 3 (September 1992): 14–25. doi:10.1111/j.1460-2466.1992.tb00794.x.

——. *The Uncensored War: The Media and Vietnam.* Berkeley: University of California Press,
1989.

Hanson, Christopher [William Boot, pseud.]. "Iranscam: When the Cheering Stopped."
Columbia Journalism Review, March/April 1987.

Hayes, Arthur S. *Press Critics Are the Fifth Estate: Media Watchdogs in America.* Democracy and
the News. Westport, CT: Praeger, 2008.

Hemmingway, Emma. *Into the Newsroom: Exploring the Digital Production of Regional Television
News.* London: Routledge, 2008.

Herbst, Susan. *Reading Public Opinion: How Political Actors View the Democratic Process.* Studies in
Communication, Media, and Public Opinion. Chicago: University of Chicago Press, 1998.

Hochman, David. "Rumor Detectives: True Story or Online Hoax?" *Reader's Digest*, April
2009. http://www.rd.com/home/rumor-detectives-true-story-or-online-hoax/.

Hoyt, Mike. "Defining Bias Downward: Holding Political Power to Account Is Not Some
Liberal Plot." *Columbia Journalism Review* 43 (January 2005). http://www.cjr.org/behind
_the_news/defining_bias_downward_holding.php.

Internet Gains on Television as Public's Main News Source. Washington, DC: Pew Research Center for the People & the Press, January 4, 2011. http://www.people-press.org/2011/01/04
/internet-gains-on-television-as-publics-main-news-source/.

Jackson, Brooks, and Kathleen Hall Jamieson. *UnSpun: Finding Facts in a World of Disinformation.* New York: Random House, 2007.

Jacobs, Ronald N., and Eleanor R. Townsley. *The Space of Opinion: Media Intellectuals and the
Public Sphere.* New York: Oxford University Press, 2011.

James, William. *Pragmatism and Other Writings*. New York: Penguin Books, 2000.

Jamieson, Kathleen Hall, and Joseph N. Cappella. "Setting the Record Straight: Do Ad Watches Help or Hurt?" *The Harvard International Journal of Press/Politics* 2, no. 1 (January 1997): 13–22. doi:10.1177/1081180X97002001003.

Kelty, Christopher M. *Two Bits: The Cultural Significance of Free Software*. Durham, NC: Duke University Press, 2008.

Kessler, Glenn. "Just the Facts." *Foreign Affairs*, December 26, 2014. http://www.foreignaf fairs.com/articles/142741/glenn-kessler/just-the-facts.

——. "The Global Boom in Political Fact Checking." Fact Checker, *Washington Post*, June 13, 2014. http://www.washingtonpost.com/blogs/fact-checker/wp/2014/06/13/the-global -boom-in-fact-checking/.

Knorr-Cetina, K. "Culture in Global Knowledge Societies: Knowledge Cultures and Epistemic Cultures." In *The Blackwell Companion to the Sociology of Culture*, ed. Mark D. Jacobs and Nancy Weiss Hanrahan. Malden, MA: Blackwell, 2005.

——. *Epistemic Cultures: How the Sciences Make Knowledge*. Cambridge, MA: Harvard University Press, 1999.

Krause, Monika. "Reporting and the Transformations of the Journalistic Field: US News Media, 1890–2000." *Media, Culture & Society* 33, no. 1 (January 2011): 89–104. doi:10.1177/0163 443710385502.

Kuhn, Thomas S. *The Structure of Scientific Revolutions*. 4th ed. Chicago: University of Chicago Press, 2012.

Lang, Thomas. "Glenn Kessler on Fact-Checking Candidates, Getting off the Bus, and Reporters Who Are Ahead of the Curve." *Columbia Journalism Review*, September 17, 2004. http://www.cjr.org/the_water_cooler/glenn_kessler_on_factchecking.php.

Latour, Bruno. *Pandora's Hope: Essays on the Reality of Science Studies*. Cambridge, MA: Harvard University Press, 1999.

——. *Reassembling the Social: An Introduction to Actor-Network-Theory*. Clarendon Lectures in Management Studies. Oxford: Oxford University Press, 2005.

——. *Science in Action: How to Follow Scientists and Engineers Through Society*. Cambridge, MA: Harvard University Press, 1987.

——. *We Have Never Been Modern*. Cambridge, MA: Harvard University Press, 1993.

Lawrence, Regina G., and Matthew L. Schafer. "Debunking Sarah Palin: Mainstream News Coverage of 'Death Panels.'" *Journalism* 13, no. 6 (August 2012): 766–82. doi:10.1177/1464 884911431389.

Lee, Angela M., Seth C. Lewis, and Matthew Powers. "Audience Clicks and News Placement: A Study of Time-Lagged Influence in Online Journalism." *Communication Research* 41, no. 4 (June 2014): 505–30. doi:10.1177/0093650212467031.

Lemann, Nicholas. "Amateur Hour: Journalism Without Journalists." *New Yorker*, August 7, 2006.

Lewis, Seth. "The Tension Between Professional Control and Open Participation." *Information, Communication & Society* 15, no. 6 (2012): 836–66. doi:10.1080/1369118X.2012.674150.

Lewis, Michael. "J-School Confidential." *New Republic*, April 19, 1993, 20–27.

Lippmann, Walter. *Public Opinion*. 1922. Reprint, New York: Free Press, 1997.

Lorentzen, Christian. "Short Cuts." *London Review of Books*, April 5, 2012.

Marchetti, Dominique. "Subfields of Specialized Journalism." In *Bourdieu and the Journalistic Field*, ed. Rodney Benson and Erik Neveu, 64–84. Cambridge; Malden, MA: Polity, 2005.

Marmor, Theodore R., and Jerry L. Mashaw. "Cassandra's Law." *New Republic*, February 14, 1994, 20.

Marx, Greg. "What the Fact-Checkers Get Wrong." *Columbia Journalism Review*, January 5, 2012. http://www.cjr.org/campaign_desk/what_the_fact-checkers_get_wro.php.

Massing, Michael. "Now They Tell Us." *New York Review of Books*, February 26, 2004.

May, Ronald. "Is the Press Unfair to McCarthy?" *New Republic*, April 1953.

Mazzoleni, Gianpietro, and Winfried Schulz. "'Mediatization' of Politics: A Challenge for Democracy?" *Political Communication* 16, no. 3 (1999): 247–61. doi:10.1080/10584 6099198613.

McCaughey, Elizabeth. "No Exit: What the Clinton Plan Will Do for You." *New Republic*, February 7, 1994, 21–25.

McPhee, John. *Silk Parachute*. New York: Farrar, Straus and Giroux, 2010.

Medvetz, Thomas. *Think Tanks in America*. Chicago: University of Chicago Press, 2012.

Molotch, Harvey, and Marilyn Lester. "Accidental News: The Great Oil Spill as Local Occurrence and National Event." *American Journal of Sociology* 81, no. 2 (1975): 235–60.

Moore, Martha T. "Fact Checkers Help Sort Through Political Claims," *USA Today*, March 21, 2012, http://www.usatoday.com/news/politics/story/2012-03-21/fact-checkers-politicians /53693798/1.

Myers, Steve. "PolitiFact Takes Lesson from Fast-Food Industry as It Franchises Fact Checking." Poynter.org, May 3, 2010. http://www.poynter.org/latest-news/top-stories/102422 /politifact-takes-lesson-from-fast-food-industry-as-it-franchises-fact-checking/.

Nerone, John. "History, Journalism, and the Problem of Truth." In *Assessing Evidence in a Postmodern World*, ed. Bonnie Brennen, 11–29. Diederich Studies in Media and Communication, no. 3. Milwaukee, WI: Marquette University Press, 2013.

Neveu, Erik. "Four Generations of Political Journalism." In *Political Journalism: New Challenges, New Practices*, ed. Raymond Kuhn and Erik Neveu, 22–44. ECPR Studies in European Political Science. London: Routledge, 2002.

Nielsen, Rasmus Kleis. *Ground Wars: Personalized Communication in Political Campaigns*. Princeton, NJ: Princeton University Press, 2012.

Nyhan, Brendan. "Bill Adair, Setting Pants Ablaze No More." *Columbia Journalism Review*, April 8, 2013. http://www.cjr.org/united_states_project/bill_adair_setting_pants _ablaze_no_more.php.

——. "Does Fact-Checking Work? False Statements Are Wrong Metric." *United States Project* (blog), *Columbia Journalism Review*, March 30, 2012. http://www.cjr.org/swing_states _project/does_fact-checking_work_false.php.

——. "That's Not a Factcheck!" *United States Project* (blog). *Columbia Journalism Review*, March 12, 2013, http://www.cjr.org/united_states_project/thats_not_a_factcheck.php.

——. "Why the 'Death Panel' Myth Wouldn't Die: Misinformation in the Health Care Reform Debate." *Forum* 8, no. 1 (April 2010). doi:10.2202/1540-8884.1354.

Nyhan, Brendan, and Jason Riefler. *Misinformation and Fact-Checking: Research Findings from Social Science*. Washington, DC: New America Foundation, February 2012.

Nyhan, Brendan, and Jason Reifler. "When Corrections Fail: The Persistence of Political Misperceptions." *Political Behavior* 32, no. 2 (June 2010): 303–30. doi:10.1007/s11109-010-9112-2.

Ogburn, Jackie. "Bill Adair: Creating New Forms of Journalism." *Sanford School of Public Policy, Duke University*, September 26, 2013. http://news.sanford.duke.edu/news-type/news/2013/bill-adair-creating-new-forms-journalism.

Page, Benjamin I. *Who Deliberates? Mass Media in Modern Democracy*. American Politics and Political Economy. Chicago: University of Chicago Press, 1996.

Papper, Bob. *TV Adwatch Stories: On the Rise*. Philadelphia, PA: Annenberg Public Policy Center, November 9, 2007.

Patterson, Thomas E. *Out of Order*. New York: A. Knopf, 1993.

Peters, John Durham. *The Marvelous Clouds: Toward a Philosophy of Elemental Media*. Chicago: University of Chicago Press, 2015.

Plato. *The Republic*. 2nd rev. ed. London: Penguin, 2007.

Polanyi, Michael. *Personal Knowledge: Towards a Post-Critical Philosophy*. London: Routledge, 1998.

"Political Fact-Checking Under Fire." *Talk of the Nation*. NPR, January 10, 2012. http://www.npr.org/2012/01/10/144974110/political-fact-checking-under-fire.

Prior, Markus. *Post-Broadcast Democracy: How Media Choice Increases Inequality in Political Involvement and Polarizes Elections*. New York: Cambridge University Press, 2007.

Reese, Stephen D., and Jane Ballinger. "The Roots of a Sociology of News: Remembering Mr. Gates and Social Control in the Newsroom." *Journalism and Mass Communication Quarterly* 78, no. 4 (2001): 641–58.

Reese, Stephen D., and Lucig H. Danielian. "Intermedia Influence and the Drug Issue: Converging on Cocaine." In *Communication Campaigns About Drugs: Government, Media, and the Public*, ed. Pamela J. Shoemaker, 29–46. Hillsdale, NJ: Erlbaum Associates, 1989.

Reinemann, Carsten. "Routine Reliance Revisited: Exploring Media Importance for German Political Journalists." *Journalism and Mass Communication Quarterly* 81, no. 4 (December 2004): 857–76. doi:10.1177/1077699004081004009.

Revers, Matthias. "Journalistic Professionalism as Performance and Boundary Work: Source Relations at the State House." *Journalism* 15 (2014): 37–52. doi:10.1177/1464884913480459.

Rieder, Rem. "A Busy Season for Political Fact-Checkers." *American Journalism Review*, July 2012.

Robertson, Lori. "Campaign Trail Veterans for Truth." *American Journalism Review*, 26 (December/January 2005): 38–43, http://www.ajr.org/article.asp?id=3784.

Robinson, Sue. "The Active Citizen's Information Media Repertoire: An Exploration of Community News Habits During the Digital Age." *Mass Communication and Society* 17, no. 4 (March 17, 2014): 509–30. doi:10.1080/15205436.2013.816745.

Rosen, Jay. "Good Old Fashioned Shoe Leather Reporting," *PressThink* (blog), April 16, 2015, http://pressthink.org/2015/04/good-old-fashioned-shoe-leather-reporting/

——. "He Said, She Said Journalism: Lame Formula in the Land of the Active User." *PressThink* (blog), April 12, 2009. http://pressthink.org/2009/04/he-said-she-said-journalism-lame-formula-in-the-land-of-the-active-user/.

——. "He Said, She Said, We Said." *PressThink* (blog), June 4, 2004. http://archive.pressthink.org/2004/06/04/ruten_milbank.html.

——. "Karl Rove and the Religion of the Washington Press." *PressThink*, August 14, 2007. http://archive.pressthink.org/2007/08/14/rove_and_press.html.

——. "My Simple Fix for the Messed Up Sunday Shows." *Jay Rosen: Public Notebook* (blog), December 27, 2009. http://jayrosen.posterous.com/my-simple-fix-for-the-messed-up-sunday-shows.

——. "Politifact Chose the Vice of the Year but They Called It a Lie. That Was Dumb." *PressThink*, December 22, 2011. http://pressthink.org/2011/12/politifact-chose-the-vice-of-the-year-and-called-it-a-lie/.

——. "The View from Nowhere." *PressThink* (blog), September 18, 2003. http://archive.pressthink.org/2003/09/18/jennings.html.

——. "Why Political Coverage Is Broken." *PressThink*, August 26, 2011. http://pressthink.org/2011/08/why-political-coverage-is-broken/.

Rosenberg, Scott. *Say Everything: How Blogging Began, What It's Becoming, and Why It Matters*. New York: Crown, 2009.

Said, Edward W. *Orientalism*. Rev. ed. London: Penguin, 2003.

Schudson, Michael. *Discovering the News: A Social History of American Newspapers*. New York: Basic Books, 1978.

——. *The Good Citizen: A History of American Civic Life*. New York: Martin Kessler Books, 1999.

——. "The Objectivity Norm in American Journalism." *Journalism* 2, no. 2 (August 1, 2001): 149–70. doi:10.1177/146488490100200201.

——. "Political Observatories, Databases & News in the Emerging Ecology of Public Information." *Daedalus* 139, no. 2 (2010): 100–109.

——. "The Politics of Narrative Form: The Emergence of News Conventions in Print and Television." *Daedalus* 111, no. 4 (1982): 97–112.

——. *The Power of News*. Cambridge, MA: Harvard University Press, 1995.

——. *Watergate in American Memory: How We Remember, Forget, and Reconstruct the Past*. New York: Basic Books, 1992.

——. *Why Democracies Need an Unlovable Press*. Cambridge: Polity Press, 2008.

Schudson, Michael, and Chris Anderson. "Objectivity, Professionalism, and Truth Seeking in Journalism." In *The Handbook of Journalism Studies*, ed. Karin Wahl-Jorgensen and Thomas Hanitzsch, 88–101. New York: Routledge, 2009.

Searle, John R. *The Construction of Social Reality*. New York: Free Press, 1995.

——. *Speech Acts: An Essay in the Philosophy of Language*. London: Cambridge University Press, 1969.

——. "Why Should You Believe It?" *New York Review of Books*, September 24, 2009. http://www.nybooks.com/articles/archives/2009/sep/24/why-should-you-believe-it/.

Shapin, Steven. *A Social History of Truth: Civility and Science in Seventeenth-Century England*. Chicago: University of Chicago Press, 1994.

Shaw, Daron R., and Bartholomew H. Sparrow. "From the Inner Ring Out: News Congruence, Cue-Taking, and Campaign Coverage." *Political Research Quarterly* 52, no. 2 (June 1999): 323–51. doi:10.1177/106591299905200204.

Shepard, Alicia. "Celebrity Journalists." *American Journalism Review*, September 1997. http://ajrarchive.org/article.asp?id=247.

Sigal, Leon V. *Reporters and Officials: The Organization and Politics of Newsmaking*. Lexington, MA: D. C. Heath, 1973.

Silverman, Craig. "AP Grows Fact Checking Beyond Politics to Breaking News, Beat Reporting." Poynter.org, January 9, 2012. http://www.poynter.org/news/mediawire/158337/ap-grows-fact-checking-beyond-politics-to-breaking-news-beat-reporting/.

——. "Conferences Raise Unanswered Questions About Fact Checking." Poynter.org, December 28, 2011. http://www.poynter.org/latest-news/regret-the-error/157031/conferences-raise-unanswered-questions-about-fact-checking/.

——. "Newsweek Ditched Its Fact-checkers in 1996, then Made a Major Error." Poynter.org, August 21, 2012. http://www.poynter.org/news/mediawire/185899/the-story-of-when-newsweek-ditched-its-fact-checkers-then-made-a-major-error/.

——. *Regret the Error: How Media Mistakes Pollute the Press and Imperil Free Speech*. New York: Union Square Press, 2007.

——. "Washington Post Expands Fact-Checking Project—and Not Just to Movie Trailers." Poynter.org, February 28, 2014. http://www.poynter.org/latest-news/top-stories/241474/washington-post-expands-fact-checking-project-and-not-just-to-movie-trailers/.

——. "Washington Post's TruthTeller Project Hopes to Birth Real-Time Fact-Checking." Poynter.org, August 8, 2012. http://www.poynter.org/latest-news/regret-the-error/183774/washington-posts-truthteller-project-hopes-to-birth-real-time-fact-checking/.

Smith, Ben. "The Facts About the Fact Checkers." *Politico*, November 1, 2011. http://www.politico.com/news/stories/1011/67175.html.

Spivak, Carey. "The Fact-Checking Explosion." *American Journalism Review* 32, no. 4 (January 2011).

Star, Susan Leigh, and James R Griesemer. "Institutional Ecology, 'Translations' and Boundary Objects: Amateurs and Professionals in Berkeley's Museum of Vertebrate Zoology, 1907–39." *Social Studies of Science* 19, no. 3 (August 1989): 387–420. doi:10.1177/030631289019003001.

Stark, David. *The Sense of Dissonance: Accounts of Worth in Economic Life*. Princeton, NJ: Princeton University Press, 2011.

The State of the News Media 2010. Washington, DC: Project for Excellence in Journalism at the Pew Research Center, March 2010. http://www.stateofthemedia.org/2010/index.php.

Stencel, Mark. "Broder's Shift Key: An Unlikely Online Makeover." NPR, March 10, 2011. http://www.npr.org/2011/03/10/134421511/broders-shift-key-an-unlikely-online-makeover.

——. "'Fact Check This': How U.S. Politics Adapts to Media Scrutiny." American Press Institute, May 13, 2015. http://www.americanpressinstitute.org/fact-checking-project /fact-checking-research/u-s-politics-adapts-media-scrutiny/.

Stepp, Carl Sessions. "The State of the American Newspaper: Then and Now." *American Journalism Review* 14 (1999): 60–76.

Strömbäck, Jesper. "Four Phases of Mediatization: An Analysis of the Mediatization of Politics." *International Journal of Press/Politics* 13, no. 3 (July 2008): 228–46. doi:10.1177 /1940161208319097.

Tuchman, Gaye. *Making News: A Study in the Construction of Reality*. New York: Free Press, 1978.

——. "Objectivity as Strategic Ritual: An Examination of Newsmen's Notions of Objectivity." *American Journal of Sociology* 77, no. 4 (1972): 660–79.

Uscinski, Joseph E., and Ryden W. Butler. "The Epistemology of Fact Checking." *Critical Review* 25, no. 2 (June 2013): 162–80. doi:10.1080/08913811.2013.843872.

Usher, Nikki. *Making News at the* New York Times. The New Media World. Ann Arbor: University of Michigan Press, 2014.

Vinter, Hannah. "Bill Adair, Editor of Politifact: 'Readers Love This Kind of Accountability Journalism.'" *World Association of Newspapers and News Publishers*, August 18, 2011. http:// www.wan-ifra.org/articles/2011/08/18/bill-adair-editor-of-politifact-readers-love-this -kind-of-accountability-journal.

Waisbord, Silvio R. *Reinventing Professionalism: Journalism and News in Global Perspective*. Cambridge, U.K.: Polity Press, 2013.

Waldman, Paul. "Does Fact-Checking Work?" *American Prospect*, November 1, 2011, http:// prospect.org/article/does-fact-checking-work.

White, David M. "The 'Gatekeeper': A Case Study in the Selection of News." *Journalism Quarterly* 27, no. 1 (1950): 383–96.

Williams, Bruce A., and Michael X. Delli Carpini. *After Broadcast News: Media Regimes, Democracy, and the New Information Environment*. Communication, Society, and Politics. New York: Cambridge University Press, 2011.

Wittgenstein, Ludwig. *Philosophical Investigations*. 4th ed. Chichester, West Sussex, U.K.: Wiley-Blackwell, 2009.

Zelizer, Barbie. *Covering the Body: The Kennedy Assassination, the Media, and the Shaping of Collective Memory*. Chicago: University of Chicago Press, 1992.

——. "Journalists as Interpretive Communities." *Critical Studies in Mass Communication* 10, no. 3 (1993): 219–37. doi:10.1080/15295039309366865.

INDEX